Computer Studies *for* GCSE

Mark Bindley

New John Mansfield School, Peterborough

Basil Blackwell

For Daisy, Fred, Lina and Silo

© 1986 Mark Bindley

First published 1986

Reprinted (with corrections) 1986 (twice), 1987 (twice), 1989

Published by
Basil Blackwell Ltd
108 Cowley Road
Oxford OX4 1JF
England

British Library Cataloguing in Publication Data

Bindley, Mark
   Computer studies for GCSE.
   1. Electronic data processing—Examination,
   questions, etc.
   I. Title
   004'.076   QA76.28

ISBN 0-631-90057-8 (school edition)
ISBN 0-631-15702-6 (paperback)

Production details
Illustrated by Anne Langford and Angela Lumley.
Typeset by Katerprint Typesetting Services, Oxford in
10½ on 12pt Baskerville and 9 on 11pt Futura Book.
Printed and bound in Great Britain by
Butler and Tanner, Frome.

Contents

Acknowledgements

The author and publisher would like to thank the following for permission to reproduce copyright material:

Aileen Ballentyne; *Computing – The Magazine*; *The Guardian*; Macmillan Publishers Ltd. for the extract from *Player Piano* by Kurt Vonnegut; James Naughtie; *The Observer*; *The Sunday Times*; Syndication International for 'Computer Tut'; Clive Wilkins and Ross Speirs for 'Jargon'.

Specific illustrations
Acorn Computers Ltd cover, 17.19; Austin-Rover Exercise 36 Question 12; Barclays Bank 20.4, 20.5; BBC Ceefax 16.6; Bell and Howell 8.14; BMW 1.3; British Telecom 9.1; British Thornton 15.10; Canon (UK) Ltd Exercise 34 Question 2; C&G Concrete 14.36; Cray Research (UK) Ltd 13.11; Ferranti Electronics Ltd 1.4, 5.18, 13.5, 13.6; IBM 7.5, 8.8, 9.2, 9.6, 10.2, 10.9, 10.19, 10.20, 13.2, 13.4, 17.21; ICL 7.10, 9.5, 13.10; Kempston Microelectronics Ltd Exercise 27 Question 8; The Mansell Collection 1.1; The National Westminster Bank 7.17, Exercise 29 Question 8, 20.7; Plessey 7.19; Racal-Milgo Ltd 9.7; Rediffusion Simulation 15.6; RoboSystems 15.9; The Science Museum 7.3; Sinclair Research Ltd 1.5, Exercise 51 Question 3; Tony Sleep 2.3, 17.16, 18.4; Southern Electricity 7.16; Kerry Strand, California Computer Products Inc 21.4; Tandy Corporation Exercise 35 Questions 3 and 4, 3-M 7.9.

Examination questions
(*indicates a part question, Spec a specimen question, years are as numbered.)

The Associated Examining Board (AEB)
Associated Lancashire Schools Examining Board (ALSEB)
University of Cambridge Local Examinations Syndicate (C)
Cyd-Bwyllgor Addsyg Cymru/Welsh Joint Education Committee (WJEC)
East Anglian Examinations Board (EAEB)
East Midland Regional Examinations Board (EMREB)
University of London Schools Examinations Board (L)
Midland Examining Group (MEG)
Northern Ireland Schools Examinations Council (NI GCE) (NI CSE)
North Regional Examinations Board (NREB)
North West Regional Examinations Board (NWREB)
Oxford and Cambridge Schools Examinations Board (O&C)
University of Oxford Delegacy of Local Examinations (O)
Southern Regional Examinations Board (SREB)
Southern Universities Joint Board (SUJB)
The South East Regional Examinations Board (SEREB)
South Western Examinations Board (SWEB)
West Midlands Examinations Board (WMEB)

All efforts have been made to contact copyright holders. We apologise for any inadvertent omissions and will be happy to make corrections when reprinting.

Preface

This book has been written specifically for GCSE Computer Studies examinations. Nearly all of the material is new, apart from trial use in schools. Extensive coverage is given to all the GCSE syllabi topics, with the exception of computer programming in a specific language. Early chapters provide a comprehensive coverage of computer hardware, software and methods of use. Later chapters provide outlines of an extensive range of computer applications. Case studies often include a description of a simple manual system to compare and contrast with the computerised system.

The text is supported by numerous exercises of many different types, old and new. Role play, problem-solving and comprehension exercises are all included. The sentence-completion questions are designed to guide and test the student's reading of the text, and they can easily be used to build up a set of revision notes for the course.

Practical use of computers is essential in any Computer Studies course. It is intended that this text be used in conjunction with some of the excellent word processing, spreadsheet, graphics and database software packages already available. Special software is in preparation to illustrate those areas of the text not covered by currently available applications packages.

My thanks go to Alan Hunter for his many helpful comments on the draft manuscript of this text.

My thanks also go to my father-in-law, Silo Loubache, who produced the quiet office in France where the bulk of this text was written.

Mark Bindley
Peterborough 1986

v

1 Introduction

Computers and Information

Since the days of the earliest cave paintings (Figure 1.1), people have sought better and better ways to **record** and **communicate** information. Since the earliest abacus, people have sought better and better ways to **process** information (Figure 1.2).

Figure 1.1 A cave painting

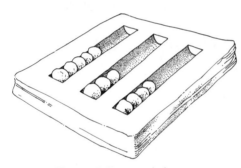

Figure 1.2 A sand abacus

The invention in the 1940s of the electronic digital computer was the natural culmination of both these developments. A computer is the best machine yet devised that can record, communicate and process information.

To be strict, computers process **data**, not information. Data is simply a collection of numbers, figures or signs without meaning. For example, consider

94 A   83 A   65 B   52 C   41 D

This data has no meaning unless we know perhaps that it represents the marks and grades of five examination candidates. Only then does it become **information**.

This distinction between data and information emphasises the fact that the computer has no understanding of the data it processes. The computer is in fact **an electronic data-processing machine**.

Computers and Programs

A computer processes data by following a set of instructions called a **program**, written by a **programmer**. **To program** means 'to write a set of instructions for the computer'.

A computer program is written in a special programming **language** such as **BASIC**, **FORTRAN** or **COBOL**.

Both the program and the data can be stored in the computer so that once the computer is started it can process the data without further help. For example, a computer may be provided with *data* on the hours worked by all a company's employees and a *program* of instruction for calculating and printing their wage slips. It can then be left to complete the task.

This apparent ability to function without human intervention makes a computer *appear* intelligent. But in fact computers have *no* intelligence of their own and cannot even recognise incorrect data (unless programmed to do so). If you were asked to sort a list of names into alphabetical order and came across JKMG AZYHTWXD, you would certainly suspect an error or even a joke. A computer would process such a name without question.

Computers and the Business World

Computers were first developed for use in military and scientific research. Because they were built as single one-off machines they often had very untidy and strange appearances. They were very large, expensive and prone to breakdowns.

Various engineering developments made it possible by the late 1950s to produce cheaper, smaller and more reliable computers. Although the costs were still measured in tens and hundreds of thousands of pounds, the use of computers in commerce and industry grew very rapidly. Today over 80% of large computer installations are to be found in offices and factories.

The great advantages that have led to such a widespread use of computers are:

* **Storage**. Computers can store and quickly retrieve vast quantities of information. Once stored, the information is never forgotten, unless it is deliberately destroyed.

1

* **Speed**. Computers can process data at very high speeds. Some can perform millions of operations in a single second.
* **Reliability**. Computers are machines. Unlike humans, they never get tired or bored and make mistakes. They may break down altogether, but when working they will always produce correct results — if provided with the correct data and programs.
* **Control**. Once programmed, computers can run automatically with minimal supervision. Not only can they control their own operation; they can also be used to control other machines and industrial processes (Figure 1.3).

Microprocessors and Microcomputers

Until the late 1960s computers were often too large and too expensive to use. Nowadays they are used in millions of devices. This is because computers have become both smaller and cheaper.

It is now possible to manufacture the main parts of a computer on tiny wafers of silicon about 6 mm square. These wafers of silicon are called **'chips'** (Figure 1.4). A chip containing a tiny but complete computer is called a **microprocessor chip**. Each chip is cheap enough to be made for a single purpose — for example, controlling a digital watch. Chips are used to control an enormous range of devices, from toys and games to washing machines. In some books these microprocessor controllers are called **microcomputers**, but this is confusing. We shall only use the term 'microcomputers' when the microprocessor has been equipped with a keyboard, TV and cassette recorder or disc drive to produce a small general purpose computer (Figure 1.5).

Computers and their Limitations

It is very difficult to specify exactly what tasks computers will always be unable to do. Certainly there are many problems they cannot yet solve. Deciding if a painting is good or bad and writing a novel are two examples.

Figure 1.3 Robots building the chassis of a BMW car

2

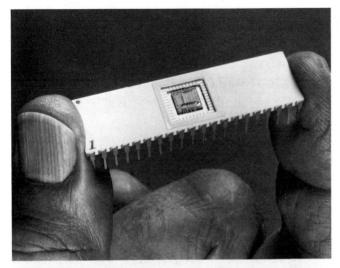

Figure 1.5 A Spectrum microcomputer

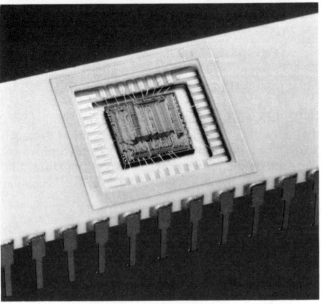

Figure 1.4 A typical chip

The computer has no in-built intelligence of its own, and no programmer can write a program to solve a problem that he or she does not understand. However, more complex programs are being written to solve problems once thought beyond the capabilities of computers. Devices are being constructed to enable computers to speak, hear, see and touch. Perhaps it would be fair to say that many tasks are beyond the present capacity of computers because nobody understands exactly how the human brain is able to accomplish them. This means that we cannot yet write programs for such tasks.

Nobody knows what may become possible. That perhaps is the most exciting aspect of computers and computing.

2 The Computer System

A Human System

Let us start by looking at a human system for problem solving. The system is shown in Figure 2.1.

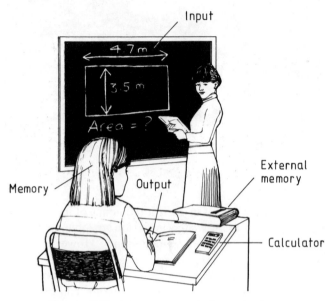

Figure 2.1 A human system in the maths class

The teacher uses a blackboard to **input** the problem.

The problem is **processed** by the student.

To help, the student has a calculator and her memory. If the student does not know the method of solution required, it can be looked up in the textbook. This textbook acts as a form of **external memory**.

The solution of the problem is **output** using a pen and exercise book.

Our problem solving system is thus divided into four parts:

* a method of input
* a method of processing
* a storage device for types of solution
* a method of output.

Most computer systems can also be divided into four parts. These are classified as:

* **Input devices**. These are used to convert information that humans can understand into the coded electrical signals that the computer can process.

* **The central processing unit**. This is where the electronic processing takes place. The unit has three parts:

  - **the control unit**, which controls all the computer's functions
  - **the arithmetic and logic unit**, which performs all the required calculations
  - **the memory unit**, which stores the program and data currently in use

* **Secondary storage devices**. These are used as an external memory. They store programs and data not in current use.

* **Output devices**. These are used to convert the computer's electrical signals back into information that humans can understand.

In the BBC microcomputer system shown in Figure 2.2, the input device is the **keyboard**. Secondary storage is provided by the **floppy disc drive**. There are two output devices: the **monitor screen** and the **printer**. The central processing unit is inside the case of the computer.

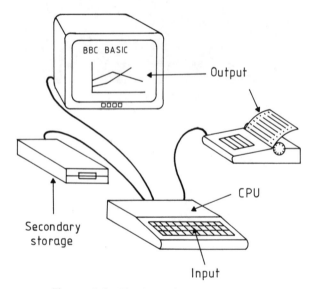

Figure 2.2 The parts of a computer system

Large computer systems often fill a whole room and have many different devices for input, output and secondary storage. Figure 2.3 opposite shows a large computer system. Later in this book we shall learn to identify the various parts of a system like this and to understand their functions.

Figure 2.3 A computer installation at the National Westminster Bank

Figure 2.4 can be applied to almost all computer systems.

The structure of the computer system affects the way in which we approach problems that require a computer solution. As we start to plan a solution we ask three questions:

* **What output is required**? This is the most important question since it will affect both the necessary input information and the processing required.

* **What information is needed to produce the required output**? This information may already be available as data held in secondary storage. Alternatively, all or some of the information may need to be input with a suitable input device.

* **What processing is required**? A suitable program may already exist in secondary storage or we may need to create a new program.

Let's look at an example. Many companies produce their workers' wage slips with a computer. Each week an input is needed giving each worker's name and the number of hours worked. A processing program to calculate and print the wage slips will be needed from secondary storage. Details of each worker's rate of pay, tax and other deductions will also be held in secondary storage.

This considerably reduces the amount of information that must be input each week. The computer will use the processing program to combine all the data and to print the wage slips. (See Figure 2.5.)

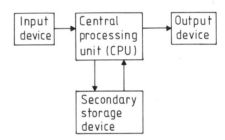

Figure 2.4 A diagram of computer parts

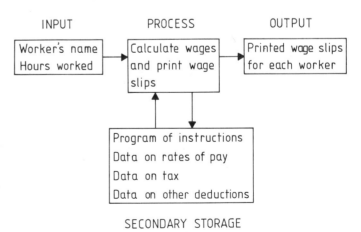

Figure 2.5 Processing wage slips

Exercise 1

1 The sketch below shows an office worker at her desk. She processes bills which are placed in an IN tray by her supervisor. To help her she has a calculator and a filing cabinet containing details of customers' accounts. When she has completed her work on a bill, she places it in an OUT tray to be collected by her supervisor. If a computer system were to be used for the same task, which parts of the system would correspond to:

  a the IN tray
  b the OUT tray
  c the filing cabinet
  d the calculator
  e the worker herself?

2 Copy and complete the following sentences.

  a The devices used to change information that humans can understand into the electrical signals that a computer can process are called _____ devices.
  b The devices used to change the computer's electrical signals back into information that humans can understand are called _____ devices.
  c The electronic processing carried out by a computer takes place in the _____ unit.
  d Programs and data that are not in current use by the computer are stored in a _____ device.
  e The three basic questions that we ask as we start to plan a computer solution to a problem are: _____.

3 The picture shows a digital watch. Inside the case is a microprocessor dedicated to controlling the watch. The buttons on the side of the watch may be used to set the time or change the display.

  a What input devices are provided on the watch?
  b What output devices are provided on the watch?
  c What kinds of information can the output devices provide?

4 In the popular home microcomputer shown below:

  a What input devices are provided on the microcomputer?
  b What output devices are provided on the microcomputer?
  c What secondary storage device is used by the microcomputer?

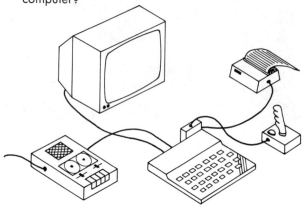

5 In each of the following cases, you are given a list of input data and a description of the processing required. Complete a list of the output data.

  a *Input* . . . Susan Jane Wendy Afifa Siloben Janet
     Process . . . Sort the names into alphabetical order.
  b *Input* . . . 3.6 3.5 3.7 3.9 3.1 3.0 3.7 3.2
     Process . . . Sort into descending numerical order.
  c *Input* . . . £2.45 £5.09 £7.86 £17.65
     Process . . . Find the total of the prices.
  d *Input* . . .

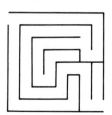

     Process . . . Find a way through the maze.

  e *Input* . . .

     Four microcomputers at £359   =
     Four disc drives at £111.50   =
     Four colour monitors at £223   =
     Two printers at £350   =

                      Total Cost =
     Process . . . Compete this bill for computer equipment.

6 Explain why the following requests for output are not clear enough to decide exactly what input and processing are required. In each case give an example of a clear request for the same kind of output.

  a Make me a pie for tea.
  b Sort the following list of numbers into order:
    1, 7, 9, 5, 2, 3, 11.
  c Prepare a list of all the pupils in your school.
  d Find Mr Smith's telephone number from the directory.
  e Buy some vegetables on your way home from school.

7 Each of the following requests for output can be met if (i) the correct input is provided and (ii) processing instructions and data are available in some form of secondary storage. In each case make a full list of all the input that must be provided and where any necessary processing instructions or data can be found.

  a An apple pie for four people, made with shortcrust pastry.
  b A customer's bill for her newspapers when she calls at the newsagents.
  c A list of all the first-year girls in your school who eat school lunches.
  d The telephone number of a garage in a particular town that sells a particular type of car.
  e A repair for a puncture in a bike tyre.

8 The picture below shows a sketch of a road crossing controlled by traffic lights.

  a What input device is provided for this system?
  b What output devices are provided for this system?
  c Write down the exact sequence of events that happens after the system receives an input signal.

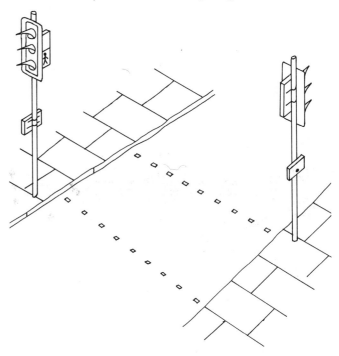

3 Problem-solving Techniques

Flowcharts and Algorithms

In the last chapter you were introduced to the three stages of data processing (Figure 3.1).

Figure 3.1 Three stages in data processing

In this chapter we will look more closely at the very systematic approach to problem solving that must be used when we work with computers.

Before we can write a computer program to solve a problem, we must first develop an **algorithm**. An algorithm is a set of instructions which, if followed exactly, will always produce a solution to a given problem. For example, we can write an algorithm to solve the problem of finding the area of any rectangle:

1 Input the base length of the rectangle.
2 Input the height of the rectangle.
3 Calculate the area by multiplying the base length by the height.
4 Output the area.

Table 3.1 Flowchart symbols

The symbol	What it is used for
(rounded box)	Start or stop the flow of data
(parallelogram)	Whenever data is input or output
(rectangle)	Whenever the data is processed
(diamond)	Whenever a decision is made
(circle)	To connect parts of a flowchart

A **flowchart** is often used to illustrate the algorithm found to solve a problem. A flowchart is a diagram which uses arrows and different shapes to show the steps in a problem solution. Some of the shapes used are shown in Table 3.1.

A flowchart for the algorithm to find the area of a rectangle is shown in Figure 3.2.

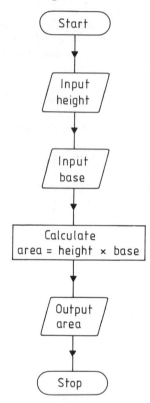

Figure 3.2 A flowchart to help find the area of a rectangle

Flowcharts are often used outside the world of computing to illustrate the solution to a problem.

For example, there is the well-known problem of a man who has a fox, a dog and a hen. If he leaves the fox alone with the dog, the dog will kill the fox. If he leaves the fox alone with the hen, the fox will eat the hen. The man comes to a river where there is only one boat, just big enough for himself and any one of the animals. How does he arrange to cross the river with all three animals still intact? The flowchart in Figure 3.3 illustrates a solution to this problem.

Flowcharts like the one above do not offer any great advantage over a simple list of instructions. It is when the consequences of decisions need to be illustrated that flowcharts are of most use. For example, suppose we wish to search a list of car owners and print out the names and addresses of all owners of red Metros. A

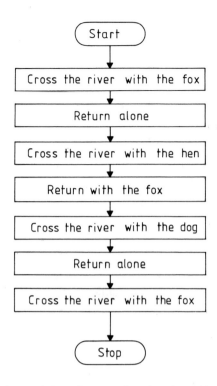

Figure 3.3 A flowchart for a beastly problem

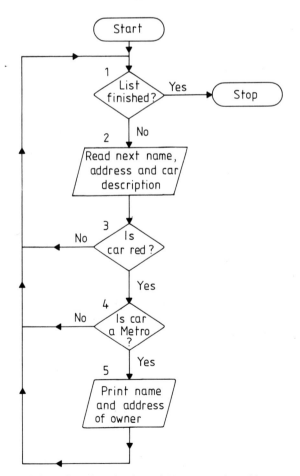

Figure 3.4 A flowchart for the red Metro search problem

computer programmer who wishes to use a computer for this task will need to break the search down into simple steps. A possible algorithm is shown below:

Step 1. If the list is finished, then stop.
Step 2. Read the next name, address and car description.
Step 3. If the car is not red, go to Step 6.
Step 4. If the car is not a Metro, go to Step 6.
Step 5. Print the name and address of the owner.
Step 6. Go to Step 1.

A flowchart drawn from this list of instructions is shown in Figure 3.4. Do you find the logic of the solution easier to follow from the flowchart than from the simple list of steps?

Notice that **Read** replaced 'Input' in the last flowchart. **Print** was also used in place of 'Output'. 'Read' indicates that the computer will find the required data either in its CPU memory or in its secondary storage memory. 'Input' indicates that the data will be entered directly. 'Print' indicates that the results will be printed, either on a monitor screen or on a printer.

Exercise 2

1 The following steps can, when placed in order, be used to make a cup of coffee. Draw a flowchart to illustrate these steps arranged into the correct order to make a cup of coffee.

Step 1. Add some sugar.
Step 2. Stir contents of the cup.
Step 3. Put some coffee powder in the cup.
Step 4. Boil some water.
Step 5. Top up the cup with milk.
Step 6. Pour boiling water into cup leaving room for the required amount of milk.

2 Imagine you have a grill that can hold exactly 2 slices of bread. The grill takes 2 minutes to toast one side of the bread. You wish to toast 3 slices of bread, slice A, slice B and slice C. Draw a flowchart to illustrate how you can toast all 3 slices of bread on both sides in only 6 minutes.

3 Draw a flowchart to illustrate an algorithm to calculate the area of any triangle.

4 To change a mark out of a total of 60 to a percentage, you first divide the mark by 60 and then multiply this result by 100. Draw a flowchart that inputs a pupil's name followed by a test mark out of a total of 60. The pupil's percentage mark should then be calculated. Finally, the pupil's name and percentage mark should be output.

5 A box contains a mixture of plastic shapes, each of which is either a rectangle, a triangle or a circle. Three empty boxes are labelled rectangles, triangles or circles. Your task is to draw a flowchart for an automatic process to sort the shapes into the correct empty boxes using the following rules:

Rule 1. If the shape has 4 sides, it is a rectangle.
Rule 2. If the shape has 3 sides, it is a triangle.
Rule 3. If the shape is not a rectangle or a triangle, it is a circle.

To help you the start of the flowchart is shown below.

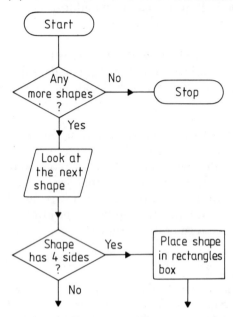

Sketch a design for a machine that you think might be capable of sorting the shapes by following the steps in your flowchart. You may assume that you have available a 'magic eye' which is capable of looking at each shape and deciding if it has 3 or 4 sides.

6 A computer has a long list of data in its secondary storage that details (i) the manufacturer of a car, (ii) the model name, (iii) the type of car (sports, saloon, hatchback or estate), and (iv) the country of manufacture.

Draw a flowchart for an algorithm to search this list and print the manufacturer and model name for all the hatchback cars that are not made in England.

7 A computer solution to many maze problems can be found by using the following algorithm.

Instruction 1. If you are home, then stop.
Instruction 2. If there is no way ahead, go to instruction 6.
Instruction 3. Move one step forwards.
Instruction 4. Turn to the right.
Instruction 5. Go to instruction 1.
Instruction 6. Turn to the left.
Instruction 7. Go to instruction 2.

Draw a flowchart to illustrate this algorithm. Test your flowchart by copying the maze below and marking the path that a computer following your flowchart would take through it.

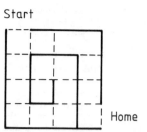

Miniature computerised machines that find their way through a maze using an algorithm like this one are called **wall followers**. Can you explain why? Can the instructions in the flowchart be reduced to a single simple instruction?

8 Many items that we use have a short list of instructions. For example a cassette recorder, a packet of frozen peas and a tin of paint each has instructions on how it should be used.

Write short, but clear, lists of instructions for **two** of the following:

  (i) Using a bicycle puncture repair outfit.
 (ii) Using an Instant Cash machine at a bank.
(iii) Correctly wiring a three-pin 13 amp electric plug.
(iv) Using a telephone in a kiosk.
 (v) Making a cake from a sponge mix.

(EAEB 83)

9 The owner of a bookshop has his own rules for deciding how many copies, if any, he will order of each book.

Using **only** the information given below, draw a flowchart to find the order required for **one** book.

Reprinted books:	do not order any copies
Non-fiction:	order 50 copies
Fiction: hard cover:	order 120 copies
paperback:	order 330 copies unless the book is written by a best selling author, in which case order 970 copies

(SERB 82)

10 The flowchart below shows how a code may be broken.

By working through the flowchart for the chosen number, a **new number** can be calculated. Use the following table to find the letter corresponding to the **new number**.

New number: 1 2 3 4 5 6 7 8 9 10 11 12 13

Letter represented:
A B C D E F G H I J K L M

New number: 14 15 16 17 18 19 20 21 22 23 24 25 26

Letter represented:
N O P Q R S T U V W X Y Z

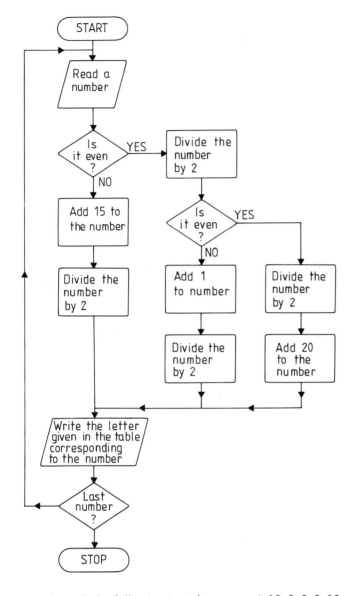

a Decode the following into characters: 4, 13, 3, 8, 2, 10.

b What number entered in the flowchart would produce the number used in the code to represent H?

(WJEB 82)

Flowcharts and Numerical Problems

When flowcharts are used to illustrate the solutions to numerical problems we need to understand some mathematical notation. If A, B, and C are any three numbers, then

$A > B$?	means 'is A greater than B?'
$A < B$?	means 'is A less than B?'
$A \geq B$?	means 'is A greater than or equal to B?'
$A \leq B$?	means 'is A less than or equal to B?'
$A = A + 1$	means 'let the number A be increased by 1.'
$B = A - C$	means 'let the number B take the value of $A - C$.'

Counter-controlled Loops

Sometimes we will wish to input and process a fixed number of data items. A flowchart can illustrate this situation by using a **counter-controlled loop**.

For example, suppose we wish to input the names and marks out of a total of 80 for 20 students. As each name is input, it should be printed followed by a percentage mark. The flowchart in Figure 3.5 illustrates the use of a counter-controlled loop to achieve this result.

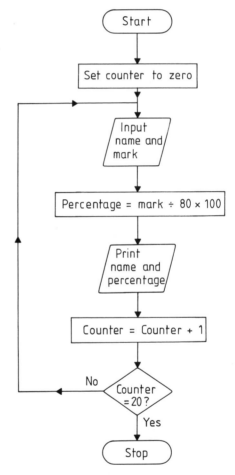

Figure 3.5 How a counter-controlled loop is used

Condition-controlled Loops and Rogue Values

Sometimes we will not know in advance the number of times that we wish a loop to repeat. The flow of data in this case can be interrupted by using a **rogue value** (sometimes called a **data terminator**). A rogue value is a data item that can be detected as different in some way from the normal data items. It can thus be used as a signal that the entry of data is completed. Because the loop will repeat until the special data item is met, it is called a **condition-controlled loop**.

For example, suppose we wish to input any number of positive numbers and, when data entry has ended, print the average of the numbers. In this case, a rogue value of -1 can be used to signal the end of data entry. A completed flowchart for this problem is shown in Figure 3.6.

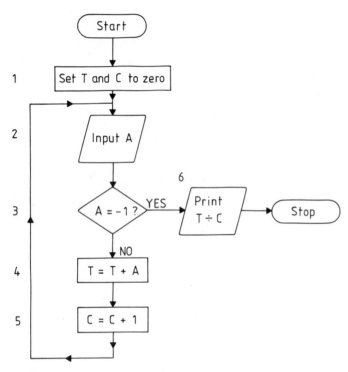

Variables used

T   the total of all input numbers
C   the number of input numbers
A   represents each input number

Figure 3.6   How a condition-controlled loop is used

Notice that all the variables used are explained below the flowchart.

Test Data and Trace Tables

Test data is data carefully designed to test that a flowchart is working correctly. Where a flowchart includes decision boxes, the data is chosen so that it tests all the branches of the flowchart. **Trace tables** can be used to show the flow of the test data through each separate step of the flowchart.

When completing a trace table, it is a good idea to number each box in the flowchart. A table is then drawn up to show the value of each of the variables used, and

the value of any output as the test data is run through the flowchart. A completed trace table for the previous flowchart using the test data 2, 5, 8 and -1 is shown in Table 3.2.

Table 3.2   Trace table for Figure 3.6

Box Number	Variables			Output
	A	T	C	
1		0	0	
2	2	0	0	
3	2	0	0	
4	2	2	0	
5	2	2	1	
2	5	2	1	
3	5	2	1	
4	5	7	1	
5	5	7	2	
2	8	7	2	
3	8	7	2	
4	8	15	2	
5	8	15	3	
2	-1	15	3	
3	-1	15	3	
6	-1	15	3	5

When our flowchart has been completed and tested, we are then in a position to turn it into a computer program. This book does not aim to teach programming in any particular language, but the example below (Figure 3.7) shows the previous flowchart changed into BASIC.

```
10 LET T = 0
20 LET C = 0
30 INPUT A
40 IF A = -1 THEN GOTO 80
50 LET T = T + A
60 LET C = C + 1
70 GOTO 30
80 PRINT T / C
```

Figure 3.7   A computer program for Figure 3.6

Exercise 3

1 A teacher wishes to use a microcomputer to process some test results. She requires a program that will allow her to enter each pupil's name and a test mark out of a total of 120. Each name should be printed after it is input, followed by a percentage mark for the test. Data entry will be ended when the rogue values **XXX** for a name and **0** for a mark are entered. Draw a flowchart to illustrate a solution to this teacher's problem.

2 In a decathlon, each competitor takes part in ten events. For each event he is awarded a score based on the amount by which he beats a set standard. Draw a flowchart for a program that will input a competitor's name followed by ten scores. The competitor's name and overall total score should then be printed.

3 On an aircraft flight, each passenger is allowed to take up to 20 kg of baggage. Any passenger over this limit is charged 1% of the first-class fare for the flight for each kilogram of excess baggage. For example, a passenger with 24 kg of baggage on a flight with a first-class fare of £300 will be charged for 4 kg of excess baggage at £3 per kilogram, a total of £12. Draw a flowchart to input the *total* weight of baggage and the first-class fare and then to calculate and output the charge (if any) for excess baggage.

4 A dice game is played by the following rules.

Step 1. Throw two dice and call the score S.
Step 2. If S = 2, 3 or 12, the player loses.
Step 3. If S = 7, the player wins.
Step 4. For any other score set D equal to S.
Step 5. Throw the dice again and call the score S, changing the old value of S if necessary.
Step 6. If S = D, the player wins.
Step 7. If S = 7, the player loses.
Step 8. Repeat from Step 5 until the player wins or loses.

Draw a flowchart to illustrate the rules of this game. You may use a process box that sets S equal to a double dice score. You may also use a single decision box to test if S is equal to 2, 3 or 12.

Obtain two dice and complete trace tables for three separate games.

5 Study this flowchart carefully and then answer the questions which follow.

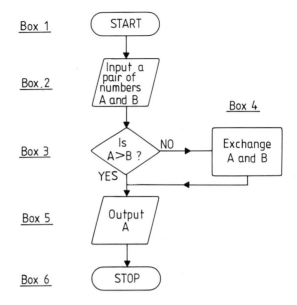

a If A = 1 and B = 2 upon input what would the value of A be on output?
b Copy and amend the flowchart so that more than one pair of numbers can be processed.
c What test could be used to stop the process, given that the normal values of A and B are never negative, and where would the test box be placed?

(ALSEB 82)

Famous Computer People: Number 1
Charles Babbage 1792 to 1871

Charles Babbage designed mechanical calculators and computers. His machines worked with gearwheels and levers and used punched cards to store data. Modern reconstructions have shown that Babbage's designs would have worked perfectly. Unfortunately, the engineers of his time could not achieve the precision needed to build the machines.

One hundred years were to pass before the development of electronics allowed Babbage's ideas to be put into practice.

6

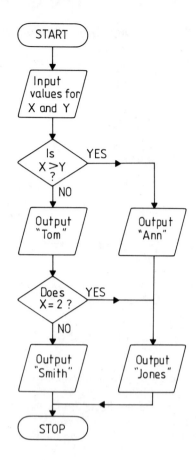

7 A flowchart and a blank trace table are given below. Copy and complete the trace table by using the following data: 0, 0, 0, 1, 1, 0, 1, 1.

(NREB 82*)

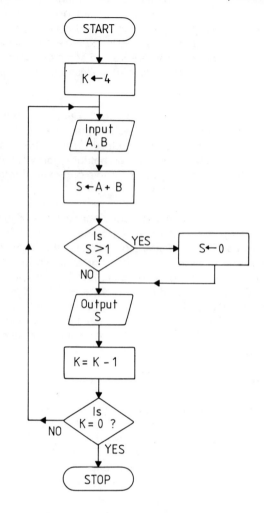

a Write down the three output names that will result from each of the following sets of test data:

Set 1. $X = 3$, $Y = 4$; $X = 4$, $Y = 5$; $X = 2$, $Y = 1$
Set 2. $X = 2$, $Y = 3$; $X = 1$, $Y = 2$; $X = 2$, $Y = 1$
Set 3. $X = 2$, $Y = 1$; $X = 2$, $Y = 0$; $X = 3$, $Y = 0$

b Which set of test data properly tests the flowchart?

(EAEB 82)

Famous Computer People: Number 2

Countess of Lovelace 1815 to 1852

The Countess of Lovelace was the daughter of the poet Byron. She knew Charles Babbage and took a keen interest in his designs for a mechanical computer. She wrote programs for the computer and can thus be regarded as the world's first computer programmer. The modern computer language ADA is named in her honour, her real name being Ada Byron.

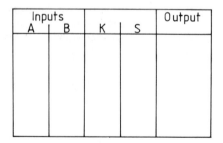

Inputs				Output
A	B	K	S	

8 Work through the flowchart below, and produce a table showing clearly the values of the printed output C, and the values for A, B and D, as the process is followed.

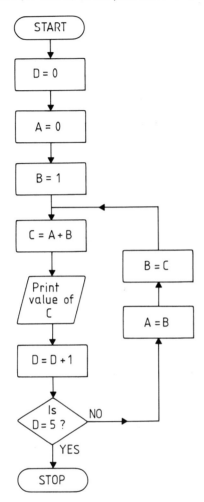

(i) What is the purpose of the variable D?
(ii) What change would you make to the flowchart to obtain TEN printed values of C?

(EMREB 82*)

9 (i) Trace through this flowchart to find what the output would be if A is 14 and B is 4.
(ii) Describe in general terms what this flowchart does.

(SUJB 81)

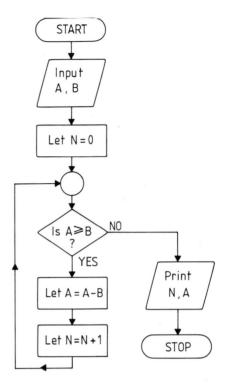

10 An examination consists of two papers each marked out of 100.

If a candidate obtains 80 or more marks on each paper he is awarded a DISTINCTION.

If he fails to be awarded a distinction, but the sum of his marks is 100 or more he is awarded a PASS.

If none of these conditions are met he FAILS.

Draw a flowchart for a computer program to process and grade the examination results for the candidates sitting this examination.

Your flowchart should:

1. Read in each candidate's name and the marks for the two papers. The list of candidates and marks is ended with the rogue data XXX,0,0.
2. Printout the candidate's name and DISTINCTION, PASS or FAIL as appropriate.
3. Printout the total number of candidates who sat the exam following the list of results.

(SREB 82)

11 Draw a flowchart, for use before writing a program, which will input a class list with seven test results for each pupil and output the list with each pupil's average mark and highest mark with appropriate messages.

(ALSEB 82)

12 Here is a detailed flowchart for finding the average of five numbers:

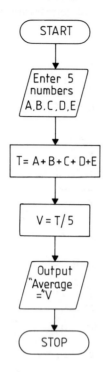

a Explain why this approach is satisfactory for 5 numbers but not for 500 numbers
b Draw a flowchart to find the average of 500 numbers.

(EAEB 83)

13 a Draw a flowchart based upon the following description of the cost of insuring a motor cycle.

"The basic cost of the annual insurance for a motor cycle is £20 for full insurance or £15 if full insurance is not required. If the rider is under the age of 25 and has

not passed the driving test the cost is increased by a further £12, however if he has passed his test the cost will be increased by only £5. A further £8 is added to the cost of the insurance if the driver has had an accident during the last three years."

b How much will it cost Fred Bloggs for full insurance if he has just become old enough (16 years of age) for a licence to drive a motor cycle?

(EAEB 82)

14 A newspaper boy has been given a microprocessor and wants to write a program to process the customers' accounts from his newspaper round.

For each customer, he inputs

1. Daily cost of morning papers (delivered Monday to Saturday)
2. Daily cost of evening papers (delivered Monday to Saturday)
3. Cost of Sunday papers.

a Draw a flow chart to input the data for *one* customer and output that customer's weekly bill.
b The customers are charged for delivery as follows:
   1. 5p per week for morning papers
   2. 5p per week for evening papers
   3. 2p for Sunday papers.

If the boy has 40 customers, draw a flow chart to *input* the cost of papers and *output* the weekly bill for *each customer in turn*.

(Notes — (1) There **must** be three inputs for every customer — if he does not buy a particular *type* of paper, the cost of that paper is input as zero. (2) Your flow chart will have to test whether or not to charge delivery for each type of paper.)

(SWEB 82)

4 Data Representation in the Computer

Binary Numbers

Normal everyday numbers are called **base ten** or **denary** numbers. This is because they are written under column headings based on the number ten. For example, the number 345 means:

Hundreds	Tens	Units
3	4	5

Binary or **base two** numbers are written under column headings based on the number two. For example, in binary, the number 101 means:

Fours	Twos	Units
1	0	1

This binary number is equal to the denary number 5.

The first ten denary numbers and the first ten binary numbers are shown in Table 4.1.

Table 4.1 Denary and binary numbers

Denary numbers		Binary numbers			
Tens	Units	Eights	Fours	Twos	Units
	0				0
	1				1
	2			1	0
	3			1	1
	4		1	0	0
	5		1	0	1
	6		1	1	0
	7		1	1	1
	8	1	0	0	0
	9	1	0	0	1
1	0	1	0	1	0

Changing binary numbers to denary numbers is easy if you first write the column headings in above the number. For example, if we wish to change the binary number 10111 into denary, we first write it down in sixteens, eights, fours, twos and ones:

16s	8s	4s	2s	1s
1	0	1	1	1

We can now see that the binary number 10111 is equal to 16 + 4 + 2 + 1, or 23 in denary.

When changing a denary number into a binary number, we also start by writing down the binary column headings. The denary number is then divided out into these new columns. For example, the denary number 45 can be divided out into binary columns in the following way:

64s	32s	16s	8s	4s	2s	1s
	1	0	1	1	0	1

45 =

We *must* remember that the binary number system only uses the digits 1 and 0. It is *completely wrong* to represent the denary number 45 in the following way:

16s	8s	4s	2s	1s
2	1	1	0	1

45 =

The binary number system is a **two-state system** because it uses only two digits, 1 and 0. Our normal everyday number system is a **ten-state system** because it uses ten digits, 0, 1, 2, 3, 4, 5, 6, 7, 8 and 9. Many two-state systems exist and they can all be used to represent binary numbers. For example, if

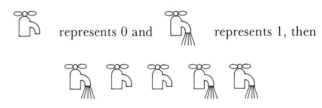

represents 0 and represents 1, then

represents the binary number 10011 which in denary is equal to 19.

Exercise 4

1 Switches can be open or closed. If represents 0 and represents 1, what binary numbers are represented in each of these lines of switches? Change each binary number to its denary equivalent.

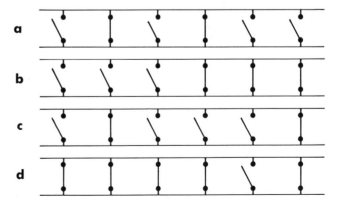

2 A hole may or may not be punched in a piece of paper tape.

If 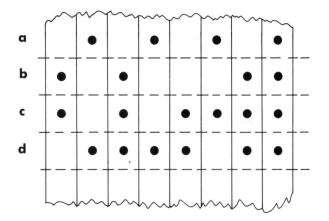 represents 0 and represents 1, what binary numbers are represented in each row (frame) across this 8-track paper tape? Change each binary number to its denary equivalent.

3 A pulse of electricity may or may not be present at any point in a circuit. If represents no pulse or 0 and represents a pulse or 1, what binary numbers do each of the following pulse patterns represent? Change each binary number to its denary equivalent.

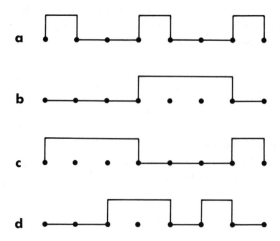

4 A small ferrite ring can be magnetized in either the clockwise or anticlockwise direction. If  represents 0 and represents 1, what binary number is represented in each of the following sets of rings. Change each binary number to its denary equivalent.

a

b

c

d

In a 2-bit binary code there are 4 different binary numbers:

0	0
0	1
1	0
1	1

In a 3-bit binary code there are 8 different binary numbers:

0	0	0
0	0	1
0	1	0
0	1	1
1	0	0
1	0	1
1	1	0
1	1	1

Binary Numbers and Computers

A binary code is used to represent all the data processed in a modern digital computer. Several different devices are used to store and process the data but they are all two-state devices. There are two reasons why digital computers are designed to use binary numbers and constructed from two-state devices:

* The construction of two-state devices is much simpler than the construction of devices with more than two states.
* Communication between the devices is very reliable because only two different signals need to be recognized when data is transmitted.

Representing Data with a Binary Code

If we wish to use a binary code to represent data, we must first decide how many **bi**nary dig**its** or **bits** we will need to represent each separate character of data. We will need a different binary code number for:

* 26 capital letters (upper case)
* 26 small letters (lower case)
* 10 numbers (0 to 9)
* 8 punctuation symbols (" ? ' ; : , ! and .)
* about 20 special symbols (* & £ % + = etc.)
* about 20 control signals (line feed, form feed etc.)
* a space.

Therefore we will need a total of about 120 different binary code numbers.

In general, the number of different numbers in a binary code can be found from the corresponding power of 2. Thus, a 5-bit code gives 2^5 ($2 \times 2 \times 2 \times 2 \times 2$) or 32 different binary numbers. Table 4.2 shows the number of different binary numbers available in codes from 1 bit to 8 bits.

Table 4.2 Number of bits against number of binary numbers

Number of bits in the binary code	Number of different binary numbers
1	$2^1 = 2$
2	$2^2 = 4$
3	$2^3 = 8$
4	$2^4 = 16$
5	$2^5 = 32$
6	$2^6 = 64$
7	$2^7 = 128$
8	$2^8 = 256$

Remember that we need a total of about 120 different binary code numbers to represent a full set of characters. This means that when a binary code is devised to represent data, a minimum of 7 binary digits is needed to represent each character of the data. A very common 7-bit code is called ASCII (pronounced *Askey*). ASCII stands for the American Standard Code for Information Interchange. Because 7 bits are used, ASCII allows 128 different representations. Some of these are shown in Table 4.3.

Table 4.3 Some of the ASCII representations

Character	Binary code							Decimal equivalent
A	1	0	0	0	0	0	1	65
B	1	0	0	0	0	1	0	66
C	1	0	0	0	0	1	1	67
D	1	0	0	0	1	0	0	68
E	1	0	0	0	1	0	1	69
F	1	0	0	0	1	1	0	70
G	1	0	0	0	1	1	1	71
H	1	0	0	1	0	0	0	72
I	1	0	0	1	0	0	1	73
J	1	0	0	1	0	1	0	74
K	1	0	0	1	0	1	1	75
L	1	0	0	1	1	0	0	76
M	1	0	0	1	1	0	1	77
N	1	0	0	1	1	1	0	78
O	1	0	0	1	1	1	1	79
P	1	0	1	0	0	0	0	80
Q	1	0	1	0	0	0	1	81
R	1	0	1	0	0	1	0	82
S	1	0	1	0	0	1	1	83
T	1	0	1	0	1	0	0	84
U	1	0	1	0	1	0	1	85
V	1	0	1	0	1	1	0	86
W	1	0	1	0	1	1	1	87
X	1	0	1	1	0	0	0	88
Y	1	0	1	1	0	0	1	89
Z	1	0	1	1	0	1	0	90
Space	0	1	0	0	0	0	0	32
0	0	1	1	0	0	0	0	48
1	0	1	1	0	0	0	1	49
2	0	1	1	0	0	1	0	50
3	0	1	1	0	0	1	1	51
4	0	1	1	0	1	0	0	52
5	0	1	1	0	1	0	1	53
6	0	1	1	0	1	1	0	54
7	0	1	1	0	1	1	1	55
8	0	1	1	1	0	0	0	56
9	0	1	1	1	0	0	1	57
+	0	1	0	1	0	1	1	43
−	0	1	0	1	1	0	1	45
=	0	1	1	1	1	0	1	61
?	0	1	1	1	1	1	1	63
.	0	1	0	1	1	1	0	46
;	0	1	1	1	0	1	1	59

Computers have been built that use a 6-bit code to represent data. Because a 6-bit code allows only 64 representations, a restricted set of characters must be used. For example, in 6-bit codes, often only capital letters can be represented.

The binary code used to represent characters in a computer is called the **internal character code** of the computer. The actual characters that can be represented are called the **character set** of the computer. A code like ASCII, which can represent letters, numbers and symbols, is called an **alphanumeric code**.

A section of computer memory that can store a single character of data is called a **byte** of memory. In most computers, each byte of memory contains 8 binary digits or bits. A representation of an 8-bit byte of memory storing the ASCII code for the letter P is shown below:

0	1	0	1	0	0	0	0

Because ASCII is a 7-bit code, each byte of memory has one spare bit. This bit is often used to provide a **parity check**. The 8th bit is added as either a 1 or a 0 so that the number of 1s in the final code is always an even number.

Thus P, with code 1010000, becomes 01010000, with two 1s. R, with code 1010010, becomes 11010010, with four 1s. Data that includes a parity bit can be checked after it has been transmitted from one part of the computer to another. If one bit has been accidentally changed, the number of 1s will no longer be even and the mistake can be detected and reported. Notice however that 2, 4 or any even number of mistakes cannot be detected.

When a computer is built it is provided with a large number of separate memory locations. Each location is numbered and the computer can use the number, called the **address** of the location, to select the data it contains. Small microcomputers often only store one byte of data in each memory location. Larger computers may store several bytes of data in each memory location. Figure 4.1 shows how the word PEAR might be stored in locations 1000 to 1011 of a microcomputer or in location 1000 of a large computer.

Address	Data	
1000	01010000	P
1001	11000101	E
1010	01000001	A
1011	11010010	R

Address	Data			
1000	01010000	11000101	01000001	11010010
	P	E	A	R

Figure 4.1 Two ways to store PEAR in a computer

The number of bits provided in each memory location is referred to as the **wordlength** of the computer. In the example above, the microcomputer uses an 8-bit wordlength and is thus an **8-bit computer**. The larger computer uses a 32-bit wordlength and is thus a **32-bit computer**.

The size of a computer's memory is the number of bytes of data storage that it provides. The size is measured using the following table.

> 1 **byte** of memory = storage for a **single character** of data.
> 1 **kilobyte** of memory = **1024** bytes.
> 1 **megabyte** of memory = **1 000 000** bytes.

'Kilobyte' is usually shortened to K. A 64K computer can store 64 × 1024 or 65 536 characters of data.

Exercise 5

1 If 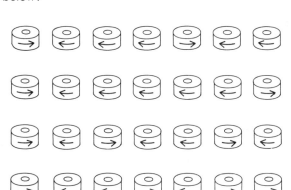 represents 0 and represents 1, what word is stored in ASCII code in the sets of rings shown below?

2 Each year the Zapper computer company has an outing. This year eight people went off to climb a hill and later the rest of the party saw seven of them signalling from the top of the hill. They were signalling in ASCII. Try to decode their message.

3 An ASCII message has been punched on this tape using the left-hand track as an eighth parity bit. If a punched hole represents a 1 and a blank represents a 0, decode the message.

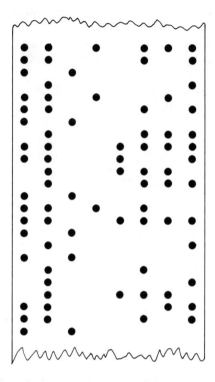

4 Using 1s and 0s, write down the ASCII code plus even parity bit for:

a N
b B
c X
d K
e ?

5 If an even parity check is in use, which of the following codes indicate that there has been a fault in transmission?

a 10010111
b 01001011
c 11011000
d 01000011

6 How many representations are possible with a 5-bit binary code?

7 Is a 5-bit code practical for use in a computer?

8 Draw diagrams to show how the word OBSTREPEROUS would be stored using even parity ASCII in:

a 12 8-bit words
b 4 24-bit words
c 3 32-bit words

9 A 6-bit code uses the binary numbers from 100000 to 111010 to encode the letters A to Z. Draw a diagram to show the word BEAD stored in 1 24-bit word using this code.

10 If a computer uses an 8-bit internal character code and 32-bit words, how many memory locations are required to store the phrase ENGAGE THE ENEMY MORE CLOSELY.

11 A computer memory is described as a 16K 16-bit memory. How many:

a words
b bytes
c bits

does the memory contain?

12 Having a 16K 8-bit microcomputer, a teacher decides to write a program which stores as data in the computer's memory the names and addresses of the 1200 pupils in the school. Is this a practical idea? Explain your answer.

13 Estimate the number of characters in this book (very roughly). Hence find the approximate number of bytes of memory needed to store the book.

14 Using any 2-state system that you like, encode a message in 7-bit ASCII. Give the message to a friend to decode.

Representing Numbers

When a number is part of a string of characters, it will be stored using the internal character code of the computer. For example, the string of characters QE2 can be stored using even parity ASCII code in the following way:

Q →	1	1	0	1	0	0	0	1
E →	1	1	0	0	0	1	0	1
2 →	1	0	1	1	0	0	1	0

There are, however, two reasons why numbers used for calculations are not stored using the internal character code:

* Arithmetic is very difficult when numbers are stored using the internal character code.
* Storage is very inefficient when numbers are stored using the internal character code.

To illustrate the second point, imagine we have a single byte of memory available to store a number.

Using even parity ASCII code, we can store any whole number from 0 to 9:

From	0	0	1	1	0	0	0	0	← 0
To	0	0	1	1	1	0	0	1	← 9

If, however, we allow each binary number to represent the equivalent denary number, we can store any whole number from 0 to 255:

From	0	0	0	0	0	0	0	0	← 0
To	1	1	1	1	1	1	1	1	← 255

Representing Negative Numbers

The bit at the left of any binary number is called the **most significant bit** because it is under the largest column heading. The bit at the right of any binary number is called the **least significant bit** because it is under the smallest column heading:

1 1 0 0 1 0 1 0

Most significant bit   Least significant bit

The most common form of representation for negative binary numbers is called the **two's complement system**. Using this system, the most significant bit of any binary number represents a negative quantity. For example, for a 5-bit two's complement number the column headings are:

$$-16s \quad 8s \quad 4s \quad 2s \quad 1s$$

In 5-bit two's complement numbers, 10001 represents $-16 + 1$ or -15.

Examples

a Change the 6-bit two's complement number 100011 into a denary number.

	$-32s$	$16s$	$8s$	$4s$	$2s$	$1s$
100011 is	1	0	0	0	1	1

Thus $100011 = -32 + 3 = -29$

b Change -3 into a 4-bit two's complement number.

	$-8s$	$4s$	$2s$	$1s$
-3 is $-8 + 5$ or	1	1	0	1

Thus $-3 = 1101$

If a single byte is available to store a number, two's complement representation will allow us to store any whole number from -128 to $+127$:

From	1	0	0	0	0	0	0	0	(-128)
To	0	1	1	1	1	1	1	1	$(+127)$

If we know the representation of any positive number in binary, the two's complement representation of the corresponding negative number is easily obtained from it. The reverse is also true. This process of reversing the sign of a binary number is called **finding the two's complement** of the number.

Examples

a Find the two's complement of 00010111

Step 1. Change each bit of the number.

0	0	0	1	0	1	1	1	(+23)
↓	↓	↓	↓	↓	↓	↓	↓	
1	1	1	0	1	0	0	0	

Step 2. Add 1.   +1

1	1	1	0	1	0	0	1	(−23)

b Find the two's complement of 10000100

Step 1. Change each bit of the number.

1	0	0	0	0	1	0	0	(−124)
↓	↓	↓	↓	↓	↓	↓	↓	
0	1	1	1	1	0	1	1	

Step 2. Add 1.   +1

0	1	1	1	1	1	0	0	(+124)

The result obtained by just changing each bit of the number is called its **one's complement**.

Exercise 6

1 Change each of the following 4-bit two's complement binary numbers into denary:

a 0011 **b** 0101 **c** 1000 **d** 1011 **e** 1111

2 Change each of the following numbers into 4-bit two's complement binary numbers:

a 6 **b** −7 **c** −2 **d** −6 **e** −4

3 What range of denary integers can be stored in 4-bit two's complement form?

4 Change each of the following 6-bit two's complement binary numbers into denary:

a 011111 **b** 100000 **c** 101011 **d** 111111
e 111000

5 Change each of the following numbers into 6-bit two's complement binary numbers:

a 30 **b** −30 **c** 10 **d** −10 **e** −4

6 What range of denary integers can be stored in 6-bit two's complement form?

7 Using the method of changing bits and adding 1, find the two's complement of each of the following numbers. Check your work by changing both the given number and your answer into denary.

a 00010111   **e** 00000001
b 10000011   **f** 11111010
c 00000011   **g** 10101010
d 10000001   **h** 11000000

8 The BBC microcomputer stores two's complement numbers in 32 bits. What range of denary integers can be stored in this way? (*Hint.* 2^{31} = 2 147 483 648)

Representing Fractions

The binary system can be extended to cope with fractions. The column headings for binary fractions are:

$$4s \quad 2s \quad 1s \quad \tfrac{1}{2}s \quad \tfrac{1}{4}s \quad \tfrac{1}{8}s$$

Examples

a Change the binary number 101.101 into denary.

	4s	2s	1s	$\tfrac{1}{2}$s	$\tfrac{1}{4}$s	$\tfrac{1}{8}$s	
101.101 is	1	0	1	1	0	1	or $5 + \tfrac{1}{2} + \tfrac{1}{8}$

$5 + \tfrac{1}{2} + \tfrac{1}{8}$ can be written as $5\tfrac{5}{8}$ or 5.625.

b Change 6.75 into binary.

	4s	2s	1s	$\tfrac{1}{2}$s	$\tfrac{1}{4}$s	$\tfrac{1}{8}$s
6.75 is $6\tfrac{3}{4}$ or	1	1	0	1	1	0

Thus 6.75 = 110.11.

Many denary decimal fractions cannot be represented as exact binary fractions. The decimal 0.8, for example, can only be represented by the recurring binary number 0.1100110011001100 . . .

When a fixed number of bits is available to store a long binary number like this, it must be **truncated** or cut to fit. For example, if 4 bits are available to store a representation of 0.8, we can truncate the recurring binary number and store 0.8 as

$\tfrac{1}{2}$s	$\tfrac{1}{4}$s	$\tfrac{1}{8}$s	$\tfrac{1}{16}$s
1	1	0	0

This binary number is exactly equal to 0.75, so we have introduced a **truncation error** of 0.05 by attempting to store 0.8 in 4 bits.

A better approximation can be found if we **round** the binary fraction. To round a binary fraction to a fixed number of places we look at the next place along. **If the bit in this place is 1, we round up; if it is a 0, we round down**. The decimal 0.8 can be stored in 4 bits as the rounded binary number 0.1101:

$$\frac{1}{2}s \quad \frac{1}{4}s \quad \frac{1}{8}s \quad \frac{1}{16}s$$
$$1 \quad\quad 1 \quad\quad 0 \quad\quad 1$$

This binary number is exactly equal to 0.8125, so we have a **rounding error** of 0.0125.

Real computers provide many more bits to store binary fractions but truncation and rounding errors still occur. There will therefore be a limit to the calculation accuracy of any computer.

Conversions between denary and binary fractions are best tackled with a calculator and the following list of conversions:

$$1/2 = 0.5$$
$$1/4 = 0.25$$
$$1/8 = 0.125$$
$$1/16 = 0.0625$$
$$1/32 = 0.03125$$
$$1/64 = 0.015625$$
$$1/128 = 0.0078125$$

Examples

a Change the binary number 1.011011 into base ten.

$$1s \quad \frac{1}{2}s \quad \frac{1}{4}s \quad \frac{1}{8}s \quad \frac{1}{16}s \quad \frac{1}{32}s \quad \frac{1}{64}s$$
$$1.011011 \text{ is } \quad 1 \quad 0 \quad 1 \quad 1 \quad 0 \quad 1 \quad 1$$

which is

$$1+0.25+0.125+0.03125+0.015625=1.421875.$$

b Find the best possible representation for the decimal 0.1 using four binary places. State the error in this representation.

Representing 0.1 in five binary places, we have:

$$\frac{1}{2}s \quad \frac{1}{4}s \quad \frac{1}{8}s \quad \frac{1}{16}s \quad \frac{1}{32}s$$
$$0.1 \text{ is } \quad 0 \quad 0 \quad 0 \quad 1 \quad 1$$

Rounding this to four binary places, we have:

0.1 (in base ten) = 0.0010 (in binary)

This binary number is exactly equal to 0.125, so the error in this representation is 0.025.

The binary point is not usually coded in the computer and can be fixed anywhere within a number. Thus the 4-bit binary number

0	1	1	1

can be interpreted as:

7 if the point is after the last bit
3.5 if the point is one place from the right
1.75 if the point is two places from the right
0.875 if the point is three places from the right
0.4375 if the point is at the start of the number.

Exercise 7

1 Change each of the following binary numbers into denary.

   a 1.1 **b** 0.11 **c** 111.111 **d** 1011.011 **e** 11.1001

2 Change each of the following denary numbers into binary.

   a $3\frac{1}{2}$ **b** $7\frac{3}{4}$ **c** $5\frac{7}{8}$ **d** 0.375 **e** 0.3125

3 Find the best possible representation in four binary places for each of the following denary numbers. In each case state the error in this representation.

   a 0.2 **b** 0.6 **c** 0.625 **d** $\frac{2}{3}$ **e** 0.95

4 Convert to denary the binary numbers shown under the following two's complement binary headings.

	$-1s$	$\frac{1}{2}s$	$\frac{1}{4}s$	$\frac{1}{8}s$	$\frac{1}{16}s$
a	0	1	0	1	1
b	0	0	1	1	1
c	1	1	0	0	0
d	1	1	1	0	0
e	1	0	1	1	0

5 Convert the binary number 00011110 into a denary number if the binary point is fixed:

   a at the right of the number
   b one place from the right
   c two places from the right
   d three places from the right
   e four places from the right
   f five places from the right
   g six places from the right
   h seven places from the right
   i at the left of the number.

Octal and Hexadecimal Numbers

If you are learning to program a computer, you are almost certainly learning a computer language such as BASIC or PASCAL or LOGO. When using these languages, the computer programmer never needs to worry about the binary numbers that are actually stored and processed by the computer. The computer system automatically converts the programmer's instructions into binary numbers and then converts any binary output back into normal characters of data.

Sometimes, however, programmers need to work at a level much closer to the actual binary numbers used in the computer. In these cases they usually write their programs using **octal** or **hexadecimal** numbers.

Octal or **base 8** numbers are written under column headings based on the number 8. For example, in octal the number 234 means:

$$\begin{array}{ccc} 64s & 8s & 1s \\ 2 & 3 & 4 \end{array}$$

which in denary is $128 + 24 + 4$ or 156.

Hexadecimal or **base 16** numbers are written under column headings based on the number 16. For example, in hexadecimal the number 234 means:

$$\begin{array}{ccc} 256s & 16s & 1s \\ 2 & 3 & 4 \end{array}$$

which in denary is $512 + 48 + 4$ or 564.

Programmers use octal or hexadecimal numbers for two reasons.

* **They are preferred to binary numbers** because it is very difficult for humans to remember binary numbers or write them down without mistakes.
* **They are preferred to denary numbers** because conversion of binary numbers to and from these bases is easier than conversion of binary numbers to and from denary.

Table 4.4 shows the first twenty numbers in denary, binary, octal and hexadecimal. Notice that it is necessary to invent some new symbols for use in hexadecimal numbers. This is because the denary numbers 10, 11, 12, 13, 14 and 15 are all single-digit numbers in hexadecimal. By common agreement, the letters A, B, C, D, E and F are used to represent these denary numbers in hexadecimal.

Table 4.4 Numbers in different bases

Denary (Base 10)		Binary (Base 2)					Octal (Base 8)		Hexadecimal (Base 16)	
10s	1s	16s	8s	4s	2s	1s	8s	1s	16s	1s
	0					0		0		0
	1					1		1		1
	2				1	0		2		2
	3				1	1		3		3
	4			1	0	0		4		4
	5			1	0	1		5		5
	6			1	1	0		6		6
	7			1	1	1		7		7
	8		1	0	0	0	1	0		8
	9		1	0	0	1	1	1		9
1	0		1	0	1	0	1	2		A
1	1		1	0	1	1	1	3		B
1	2		1	1	0	0	1	4		C
1	3		1	1	0	1	1	5		D
1	4		1	1	1	0	1	6		E
1	5		1	1	1	1	1	7		F
1	6	1	0	0	0	0	2	0	1	0
1	7	1	0	0	0	1	2	1	1	1
1	8	1	0	0	1	0	2	2	1	2
1	9	1	0	0	1	1	2	3	1	3
2	0	1	0	1	0	0	2	4	1	4

When converting between binary and octal, each group of three binary digits converts to one octal digit.

Examples

a Change the binary number 111011101 into octal.

$$\begin{array}{ccc} 111 & 011 & 101 \\ \downarrow & \downarrow & \downarrow \\ 7 & 3 & 5 \end{array}$$

111011101 (in binary) = 735 (in octal)

b Change the octal number 205 into binary.

$$\begin{array}{ccc} 2 & 0 & 5 \\ \downarrow & \downarrow & \downarrow \\ 010 & 000 & 101 \end{array}$$

205 (in octal) = 010000101 (in binary)

When converting between binary and hexadecimal, each group of four binary digits converts to one hexadecimal digit.

Examples

a Change the binary number 10111101000 into hexadecimal.

$$\begin{array}{ccc} 101 & 1110 & 1000 \\ \downarrow & \downarrow & \downarrow \\ 5 & E & 8 \end{array}$$

10111101000 (in binary) = 5E8 (in hexadecimal)

b Change the hexadecimal number A7C into binary.

A7C (in hexadecimal) = 101001111100 (in binary)

Exercise 8

1 Convert each of the following binary numbers into octal:

a 111000   **c** 111100001010011
b 101001100   **d** 10111

2 Convert each of the following octal numbers into binary:

a 26   **c** 5555
b 174   **d** 30002

3 Convert each of the following binary numbers into hexa-decimal:

a 11110000   **c** 1010101111001101
b 10010111   **d** 1001000000001111

4 Convert each of the following hexadecimal numbers into binary:

a 111   **c** E09FD
b 2A5   **d** CC74B

Addition of Binary Numbers

When adding together two binary numbers there are only four basic rules to consider. These are:

* $0 + 0 = 0$
* $1 + 0 = 1$
* $1 + 1 = 0$ with 1 to carry
* $1 + 1 + 1 = 1$ with 1 to carry

Applying these rules to the problem $1101100 + 1011010$, we have

```
  1   1   1   1
    1   1   0   1   1   0   0
 +1   0   1   1   0   1   0
  1   1   0   0   0   1   1   0
```

In a computer a fixed number of bits will be available to store each number. An **overflow** error will occur if the result of a binary calculation is too long for the available number of bits. For example, suppose a computer is storing two's complement numbers in 8 bits. Location A is storing 01111110 and location B is storing 00000010. If the contents of these two locations are added together and stored in location C, we have:

Location A   0 1 1 1 1 1 1 0 (+126)

Location B   0 0 0 0 0 0 1 0 (+2)

Location C   1 0 0 0 0 0 0 0 (−128)

The negative result stored in location C is quite clearly incorrect. An overflow error has resulted because the correct result +128 cannot be stored in 8 bits as a two's complement number. A real computer will provide many more than 8 bits to store binary numbers, but for any computer there is always a limit on the largest number that can be stored.

Exercise 9

A section of computer memory is shown below, storing numbers in 8-bit two's complement form.

Location A   0 0 0 1 1 0 1 1

Location B   0 1 0 1 1 1 0 0

Location C   0 1 0 0 0 1 1 0

Location D   0 0 1 1 0 0 0 0

Location E   1 0 0 0 0 1 1 1

For each of the following instructions, show the contents of the new location and state if an overflow error has occurred.

1 Add the contents of A to the contents of B and store in F.
2 Add the contents of A to the contents of C and store in G.
3 Add the contents of A to the contents of D and store in H.
4 Add the contents of A to the contents of E and store in I.
5 Add the contents of B to the contents of C and store in J.
6 Add the contents of B to the contents of D and store in K.
7 Add the contents of B to the contents of E and store in L.
8 Add the contents of C to the contents of D and store in M.
9 Add the contents of C to the contents of E and store in N.
10 Add the contents of D to the contents of E and store in O.

Subtraction of Binary Numbers

Subtraction is usually performed in a computer by **adding** the two's complement of the second number. Remember, the two's complement of any binary number is the number formed by changing each bit and adding one.

The following example shows how the calculation $37 − 18$ is performed in 8 bits.

Example

Using two's complement addition, calculate 00100101 −00010010. First, the two's complement of the second number is found.

$$
\begin{array}{cccccccc}
0 & 0 & 0 & 1 & 0 & 0 & 1 & 0 \quad (+18)\\
\downarrow & \downarrow & \downarrow & \downarrow & \downarrow & \downarrow & \downarrow & \downarrow \\
1 & 1 & 1 & 0 & 1 & 1 & 0 & 1 \\
 & & & & & & & \downarrow \\
 & & & & & & & +1 \\
 & & & & & & & \downarrow \\
1 & 1 & 1 & 0 & 1 & 1 & 1 & 0 \quad (-18)
\end{array}
$$

This complement is now added to the first number.

$$
\begin{array}{ccccccccc}
 & 0 & 0 & 1 & 0 & 0 & 1 & 0 & 1 \quad (+37)\\
+1 & 1 & 1 & 0 & 1 & 1 & 1 & 0 \quad (-18)\\
\hline
(1) & 0 & 0 & 0 & 1 & 0 & 0 & 1 & 1 \quad (+19)
\end{array}
$$

If we ignore the carry past the 8th bit, the result is correct.

It is easier to construct a computer with circuits for adding and complementing rather than for adding and subtracting. This is why two's complement representation is chosen for negative numbers in many computers.

Exercise 10

1 Using 5-bit two's complement numbers, show the stages in obtaining a computer solution to 13–7, using two's complement addition.

2 Using 6-bit two's complement numbers, show the stages in obtaining a computer solution to each of the following problems, using two's complement addition.

    a 25–17   **b** 24–8   **c** 5–13   **d** 20--15

3 Using 8-bit two's complement numbers, show the stages in obtaining a computer solution to each of the following problems, using two's complement addition.

    a 60–40   **b** 127–64   **c** 1–98   **d** 50--50

Multiplication of Binary Numbers

Multiplication is usually performed in a computer by a combination of **shifting** and **adding**. The following example shows how the calculation 12×10 is performed.

Example

Using only shifting and addition, calculate 1100×1010

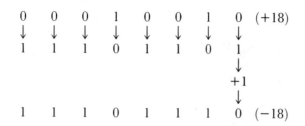

The result 1111000 is equal to 120, which is correct.

Division of Binary Numbers

The process of division can be reduced to a series of subtractions. For example, the calculation $13 \div 5$ can be completed by

$$
\begin{array}{r}
13 \\
-5 \\
\hline
8 \\
-5 \\
\hline
3 \\
\hline
\end{array}
$$

$13 \div 5 = 2$ with a remainder of 3.

In a computer, binary divisions are often completed by a series of shifted subtractions. These subtractions can be achieved by adding complements. The process is rather complicated and it is not demonstrated here.

We have now shown that all arithmetic in a binary computer can be reduced to the steps of **adding**, **complementing** and **shifting**.

Exercise 11

1 Copy and complete the following passages:

    a The binary number system is called a _____ system because it uses only two digits, _____ and _____. There are two reasons why digital computers use binary numbers. These are:
    1. _____
    2. _____

b A full binary code for use in a computer requires about _____ different code numbers. This means that a minimum of _____ bits must usually be used for each code number. One very common _____ bit code is called _____. This code provides _____ code numbers and can represent letters, _____ and _____. Because it can represent letters, _____ and _____ it is called an _____ code.

c The binary code used to represent characters in the computer is called the _____ of the computer. The actual characters that can be represented are called the _____ of the computer. Some computers use a 6-bit code, but this means that they can only store a restricted _____.

d A _____ is called a bit. A section of computer memory that can store a single character of data is called a _____. Usually 8 bits are available in each _____ of memory. If a 7-bit code like _____ is used, the spare 8th bit is often used to provide a _____. The 8th bit is added as either a one or a _____ to make the number of _____ in the final code an _____ number.

e Every computer is provided with a large number of memory locations. The computer can select the data stored in any one of these locations by using its _____. Small computers usually store one _____ in each location. Large computers may store several _____ in each location. The number of bits available in each location is called the _____ of the computer.

f The bit at the left of a binary number is called the _____. The bit at the right of a binary number is called the _____. In two's complement binary numbers, the _____ always represents a _____ quantity. For example, the column headings for an 8-bit two's complement numbers are _____.

g Many decimal fractions cannot be expressed as exact binary fractions. This means that many decimals must be represented by binary numbers that have been _____ or cut short. This produces _____ errors. _____ errors can be reduced if the binary numbers are rounded. Because of _____ errors and _____ errors, there is a limit to the _____ of any computer.

h Both octal numbers and _____ numbers are used by programmers to write down the equivalents of binary numbers. Octal numbers and _____ numbers are preferred to binary numbers because _____. Octal numbers and _____ numbers are preferred to denary numbers because _____.

i An _____ error occurs if the results of a binary calculation are too large to store in the available number of bits.

j Subtraction of binary numbers is usually achieved by adding the _____ of the second number. Many computers reduce all binary calculations to the steps of _____, _____ and _____.

For Questions 2–4 look at the following diagram which shows some sets of transistors. [symbol] represents a transistor that is conducting current and is storing a 1. [symbol] represents a transistor that is not conducting current and is storing a 0.

a [transistor row]
b [transistor row]
c [transistor row]
d [transistor row]
e [transistor row]

2 If the transistors are storing ASCII characters to which an even parity bit has been added, what characters are being stored?

3 If the transistors are storing two's complement binary numbers, what base ten numbers are being stored?

4 If the transistors are storing fixed point binary numbers with the bits designated 8s 4s 2s 1s $\frac{1}{2}$s $\frac{1}{4}$s $\frac{1}{8}$s and $\frac{1}{16}$s, what base ten numbers are being stored?

5 Computers store and manipulate data in binary form because

A It isn't possible to build circuits that work in base 10.
B The computer is constructed from two state devices.
C More digits are required to represent numbers in binary than in decimal.
D Fewer digits are required to represent numbers in binary than in decimal.
E Logic circuits are very small.

(NI CSE 82)

6 a How many different characters can be represented in a four-bit character code?

b Design your own three-bit codes to represent a, b, c, and d using the third for an even parity check.

[□□□ □□□ □□□ □□□]
↑
parity bit

(ALSEB 82)

7 A computer stores whole numbers in a five-bit register with the left hand bit as the sign bit. Negative numbers are held in the two's complement form.

a Write in denary (base ten) the negative number which would be held in this register as

| 1 | 0 | 1 | 0 | 0 |

b Write each of the positive numbers nine and eleven as they would appear in this register.

c Add together *your* answers to part b and write down the resulting binary number.

d Explain why the five-bit register cannot hold the result of adding nine and eleven.

(NREB 82)

8 a Convert the decimal number 29 to binary. Show your working.

b The following sum was performed in a computer with 6-bit locations. Why must the answer be wrong?

0	1	1	1	1	1

$+$

0	0	0	0	0	1

1	0	0	0	0	0

(SEREB 81)

9 What is the minimum number of bits needed to represent uniquely the 26 letters of the English alphabet? Explain briefly how you arrived at your answer.

(O 82)

10 a Convert the positive decimal integer 536 to binary.

b Calculate by binary arithmetic the product $10010_2 \times 11011_2$

c Find the two's complement of the 10-bit positive binary number 0001010111.

(O)

11 In a particular computer integers are stored in 6 bits where the first bit is used to indicate the sign (0 for a positive integer and 1 for a negative integer). Negative integers are stored in two's complement form.

a What base 10 numbers are represented by:
(i) 010011, (ii) 001010?

b What is the two's complement of 001010?

c What is the largest positive integer which can be stored?

d What is the largest negative integer which can be stored?

e Explain how the answer to part **b** can be used to do the binary subtraction sum corresponding to $19-10$ in base 10.

(SUJB 80)

12 A computer stores a representation of integers in 4-bit words using two's complementation.

a What is the largest possible integer represented in a 4-bit word?

b What number is represented by 1000?

c Show how you would represent the integer -3 in the 4-bit word.

(AEB 81)

13 The display element of a calculator is designed to display number shapes (0 to 9) and consists of a seven bar display like this:

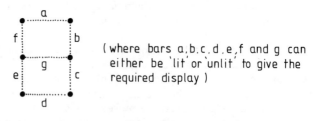

(where bars a,b,c,d,e,f and g can either be 'lit' or 'unlit' to give the required display)

We can represent a number shape by means of a binary code, with the positions as follows:

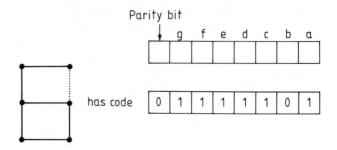

a What is the code for the shape shown in Fig. 3?

b What shape has the following code?

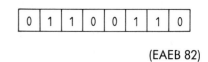

(EAEB 82)

14 a Convert (i) 17 (ii) 26 from base 10 to base 2.

PARTS **(b)** to **(g)** REFER TO A 6-BIT INTEGER REGISTER IN WHICH TWO'S COMPLEMENTS ARE USED FOR NEGATIVE NUMBERS.

b How would 17 be stored in this register?

c What is the two's complement of 17 in this register?

d How would a computer carry out $26-17$ in this register? Give the answer to its calculation in binary and in denary.

e What would happen if $26 + 17$ was carried out in this register?

f The register holds 111100; what denary number does this represent?

g What are the largest (most positive) and smallest (most negative) numbers which this register can store? Give your answers in denary.

(SWEB 82)

15 a Three decimal numbers are $a = 7$, $b = 15$, and $c = 33$.
   (i) Express a, b, and c as seven-bit binary numbers.
Find from these seven-bit binary numbers, using binary arithmetic throughout:
   (ii) $a \times b$;
   (iii) $a + b + c$.
b State and explain the processes by which an adder can be used to carry out a subtraction.

(O 82)

16 a Convert the decimal integer 23 to binary. Show all your working.
b A computer uses 8-bit storage cells like the one shown here.

   (i) Show how the binary representation of the decimal integer 23 would be stored in these cells.
   (ii) Show how its 1's complement would be stored.
   (iii) Show how its 2's complement would be stored.
c Why are complements of numbers used in computers?
d Noticing that $46 = 23 \times 2$, use your answer to (**b**) (i) to write down the binary representation of the decimal integer 46 in an 8-bit cell.
e (i) Show how to do the sum $46 - 23$ in 8-bit cells using 1's complement binary arithmetic.
   (ii) Why could you not do the same sum in 6-bit cells?

(WMEB 82)

17 a (i) Describe a system you might use for representing alphabetic characters in binary so that they can be stored in a computer.
   (ii) Similarly describe a system you might use for representing two digit integers in binary.
b Postal codes are made up in any of the following formats:

L25 2RB,   SH5 7TN,   EH5 12RY,   SWW6 4BH,
NW1X 3QR

   (i) Suggest a way in which the above postal codes could be encoded in binary in an economic manner (i.e. using as few bits as possible).
   (ii) Using the method you have described in (b(i)) encode the following:
   NW1X 14ZQ

(AEB 81)

18 Which one of the following octal numbers represents the hexadecimal value 14?

   a   14
   b   20
   c   24
   d   1100

(WMEB 82)

19 What is the hexadecimal result of adding together the hexadecimal numbers 2 and A?

5 The Processing of Binary Data

Switching Circuits

Look at the simple electrical circuit shown in Figure 5.1.

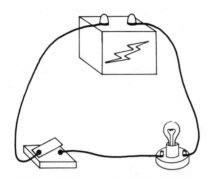

Figure 5.1 A simple electrical circuit

When the switch is closed the lamp will be on and when the switch is open the lamp will be off. We summarise this in Table 5.1.

Table 5.1

Switch	Lamp
Open	Off
Closed	On

So, if we use 1 to represent a closed switch or a lamp on, and 0 to represent an open switch or a lamp off, we produce Table 5.2.

Table 5.2

Switch	Lamp
0	0
1	1

If we include two or more switches in a circuit, the situation becomes more complicated. To describe the action of the circuit we must consider every possible combination of open and closed switches. This is easily done if the representation of 1 for a closed switch and 0 for an open switch is used.

For example, look at the circuit shown in Figure 5.2.

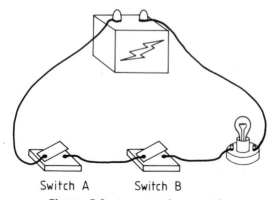

Figure 5.2 A circuit with two switches

For this circuit we can produce Table 5.3.

Table 5.3

Switch A	Switch B	Lamp
0	0	0
0	1	0
1	0	0
1	1	1

Notice that the pattern of open and closed switches is arranged as the first four binary numbers. This is an easy way to make certain that you consider every possible combination.

If we were asked to describe the action of this circuit in words, we might say 'The lamp is on only if both Switch A and Switch B are closed'.

A table drawn up to describe a circuit is called an **operation table** or **truth table** for the circuit.

Exercise 12

It is suggested that you obtain batteries, switches and lamps and treat this as a practical exercise.

1 Complete a truth table for each of the following circuits and describe the action of the circuit in your own words.

a

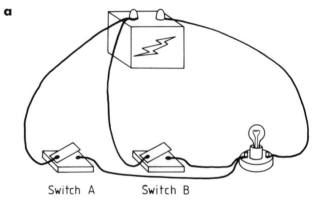

b

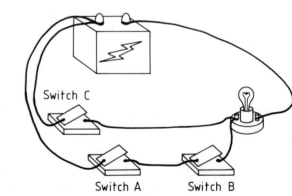

c

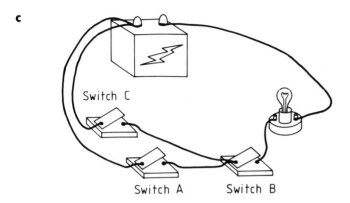

Switch C

Switch A Switch B

d

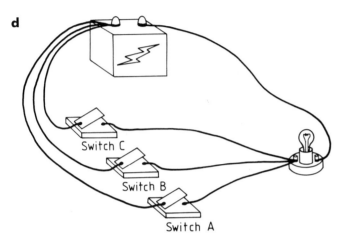

Switch C

Switch B

Switch A

2 A double switch can be made by linking two switches with a metal rod. The action of the switches can be arranged so that when one switch is open the other is closed. The circuit below shows a double switch like this. Complete a truth table for the circuit and describe the action of the circuit in your own words.

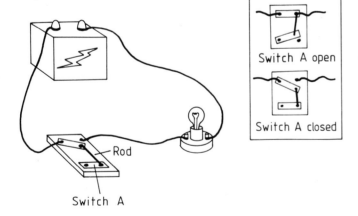

Switch A

Rod

Switch A open

Switch A closed

Logic Gates

We have been looking at switching circuits. They can be designed so that a fixed input (switches open or closed) produces a specific output (lamp on or off). Inside the CPU of a computer are many thousands of electronic switches. These switches can be opened or closed automatically by the pulses of electricity that communicate

data in the computer. These pulses carry binary data around the computer. A pulse of electricity represents a 1 and the absence of a pulse represents a 0. Figure 5.3 represents a train of pulses carrying the binary code for the letter R.

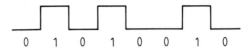

0   1   0   1   0   0   1   0

Figure 5.3 A train of pulses for the letter R

By using two or more of these pulses as inputs to control the switches in a circuit it is possible to combine them into a single output. Very complex circuits may be required but they are all built up from simple components called **logic gates**. In this book we will not be concerned with the way that logic gates are made, only in the way they are used to build the circuits needed in computers. In circuit diagrams a logic gate is usually shown as a circle. Into the circle come the inputs, and from it comes an output. There are three basic types of logic gate. A description of each with its truth table is given in Figure 5.4.

Figure 5.4 AND, OR and NOT gates

An **AND gate** combines two bits so that the output is a 1 only if both inputs are 1.

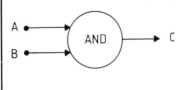

Truth Table

A	B	C
0	0	0
0	1	0
1	0	0
1	1	1

An **OR gate** combines two bits so that the output is a 1 if either of the inputs is a 1.

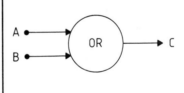

Truth Table

A	B	C
0	0	0
0	1	1
1	0	1
1	1	1

A **NOT gate** reverses the pattern of a bit. If the input is a 1, the output is a 0. If the input is a 0, the output is a 1.

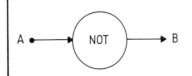

Truth Table

A	B
0	1
1	0

If we are asked to complete a truth table for a circuit built from several gates, it is helpful to label each output with a letter. This allows us to work carefully through the circuit to the final output.

Example

Complete a truth table for the circuit below.

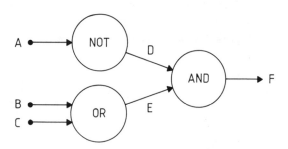

We draw up a table as shown below and work across from left to right for each of the possible combinations of inputs.

Inputs			D	E	F
A	B	C	Not A	B or C	E and D
0	0	0	1	0	0
0	0	1	1	1	1
0	1	0	1	1	1
0	1	1	1	1	1
1	0	0	0	0	0
1	0	1	0	1	0
1	1	0	0	1	0
1	1	1	0	1	0

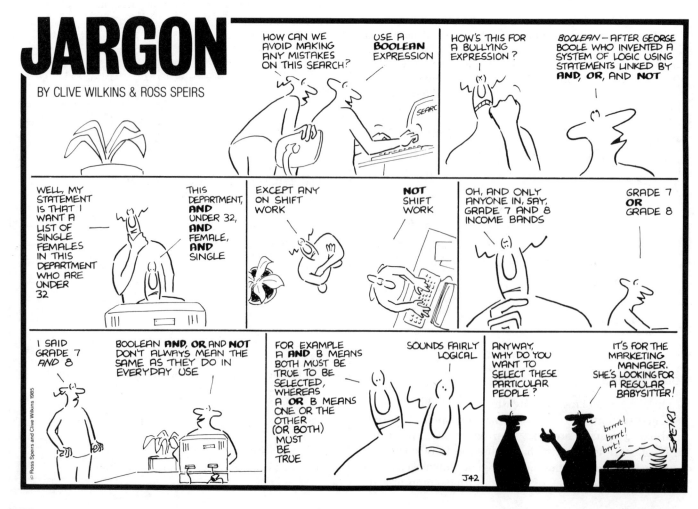

Exercise 13

Complete truth tables for each of the following logic circuits.

1

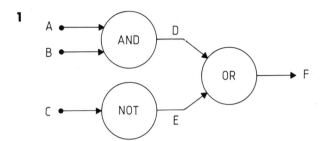

7

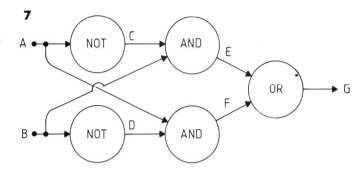

2

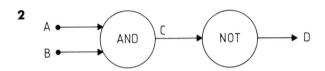

3

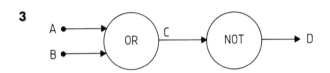

8

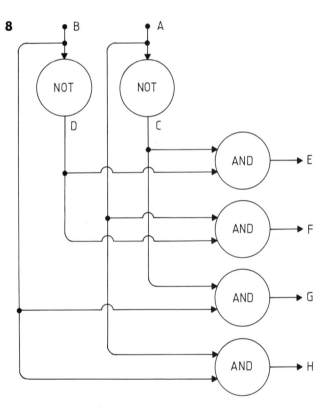

4

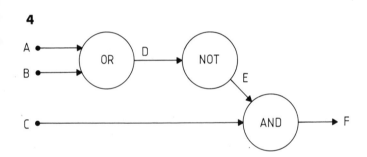

5

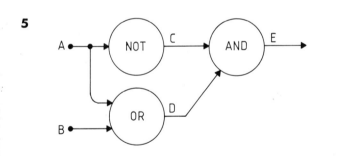

6

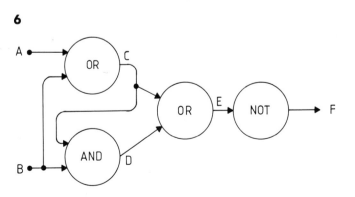

9

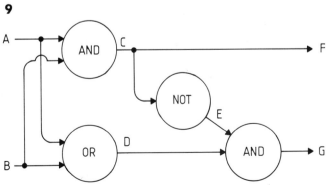

10 On the control panel of a machine there are three switches. The switches are connected to the motor of the machine with the circuit shown below.

By drawing a truth table for the circuit, discover which switches must be on and which must be off in order for the machine to work.

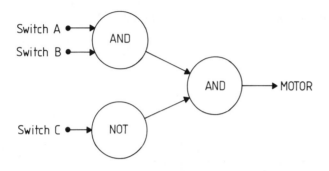

11 Design a circuit for a similar machine that will turn the motor on when either Switch C or Switch B is on but Switch A is not on.

12 Three people, Alan, Betty and Cindy, have a key to the safe at the Zapper Computer Company. The door of the safe can be opened with any two of the three keys. Draw a logic circuit using three AND gates and one OR gate that produces this required output. Label your input A, B and C to represent the three keys. Label your output S to represent an open or locked safe.

Uses of Logic Circuits

In this section we will turn our attention to the practical uses of logic circuits in the construction of computers.

Building a Binary Adding Machine

A simple binary adding machine will need two inputs and two outputs. An outline of the required machine is shown in Figure 5.5.

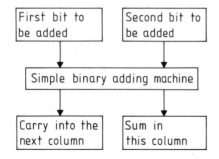

Figure 5.5 The outline for a binary adding machine

The rules that this machine must follow are:

Inputs		Outputs	
First bit	Second bit	Carry	Sum
0	0	0	0
0	1	0	1
1	0	0	1
1	1	1	0

Look at the circuit in Figure 5.6 and its truth table.

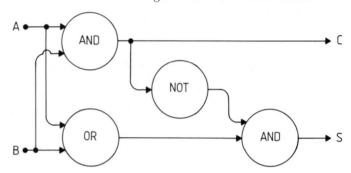

Figure 5.6 The circuit for an adding machine

Truth table

A	B	C	S
0	0	0	0
0	1	0	1
1	0	0	1
1	1	1	0

The circuit produces the exact results required for a simple binary adding machine!

If you attempted Question 9 of Exercise 13 (p. 35), you have already completed a truth table for this circuit. If not, you may like to check that the circuit does produce the required truth table.

This simple binary adder cannot cope with a carry from a previous column. It is thus called a **half adder** circuit.

Exercise 14

In the diagram below, a half adder is shown completing the addition 1 + 0. Connections carrying a 1 are shown as solid lines and connections carrying a 0 are shown as broken lines.

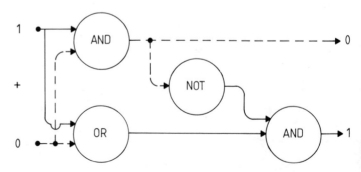

1 Draw a diagram to show a half adder completing the addition 0 + 0. Use solid lines for connections carrying a 1 and broken lines for connections carrying a 0.

2 Draw a diagram to show a half adder completing the addition 0 + 1. Use solid lines for connections carrying a 1 and broken lines for connections carrying a 0.

3 Draw a diagram of a half adder completing the addition 1 + 1. Use solid lines for connections carrying a 1 and broken lines for connections carrying a 0.

A Full Binary Adding Machine

An outline for a full binary adding machine is shown in Figure 5.7.

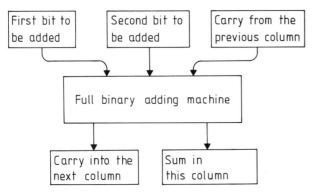

Figure 5.7 The outline for a full binary adding machine

The rules that this machine must follow are:

Inputs			Outputs	
Carry	First bit	Second bit	Carry	Sum
0	0	0	0	0
0	0	1	0	1
0	1	0	0	1
0	1	1	1	0
1	0	0	0	1
1	0	1	1	0
1	1	0	1	0
1	1	1	1	1

The circuit required for this full adder can be built from two half adders joined with an OR gate. The circuit is shown in Figure 5.8. It is left as a challenge to the reader to check that it does produce the required truth table.

Exercise 15

1 Draw a diagram to show a full adder completing the addition 1 + 0 + a carry of 1. Use solid lines for connections carrying a 1 and broken lines for connections carrying a 0.

Serial and Parallel Adders

A single full adder circuit can be used to add together two binary numbers of any length. The successive pairs of bits are fed into the circuit together with any carry from the last pair. The results are stored bit by bit in the answer location. A device like this is called a **serial adder**.

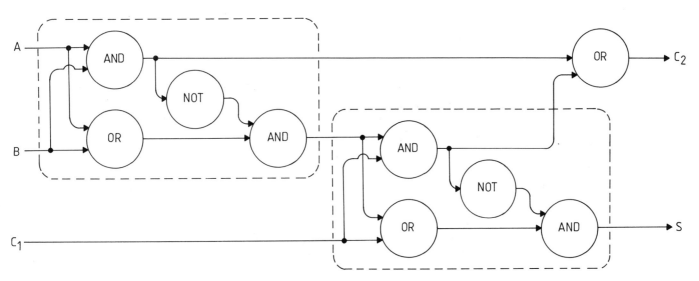

Figure 5.8 The circuit for a fully binary adder

An outline of a serial adder is shown below in Figure 5.9.

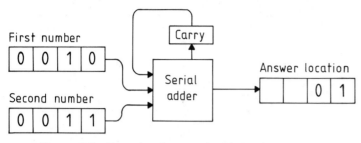

Figure 5.9 The outline for a serial adder being used to add two numbers

If several full adder circuits are linked, all the pairs of bits in two numbers can be added together at the same time. A device like this is called a **parallel adder**. A parallel adder will be faster than a serial adder, but it is a more complicated device to build. A parallel adder designed to add two 4-bit numbers is shown in Figure 5.10. Each separate full adder circuit is shown as a single box with three inputs and two outputs.

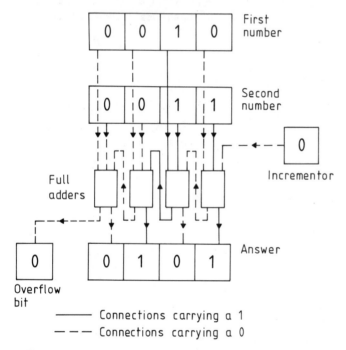

Figure 5.10 A 4-bit parallel adder completing the calculation 0010 + 0011

The extra bit in the answer location is provided to store any overflow that may occur. The **incrementor** is provided so that the first carry can be set to 1 or 0. For all normal additions this will be set to zero.

That completes the design of our binary adding machine. There is, however, one final point to note. Our design for a parallel adder only copes with 4-bit numbers. In general, a parallel adder must be built that can cope with numbers of the computer's wordlength. Thus an 8-bit computer will need an 8-bit parallel adder and a 32-bit computer will need a 32-bit parallel adder.

Subtracting Binary Numbers

Our binary adding machine can also be used for subtractions if we add a set of NOT gates. Figure 5.11 shows two numbers being subtracted in this way. The bits of the second number are passed through the NOT gates and the incrementor is set to 1. This finds the two's complement of the second number. This complement is then added to the first number to perform the required subtraction. As usual with two's complement subtraction, the carry into the overflow bit is ignored.

In our combined binary adder/subtractor, the NOT gates must be switched in when subtraction is required and switched out when addition is required. For simplicity, the circuit required to switch the NOT gates in and out is not shown in Figure 5.11.

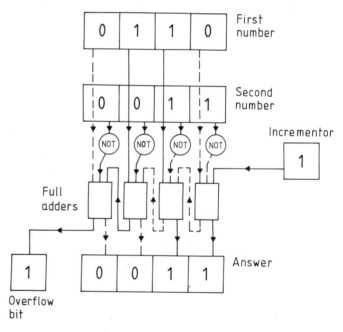

Figure 5.11 A 4-bit parallel adder and a set of NOT gates completing the calculation 0010 − 0011

Exercise 16

1 Draw a diagram to show a 4-bit parallel adder completing the calculation 0001 + 0011. Use solid lines for connections carrying a 1 and broken lines for connections carrying a 0.

2 Draw a diagram to show a 4-bit parallel adder and a set of NOT gates completing the calculation 0110 − 0101. Use solid lines for connections carrying a 1 and broken lines for connections carrying a 0.

Controlling the Flow of Data

If the computer is to use the same machine for both additions and subtractions, it must have ways to select the required function. The next two sections look at how devices can be built to select and control the way that data flows through the computer.

Control Switches

In a parallel computer, data flows around the computer along **data buses**. These buses have one wire for each bit of a word. Thus an 8-bit computer will have data buses with 8 wires. The flow of data along the data buses is controlled by switches. These switches consist of a set of AND gates built into the data bus. Each AND gate is linked to one wire from the data bus and to a wire from the control unit of the computer. Figure 5.12 shows the way in which a signal from the control unit can either block the flow of data in 4-bit data bus or allow it to pass.

In (a) the control unit sends a 0 signal along the control wire and the data flow is blocked. In (b) the control unit sends a 1 signal along the control wire and the data flow passes through the control switch.

Decoders

DECODERS are used to select individual memory locations and to allow the computer to produce different responses to different binary instructions. A decoder can select a single output line corresponding to an input binary pattern. For example, 3 data lines can carry 8 different binary patterns, from 000 to 111. A 3-bit decoder will separate the 8 possible input signals into 8 different output data lines. An outline of a 3-bit decoder is shown in Figure 5.13.

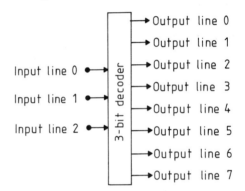

Figure 5.13 The outline for a 3-bit decoder

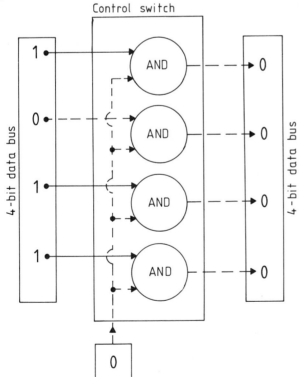

A 0 signal from the control unit

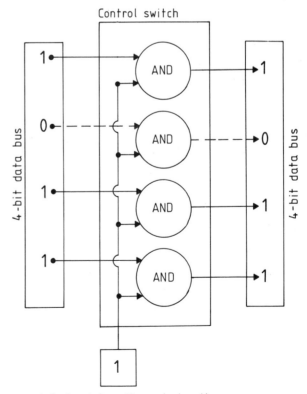

A 1 signal from the control unit

Figure 5.12 How the flow of data is controlled in a control unit

If the binary pattern 101 is input, there will be an output on line 5 only. If the binary pattern 011 is input, there will be an output on line three only. This is shown in Figure 5.14.

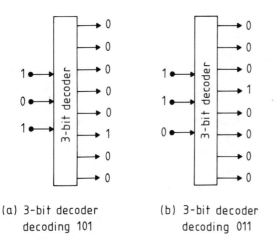

(a) 3-bit decoder decoding 101

(b) 3-bit decoder decoding 011

Figure 5.14 How a 3-bit decoder decodes

The logic circuit for a 2-bit decoder is shown in Figure 5.15 with its truth table.

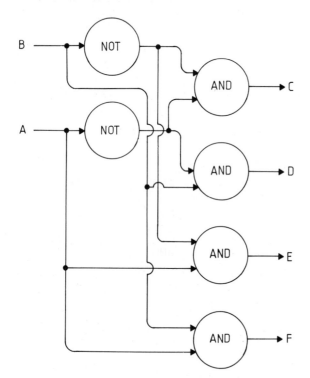

Figure 5.15 A 2-bit binary decoder

Truth table

Inputs		Outputs			
A	B	C	D	E	F
0	0	1	0	0	0
0	1	0	1	0	0
1	0	0	0	1	0
1	1	0	0	0	1

You can see from the truth table that there are four possible input combinations. Each of these input patterns produces an output signal on only one of the four output lines.

Exercise 17

1 Draw a diagram to show a control switch in a 4-bit data bus allowing the signal 1001 to pass. Use solid lines for connections carrying a 1 and broken lines for connections carrying a 0.

2 Draw a diagram to show a control switch in a 4-bit data bus blocking the signal 1001. Use solid lines for connections carrying a 1 and broken lines for connections carrying a 0.

3 Draw a diagram to show a 2-bit decoder decoding the signal 10. Use solid lines for connections carrying a 1 and broken lines for connections carrying a 0.

Flip Flops and Registers

Flip-flops are used to store the binary data in the CPU of all modern computers. A flip-flop is a logic circuit with two output lines. If one output is a 1, the other is always a 0. The outputs remain fixed unless changed or 'flipped over' by input signals. The flip-flop is thus a two-state device or **bistable** and each flip-flop can be used to store a single bit of data. Figure 5.16 shows a flip-flop in its two steady states.

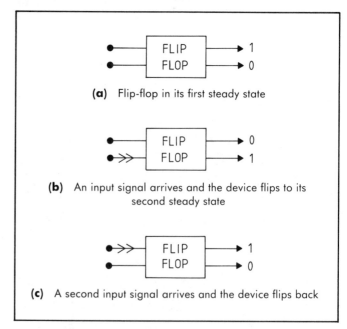

(a) Flip-flop in its first steady state

(b) An input signal arrives and the device flips to its second steady state

(c) A second input signal arrives and the device flips back

Figure 5.16 The two steady states of a flip-flop

The logic circuit for a simple flip-flop is shown in Figure 5.17. As you can see, the circuit is complicated because outputs are fed back into the gates that produce them. No attempt will be made to describe the detailed action of this circuit, and it is included only for the reader's interest.

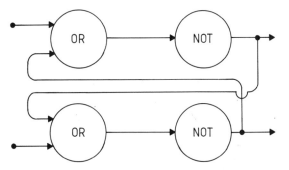

Figure 5.17 The logic circuit for a flip-flop

One flip-flop can only store one bit of data. To store bytes or data words, several flip-flops must be linked together. For example, in an 8-bit computer, each memory location will require 8 flip-flops. A set of flip-flops linked together to store data is called a **register**.

The Connection Between Gates and Chips

The **integrated circuits** or **chips** in a modern computer may contain tens or even hundreds of thousands of logic gates. These and all their necessary connections are squeezed into a space just a few millimetres square. Figure 5.18 below shows an enlarged circuit diagram of a microprocessor chip.

We will end this chapter with a description of three more gates. These are the NAND gate, the NOR gate and the EX-OR gate (Figure 5.19). Computer manufacturers often design their circuits using only NAND or NOR gates. As you will see if you complete the following exercise, all other gates can be constructed from combinations of NAND or NOR gates.

Figure 5.18 The gates on a Ferranti microprocessor

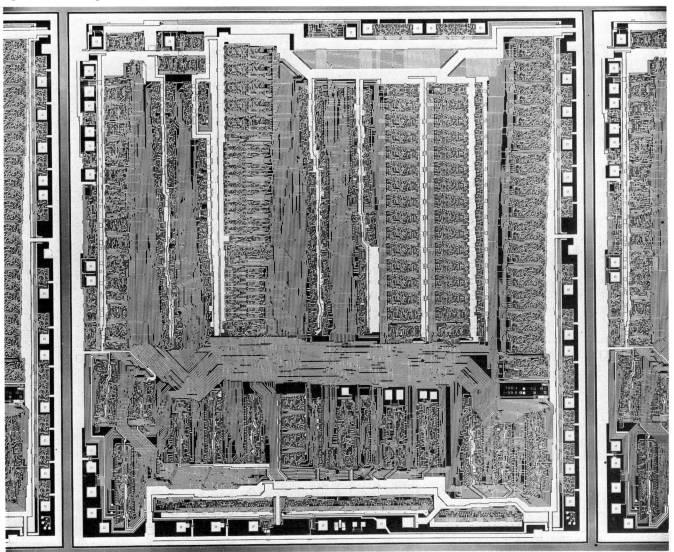

The **NAND** gate functions like an AND gate followed by a NOT gate:

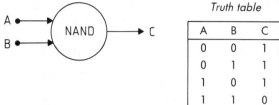

Truth table

A	B	C
0	0	1
0	1	1
1	0	1
1	1	0

The **NOR** gate functions like an OR gate followed by a NOT gate:

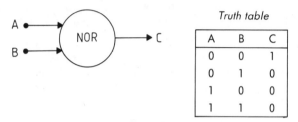

Truth table

A	B	C
0	0	1
0	1	0
1	0	0
1	1	0

The **EX-OR** (or **EXCLUSIVE OR**) gate produces an output of 1 only when the inputs are different:

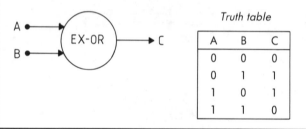

Truth table

A	B	C
0	0	0
0	1	1
1	0	1
1	1	0

Figure 5.19 NAND, NOR and EX-OR gates

Exercise 18

1 Copy and complete the following sentences:

a Switching circuits can be designed so that a fixed _____ produces a specific _____.

b The CPU of a computer contains many thousands of _____ which can be opened or closed automatically by the pulses of electricity used to communicate data in the computer.

c In a computer, a single pulse of electricity represents a _____ and the absence of a pulse represents a _____.

d A logic gate that produces a 1 only if both inputs are 1 is called an _____.

e A logic gate that produces a 0 only if both inputs are 0 is called an _____.

f A gate that reverses a single input is called a _____.

g A device that can add two bits without a carry from the previous column is called a _____.

h A device that can add two bits with a carry from the previous column is called a _____. It is built from two _____ circuits, joined with an _____ gate.

i A _____ is a device that can add two binary numbers, one pair of bits at a time.

j A device that can add all the pairs of bits in two binary numbers at the same time is called a _____.

k Subtraction which is performed by a special form of addition is called _____. A parallel adder can use this form of subtraction if a set of _____ gates is added to its construction.

l A control switch consists of a set of _____ gates built into a _____ and linked to the control unit of the computer.

m A decoder is used to select _____ and to produce different responses to different _____.

n A 3-bit decoder has 3 inputs which can carry a total of 8 _____. It has _____ output lines, one for each input signal.

o The device in a computer that can store either a 1 or a 0 and rapidly change from one to the other is called a _____. Several _____ must be linked together to store _____ or data words. A set of linked _____ is called a register.

p A logic gate which functions like an AND gate followed by a NOT gate is called a _____.

q A NOR gate functions like an _____ gate followed by a _____ gate.

r A logic gate that produces a 1 only if the inputs are different is called an _____.

2 In switching circuit diagrams, the following symbols are often used.

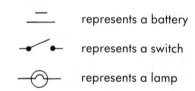

_____ represents a battery

represents a switch

represents a lamp

Complete a truth table for the switching circuit shown below.

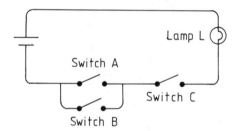

3 a Name the logic gate that is equivalent to the switching circuit shown below.

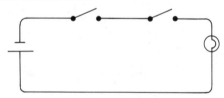

b Complete a truth table for this logic (switching) circuit.

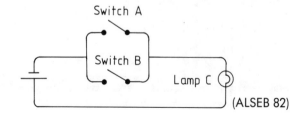

(ALSEB 82)

42

4 Each of the following logic circuits shows a combination of NAND gates. By completing truth tables for the circuits, discover which single gate the circuits can replace.

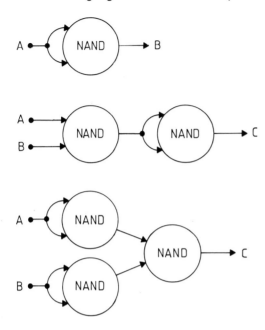

5 Each of the following logic circuits shows a combination of NOR gates. By completing truth tables for the circuits, discover which single gate the circuits can replace.

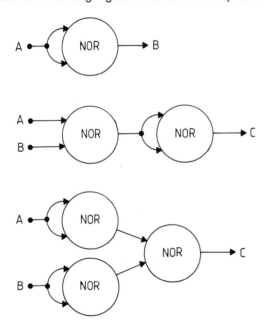

6 Design a circuit using only NAND gates that can replace a single NOR gate

7 Design a circuit using only NOR gates that can replace a single NAND gate.

8 Complete a truth table for the following logic circuit and hence explain how such a circuit might be used.

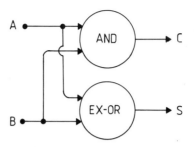

9 A microcomputer has an 8-bit output port which allows it to be connected to other devices. The circuit below was built to allow the computer to switch on the motor in a small electric train. It uses two four-input AND gates. These gates produce an output of 1 only if all four inputs are 1. The motor is switched on only if the final output of the circuit is 1. What binary signal must be sent from the output port to switch on the motor?

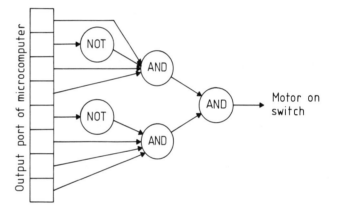

10 In Question 9, the motor of the train continues to run once it has been switched on by the microcomputer. To switch the motor off again, the computer sends the signal 10110011 from its output port. Draw a design for a circuit which will decode this signal into a single output of 1 to be sent to the motor's off switch.

11

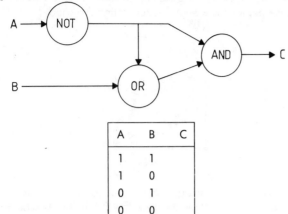

A	B	C
1	1	
1	0	
0	1	
0	0	

a Copy and complete the table for the output at C for the above circuit.
b Comment on the results in part **a** and their implications for the above circuit.

(SUJB 80)

12 Copy and complete the table for this logic circuit.

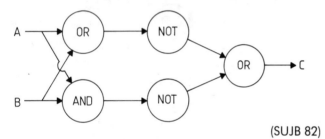

(SUJB 82)

A	B	C
0	0	
0	1	
1	0	
1	1	

13 The logic network below obeys the given truth table.

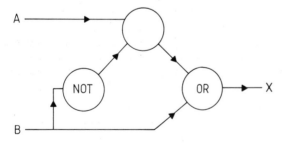

Inputs		Output
A	B	X
0	0	0
0	1	1
1	0	1
1	1	1

a What type of logic gate is represented by the empty circle?
b What single logic gate has the same truth table as this network?

(NREB 82)

14 The diagram shows a piece of decoding logic.

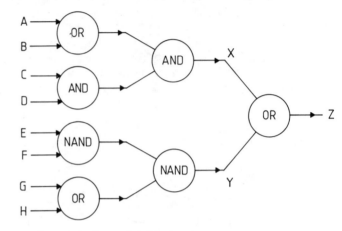

Complete the truth table for the inputs given:

A	B	C	D	E	F	G	H	X	Y	Z
1	1	1	1	1	1	1	1			
0	0	1	1	1	1	1	1			
0	0	1	1	1	1	0	0			
1	1	0	0	0	0	1	1			
1	0	1	0	1	0	1	0			

(AEB 81)

15 a Complete truth tables for the two circuits given below and hence show that they both produce the same output.

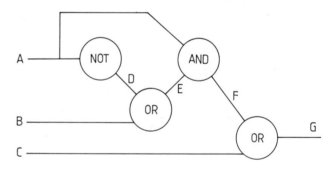

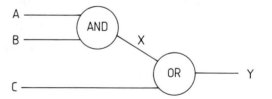

44

b Three registers P, Q, R are connected by an AND gate as shown below.

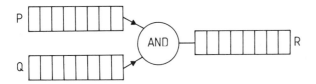

The contents of the register P and Q are shifted to the right, one bit from each register at a time, into the AND gate and the result is stored in the left hand bit position of R.

The contents of R are shifted to the right one place to accommodate each new bit output from the AND gate. This will continue until P and Q are both empty and R is filled.

(i) If register P contains the pattern 11001011 and we want this same pattern copied into R what pattern should Q contain?

(ii) If register P contains 11111011 and we want R to contain 11100000 what pattern should Q contain?

(NI CSE 82)

16 a Complete the truth table below by using the flowchart for each pair of bits.

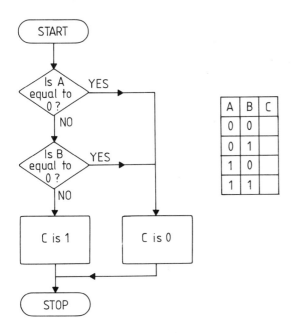

A	B	C
0	0	
0	1	
1	0	
1	1	

b Which single logic gate, if any, does this truth table represent?

(SEREB 81)

17 A gallery displaying a famous diamond uses a special Security Unit to protect access to the Display Room (D). The diagram below shows the layout of the system.

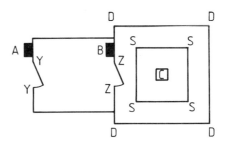

The display cabinet (C) is surrounded by a screen of electronic eyes (S).
Access to the display room is through doors (Y), (Z).
Boxes (A), (B) are used in the system.
The following persons are involved in the system

Manager, Deputy Manager, Chief Security Officer

The Display Room is opened as follows:

The Unit must be activated at box A.
Door (Y) is opened by any two of the above persons at box A.
Box B is activated by the Manager and Deputy Manager together.
The Screen (S) is activated by the Chief Security Officer alone at box B only.
Door (Z) can only be opened once the screen (S) is activated.

Draw the logic circuit required inside the Unit to operate it. Ensure your diagram is documented.

(AEB 82)

Famous Computer People: Number 4

Herman Hollerith 1860 to 1929

Herman Hollerith was a German immigrant to America. He designed and built machines to sort and process punched cards. In 1890 Hollerith's machines were used to process the data for the American Census. All the data collected for the census was transcribed on to punched cards and these were sorted and counted by the machines in only three years. Manual processing of the 1880 Census had taken seven years.

Hollerith formed the Hollerith Tabulating Machine Company in 1897 which, after a series of mergers, became part of International Business Machines (IBM). Today, IBM is the largest computer manufacturer in the world.

18 The diagram below shows the outline of a circuit designed to perform both addition and subtraction.

- **a** Write down the answer and overflow bit that will be produced if the incrementor is set to zero.
- **b** Write down the answer and overflow bit that will be produced if the incrementor is set to one.
- **c** Explain why the EX-OR gates are used in this circuit design.

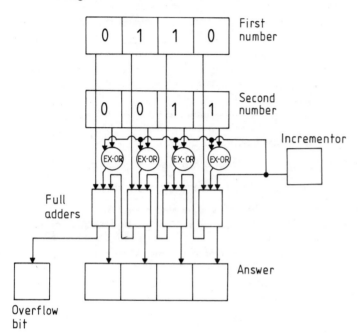

6 Inside the Central Processing Unit

The ZAP-1 Model Computer

ZAP-1 exists only on paper. It is a model computer designed to help you understand the workings of a real computer. To keep ZAP-1 as simple as possible, we have omitted or modified many of the features of a real computer. Two important differences between ZAP-1 and a real computer are:

* ZAP-1 works with normal base 10 numbers. All real computers work with *binary* numbers.
* There is no clock in ZAP-1. In all real computers very precise timing is needed and this is provided by an electronic clock.

Buses are the pathways of wires and connectors that are used to link together the components of the computer. To reduce the need for duplicated connections, all the components are linked to a small number of common buses shared between them. A **data channel** is the physical path followed by data as it passes from one component to another. Switches built into the computer's buses allow the control unit to select many different data channels. A small number of buses can thus provide many different data channels. Figure 6.1 shows the ZAP-1 model computer. The dotted lines show all the different data channels that can be selected by the control unit.

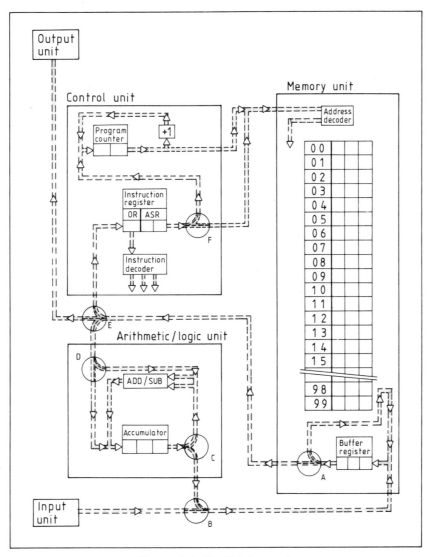

Figure 6.1 The ZAP-1 computer

Data Storage in ZAP-1

Figure 6.2 shows the memory unit of the ZAP-1 computer.

Memory unit

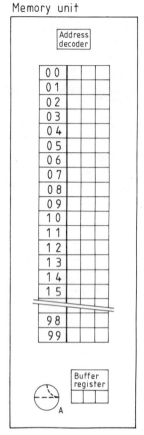

Figure 6.2 The memory unit of ZAP-1

As you can see, the memory unit has one hundred locations with addresses from 00 to 99. Each location can store any three-digit base 10 number. This memory is often called the **immediate access store**. At the top of the memory unit is the **address decoder**. This device allows any one of the addresses to be selected. After the address is selected, data can either be read from or written to that location. Any data entering or leaving the memory unit passes through the **buffer register**.

The buffer register provides a temporary store to hold data while the correct data channel is selected.

Data Codes Used in ZAP-1

ZAP-1 uses the following codes to store data in its memory unit:

* **Numbers**

  The first digit is used as a code for plus or minus. A 0 is used for plus and a 1 is used for minus. Thus 067 represents +67 and 145 represents −45. The range of numbers that can be coded is from 199 (−99) to 099 (+99).

* **Symbols**

  200 represents a space.
  201 represents the letter A
  202 represents the letter B
  ....
  226 represents the letter Z.

The section of memory shown below is storing the name 'QE2'.

0	0	2	1	7	Q
0	1	2	0	5	E
0	2	0	0	2	2

There is never confusion between numbers and symbols. If the first digit is a 1 or a 0, the data item *must* be a number. If the first digit is a 2, the data item *must* be a symbol. All the other possible codes are not used. If we wished, they could be selected to represent any required data item.

Exercise 19

1 Write down the ZAP-1 code for each of the following:

a	18	**f**	Y
b	−18	**g**	60
c	J	**h**	−60
d	M	**i**	T
e	R	**j**	zero

2 Draw a section of the ZAP-1 memory unit storing the message 'KILROY WAS HERE'. How many memory locations are required to store this message?

Program Storage in ZAP-1

Programs are also stored in the immediate access store. Each separate instruction always has the structure shown in Figure 6.3.

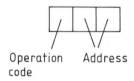

Operation   Address
code

Figure 6.3 The structure of an instruction

The following instructions are provided:

0 X X   Stop

1 X X   Input a number and store it in location XX

2 X X   Output a number from location XX

3 X X   Copy the contents of location XX into the accumulator

4 X X   Copy the contents of the accumulator into location XX

5 X X   Add the number in location XX to the number in the accumulator

6 X X   Subtract the number in location XX from the number in the accumulator

7 X X   Jump to the instruction in location XX

8 X X   Jump to the instruction in location XX if the number in the accumulator is negative

9 X X   Jump to the instruction in location XX if the number in the accumulator is zero.

The XX included in the instructions can be any one of the 100 possible address numbers. Data input or copied into a memory location will automatically replace any data already stored there.

There can be confusion between the data codes used in ZAP-1 and the codes used for instructions. Both are stored in the memory unit. A location storing 118 could be storing either −18 or the instruction to input a number into location 18. It is the task of the programmer to make sure that the contents of a memory location are always interpreted in the correct way.

Exercise 20

1 Interpret each of the following ZAP-1 instructions:

a	423	**f**	913
b	810	**g**	000
c	100	**h**	345
d	699	**i**	769
e	222	**j**	514

2 Write down the ZAP-1 code for each of the following instructions:

  a Jump to the instruction in location 13

  b Add the number in location 16 to the number in the accumulator

  c Input a number and store it in location 07

  d Output a number from location 07

  e Jump to the instruction in location 46 if the number in the accumulator is zero.

The Control Unit in ZAP-1

The function of the control unit is to control all the operations of the computer. To enable it to do this, the control unit has control links to all the other units of the computer. For simplicity, these links are not shown in Figure 6.1. Some of the control switches are shown, however. They are lettered A–F. These switches are used to select the correct path for data as it flows through the computer. Figure 6.4 shows that the control unit contains three main parts.

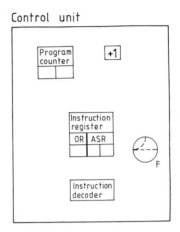

Figure 6.4 The parts of a control unit

The **program counter** always stores the address of the next instruction in the computer program. This address can be selected by sending the contents of the program counter to the address decoder. As this is done, the contents of the program counter are automatically increased by 1. The program counter is thus always ready to select the next instruction when it is required.

The **instruction register** stores a copy of the instruction being processed. This register has two parts: the **operation register** and the **address selection register**. The operation register stores the operation code and is connected to the **instruction decoder**. The instruction decoder decodes the operation code and sends signals to the control switches in the computer. The address selection register stores the address part of each instruction. Its contents are passed to the address decoder to select the required address.

The program counter is sometimes called the **sequence control register**. The instruction register is sometimes called the **current instruction register**.

The Arithmetic/Logic Unit in ZAP-1

The arithmetic/logic unit of a computer is where all the calculations and logic operations take place. The unit in ZAP-1 is a very simple one as Figure 6.5 shows.

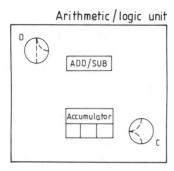

Figure 6.5 The parts of an arithmetic/logic unit

The **accumulator** is a register used to store the results of calculations.

The **ADD/SUB** unit can add or subtract the contents of any memory location to or from the accumulator.

ZAP-1 in Action

ZAP-1 works through a program of instruction using a two-phase cycle called the **fetch/execute** cycle:

* During the fetch part of the cycle the next instruction is fetched from the memory and stored in the instruction register.
* During the execute part of the cycle the instruction is decoded and carried out.

We will illustrate this cycle by following the execution of a very simple program. The program inputs two numbers, adds them together and outputs the result. The instructions required are shown below:

113	Input a number and store it in location 13
114	Input a number and store it in location 14
313	Copy the contents of location 13 into the accumulator
514	Add the number in location 14 to the number in the accumulator
415	Copy the contents of the accumulator into location 15
215	Output a number from location 15
000	Stop.

Figure 6.6 shows ZAP-1 loaded with the program and ready to start. The program is stored in locations 00–06. The program counter is set to 00. As we work through the program we will use 025 and 031 as our two input numbers.

Figure 6.7 shows the position at the end of the first fetch phase. The contents of the program counter have been passed to the address decoder and used to select location 00. The contents of location 00 have been passed via the buffer and switches A and E into the instruction register. The program counter has been increased and is now ready to select address 01.

The fetch phases of a program with no jump instructions are all repetitions of Figure 6.7. Each successive location is selected and its contents fetched into the instruction register. The figures that follow show only the execute phase of the fetch/execute cycle.

Figure 6.8 shows the position at the end of the first execute phase. The instruction decoder has decoded the contents of the operation register and opened a data channel from the input unit to the memory buffer. The address decoder has selected the address in the address selection register and the first input number has been stored in this location.

Figure 6.9 shows the position at the end of the second complete fetch/execute cycle. The second input number is now stored in location 14. The program counter has again been increased and is now ready to select address 02.

Figure 6.10 shows the position at the end of the third complete fetch/execute cycle. The third instruction has been fetched from location 02 and executed. The address decoder and the address selection register have selected address 13. The operation register and the instruction decoder have opened a data channel from the memory to the accumulator. The contents of location 13 have been copied into the accumulator. The program counter has again been increased and is now ready to select address 03.

Figure 6.11 shows the position at the end of the fourth complete fetch/execute cycle. The fourth instruction has been fetched from location 03 and executed. The address decoder and the address selection register have selected address 14. The operation register and the instruction decoder have opened data channels to add the contents of location 14 to the accumulator. This was done by inputting both the contents of location 14 and the contents of the accumulator into the ADD/SUB unit. The result has been stored back in the accumulator. The program counter has again been increased and is now ready to select address 04.

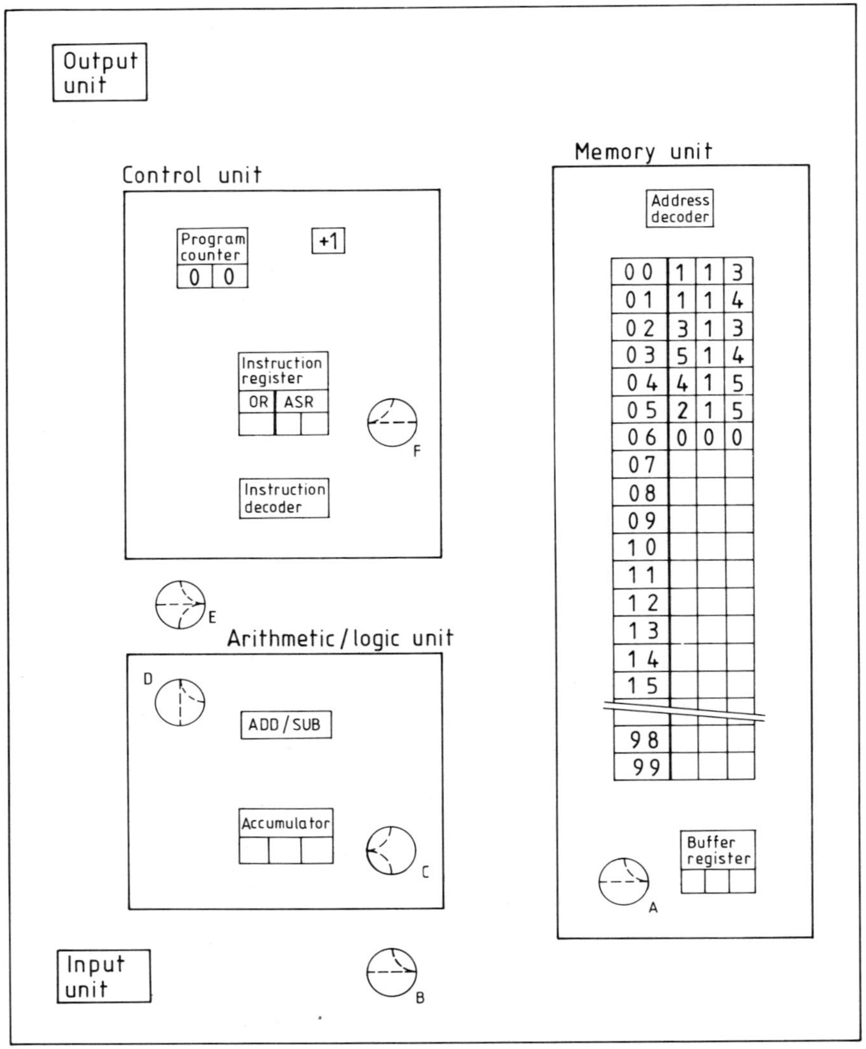

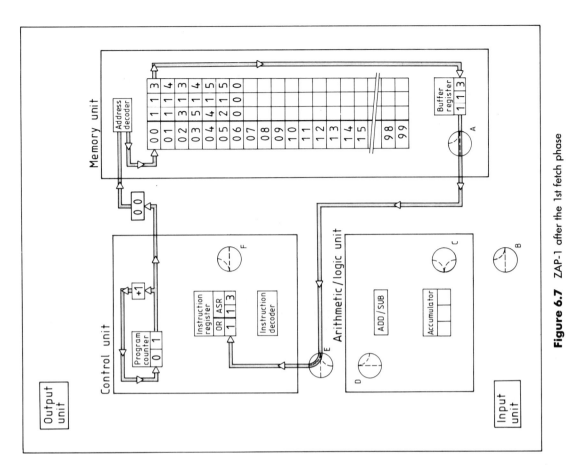

Figure 6.7 ZAP-1 after the 1st fetch phase

Figure 6.6 ZAP-1 loaded and ready to start

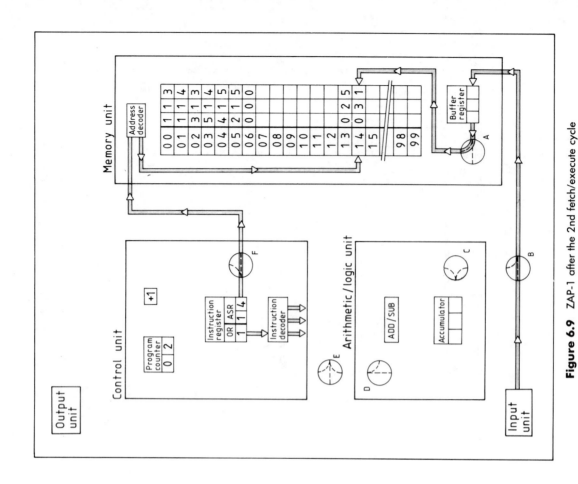

Figure 6.9 ZAP-1 after the 2nd fetch/execute cycle

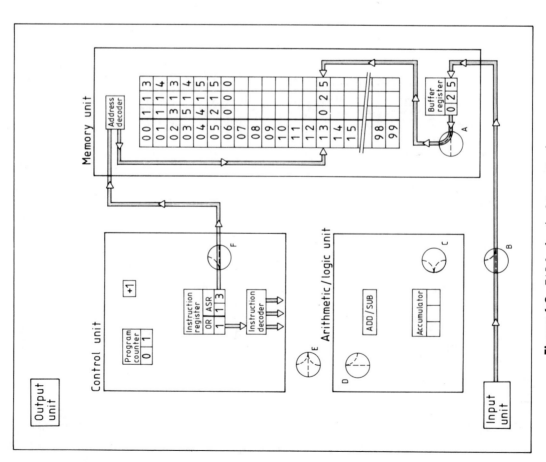

Figure 6.8 ZAP-1 after the 1st execute phase

52

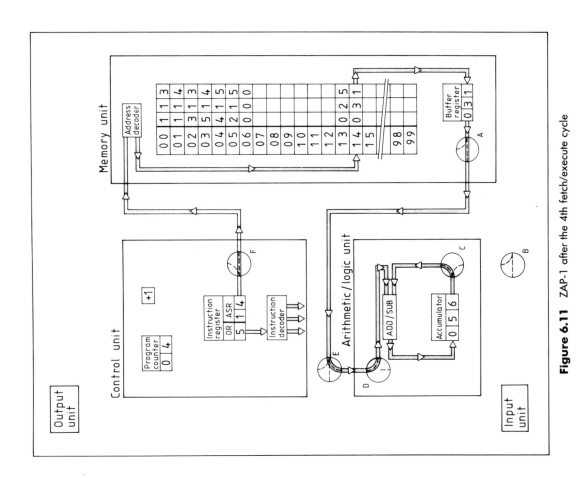

Figure 6.11 ZAP-1 after the 4th fetch/execute cycle

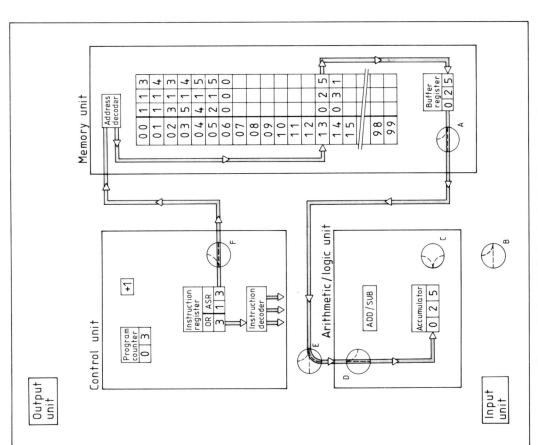

Figure 6.10 ZAP-1 after the 3rd fetch/execute cycle

53

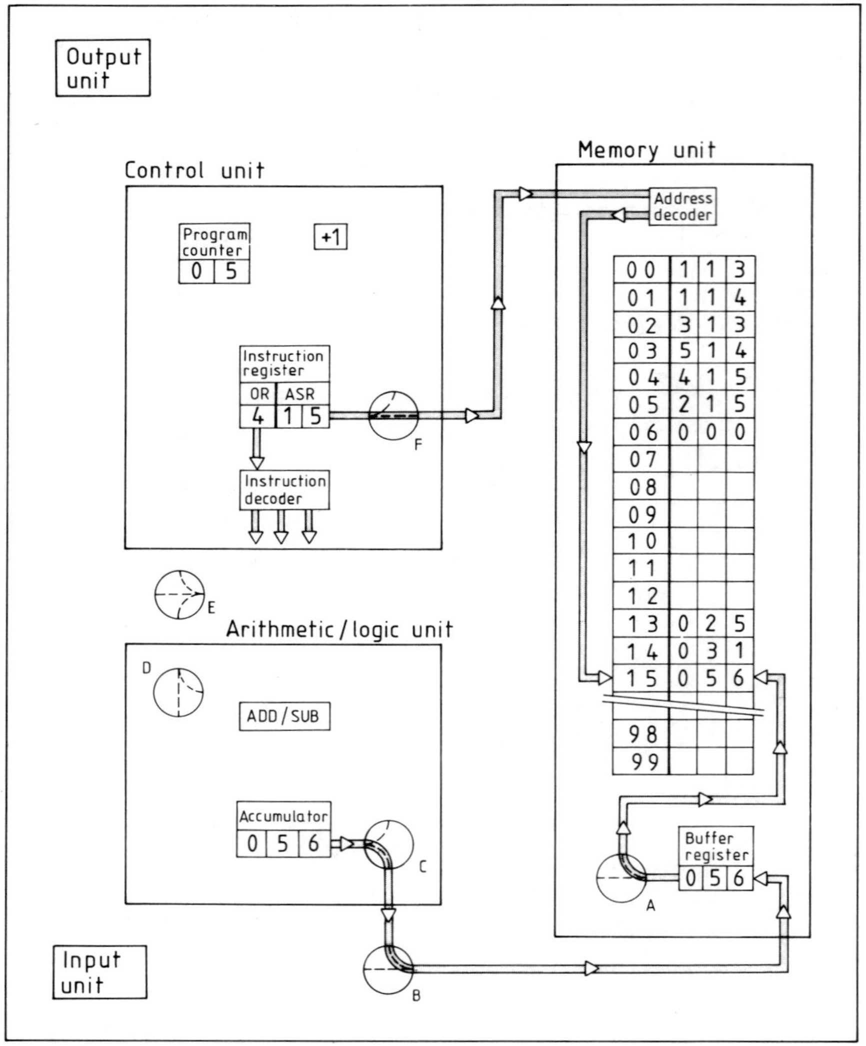

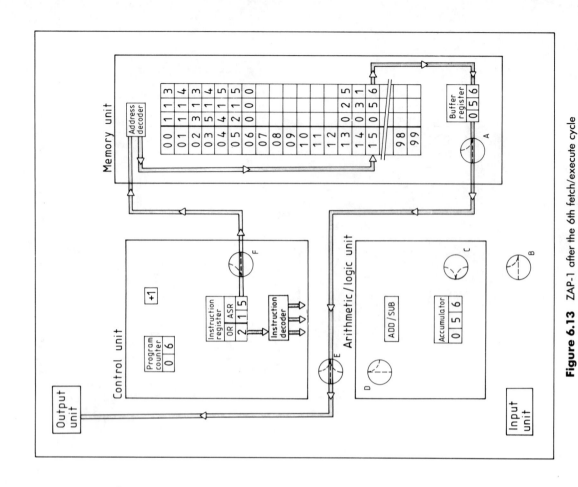

Figure 6.13 ZAP-1 after the 6th fetch/execute cycle

Figure 6.12 ZAP-1 after the 5th fetch/execute cycle

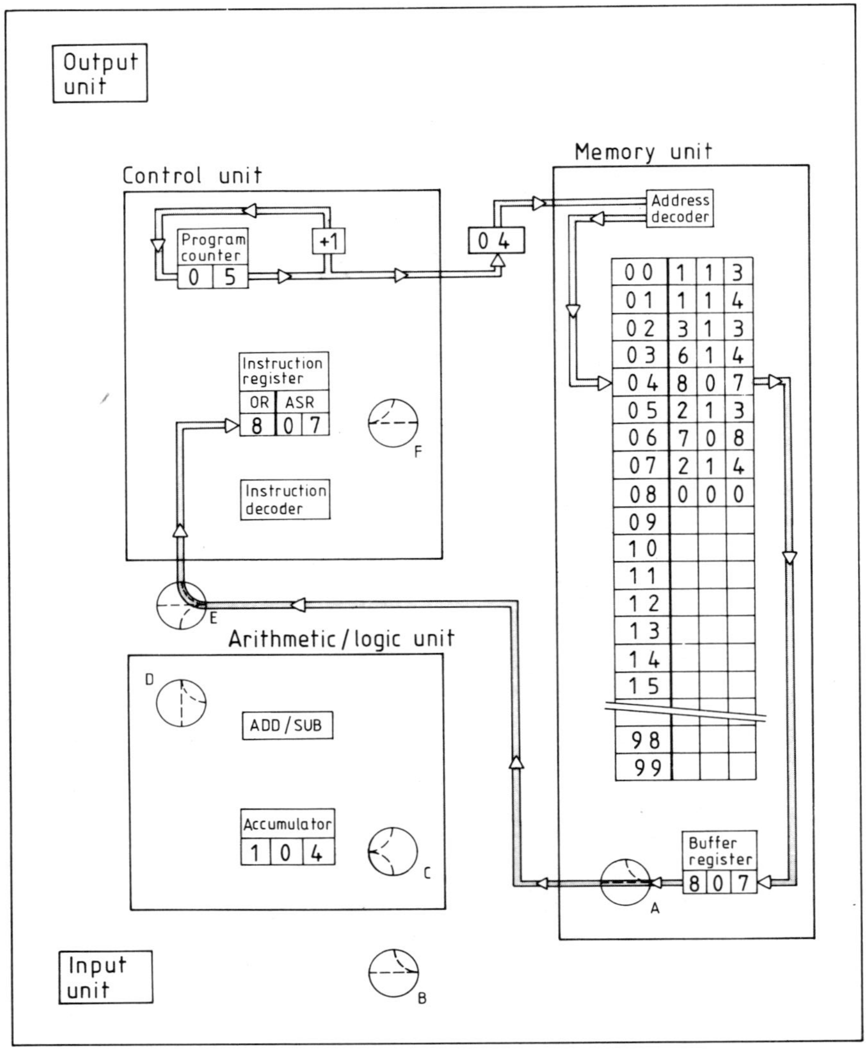

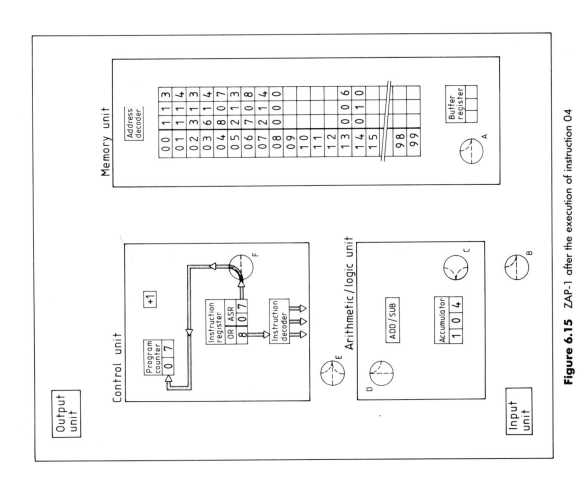

Figure 6.15 ZAP-1 after the execution of instruction 04

Figure 6.14 ZAP-1 after the fetch phase for instruction 04

Figure 6.12 shows the position at the end of the fifth complete fetch/execute cycle. The fifth instruction has been fetched from location 04 and executed. The address decoder and the address selection register have selected address 15. The operation register and the instruction decoder have opened a data channel from the accumulator to the memory. The contents of the accumulator have been copied into location 15. The program counter has again been increased and is now ready to select address 05.

Figure 6.13 shows the position at the end of the sixth complete fetch/execute cycle. The sixth instruction has been fetched from location 05 and executed. The address decoder and the address selection register have selected address 15. The operation register and the instruction decoder have opened a data channel from the memory to the output unit. The contents of location 15 have been sent to the output unit.

The program counter has again been increased and is now ready to select address 06. When it is fetched and executed, the instruction in location 06 will stop the program.

Data and Instructions

The possible confusion between the codes used for data and program instructions has already been mentioned. Both occupy the same immediate access store, and it is the task of the programmer to make sure that the contents of a memory location are correctly interpreted. For example, if the fourth instruction had been incorrectly coded as 504, then the contents of location 04 and not location 14 would have been added to the accumulator. This would cause an error because location 04 contains 415, which is beyond the range of numbers allowed in ZAP-1. In a similar way, if the program counter had ever been allowed to read 13, then the contents of location 13 would have been fetched as an instruction, not a number. Because location 13 contains 025, the program would stop.

Jump Instructions

Jump instructions allow a programmer to alter the sequence in which program instructions are executed. Figures 6.14 and 6.15 show the way that a jump instruction is executed. The complete program stored in the memory unit is designed to input two numbers and output the larger of the two (it assumes the numbers will be different). You may wish to trace through the complete program, but the diagrams show only the execution of instruction 04.

Figure 6.14 shows the position at the end of the fetch phase for instruction 04. The instruction has been fetched into the instruction register and the program counter has been increased to 05.

Instruction 04 will cause a jump to the instruction stored in location 07 if the contents of the accumulator are negative. In this case, because the accumulator contains 104 (or −4), the jump will take place.

Figure 6.15 shows the position after the execution of instruction 04. The operation register and the instruction decoder have opened a data channel from the address selection register to the program counter. The contents of the address selection register have been copied into the program counter. At the start of the next fetch phase, the instruction in location 07 will now be fetched.

If the contents of the accumulator were not negative, then nothing would happen during the execute phase. The contents of the program counter would remain unchanged and the program would fetch the instruction in location 05.

You may wonder how ZAP-1 knows that the contents of the accumulator are negative or positive. In fact, in our simple model no data channels exist between the accumulator and the control unit. We are cheating a little by assuming that conditional jumps can be made. In a real computer a **status register** exists in the arithmetic/logic unit. The individual bits of this register indicate various conditions, such as an overflow or a negative result in the accumulator. The control unit can test each bit in the status register and proceed accordingly.

Dry Running

Dry running a program means testing it with pencil and paper rather than a computer. ZAP programs can only be dry-run because ZAP-1 is a paper computer.

A trace table like the ones to test flowcharts is used. In the example that follows, the lines in the trace table show the contents of the registers and locations at the END of each complete fetch/execute cycle.

Example

Dry-run the following ZAP program using the number 3 as test data. What output will be produced?

Location	Instruction
00	113
01	313
02	907
03	213
04	607
05	413
06	702
07	001

Trace table

Contents of registers and locations at the end of each cycle				
Program counter	Instruction Register	Accumulator	Location 13	Output
01	113	–	3	
02	313	3	3	
03	907	3	3	
04	213	3	3	3
05	607	2	3	
06	413	2	2	
02	702	2	2	
03	907	2	2	
04	213	2	2	2
05	607	1	2	
06	413	1	1	
02	702	1	1	
03	907	1	1	
04	213	1	1	1
05	607	0	1	
06	413	0	0	
02	702	0	0	
03	907	0	0	
08	001	0	0	

As you can see from the trace table, the program counts down from the input number. In this case the output produced is 3, 2, 1. Using location 07 as both an instruction and as data is not very good programming practice, but it does demonstrate that instructions and data items are indistinguishable.

Exercise 21

1 Dry-run the following ZAP program using the test data A, 23, B, 20. What output will be produced?

Location	Instruction
00	113
01	114
02	115
03	116
04	314
05	616
06	810
07	213
08	214
09	712
10	215
11	216
12	000

2 Dry-run the following ZAP program using the test data 4, 3. What output will be produced?

Location	Instruction
00	113
01	114
02	315
03	513
04	415
05	314
06	611
07	414
08	910
09	702
10	215
11	001

3 Write and dry-run a ZAP program that inputs two numbers, outputs the smaller number if they are different and the letter E if they are equal.

4 Assume that ZAP-1 can subtract the code for one letter from the code for another letter and detect if the result is negative. Write and dry-run a program that inputs two letters in any order and then outputs them in alphabetical order. You may assume that the letters will not be the same.

Binary Instruction Codes

ZAP-1 uses normal numbers for operation codes, addresses and data but all real computers use binary numbers. Unfortunately each type of computer has its own binary codes or **machine language**. Thus a program written in the **machine code** of one computer cannot be used on a computer of a different type.

A possible machine code using a single byte for each instruction is shown below (Figure 6.16). This is not a practical system for a real computer, but it illustrates the principles of binary machine codes.

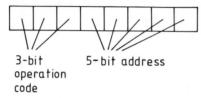

3-bit operation code   5-bit address

Figure 6.16 A binary machine code

A 3-bit operational code gives 8 possible codes and a 5-bit address code gives 32 possible codes. Thus we can code 8 operations and 32 addresses. We will use the following operation codes:

000   Stop
001   Load the accumulator from a memory location
010   Store the contents of the accumulator in a memory location
011   Add the contents of a memory location to the contents of the accumulator
100   Subtract the contents of a memory location from the contents of the accumulator
101   Jump to the instruction in a memory location
110   Jump to the instruction in a memory location if the contents of the accumulator are negative
111   Jump to the instruction in a memory location if the contents of the accumulator are zero.

The meaning of the complete instruction 01100101 is shown in Figure 6.17.

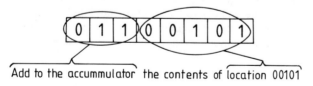

Add to the accummulator the contents of location 00101

Figure 6.17 What a machine code means

Exercise 22

1 Using the codes given in the text, explain the meaning of the following instructions:

a	11100111	**e**	10110101
b	00000000	**f**	01001111
c	11011101	**g**	10000000
d	00111111	**h**	01111100

2 Dry-run the following program. Your trace table should have columns for a 5-bit program counter, an 8-bit instruction register, an 8-bit accumulator, and the 8-bit contents of location 00110. What are the contents of location 00110 at the end of the program?

Location	Instruction
00000	00100100
00001	01100101
00010	01000110
00011	00000000
00100	00000101
00101	00000010

3 A computer using the codes given in the text would need a 5-bit binary decoder to select individual memory locations. Part of the necessary logic circuit is shown below. What pattern of bits must the address selection register contain in order to produce an output of 1?

Inputs from the address selection register

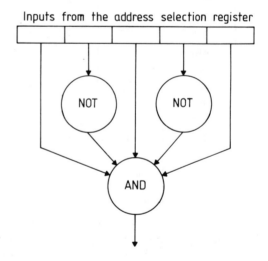

4 Design the part of the address decoder's logic circuit needed to select the address 00111.

5 Part of the logic circuit needed to decode the operation codes given in the text is shown below.

  a What operation code produces an output of 1 at A?
  b What operation code produces an output of 1 at B?

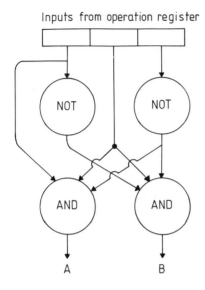

Inputs from operation register

6 Design the part of the instruction decoder needed to select either 'Load the accumulator' or 'Add to the accumulator'.

7 A computer uses a 12-bit word for each machine instruction. 4 bits are used for the operation code and 8 bits for the address.

  a How many bits are needed in the program counter?
  b How many bits are needed in the instruction register?
  c How many different operation codes can be used?
  d What is the maximum size for the immediate access store?

8 Repeat Question 7 for a computer that uses a 16-bit word, with 6 bits for the operation code and the rest for the address.

Practical Considerations

We will end this chapter by considering some of the practical problems that exist in real computers and which are not included in our simple model.

Data buses. In ZAP-1, all the data buses are shown with a single line. It is possible to transmit binary signals along a single wire, with the separate bits of a byte or word following one after the other. This is called **serial transmission** and computers that use serial transmission are called **serial computers**. In most modern computers, however, the separate bits in a byte or word are transmitted along a set of parallel wires. This is called **parallel transmission** and computers that use parallel

transmission are called **parallel computers**. Thus, unlike our simple model, a modern parallel computer will require data buses with a number of wires equal to the wordlength of the computer. Figure 6.18 shows the pulse pattern 01000001 transmitted in serial form and in parallel form.

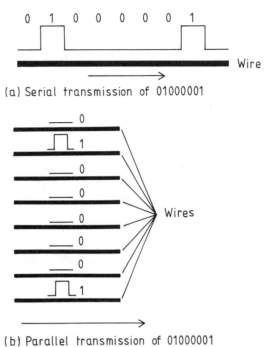

(a) Serial transmission of 01000001

(b) Parallel transmission of 01000001

Figure 6.18   The transmission of 01000001

Timing. During each complete fetch/execute cycle many different control signals must be generated. For example, at the start of each fetch phase a data channel must be opened from the program counter to the address decoder. Almost immediately after this, during the execute phase, a data channel must be opened from the address selection register to the address decoder. Very accurate timing of the control sequence is essential. An electronic clock is provided in all computers. This sends out a very rapid sequence of pulses of electricity. These pulses are used to open and close control switches and to synchronise all the step-by-step operations of the computer. The frequencies used by the clocks are very high. Several million pulses or more every second may be used. To measure such small time intervals we have:

  * 1 millisecond = 1 thousandth of a second
  * 1 microsecond = 1 millionth of a second
  * 1 nanosecond = 1 thousand millionth of a second

A Final Block Diagram

We can now draw a final block diagram of a simple computer showing all the necessary control and data links (Figure 6.19). Beware, however. As you will see in later chapters, large modern computers have many extra complications.

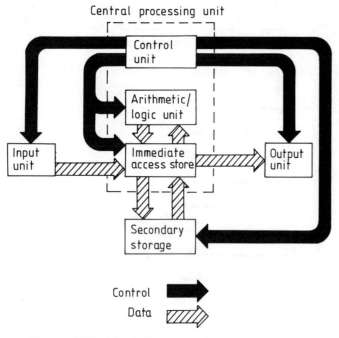

Figure 6.19 A block diagram of a basic computer system

Exercise 23

1 Copy and complete the following passages:

a Two of the most important differences between ZAP-1 and a real computer are _____.

b There are _____ memory locations in ZAP-1. Each location can store any _____ number. The memory unit is called the _____.

c The device that allows any memory address to be selected is called the _____.

d Data entering or leaving the memory passes through the _____.

e Program instructions and _____ codes are stored in the memory unit.

f The function of the control unit is to _____.

g The register that stores the address of the next program instruction is called the _____.

h The _____ stores a copy of the instruction being executed. It has two parts, the _____ and the _____.

It is sometimes called the _____.

i The _____ decodes the operation part of each instruction and sends signals to the _____.

j The address part of each instruction is stored in the _____. It is passed to the _____ or, in the case of a jump, to the _____.

k Another name for the program counter is the _____.

l All calculations and logic operations take place in the _____.

m The register that stores the results of calculations is called the _____.

n An instruction that allows the programmer to alter the sequence of program instructions is called a _____.

o Each computer has its own set of binary instructions, called the _____ of the computer.

p _____ computers transmit data bit by bit along a single wire. _____ computers transmit data several bits at a time along a set of parallel wires.

q An electronic _____ is needed in all computers. This sends out a very rapid series of timing pulses. These are used to _____.

2 Explain the meaning of the byte 01000001:

a if it is fetched as an instruction, using the machine code given in this chapter

b if it represents a number stored in two's complement form.

3 The diagram below shows the program counter and the instruction register of a computer that uses the machine code given in this chapter. Draw diagrams to show the contents of these registers:

a if the accumulator is storing a negative number

b if the accumulator is storing a positive number.

Program counter				
0	0	0	1	1

Instruction register							
OR			ASR				
1	1	0	0	1	1	1	0

4 Describe with as much detail as possible the sequence of events that happens during each of the following:

a the fetch phase of the fetch/execute cycle

b the execute phase of the fetch/execute cycle for an instruction to copy the contents of a location into the accumulator

c the execute phase of the fetch/execute cycle for an instruction that adds the contents of a location to the contents of the accumulator

d the execute phase of the fetch/execute cycle for an instruction that outputs a number from a location.

5 Explain the function of the sequence control register (also called the program counter). Illustrate your answer by describing the execution of a jump instruction.

(L 81)

6 a With suitable examples explain fully each of the following programming terms: loops; conditional jump; subroutine.

b A machine code program has an instruction word of 16 bits of which 6 bits are used for the function (operation) code.

(i) How many different codes can be specified?

(ii) Using a diagram, show how machine code programs are executed sequentially.

c If the code for INPUT is 001101, show with a logic diagram how this signal could be decoded in the execute cycle.

(AEB 82)

7 A small computer uses an 8 bit word. When storing an instruction the first 3 bits starting from the left represent an operation code, the remaining 5 bits the address in memory to which the operation refers.

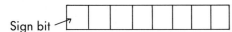

When storing a number, the left most bit is the sign bit, and negative numbers are represented in 2's complement form.

Sign bit

Listed below are some of the operation codes and their meanings. All operations use the accumulator.

Operation Code	Meaning
001	Load the contents of the given location into the accumulator.
010	Add the contents of the given location to the accumulator.
011	Subtract the contents of the given location from the accumulator.
100	Store the contents of the accumulator in the given location.
101	Jump unconditionally to the given location.

a How many instructions are possible?

b How many locations can be directly addressed?

c The contents of three locations are given in the following table.

LOCATION ADDRESS	CONTENTS
10001	00001001
10010	00001101
10100	00011001

Showing all necessary work answer the following questions:

(i) What binary value will be in the accumulator after the following two instructions have been executed?

001   10001
010   10010

(ii) What is the equivalent decimal value?

(iii) If the next instruction executed is 011 10100 what value will the accumulator then contain?

(iv) What is the equivalent decimal value?

(v) When the instruction 101 00101 has been executed what will be the address of the next instruction to be obeyed?

(NI CSE 82)

8 A certain computer uses 12-bit words, each of which can contain one machine code instruction. In each machine code instruction, the operation code occupies 4 bits. A single accumulator is used.

(i) Within the central processing unit, data may be transferred in *serial* or in *parallel*. Distinguish between these methods of transfer and briefly indicate the advantages and disadvantages of each. In each case, state the width of the data bus (data highway) which would be used.

(ii) The machine code instruction

1 0 0 0	1 1 0 1 0 1 1 1

indicates that data should be loaded into the accumulator from the location in main store having the binary address

1 1 0 1 0 1 1 1.

Draw a simple diagram showing the principal elements of the central processing unit. On this diagram, show the data paths and control signals which would be needed to decode and execute the instruction shown above, after it has been fetched from store. Write notes to describe this process of decoding and execution.

(iii) Why is it likely that, in practice, a computer would use

a operation codes occupying more than 4 bits?

b machine code instructions occupying more than 12 bits?

(C 82)

9 A certain computer's machine language contains the following instructions:

FETCH n – copy the contents of the location whose absolute address is n into the accumulator;

ADD n – add the number contained in location n to the contents of the accumulator;

STORE n – copy the contents of the accumulator into location n;

JNEG n – jump (branch) to location n if the number in the accumulator is negative;

STOP – end of program.

Part of a program is stored in locations 20 to 25 as follows:

location	20	STORE	102
	21	FETCH	100
	22	ADD	101
	23	JNEG	22
	24	STORE	103
	25	STOP	

a If, before execution of the program, the accumulator contains +50, location 100 contains −70, location 101 contains +20, what will be the contents of locations 100, 101, 102, 103 and the accumulator when the STOP statement is executed?

b If, before execution of the program, the accumulator contains −50, location 100 contains +70, location 101 contains −10, what will be the contents of locations 100, 101, 102, 103, and the accumulator when the STOP statement is executed?

(O 82)

10 A simplified system of machine instructions uses the first 3 bits of an 8 bit instruction for the operation code and the other 5 bits are used for the binary number representing the memory address. The following table gives the interpretation of a selection of the operation codes.

Operation Code	Interpretation
010	Copy number from accumulator to memory
100	Copy number from memory to accumulator
110	Add number in memory to accumulator.

a Explain the instruction 10000101, specifying the memory address in base 10.

b Write 2 further instructions to follow that in part **a** which would add the number in memory 6 to the accumulator and store the result in memory 15.

(SUJB 82)

11 Data for input to a computer can be represented as either:

numeric
alphanumeric

a Explain how each form of data is stored internally.

b Explain how positive and negative numbers are stored in binary showing how addition and subtraction are performed.

c Explain the function of each of the following within the computer:

accumulator;
buffer;
sequence control register

(AEB 82)

12 The sixteen bit word of a computer contains the following bit pattern:

16	15	14	13	12	11	10	9	8	7	6	5	4	3	2	1
1	1	0	1	0	0	1	1	0	1	0	1	1	0	1	0

Describe three possible interpretations of this pattern.

(O&C 82)

7 The Capture, Input and Checking of Data

Data Capture

Collecting information to be processed by a computer is called **data capture**. The expression

garbage in = garbage out (GIGO)

is commonly used in the computer world. It means that a computer provided with inaccurate input will certainly produce inaccurate output. If we want the computer to produce accurate results, then we must obviously collect and input accurate information.

Forms and Documents

Forms and documents are often used to capture data. Think of the many hundreds of reasons for filling out forms: to obtain a driving licence or a passport, to open an account, to make a claim, to join an organization, to complete a survey, to apply for a job, to order some goods, to send a bill, and so on. The British Government uses an estimated 104 000 different types of form to collect and transmit information! Today more often than not, the information collected on a form will be processed by computers.

Many people complain that a lot of the forms they are asked to use are difficult to complete. It is certainly very easy to design a bad form. The topic of form design could fill a whole book but some simple points to note are:

* All questions and requests for data should be worded as simply as possible.
* All questions should be unambiguous. This means that there should be a single clear meaning for each question on the form.
* Examples should be provided to demonstrate how to answer difficult or complicated questions.
* A clear space should be provided for each answer, large enough to contain any expected answer.
* The form must accurately collect *all* the required information.
* The form should be produced on a standard size of paper, for example A4 or A5.
* If possible, different typefaces and colours should be used to improve presentation and to emphasise important information.
* The form design should make it easy to prepare the data for input to a computer.

Suppose we wished to conduct a survey on the accommodation available in a small town. We might decide to use a survey form to collect information from a sample of 200 people. Look at each of the following possible survey questions:

a Please state the form of your abode. _____

b What kind of accommodation do you live in? _____

c Please tick one box for the kind of accommodation that you live in:

Detached house	☐
Semidetached house	☐
Detached bungalow	☐
Semidetached bungalow	☐
Terraced house	☐
Cottage	☐
Farmhouse	☐
Flat or apartment	☐
Hotel	☐
Hostel	☐
Other (please specify: _____)	☐

Question **a** is set in a very formal way. Some people will not understand it.

Both Question **a** and Question **b** may produce either less or more information than we require. If we wish to identify all the options given in Question **c**, an answer of 'house' may not be sufficient. On the other hand, an answer of 'a four-bedroom, detached, non-estate, neo-Georgian style house in a quiet road' may contain far more information than needed. Time will be wasted picking out the required details from this answer. Question **c**, though, can be answered quickly and accurately. It is designed to obtain the exact information that we require.

It is essential when designing a form to consider exactly *what* information we wish to collect. If Question **c** is used in the example above, no information will be collected on the number of bedrooms in the accommodation or whether it is owner occupied. If we require this information, other questions must be included on the survey form to collect it.

It is always preferable to provide a definite number of options for any question designed to collect information. This can even be done when we ask people for their opinions. For example, suppose we wish to conduct a survey on people's opinions of the Prime Minister. If we simply ask one thousand people the question 'What do you think of the Prime Minister?' we are likely to get one thousand different replies ranging from a single word to an essay. While the data collected may be interesting, it will be virtually impossible to process.

It would be much better to decide in advance what attributes we wished to collect opinions on. For example, successful or unsuccessful, friendly or unfriendly, powerful or not powerful, hardworking or lazy. For each attribute we could then design a question like the one below.

THE PRIME MINISTER IS (please tick one box):

SUCCESSFUL			Neither	UNSUCCESSFUL		
Extremely	Fairly	Slightly		Slightly	Fairly	Extremely

The data this question will collect can be processed, average opinions can be found, and conclusions made.

Even with a simple question like 'What is your age?' we might provide a box like this:

AGE   YEARS ☐☐   MONTHS ☐☐

Alternatively, if we are only interested in a person's approximate age we might provide this:

Please tick one box for your age range.

18–24 years	☐
25–34 years	☐
35–44 years	☐
45–54 years	☐
55–64 years	☐
65 and over	☐

This will save time if we only need approximate ages but will be useless if we need to know exact ages! Full instructions, or even better examples, must be provided. It may be obvious to you how to fill in the question on the Prime Minister, but you may like to check if it is obvious to everyone in your class!

When information must be written on the form, it is a good idea to divide the answer space into separate squares and to ask for capital letters. This usually produces replies that are much easier to read. Compare the following examples of questions and replies:

* Please write your name and address in the space below:

J. Smith
33 Upton St
Downtown
Lincs

* Please write your name and address in the space below in CAPITAL letters. Use one square for each letter.

J		S	M	I	T	H							
3	3		U	P	T	O	N		S	T			
D	O	W	N	T	O	W	N						
L	I	N	C	S									

Coding or numbering the answers will speed the process of collecting and inputting the data from completed forms. For example, suppose we had used the age range question and wished to input and process the information from two hundred forms. Coding the replies from 1 to 7 will save us a lot of entry time because it will reduce the volume of data to be input. The computer program to process the data will of course need to be written so that it accepts these codes. Here is an example:

Please tick one box for your age range.

1	☐	18–24 years
2	☐	25–34 years
3	☐	35–44 years
4	☐	45–54 years
5	☐	55–64 years
6	☐	65 and over

The code number 7 will not appear on the form but will be used to code anyone who fails to complete the question. This is an important provision because we will not wish to discard all the information just because one question was refused or overlooked. Indeed, in some cases the number of 'don't knows' or 'won't tells' may be interesting information.

Having completed the design for a form, you should test it with a small sample of people. This will show up faults in the design that can be corrected before a form is printed in large numbers.

Codes are also commonly used on business forms to speed the entry of data. Look at the Zapper Radios order form (Figure 7.1).

Zapper Radios only sell their products to shopkeepers through representatives who call each month. The representative completes the order form and returns it to headquarters. The details on the form are entered into the firm's computer which deals with delivery of the radios and charging the shopkeepers for them. A code is used for:

* Each representative. Ann Jones is representative 2375.
* Each customer. The Radio Shop is customer 04732A.

ZAPPER RADIOS INTERNATIONAL LTD.

ORDER FORM

REPRESENTATIVE _ANN JONES_   REF. NO. [2][3][7][5]

CUSTOMER DETAILS

NAME _THE RADIO SHOP_   ADDRESS _38 HIGH ST., DOORPEN,_
ACCOUNT NO. [0][4][7][3][2][A]   _LINCS_

ITEM	CATALOGUE NO.	QTY.	PRICE	TOTALS
Zappette M/B Yellow	0827/3/5/4	5	10.50	52.50
SuperZap B Red	0834/2/2/9	4	12.00	48.00
HASH TOTAL	1661583		TOTAL	100.50
			DISCOUNT	5%

Please supply the goods shown above subject to all the terms and conditions shown overleaf.

CUSTOMER SIGNATURE _H. Bloggs_   DATE _4/2/86_

Figure 7.1   The use of codes on a business form

* Each type of radio made by Zappers. This code has four parts:

Four digits	One digit	One digit	One digit
↓	↓	↓	↓
Model of radio	Power supply	Colour	Check digit
	1=Mains only	1=Black	
	2=Battery only	2=Red	
	3=Mains or battery	3=green	
		4=Blue	
		5=Yellow	
		6=White	

The only information that needs to be input from this form into the computer is:

2375   04732A   0827354   5   0834229   4
040286   1661583

The use of 'hash totals' and 'check digits' will be explained in the section on data validation.

Exercise 24

1 Copy and complete the following passages:

a Collecting information to be processed by a computer is called _____. The expression GIGO is commonly used. It means _____.

b Some of the points to note when designing a form are _____.

c It will be easier to read answers if we ask for _____ in all replies and provide _____. If we code the answers, it will speed input to a computer. This is because codes reduce the _____ of data to be input.

d Completed designs should always be _____ before they are printed in large numbers.

2 In each of the following cases design a suitable question to capture the required information. Whenever possible provide an answer box to be ticked. Where answers may be in a wide range, you must decide suitable division points to divide the range.
  a the eye colour of every pupil in your school
  b the political party that a group of people intend to vote for at the next election
  c the academic qualifications of a group of people
  d the weekly earnings after tax of a group of people.

3 Design a short survey form to collect pupil's opinions of your computer studies course.

4 It has been decided that every teacher in your school will complete a slip each lesson showing the names of all pupils absent from the class. These slips will be sent to the office to be checked against the school registers.
  a Design a suitable slip for the teachers to use.
  b How many slips will the office staff receive each lesson? How many will they receive each day?
  c Describe the best way for the office staff to sort the slips before starting to check them against the registers.
  d State the advantages to the school in using a system like this.
  e State the disadvantages to the school in using a system like this.
  f Do you think this is a sensible plan, considering the advantages and disadvantages you have stated?
  g What actions need to be taken if:
    (i) a pupil marked absent in the register is not marked absent on a slip?
    (ii) a pupil marked present in the register is marked absent on a slip?
  h Describe how you think a computer could be used to help with this task. In your answer list:
    (i) the input data needed
    (ii) the data required from secondary storage
    (iii) the processing required
    (iv) the presentation of the output.

5 When information is hand written on a form, letters and numbers can be confused. For example, the number 2 may be confused with the letter Z. Make a list of some other pairs of letters and numbers that could cause confusion.

6 Identify the code shown in each of the following cases and state what the code is used for:
  a FPL 875 V,   WWR 308 Y,   B 347 FGT
  b WIM OBP, RG3 1NR, SE1 7BP
  c JS. 18 4A CHEM,   TW. 19 4B PHYS,   CW. 20 4C BIOL
  d ·—, ··· ·—, —· ·—, ·——·
  e
  f
  g

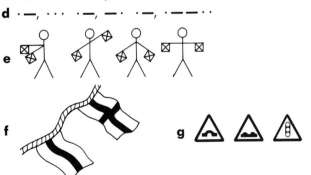

7 Read the following article

Jargon pruned from forms

by Aileen Ballantyne

THE PRIME Minister yesterday inspected the progress of a campaign to banish gobbledegook from government forms, but found that there are about 35,000 still to be ploughed through.

Forms on policies such as the right to buy a council house and grants for small businessmen were displayed for Mrs Thatcher's inspection at the Treasury Chambers in London.

She was able to study the management and efficiency department's new improved versions at the exhibition, mounted by the Plain English Campaign and opened yesterday by Lord Gowrie, the Civil Service Minister.

One old form from the Lord Chancellor's department, intended for elderly bereaved people who wished to apply to adminster the estate of someone who has died, was "too concentrated," said Mrs Thatcher. The form asks if the deceased left "a husband or widow" and asks for reasons why other executors are not now applying, to be ticked where applicable. These include, "is dead," and "does not wish to apply now, but may wish to do so later."

The new form, much simplified and with space left for the applicant to give a legible answer, appeared to meet with Mrs Thatcher's approval. Of 143,000 of the original forms sent out, 25,000 were returned incorrectly.

The Government published a white paper three years ago which required its departments to reduce the number of forms and to simplify those still needed. There remain an estimated 104,000 different types of government form. The "management and efficiency" department have examined about 69,000 of these and found nearly 16,000 that were so far beyond redemption that they had to be abolished.

A further 21,000 forms have been significantly improved, according to a spokesman who said he was from the "ME" department, then apologised for using jargon.

(*The Guardian* 8 August 1985)

a Explain in your own words the meaning of the following:

  (i) *jargon*
  (ii) *gobbledegook*
  (iii) *Plain English Campaign*
  (iv) *too concentrated*
  (v) *a white paper*

b What were the design faults of the form mentioned in the article? How has the design been improved?

c What percentage of Government forms have been examined?

d Of these, what percentage have had to be abolished?

e What percentage of examined forms have been significantly improved?

8 a Give **two** different benefits from encoding information (such as the postal code GU11 1BQ).

b A company manufactures drums for washing machines. The drums are different sizes, for different washing machine manufacturers and for different models of washing machine. Devise a code which this company could use in its catalogues. Explain each part of the code.

(AEB 85)

9 A questionnaire has been designed to collect data about the reading habits of pupils at a school.
Explain why

a the pupil's name is not included,

b a list of newspapers is provided which is ticked by the respondent,

c for magazines respondents are asked to name their area of interest and give the number bought per week and per month in each area,

d asking for both age and date of birth so that a validity check can be made affects the privacy of the information.

(L 79)

Data Preparation and Input

As a student of computer studies, you are probably more familar with microcomputers than with **mainframe** computers. A microcomputer's input data is usually entered directly at the keyboard as the program runs. Often this is not a suitable input method for mainframe computers. These computers cost hundreds of thousands of pounds. For them to be economical they must be used for as much data processing as possible. Entry of data at a keyboard while a program runs may sometimes be essential but it is a very slow input method.

Some scientific mainframe computer applications input a relatively small volume of data and exploit the computer's power by carrying out a large number of calculations at very high speeds. In this case, the time taken to enter the data is not important. Many commercial applications, however, input a large volume of data and carry out only very simple calculations on each item. In this case, it is essential that the computer is not kept waiting while the large volume of data is input at a keyboard.

Therefore, whenever possible, a faster input method is used. All the methods used require a **medium** (material) for data storage that can be 'read' at high speed by an input device. We will look first at three methods by which data from source documents is **transcribed** (copied) on to computer media. This stage of translating data into a machine-readable form is called **data preparation**. Figure 7.2 is an outline sketch of data preparation systems.

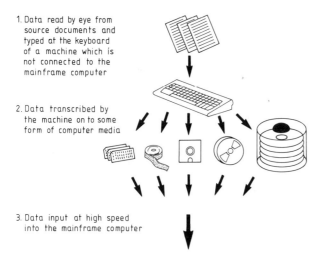

1. Data read by eye from source documents and typed at the keyboard of a machine which is not connected to the mainframe computer
2. Data transcribed by the machine on to some form of computer media
3. Data input at high speed into the mainframe computer

Figure 7.2 Data preparation systems

"HOLLERITH"
KEEP THIS DOOR CLOSED

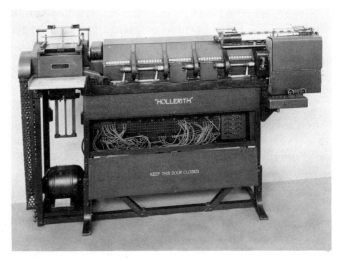

Figure 7.3 An early tabulator

Punched Cards

Punched cards were in use long before the invention of computers. They were used to store data which could then be processed by electromechanical machines designed to sort and count the cards. For example, when the American Census Bureau completed the 1890 census of the American population, all the information collected on the census forms was transferred to punched cards. These cards were then processed by machines invented by Dr Herman Hollerith. Hollerith's machines took three years to sort and count the cards. Manual counting methods used for the 1880 census had taken seven years! The use of punched card machines or **tabulators** grew and they were used in many commercial applications to store and process data until computers came into general use in the early 1960s. Figure 7.3 shows an early tabulator.

In the early days of computing, punched cards were adapted for use as a storage and input medium. Today, their use is declining and the following section is included mainly for historical interest.

A typical modern card is about 18 cm by 8 cm and has 80 columns and 12 rows of punching positions. One complete column is used for each character. Because each card can only store 80 characters, many cards are necessary to store a complete program or collection of data. The complete set of cards used is called a **pack** or **deck**. Cards are often **interpreted** so that they can be read by both humans and computers. Interpreted cards have the stored data printed in normal characters across the top of the card. Figure 7.4 shows a typical card punched with a complete character set. One corner of the card is clipped off so that any upside-down or back-to-front cards in a deck can be spotted at once.

Figure 7.4 A punched card

CDL 5081
Printed in the U.K.

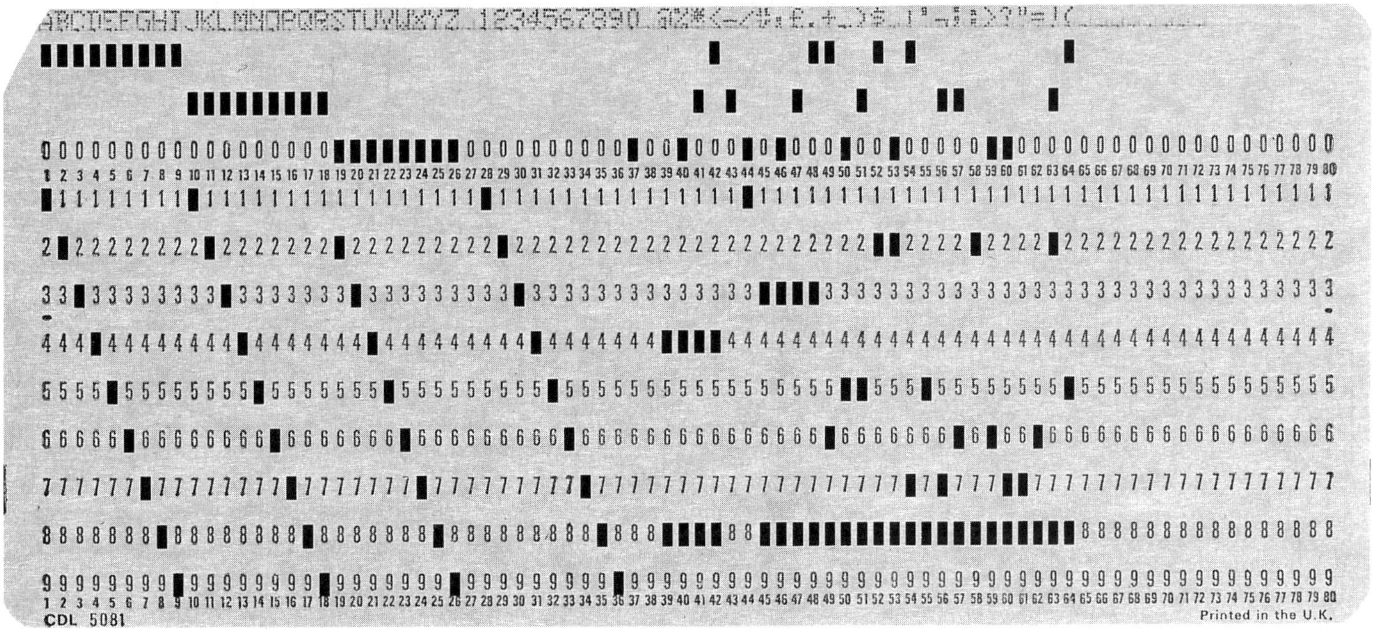

Cards are punched using a machine called a **keypunch**. This machine has a normal keyboard like a typewriter. A **keypunch operator** reads the data from source documents and types it at the keyboard. As each character is typed, the machine uses a set of small knives to punch out the correct holes in the card automatically.

After a set of cards has been punched, they are **verified** to check that the data has been correctly transcribed onto the cards. This may require a separate machine, or a combined **punch/verifier** may be used (Figure 7.5). The verifier feeds in the cards for a second time. A different operator also types in all the data again. As each character is retyped, the verifier compares it with the character punched on the card. If the characters match, the card is advanced and the next character checked. If the characters do not match, the keys on the keyboard are locked. The operator must now check to see if the mistake is in the card or the second typing. If the mistake is in the second typing, pressing the correct key will unlock the keyboard. If the mistake is in the card, a whole new card must be punched and then reverified.

Figure 7.5 An IBM punch/verifier

When a set of cards has been punched and verified, the data is input using a **card reader**. As the cards are fed through this machine, they pass between a light and a set of twelve photoelectric cells. Where there is a hole in the card, light shines through onto one of the cells and a pulse of electricity is produced. Where no hole has been punched, no light can pass and no pulse is produced. In this way the two-state system in the card (hole or no hole) is changed to the two-state system in the computer (pulse or no pulse).

Figure 7.6 shows the outline of a card reader.

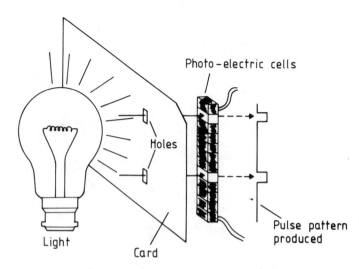

Figure 7.6 How a card reader works

Card reader speeds vary considerably. Speeds of up to 2000 cards per minute are possible, but 1000 cards per minute is a more typical rate.

Paper Tape

Punched paper tape can be used as an alternative to punched cards. A typical paper tape is 2.5 cm wide and has 8 punching positions called **tracks** across its width. 7- or 5-track tape may also be used. With 8-track tape, a 7-bit code is often used and the eighth track is used for a **parity check**. Four characters can be punched in each centimetre of tape and a complete reel may be over 100 metres long. One complete column or **frame** across the tape is used to code each character. Figure 7.7 shows a section of paper tape with some characters punched into it. If you look closely you may spot that the code used is one we have met before. The small **sprocket holes** are not part of the code, they are used to feed the tape through punching and reading machines.

Paper tape is also punched using a machine called a **keypunch**. This paper tape machine is very similar to the card machine. The main difference is the provision of an **erase key**. If paper tape punch operators know they have made a mistake, the tape can be moved back and the erase key used. This key will punch out holes in all the frames to form the erase code. This code is ignored when the tape is read. An erase key is not provided for punched cards because of the limited space on each card. A paper tape can be as long as required.

Paper tape is verified like punched cards by typing the data a second time. When punched cards are verified, single incorrect cards can be taken from the deck and repunched. It is not possible to repunch a section of a paper tape, so the verifier always produces a completely new tape. As each character is retyped, the verifier compares it with the character punched on the old tape.

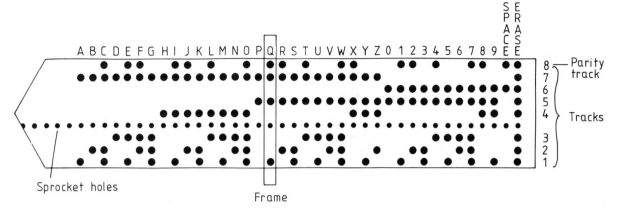

A B C D E F G H I J K L M N O P Q R S T U V W X Y Z 0 1 2 3 4 5 6 7 8 9 SPACE ERASE

Parity track
Tracks

Sprocket holes

Frame

Figure 7.7 A section of 8-track paper tape

If the characters match, this character is punched into the new tape. If the characters do not match, the keyboard locks. The operator must then check whether the mistake is in the old tape or the second typing. When this has been decided, the correct character is typed and punched into the new tape.

Any keypunch operator can be expected to make at least one mistake in every one hundred characters typed. Verification of cards and tape is thus a very important stage in data preparation.

When a paper tape has been punched and verified, it is input using a **paper tape reader**. This works in a very similar way to a punched card reader and converts the two-state system of punched holes in the tape into the two-state system of electrical pulses in the computer. Figure 7.8 shows an outline sketch of a paper tape reader.

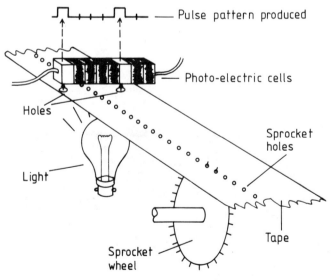

Pulse pattern produced

Photo-electric cells

Holes

Light

Sprocket holes

Sprocket wheel

Tape

Figure 7.8 How a paper tape reader works

Speeds of paper tape readers vary considerably, they can be as low as 100 characters per second or as high as 2000 characters per second.

A Comparison Between Punched Cards and Paper Tape

Advantages of cards
* Interpreted cards can be read by eye. Paper tape cannot be easily read by eye.
* Some of the data in a set of cards can be changed by repunching a few cards. To change any data on a tape it must be completely repunched.
* In general, cards are more robust than tape. This makes cards more suitable for applications where the input medium may be handled several times before it is input.

Advantages of tape
* Tape is continuous (all in one piece) so the order of the data cannot be accidently changed. Cards can become misplaced in a deck.
* Tape is less bulky than cards. It takes up less space to store the same amount of data.
* Because tape is continuous, records can be more flexible in length. Each card is restricted to a maximum of eighty characters of data.
* Paper tape is a cheaper storage medium than punched cards.
* Paper tape readers are simpler devices and therefore cheaper to produce.

On-line and Off-line Devices

Keypunches for either cards or tape are not connected to the computer. They are electrical and mechanical devices and are controlled by a keypunch operator. When we wish to input the prepared tape or cards, they are transferred to a reader which is directly connected to the computer. Keypunches are called **off-line** devices because they have no connection to the computer and

69

Figure 7.9 Magnetic media: floppy discs (*above*) and tape reels and disc packs (*below*).

Key-to-disc and Key-to-tape Systems

Key-to-disc and key-to-tape systems input data directly on to the discs and magnetic tapes used for secondary storage in the computer. As an input method this is increasing in importance and has largely superseded punched cards and paper tape. Three main types of magnetic media are used: **magnetic tapes**, **floppy discs** and **hard discs** (Figure 7.9). A detailed explanation of data storage on these media will be given in a later chapter.

The following pattern of data preparation can be applied to most key-to-disc or key-to-tape systems:

1 The data is read by eye from source documents and typed at a **data entry station**. Each station has a keyboard and a display screen. The screen displays the data as it is typed so that it can be checked and corrected. If the data is from a standard form, a blank form outline may be displayed on the screen.
2 As the data is entered and visually checked, it is stored on some form of magnetic media.
3 The data is verified with a second typing by a different operator. Any errors detected can be corrected at once by overwriting the incorrect data on the magnetic media.
4 The verified data is input to the computer at very high speeds from the magnetic media.

In small systems, each station is usually controlled by its own microcomputer. The task of this microcomputer is to supervise data entry and verification. The data input at each station is normally stored on a floppy disc. The system may have facilities for 'pooling' the data from several floppy discs on to one magnetic tape or hard disc. If these facilities do not exist, the data is input to the mainframe computer directly from the floppy discs. Figure 7.10 shows a typical microcomputer-controlled data entry station.

are not under its control. The card or tape reader is an **on-line** device because it is connected to the computer and under its control. Keypunches are sometimes *wrongly* called **card punches** or **paper tape punches**. These terms should be reserved for the on-line **output** punches used by the computer to produce its own cards or tape.

Figure 7.10 An IBM data entry station

Large key-to-disc or key-to-tape systems often have over 30 work stations controlled by a single minicomputer. The task of this minicomputer is to supervise data entry and verification and to build up all the data onto a single hard disc or magnetic tape. In key-to-tape systems, the data may first be built up on a disc and then transferred to a magnetic tape. This is because verification and editing are easier when the data is held on a disc.

The final verified magnetic tape or disc is then used as input for a mainframe computer system. Figure 7.11 shows an outline sketch of a minicomputer-controlled system.

1. Data read from documents and input at work stations

2. Minicomputer supervises work stations and builds data on to a tape or disc

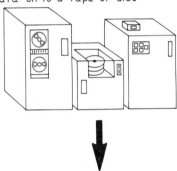

3. Final verified tape or disc

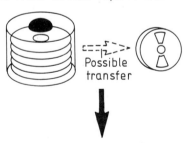

Possible transfer

4 Input to mainframe computer

Figure 7.11 The components of a mini computer-controlled key-to-disc or key-to-tape system

A Comparison Between Key-to-disc or Key-to-tape Systems and Punched Cards or Paper Tape

Advantages of key-to-disc or key-to-tape

1 Data stored on magnetic media can be input much more rapidly than data stored on paper media. A fast card or paper tape reader may work at 2000 characters per second. Data can be read from magnetic tapes at speeds up to 300 000 characters per second and from discs at speeds of up to 2 000 000 characters per second.

2 When data is verified, mistakes on magnetic media can be overwritten. With paper media, mistakes will require the punching of new cards or paper tape.

3 Magnetic tapes and discs can be re-used many times.

4 Data entry stations have far fewer moving parts than keypunches. They will break down less often.

5 The microcomputer or minicomputer controlling the data entry station can run a program of validation checks on the input data.

6 Data entry stations are quieter and cleaner than keypunches.

7 Data storage on magnetic media is much more compact than data storage on paper media. A single floppy disc can store the same quantity of information as 3000 punched cards. One centimetre of paper tape can store 4 characters; one centimetre of magnetic tape can store 600 characters. Storage space is thus much reduced and handling made easier when magnetic media are used.

8 Because the data input at a key-to-disc or key-to-tape station is displayed on a screen, it can be visually checked as it is entered.

9 Because of all the above advantages, each data entry station can cope with more work than each keypunch. It is estimated than 10 data entry stations can do the work of 16 keypunches.

Advantages of cards and paper tape

1 Interpreted cards can be read by eye.
2 Magnetic media is more fragile than paper media. Dust, heat, moisture and magnetic fields must all be carefully controlled.

Because paper media were in use first, an organization may already have extensive card or paper tape data preparation systems. Changing to a key-to-disc or key-to-tape system will be expensive. These costs must be carefully considered against the advantages to be gained. It is, however, very unlikely that any new system installed will include paper media data preparation systems.

Direct Data Entry

Key-to-disc and key-to-tape systems are often called **direct data entry systems**. Unfortunately, entering data at a keyboard while a program is running is also often called direct data entry. This can cause confusion. In the first case the direct entry is to the computer's secondary storage. In the second case the direct entry is to the processing program being run by the central processing unit. Because of this possible confusion, the use of this term is perhaps best avoided.

Exercise 25

1 Copy and complete the following passages.

a Input data for a microcomputer is usually entered through a _____ while the program runs.

b Fast input methods are usually needed when working with _____ computers. This is because these computers are very _____ and must be used for as much data processing as possible to justify their cost.

c All fast input methods require a _____ that can be read _____ by an input device.

d To _____ data means to copy it from a source document on to a computer medium. This stage of data processing is called _____.

e A typical punch card is _____ by _____. It has _____ columns and twelve _____ of punching positions. Each _____ stores the code for one character. A complete card can store _____ characters. _____ cards have the data printed across the top. One corner of each card is clipped so that _____.

f Cards are punched using a _____. This machine has a _____ to enter data and a set of knives to _____.

g When cards and paper tapes are input they pass between a light and a set of _____. Light passes through the _____ on the card or tape and produces electrical pulses in the _____. This changes a two-state system of holes in the cards or tape into a two-state system of _____.

h A typical paper tape is _____ wide. It has _____ tracks. One complete column or _____ is used for each character of data. One centimetre of tape can store _____ characters. Sprocket holes in the tape are used to _____.

i The erase key on a paper tape punch is used to _____.

j _____ or _____ systems input data directly onto the magnetic media used in the computer's _____. Small systems are usually controlled with _____. Large systems may be controlled with a _____.

2 Estimate (very roughly) the number of characters in this book. Remember to allow for the spaces between the words!

a How many punched cards would be required to store a copy of this book?

b What length of paper tape would be required to store a copy of this book?

c How long would a card reader working at 2000 cards per minute take to input a copy of this book?

d How long would a paper tape reader working at 1000 characters per second take to input a copy of this book?

e How long would it take to type a copy of this book at a speed of 15 characters per second?

f How long would it take to input a copy of this book from a magnetic tape reader working at 300 000 characters per second?

g How long would it take to input a copy of this book from a disc drive working at 2 000 000 characters per second?

3 Using the character set given in this chapter, find out what message has been punched on this card.

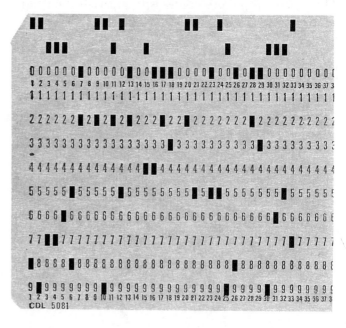

4 Using the character code given in this chapter, find out what message has been punched on this paper tape.

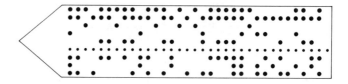

5 While a computer is inputting data with a paper tape reader, one of the photoelectric cells in the reader stops working. Explain the check included on an 8-track paper tape that will allow the computer to detect this fault.

6 The erase code is a punched hole in every track. Why do you think this particular code was selected?

7 Draw a flowchart to illustrate the stages in verifying a deck of punched cards.

8 Draw a flowchart to illustrate the stages in verifying a punched paper tape.

9 At the moment, Zapper Radios uses 16 card punches and a card reader for data preparation and input. A plan is being considered to change to 10 key-to-disc stations. This will initially cost the company quite a lot of money, but they hope the expenditure can be justified if they go ahead with the plan. Put yourself in the place of each of the following people and write down what you think you would see as the advantages and disadvantages of the plan.

a Henry Zap, the owner of Zapper Radios. He will have to persuade the bank to lend the money to buy the equipment. The bank manager will need to be convinced that it is a good investment.

b Wendy Jones, the manager of all data processing at Zappers. She first proposed the plan. She would be responsible for the detailed costing of the plan, selecting and buying the equipment and supervising its installation and implementation.

c Betty Clark, who is in charge of the data preparation room. Betty is 54 years old and has worked with punched cards for 20 years. She will first need to go on a course to learn to use the new equipment and then be responsible for training the other data preparation staff to use it. Betty will also be involved with Wendy Jones in negotiations to make some staff redundant.

d Afifa Patel, one of the keypunch operators. She has two friends, both of whom worked at Zap Insurance when they introduced a key-to-disc system. One tells Afifa she is very happy with the new equipment and gives her several reasons why she should look forward to using it. The other friend was made redundant when the new equipment was installed and has not yet found another job.

Data Capture and Input From Source Documents

In the previous sections we looked at three methods of preparing data for input. All three methods had one thing in common, a keyboard operator was needed to transcribe the source documents on to either paper or magnetic media.

In the next sections we will look at various methods that allow the source document to be read directly by an input device. These methods reduce or eliminate completely the data preparation stage. They thus offer considerable savings in staff wages, media costs and time.

Optical Mark Recognition (OMR)

Optical mark readers can detect marks made on specially prepared source documents. These documents are often used to record the answers to multi-choice questions in examinations and to record gas and electricity meter readings. Figure 7.12 shows part of the answer sheet used in an examination. The full test consists of 50 questions, each provided with 5 alternative answers. The candidate selects the answer he or she thinks is correct and marks the appropriate box on the answer sheet. In this case, answers A, D, B, C, C, B, D, B, A and D have been selected. Question 10 shows how a candidate changes an answer if they decide it is wrong. In this case the answer has been changed from B to D.

The completed document is input using an optical mark reader. In this device, a light is shone on the document and reflected back onto photoelectric cells. The black marks can be detected because they reflect less light than the white paper.

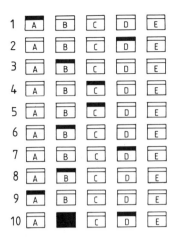

Figure 7.12 An answer sheet for an examination

An alternative device is called a **mark sense reader**. This makes use of the fact that a mark made with a soft pencil will conduct electricity. Small metal brushes pass over the surface of the document. When a brush touches a pencil mark a circuit is completed and the mark is detected.

Optical mark readers read documents at between 100 and 200 documents per minute.

Advantages of mark readers

1 Data is quickly and usually accurately captured.
2 No machine is needed to complete the source document.
3 The data preparation stage is largely eliminated.

Disadvantages of mark reading

1 The mark/no mark system can only be used if there are a limited number of alternatives for each response.
2 The marks must be accurate and clear or they will be misread.
3 The source documents must be handled with care. If they are creased, dirty or torn they cannot be read.
4 The cost of designing special forms and purchasing reading equipment is high and must be justified. Mark reading is thus a suitable choice only when a high volume of simple repetitive data is input.
5 Some data preparation staff will still be needed to correct and re-enter misread or rejected documents.

Optical Character Recognition (OCR)

Optical character readers are a more sophisticated development of the optical mark reader. As the name suggests, they can read letters and numbers, rather than just detect marks. The same process of shining a light on the document is used, but each character produces a characteristic pattern of electricity. This pattern is matched with a set of stored patterns, and thus the character can be recognised. If a satisfactory match cannot be found, an error will be reported. Early versions of the device could only read information printed in a special typeface or **font** (an example is shown in Figure 7.13). Later versions are able to read typed or hand-printed characters. A device to read handwriting is difficult to produce because there are so many different styles (you probably know people with handwriting you cannot read). However, such devices may eventually be developed. The advantage of source documents that can be read by both people and machines is considerable and the use of optical character readers is increasing.

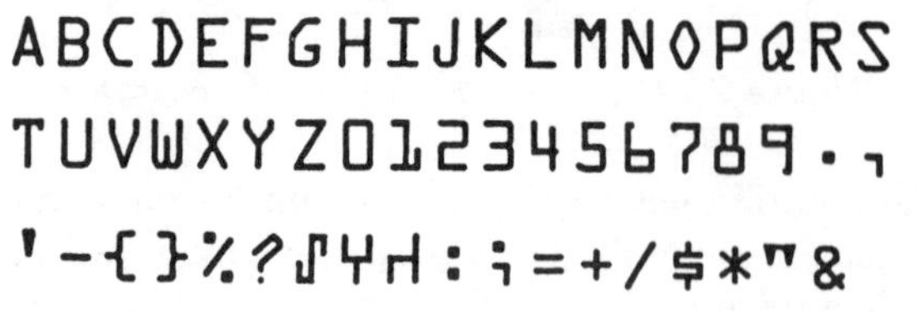

ABCDEFGHIJKLMNOPQRS
TUVWXYZ0123456789.⌐
'-{}%?⌠⌡YH:⌐=+/$*"&

Figure 7.13 A font for optical character recognition

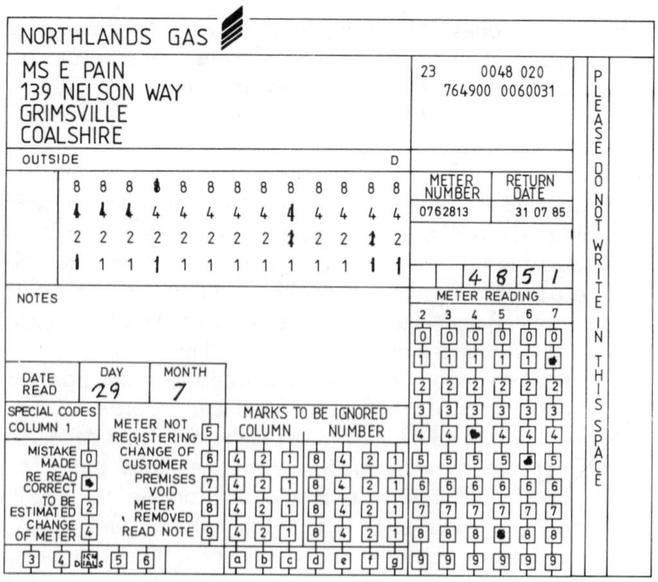

Figure 7.14 An OCR meter reading sheet

One particularly useful application of OCR (optical character recognition) is in the production of **turnaround documents**. A turnaround document is a document printed by a computer, usually in an OCR font. Later, when extra data has been added, the document can be 'turned around' and used for input.

For example, turnaround documents may be used by gas or electricity boards to collect meter readings for all their customers. The stages in this data processing are:

1 The computer prints out a meter reading sheet for each customer in an OCR font showing their name, address, account number and other details.
2 The meter readers read the meters and add the readings to each sheet. They may use careful hand printing to record the readings or optical marks may be used.
3 The completed meter reading sheets are input. This completely eliminates the data preparation stage. (See Figure 7.14.)

Optical character reader speeds vary considerably. Speeds of between 100 and 1500 documents per minute are to be expected.

Advantages of optical character recognition

1 Data is quickly and usually accurately captured.
2 The data preparation stage is largely eliminated.
3 The computer can produce documents in an OCR font. These can be used as turnaround documents.
4 OCR characters can be read both by eye and by machine.

Disadvantages of optical character recognition

1 High-quality printing may be required.
2 The documents must be handled with care. If they are creased, dirty or torn they cannot be read.
3 The cost of designing special forms and purchasing reading equipment is high and must be justified. Character reading is thus a suitable choice only when a high volume of repetitive data is input.
4 Some data preparation staff will still be needed to correct and re-enter misread or rejected documents.

Magnetic Ink Character Recognition (MICR)

Magnetic ink characters are, as the name suggests, printed in a special ink that can be magnetized. Two character fonts are in common use, one mainly in the UK and USA, the other mainly in the rest of Europe. Figure 7.15 shows these magnetic ink fonts. Notice that the UK font only contains fourteen characters.

Magnetic ink documents are input using a **magnetic ink reader**. Characters are read by magnetizing the ink and passing it under a reading head.

Each character printed in the UK font produces a characteristic electrical pattern. When the pattern produced is compared with a set of stored patterns, the character can be recognised. If a satisfactory match cannot be found, an error will be reported.

1234567890

(a) UK and USA character font

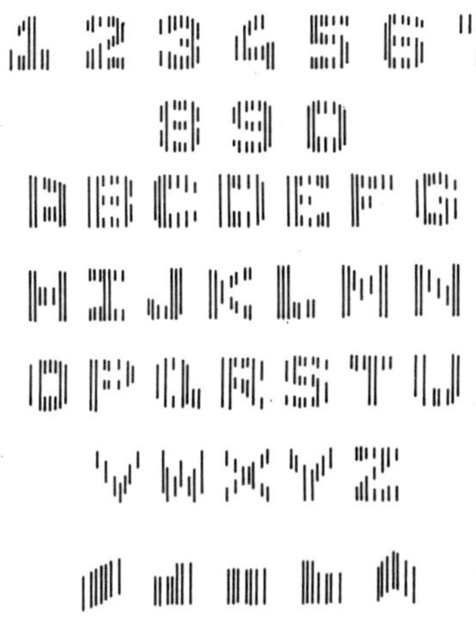

1 2 3 4 5 6 7
8 9 0
A B C D E F G
H I J K L M N
O P Q R S T U
V W X Y Z

(b) Character font used mainly in the rest of Europe

Figure 7.15 Magnetic ink fonts

Each character in the European font is printed with seven lines. The six gaps between these lines form a binary code. Wide gaps represent a 1 and narrow gaps represent a 0. Each character can thus be read as a 6-bit binary code. Figure 7.16 below shows how the eighth character is interpreted as a binary code.

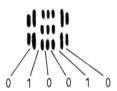

0   1   0   0   1   0

Figure 7.16 A magnetic ink character and its binary code

The most common use of MICR is in banks. The bank cheque in Figure 7.17 shows printing in the UK font.

When the cheque is paid into a bank, a **magnetic ink encoder** will be used to print the amount of the cheque in the space provided. All the necessary details for processing the cheque can then be input to a computer using a magnetic ink reader. Magnetic ink character recognition is a very specialised technique and the equipment used is comparatively expensive. Input speeds of up to 2500 documents per minute are possible with some magnetic ink readers.

Advantages of magnetic ink character recognition

1 The data preparation stage is largely eliminated.
2 MICR characters can be read both by eye and by machines.
3 MICR documents can be read even when creased and dirty. This is an important advantage with documents like cheques which may be handled several times before they are paid into a bank.
4 MICR offers very high security. Even if the printing is 'doctored' with black ink, the reader will still read the original magnetic printing. This is another important advantage for banks because it makes it impossible for a criminal to change the details printed on a cheque.
5 To deter forgers, cheques are not printed on plain paper but on paper covered with an intricate pattern of lines and words. Magnetic ink readers can easily distinguish magnetic printing from these complex background patterns.

Figure 7.17 The use of MICR on a bank cheque

0   30th May   19 86   00-00-00

National Westminster Bank PLC
Anytown Branch
41 High Street, Anytown, Berks.

Pay   Mark Brindley
Ten pounds 75p   or order
                                      £10 − 75
                                      A SPECIMEN

A. Specimen

⑈123456⑈ 00⑈0000⑈ 999999999⑈

1 Very-high-quality printing is required.
2 MICR readers must position the magnetic printing very accurately under the reading head?
3 The cost of the equipment is high and must be justified. MICR is thus only a suitable choice when a high volume of repetitive data is input and high security and resistance to wear and tear are needed.

Bar Codes

Bar codes are being used on an increasing range of items. They are used to store coded information about the item and can be read directly with an input device. The bar code is formed with a pattern of wide and narrow lines printed on the item. The data stored in the bars is usually also printed in normal characters so that it can be read by eye. The most common uses of bar codes are inside library books and on food products. You will certainly find that most of the items in your local shop or supermarket carry a bar code. Figure 7.18 shows a typical bar code.

Figure 7.18 The different parts of a bar code

Bar codes are read with a **bar code reader**. This passes a light beam over the bars and reflects it back on to a photoelectric cell. The bars can be detected because they reflect less light than the background on which they are printed.

In shops or libraries, the bar codes are often read with a small hand-held bar code reader. In the latest supermarket installations, a laser light beam is used to scan the bar code. This beam can scan the code several times as it is passed before a small opening at the checkout counter. This produces very reliable readings, even if the bar code is upside down. Some bar code readers are shown in Figure 7.19.

Price information is not included in the bar codes used in shops and supermarkets. If the price is needed to produce a bill, it must either be entered with a keyboard or called up from storage in the computer.

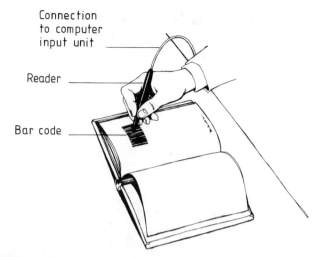

Figure 7.19 A bar code reader as used *above* in a library *below* in a supermarket

Advantages of bar codes

1 Quick and accurate data capture.
2 The data preparation stage is eliminated.
3 High-quality printing is not required. The bar code is usually included as part of the design for the packet or label. It is thus printed at no extra cost.

Disadvantages of bar codes

1 Bar codes can only be used for relatively simple codes and reference numbers.
2 Unlike optical marks and characters, bar codes cannot be used to collect additional data. They can only input the code with which they are printed. Their main use is to input the *identity* of the item to which they are attached rapidly.

The full advantages of bar codes in a specific application will be considered in a later chapter.

Merchandise Tags

Merchandise tags are a special form of price ticket that can be read both by eye and by a machine. The earliest form, still in common use particularly in clothes shops, was the **Kimball tag**. This holds printed information about the size, colour, price and other details of the garment. All this information is also held on the Kimball tag using a punched hole code. When a garment is sold, the tag is removed and becomes a record of the sale. The details on the tag can then be input directly into a computer system. This may be done by reading the tags with a small reader connected to the sales terminal. Alternatively the tags may be sent by post to a central computer installation.

A more modern form of merchandise tag uses a small strip of magnetic material to replace the punched holes. These **magnetic stripe labels** are read with a hand-held reader connected to the sales terminal. OCR and OMR merchandise tags are also used in some applications. Full details of the operation of sales terminals will be given in a later chapter.

Figure 7.20 shows some merchandise tags.

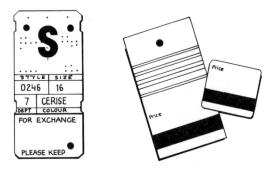

Figure 7.20 A Kimball tag (left) and a magnetic stripe tag (right)

Advantages of merchandise tags

1 Quick and accurate data capture.
2 The data preparation stage is eliminated.
3 The work of the sales staff in recording sales is much reduced. This leads to faster customer service and more accurate stock records.

Disadvantages of merchandise tags

1 Merchandise tags can record more information than bar codes but their capacity is still limited. A maximum of about 50 characters or so is to be expected.
2 If the price is included, it cannot be changed. This can lead to problems if goods are put in a sale or increased in price.
3 Tags are easily damaged by creasing or tearing.
4 Clothes shops often allow their customers to return garments. A new tag will be needed if the garment is put back on sale.
5 Unlike optical marks and characters, merchandise tags cannot be used to collect additional data. They can only input the information with which they are produced. Their main use is thus to identify to a computer the items which have been sold by a shop.

The full advantages of merchandise tags in a specific application will be considered in a later chapter.

Exercise 26

1 Copy and complete the following passages.

a The main advantage of inputting data directly from source documents is that it eliminates _____. It thus offers savings in _____, _____ and _____.

b _____ readers can detect marks made on source documents. They are often used for _____. The main advantages of this form of input are _____. The main disadvantages of this form of input are _____.

c _____ readers can read characters printed in special typefaces called _____. They may also be able to read typed or _____ characters. The main advantages of this form of input are _____. The main disadvantages of this form of input are _____.

d A _____ document is produced by the computer. After more data has been added to it, it is later used as an input document.

e _____ readers can be used to read characters printed in a special ink that can be magnetised. One type of font can be read by machine because each character produces a _____. Another type of font can be read by machine because each character is printed as a pattern of _____. The main advantages of this form of input are _____. The main disadvantages of this form of input are _____.

f A bar code is a pattern of _____ printed on an item. The most common use of bar codes is on _____. The bar code reader reads the bars by _____. The bar code reader may be a small _____ device. Alternatively, a _____ may be used to scan each bar code. The main advantages of this form of input are _____. The main disadvantages of this form of input are _____.

g Merchandise tags are a special form of _____. They can be read both by eye and by a _____. An early form was called a _____. It is still in common use, particularly in _____ shops. A more modern merchandise tag was a strip of magnetic material to replace the punched holes. It is called a _____ label.

As goods are sold, the tags are detached and used to form a _____ record for the shop. The main advantages of this form of input are _____. The main disadvantages of this form of input are: _____.

2 What are the advantages in using a computer to mark examination papers?

3 What limitations are placed on questions set in computer-marked examination papers.

4 For each of the following subjects:
(i) Prepare a question that could be set as part of a multi-choice computer-marked examination.
(ii) Prepare a question that could not be set as part of a multi-choice computer-marked examination.
a Mathematics **b** English **c** Art

5 The article below describes one very specialised use of OCR equipment. Explain why some people might be worried about this application of the technology. Explain how this application could be of use to the police in their efforts to catch criminals.

In the UK, the Home Office is using machine vision techniques experimentally, to read the number plates of cars travelling on the M1 motorway. Rapid motion and variable lighting and visibility conditions make this a challenging environment for a vision system.

Fortunately for the Home Office, number plates are retro-reflective. They can therefore be highlighted by an infra-red source mounted close to the camera.

Ingenious as it is, this rather specialised technology seems to be more useful for surveillance and detection on the roads than for any general industrial or commercial application. Once extracted from the background and 'cleaned up', a number plate does not present a very severe character recognition problem.

(*Computing*, 9 February 1980)

6 Wendy Smith's bank account number is 00132241. Harry Smith's account number is 00182241. Wendy uses black ink to change the number printed on one of her cheques to 00182241. She then uses it to buy a radio.

a What does Wendy hope will happen?
b Will Wendy succeed in this crime and if not, why not?
c If Wendy did succeed, would she have stolen from the radio shop, the bank or Harry?
d What would be the effects if Wendy were able to successfully alter:
(i) the account number printed on her cheques?
(ii) the branch number printed on her cheques?

7 Select five characters from the 6-bit magnetic ink font. Draw a diagram of each character and underneath each diagram write the binary code for the character.

8 The code used in the right-hand side of a standard UK article bar code is shown below. The code for each digit is made up from seven segments. These are coloured in so that the digit is represented by four alternate light and dark bars. Each code always starts with a dark bar and ends with a light bar. A single dark segment represents a 1 and a single light segment represents a 0. Thus the binary code used for the number 3 is 1000010.

0 1 2 3 4 5 6 7 8 9

a In the left-hand side of the bar code, two further codes are used. One is obtained by reversing the colour of the segments in the code above. The code for the number 3 thus becomes 0111101 or  Draw a full diagram for this code. We will call this Code A.

b The other code used in the left-hand side is obtained by reversing the order of the segments in the code above. The code for the number 3 thus becomes 0100001 or  Draw a full diagram for this code. We will call this Code B.

c A country of origin digit is always printed outside each UK article bar code. This code was designed to fit in with other existing systems, and there was not enough room to include this digit in the bars. Instead, the order in which codes A and B are used in the left-hand side is the code for this country of origin digit. Thus for French products, codes A and B will always be used in one particular order. For UK products, codes A and B will always be used in another particular order. By studying the UK article bar codes shown below, can you discover the order in which codes A and B are used for products made in the UK and in France?

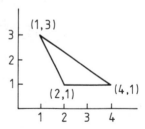

3 020640 111611   5 010067 301502

The Input of Pictures and Diagrams

Pictures and diagrams are stored in the computer as a series of **coordinates** or pairs of numbers. For example, a computer could store the data for the triangle in Figure 7.21 as (2,1), (1,3) and (4,1). The computer of course stores the coordinates as binary numbers!

Figure 7.21 Coordinates

Simple pictures require only a few pairs of coordinates, and these can easily be entered with a normal keyboard.

More complex pictures may require thousands of coordinates and it would be very tedious to enter these in the same way. A **digitiser** (or **graphics tablet**) allows picture coordinates to be entered directly.

The picture we wish to input is first placed on the pad of the digitiser. The picture outline is then followed with a small lens fitted with cross-wires or a simple pointer. The computer can sense the position of the lens and a continual series of coordinates is recorded as the picture outline is followed. Figure 7.22 shows two different designs for digitisers. In the first design, the lens is mounted on an arm with two swivel joints. The computer can detect the setting of each joint and hence calculate the position of the lens.

In the second design, a fine wire grid is embedded in the pad. The wires in this grid correspond directly to the coordinates used for the picture. The computer can detect which horizontal and vertical wire the lens is over and hence obtain the coordinates directly.

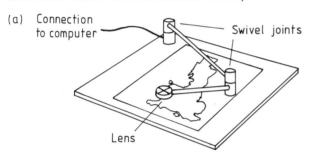

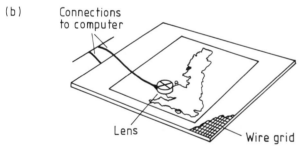

Figure 7.22 Digitisers: (a) has a swivel arm, (b) has an embedded wire grid

You may well be wondering *why* anybody should want to store pictures in a computer. The great advantage to be gained is the computer's ability to process the input picture. Simple arithmetic performed on the coordinates can reflect, rotate, enlarge, reduce and stretch the shape automatically. Thus any input picture can be modified very easily before it is reproduced with a suitable output device.

Input of Analogue Measurements

Data can be classified as either discrete data or continuous data. **Discrete data** can only take certain fixed values within a given range. For example, the number of children in a family. This can only be 1 or 2 or 3 and so on.

Continuous data can take any value within a given range. For example, the speed of a car. This might be 65 mph or 65.3 mph or 65.3724 mph and so on. Almost all physical measurements are continuous data. For example, length, weight, speed, temperature, sound level, voltage, time and pressure. Such data is often measured with an **analogue device**. This represents the physical measurement on a continuous analogue scale. For example, traditional car speedometers represent a car's speed with a needle moving round a circular dial, and traditional thermometers represent temperature with the height of a column of liquid (Figure 7.23).

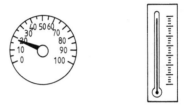

Figure 7.23 Familiar analogue measuring devices

It is often convenient to reduce continuously varying data to a discrete or **digital** scale. For example, feet come in all kinds of lengths but for the convenience of shoe manufacturers these continuously varying lengths are reduced to a discrete range of shoe sizes. In the same way, digital clocks and watches reduce continuously varying time to a discrete digital display. This process is illustrated in Figure 7.24.

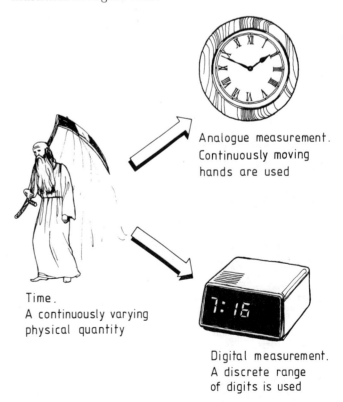

Analogue measurement. Continuously moving hands are used

Time. A continuously varying physical quantity

Digital measurement. A discrete range of digits is used

Figure 7.24 Time: analogue and digital

If we wish to input physical measurements directly, they must be reduced to a fixed range of discrete binary numbers. This process is called **digitising the measurements**. It is normally done in two stages:

1 The physical quantity is measured with an analogue device that represents the data as a continuously varying electrical voltage. The device used is called a **sensor**.

2 This analogue voltage is converted to a digital binary signal with a device called an **analogue-to-digital converter**.

Thus, the two stages in measuring and inputting a temperature might be as shown in Figure 7.25:

1 A sensor measures a temperature between 0 °C and 100 °C and changes it to a voltage between 0 V and 1.5 V.

2 An analogue-to-digital converter converts this analogue voltage to a digital signal representing an 8-bit binary number between 00000000 and 11111111.

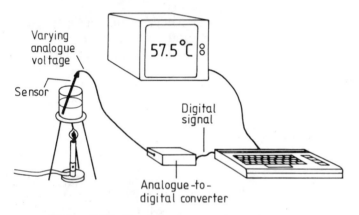

Figure 7.25   The stages in measuring a temperature

Games Paddles, Joysticks and Mice

Games paddles, joysticks and **mice** are all used with graphics displays. They allow the user to input instructions rapidly so as to control the position of an object on the display screen. They all contain an analogue device to represent the position of the object on the screen. The user moves this device and its movements are converted to digital input signals.

Games paddles can only move an object in a horizontal or a vertical direction. The movements of a small wheel on the device are converted to input signals to move the object. Figure 7.26 shows a typical games paddle.

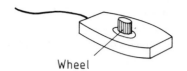

Figure 7.26   A typical games paddle

A joystick can move an object in any direction on the screen. The movements of a small lever, which can move in any direction, are converted to input signals to move the object. Cheap joysticks contain a ring of usually eight switches and can therefore only detect eight positions of the joystick. More expensive joysticks contain devices that can detect any position of the joystick. Figure 7.27 below shows a typical joystick.

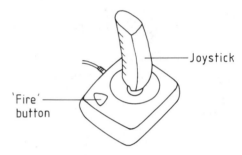

Figure 7.27   A typical joystick

A mouse can also move an object in any direction on the screen. The device contains a large steel ball which rolls as the mouse is moved around a desk top. The movements of this ball are converted to input signals to move the object. Games paddles and joysticks are usually associated with computer games. A mouse is more usually associated with small business computers. It is used as an easy way to move a pointer and select options from a screen menu. Figure 7.28 shows a typical mouse.

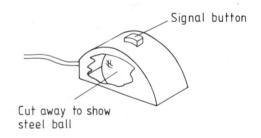

Figure 7.28   A typical mouse

Voice Recognition

Direct spoken input to the computer would be an ideal solution in many applications. It would not be a very fast form of data entry, but it would certainly remove most of the need for typing and keyboards. Unfortunately, this remains a dream for the future, although perhaps the not too distant future. At the moment, voice input is usually restricted to a limited range of previously stored words. These words are first spoken several times and recorded as electrical patterns. When a command is received, it is compared with the stored patterns and identified if possible. More sophisticated systems which can offer the user a full conversation with the computer are the aim of several research projects. The problems of regional accents, slang, heavy colds, words with two meanings and tones of voice, however, are proving to be considerable barriers – in 1986, at any rate.

Exercise 27

1 Copy and complete the following passages.

   a A computer stores pictures as a series of _____. A _____ allows this series of _____ to be input directly. The picture is placed on a pad and its outline is followed with a _____. A continual series of _____ is recorded as the outline is followed.

   b Discrete data can only take _____ within a given range. Continuous data can take _____ within a given range. Continuous data is often measured with an _____ device. Before _____ signals can be input they must be changed into digital signals using an _____.

   c The movement of an object on a display screen can be controlled with _____, _____ and _____. All these devices contain an _____ to represent the position of the object on the screen. The movements of the _____ device are converted to digital input signals to move the object.

   d Voice input would be an _____ in many applications. At the moment voice input is restricted to a limited range of _____ words. Full voice recognition systems remain a _____ for the future.

2 This question is included to illustrate the stages in digitising, modifying and reproducing pictures. It is rather mathematical in content, but if you work through it you will gain some understanding of the computer's ability to process pictures.

   a The diagram below shows a simple shape drawn on a grid. On squared paper make a copy of the diagram.

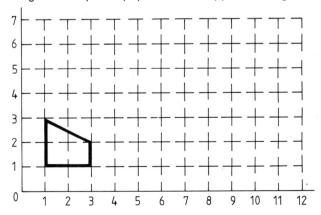

   b Digitise the diagram into coordinates, one pair for each corner.

   c Suppose a computer were instructed to add 4 to both numbers in each coordinate pair. The coordinates (1,1) would for example become (5,5). Show on your diagram the effect that this would have on the shape.

   d Suppose a computer were instructed to multiply both numbers in each coordinate pair by 2. The coordinates (1,1) would for example become (2,2). Show on your diagram the effect that this would have on the shape.

   e Suppose a computer were instructed to subtract the first number in each coordinate pair from 12. The coordinates (1,1) would for example become (11,1). Show on your diagram the effect that this would have on the shape.

   f Suppose a computer were instructed to subtract the first number in each coordinate pair from 12 and the second number from 8. The coordinates (1,1) would for example become (11,7). Show on your diagram the effects that this would have on the shape.

3 The diagram below shows a car's combined speedometer and odometer (distance recorder). Which part of the device uses an analogue scale and which part of the device uses a digital scale?

4 An example is given in the text of the way in which shoe manufacturers reduce a continuously varying measurement to a discrete set of sizes. Give some other examples of this technique.

5 Draw sketches of three different analogue measuring instruments and three different digital measuring instruments.

6 Why is voice recognition such a difficult challenge for computer scientists and engineers?

7 Select one job and one device. Write down the effects that you think voice recognition computers would have on your selected job and device.

8 A friend reads the advertisement shown below and asks you to describe the device and its uses. Write a short account of what you might say.

Data Checking

Data that has been captured and input may be incorrect for three reasons:

1 The data on the source documents may be incorrect. For example, the name BINDLEY is often recorded as BRINDLEY or BINLEY. In the same way, the number 579 000 may be recorded as 5 790 000.

2 Correct data on the source documents may be incorrectly transcribed on to computer media. For example, the reference number 127859 may be copied as 128759 or 127589. Some letters and numbers are very easily misread, particularly from handwritten source documents. For example, the part number 5749/Z may be read as 5749/2.

3 Correct data may be corrupted by the computer. Modern computers are very reliable, but mechanical, electrical and programming faults can all corrupt the correct input data.

The term GIGO has already been mentioned. The following sections look at the various techniques used to ensure that as many errors as possible are detected before they lead to incorrect output.

Data Verification

To **verify** data means to check that it has been accurately copied from one medium to another – for example, from a printed form to a punched card. No check is made to see if the data is sensible, only that it has been correctly copied. The verifying systems used for punched cards, paper tape and key-to-disc or key-to-tape systems have already been described.

Parity Checks

Parity checks are used to ensure that binary codes have been correctly transmitted from one part of the computer to another. The use of a parity bit is described in Chapter 4. Parity checks can also be made on a group of transmitted numbers. After the last number in the list, an extra number is included. This number is designed to make the number of 1's in every column of the transmitted list an even number (if even parity is used). The diagram below shows how this is done:

To:

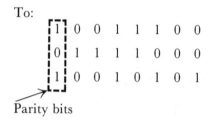

Parity bits

We add:

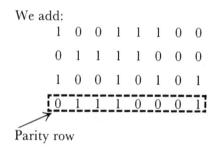

Parity row

Notice that the extra row also has even parity. A system like this may allow the computer to correct some errors in data transmission.

Data Validation

After data has been input it is **validated** before it is processed. Validating data means to check that it is accurate, complete and reasonable. As it is input, a computer program subjects the data to a series of **validation checks**. If it is reading in prepared data, the computer will not stop each time it finds an error. Instead, the computer will print out a full list of all the errors that are found in the data. These errors can then be corrected and re-input at a later stage.

If entries are made directly using a keyboard and screen, the checks can be made as each item of data is input. In this case, the computer will refuse to accept invalid data and will display an immediate error message on the screen. A description of the main types of validation checks is given below.

1. Control Totals. A control total check is designed to detect errors in entering numeric data. The control total is calculated by adding together similar data items. For example, suppose we are entering the following data:

Payroll number	Name	Hours worked
3454	S Smith	40
1243	T Jones	42
3355	M Patel	44
2189	R Singh	61

Before we enter the data we can calculate a control total by adding together all the hours:

Payroll number	Name	Hours worked
3454	S Smith	40
1243	T Jones	42
3355	M Patel	44
2189	R Singh	61
	Control total =	187

This control total is entered with the rest of the data. The computer then recalculates the control total and compares it with the one entered. If the two control totals do not match, there has certainly been some mistake in entering the numbers of hours worked. This entry error can be reported by the computer.

2. Hash Totals. A hash total is a control total calculated in a way that would normally be meaningless. For example, we could add together a list of payroll numbers. The total formed would be meaningless but it could still be used to check the entry of the payroll numbers.

	Payroll number	Name	Hours worked
	3454	S Smith	40
	1243	T Jones	42
	3355	M Patel	44
	2189	R. Singh	61
Hash total =	10241	Control total =	187

3. Invalid Character Checks. An invalid character check is used to ensure that all the characters entered are of the right kind. For example, it may be necessary to check that names contain only alphabetical characters or spaces and that payroll numbers contain only numerical characters.

4. Field Length Checks. Each separate data item is called a **field**. Thus, in the example below, there are fields for the payroll number, name and hours worked:

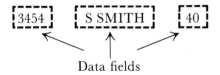

Data fields

Often, fields will have a fixed number of characters. For example, a date field may need exactly six characters: two for the day, two for the month and two for the year. In the same way, all the payroll numbers used by a company may have exactly four digits. In such cases, field length checks are used to count the number of characters in each field and make sure this is correct.

5. Range Checks. Range checks are used to ensure that numbers entered are within a sensible range. For example, we might decide that a sensible range for hours worked was between 20 and 70 hours per week. The computer would be programmed to carry out a range check on all entries and to query any that were outside this range. In the same way, a range check could be used to reject an entry for a day of the month that was not between 1 and 31.

6. Check Digits. A check digit is an extra digit calculated from a number and attached to it. This check digit can then be used to check the accuracy of the number it is attached to. Two examples follow to illustrate the use of a check digit.

Example 1.

Check digits attached to payroll numbers.

We have used the following data in several examples:

Payroll number	Name	Hours worked
3454	S Smith	40
1243	T Jones	42
3355	M Patel	44
2189	S Singh	61

In fact, all the payroll numbers started as three digit numbers. An extra digit was calculated from each and then added to it in the following way:

$$11 \overline{)345}$$
$$31 \text{ remainder } 4$$

The payroll number changes to 3454.

As you can see, the number is divided by 11 and the remainder is added as a fourth digit. A remainder of 10 would be treated as a remainder of 0. If you check, you will find that all the payroll numbers have been calculated in this way.

Suppose an entry error is made and the payroll number 3454 is incorrectly input as 3544. The computer can calculate its own check digit from the number 354. This number divided by 11 gives the result 32 remainder 2, producing a check digit of 2. This does not match the check digit of 4 attached to 3544. The entry error can thus be detected and reported.

This simple form of check digit is called a **modulus eleven check digit**. Unfortunately it cannot detect all possible errors and some incorrect numbers will produce the correct check digit by coincidence.

Example 2.

International Standard Book Numbers.

If you look at the back cover of this book you will find an International Standard Book Number (ISBN):

$$0\ 631\ 90057\ 8.$$

The last digit is a check digit calculated in the following way.

1 The digits of the ISBN are multiplied by the numbers from 10 to 2 and these results are added together.

$$
\begin{array}{rcr}
0 \times 10 &=& 0 \\
6 \times 9 &=& 54 \\
3 \times 8 &=& 24 \\
1 \times 7 &=& 7 \\
9 \times 6 &=& 54 \\
0 \times 5 &=& 0 \\
0 \times 4 &=& 0 \\
5 \times 3 &=& 15 \\
7 \times 2 &=& 14 \\
\hline
\text{Total} &=& 168
\end{array}
$$

2 This total is divided by 11 and the remainder found:
$$168 \div 11 = 15 \text{ remainder } 3$$
3 This remainder is subtracted from 11 to find the check digit:

$$11 - 3 = 8$$

Thus the full ISBN in this case is, ISBN 0 631 90057 8. A check digit of ten is recorded as an X.

Because all ISBNs have a check digit, computers in bookshops, publishers and libraries can always detect invalid entries.

This form of check digit is called a **weighted modulus eleven check digit**. It cannot detect all entry errors but it can detect more errors than the simple modulus eleven check. It is more difficult to calculate but it is a more powerful check.

Exercise 28

1 Copy and complete the following passages.

a _____ data means to check that it has been accurately copied from source documents on to _____. This is normally done by typing the data _____ and checking it against the first typing.

b A _____ check is used to check binary data after it has been transmitted from one part of the computer to another. A simple _____ check can only detect an error that changes a 1 to a 0. More powerful _____ checks may allow the computer to correct errors.

c 'Validating data' means to check that it is _____.

d A _____ is designed to detect errors in numeric data. It is calculated by adding together similar data items. For example, we might add together _____. A _____ is a _____ calculated in a way that would normally be meaningless. For example, we might add together _____.

e A check that only the correct type of characters are present in a field is called a _____. A check that the correct number of characters has been entered in a field is called _____.

f A check that the number in a field is neither too big nor too small is called a _____. An extra digit attached to a number for checking purposes is called a _____. Two examples are the _____ and the weighted _____.

2 The data below was transcribed onto punched cards and input. Unfortunately it contains many errors. Find as many errors as you can and make a note of each and the validation check needed to detect it. Assume that the data follows all the examples given in the text.

Payroll number	Name	Hours worked
34540	S Smish	40
1233	T Jones	82
335E	M Pat3l	44
2198	R S*ngh	16

3 Calculate a modulus eleven check digit to add to each of these Zapper Radios catalogue numbers.

a 0844/1/4 **b** 0901/3/6 **c** 0999/1/1

4 Which of these Zapper Radios catalogue numbers is incorrect if the final digit of each is a modulus eleven check digit?

a 0983/1/1/2 **c** 0932/2/4/3
b 0999/3/6/4 **d** 0781/3/4/1

5 Calculate the check digit required for each of these incomplete ISBN numbers:

a ISBN 0 7063 1895 **b** ISBN 0 550 11821

6 Draw a flowchart to show the stages in a range check that an input temperature is between −10 °C and 35 °C. If either part of the check fails, a suitable error message should be output and the data re-entered.

7 Gas and electricity boards often send out bills to customers every quarter. This means that a bill is sent every thirteen weeks, or four times a year. One gas board always checks that a customer's bill is between 50% and 150% of the total for the equivalent quarter of the previous year.

    a What kind of check is this?

    b Why does the gas board not simply check that the new bill is equal to the old bill?

    c Why is the equivalent quarter from the previous year used and not simply the last quarter?

    d Draw a flow diagram that inputs the NEW TOTAL and the OLD TOTAL and carries out all the arithmetic and checking necessary either to produce an error message or to print the bill.

8 Explain the difference between the *verification* and the *validation* of data.

                                                     (UCLES 82)

9 a Below is an ISBN (International Standard Book Number).

    ISBN 0 903885 19 0

    Explain how a check digit may be used to detect a transposition error in the above code number.

    b Explain what a hash total is and how it is used.

                                                     (AEB 82)

Exercise 29

1 A large hospital provides a menu service at meal times for its 2,000 patients. Every afternoon each patient chooses the next day's midday meal. The choice is one first course, one main meal and one dessert from a choice of 3 first courses, 4 main meals and 3 desserts. The meals are cooked in a central kitchen and distributed to the wards.

    a Design a suitable data capture form for collecting the patients' choice and other essential details.

    b Explain **one** method, other than using a keyboard, which could be used to input patients' choices to the computer. Include an explanation of relevant hardware.

    c Explain **one** benefit of computerising the system for:
      (i) the head chef,
      (ii) hospital finances.

                                                     (AEB 85)

2 The following is a car paint code:

    OC 936 D

    a Suggest possible meanings for the parts of this code.

    b Explain why such codes are used. Give one example of another such code and its meanings.

                                                     (AEB 82)

3 In many computer applications the collection of data is an error-prone and time-consuming activity.

    a Describe three possible causes of errors when data is collected and prepared manually for input.

    b Name three ways of collecting data without the need for data preparation. In each case describe how the data is represented in machine-readable form and how it is read.

    c Describe two different applications where automatic collection of data is an important feature. In each case, explain the advantages gained by automatic data collection.

                                                    (SREB 82)

4 The following information is to be collected about each pupil in a certain secondary school:

    Name, date of birth, sex, height(m), weight (kg).

    a The information about each pupil is to be coded as a data record on to a separate 80 column computer card. Design a card layout and explain why it is suitable.

    b State four of the data validation tests that it might be sensible to apply to the coded information.

    c With reference to your answer to **b**, construct a program flowchart for the required data validation routine. Make it clear as to what messages would be printed out if a particular data item fails a test.

                                                     (L Spec)

5 For a period of five days – Monday to Friday – a survey is made of every 100th passenger using a river ferry crossing. For each passenger the following data is collected and coded into a record on magnetic tape,
      (i) whether male, female or child (of either sex),
      (ii) whether using season, day return or other type of ticket,
      (iii) whether on business, pleasure, shopping trip or other.

    a Draw a suitable data capture form for this survey.

    b Draw a flowchart for the analysis of the above data, i.e., to read, to calculate, to print out for a Wednesday:
      (i) the total number of passengers travelling,
      (ii) the number of children with season tickets,
      (iii) the number of females going shopping on a day return.

                                                     (AEB 81)

6 The following are special methods of entering information into a computer system. Briefly describe an application of each.

    a Magnetic Ink Character Recognition.

    b Optical Mark Recognition.

    c Bar Codes.

    d Kimball Tags.

                                                    (EAEB 82)

7 The examples below are all used to input data directly into a computer. Give an example of where **each** could be found.

a

b

c
```
0000000
4 5 6 7 8 9 10
1111111

2222222

3333333
```

(SEREB 82)

8 The Bank Clearing House uses a Magnetic Ink Reader/Sorter to read a cheque as shown below.

(i) The above cheque has three separate codes printed on it. Write down each code and explain what it could mean.
(ii) Explain the function of the MICR device and say why it is necessary. (AEB 82)

9 a Name **one** type of document on which magnetic ink character recognition (MICR) is used.
b Name **one** type of document on which optical character recognition (OCR) is used.
c Name **one** type of document on which mark reading is used.
d (i) How is a magnetic ink character recognised?
(ii) What must be done to a magnetic ink character before it can be read by a machine?
e How is a character like the one shown here recognised?

f Give **one** advantage and **one** disadvantage of each of the following.
(i) Magnetic ink character recognition
(ii) Optical character recognition.
(iii) Mark reading.
g These numbers are copied from the bottom of a cheque. What do they tell you?

(WMEB 82)

10

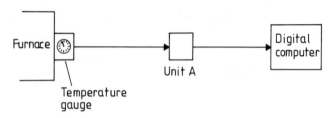

In the diagram, if a digital computer is to receive signals from a furnace temperature gauge it will need the unit (labelled A in the diagram) called a _____.

(SREB 82)

11 An Examinations Board uses a computer to process marks obtained by candidates. When a script has been marked the examiner uses a black felt tip pen to enter the mark as bars (lines) on a specially printed form. The maximum mark for the paper is 80. Part of the form is shown below.

0 8 9 2	BODY N.E.	Abs	10	20	30	40	50	~~60~~	70	80	90	tens
		0	1	2	3	~~4~~	5	6	7	8	9	units

a (i) How many marks was this candidate awarded?
(ii) Name the device that would be used to read the marks into the computer.
(iii) Name a programming language suitable for this application.
b (i) Give an example of a **validation** check that would be made on this input data.
(ii) Give an example of output that might be produced.
c State **two** reasons why the Examinations Board use a computer to process candidates' marks and give an explanation for **each**.

(SREB 82)

12a State what is meant by data validation and explain why it is used.
b Give three examples of simple data validation procedures.

(NI 81)

13 Dates are read into a computer as a numeric code, e.g. 010270 means 1 February 1970.

Explain how (i) type and (ii) range checks can be performed on this data. Clearly define any data structure which you use.

(L 81)

14 A computerised library system has been designed so that when a book is borrowed, the borrower's code number and the code numbers of the books have to be recorded onto the computer's files.

a Suggest, with reasons, a suitable method of data capture.

b Explain why the data validation techniques used will depend upon whether or not the recording device is online to a computer system which has direct access to the borrowers file and the book file.

c State one way in which a computerised library system might affect the privacy of a borrower.

(L 81)

15 The head teacher of a secondary school wishes to create a data file relating to all the pupils in the school, by collecting the following items of data for each pupil:

– name;
– date of birth;
– sex of pupil;
– class (each class is given a number between 1 and 5, followed by the initials of the class teacher, e.g. 3JLH);
– address;
– telephone number;
– name of parent or guardian.

a Design a form which, without further explanation or assistance, could be completed by a pupil to provide the required data.

b If the data were input to a computer, describe tests which the computer could perform to check the accuracy of the data.

c For any data item which is found to be in error, it will be necessary to produce an appropriate error report. Design a suitable format for error reports, giving examples of **three** types of error which might be detected.

(C 83)

16 This diagram shows the basic stages in a data processing system

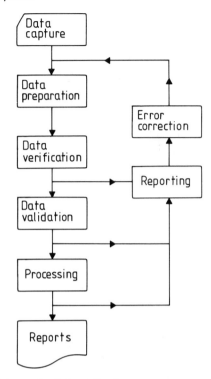

Explain each of the following stages.

a Data capture.
b Data validation.
c Reporting.

(AEB 83)

17a Explain the difference between analogue data and digital data.

b Give an example of data which would be represented in:

(i) analogue form,
(ii) digital form.

(C 83)

18a Briefly describe a key-to-disk system.

b Why is the use of key-to-disk systems in business increasing?

c Give an advantage of a key-to-disk system.

(EAEB 83)

8 Data Output and Output Devices

After data has been input and processed, some form of output will be produced by the computer. This chapter looks at the types of output produced and the devices used to produce it.

On-line Card Punches and Paper Tape Punches

In some computer systems the computer may have direct control over **card punches** and **paper tape punches**. These are on-line devices used for *output*, not to be confused with off-line *keypunches* used to prepare cards and tape for *input*.

Punched cards may be produced by the computer for use as turnaround documents, and paper tape may be produced to control engineering machines. The use of punched cards or paper tape for output is declining. Modern methods using OCR, magnetic media and direct control links have largely replaced the use of paper media.

Printed Output (Hard Copy)

Printed output is required in almost all computer systems. A vast variety of types and models of printers exist to meet this need. When a printer is selected for a particular application several factors must be considered.

1. Printing speed. This can vary from 10 to 40 000 characters per second. A printer must be selected that can produce the required volume of printing in an acceptable time.

2. Printing quality. This varies from low-quality printing with an untidy appearance to high (letter) quality printing intended for documents where presentation is important. High-quality printers tend to be slower and/ or more expensive than comparable low-quality printers. A high-quality printer must be selected for any application where presentation is important, for example, producing letters to send to company customers. On the other hand, it is a waste of time and money to buy a slow high-quality printer for an application where presentation is not important.

3. Special printing requirements. Special printing equipment may be needed to produce OCR or MICR printing.

4. Printing flexibility. This varies from printers that can only produce printing in one style to very flexible printers that can produce printing in a wide range of styles and can also produce simple pictures and diagrams.

5. Noise of operation. This varies from printers that are almost silent to very noisy printers that need sound proof covers or even separate rooms.

6. Cost. This can vary from £50 to over £100 000! The cost will increase as the speed and quality of the printing required increases.

Printer Classification

There are many possible classifications of printers. The following list shows the most common classifications.

Unit of printing
> **Character printers** print one character at a time.
> **Line printers** print a line of characters at a time.
> **Page printers** print a page of characters at a time.

Both cost and speed will increase considerably as we move from character to line to page printers.

Method of printing
> **Impact printers** work by hitting an inked ribbon against the paper.
> **Non-impact printers** use a variety of techniques to produce characters without a physical impact on the paper.

Impact printers are noisier than non-impact printers but can be used with 'carbons' to produce multiple copies from a single printing.

Type of character produced
> **Shaped characters** are like those printed in this book or produced with a typewriter.
> **Dot matrix characters** are formed by printing a pattern of dots. To print each character, the appropriate dots are selected from a rectangle of available dot positions. Print quality depends on the number of dots available in the rectangle. (See Figure 8.1.)

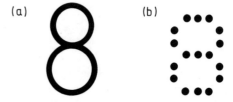

Figure 8.1 (a) A shaped character and (b) a dot matrix character

Paper feed used

Friction feed printers advance the paper by squeezing it between two rollers, just like a normal typewriter.

Tractor feed printers use special paper with a line of holes punched down each side. These holes engage toothed wheels and the paper is pulled or pushed through the machine.

Both types of feed will normally use **continuous stationery**. **Fanfolded** paper is a long strip of paper perforated into page lengths and folded into a pile. Alternatively, a roll of paper may be used. Tractor feeds allow very accurate positioning of the paper and are used on most printers. On the other hand, friction feeds have the advantage that single sheets of paper can be easily used when required. (See Figure 8.2.)

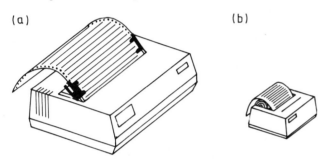

Figure 8.2 (a) A tractor feed printer using paper from a pre-perforated pile, (b) a small friction feed printer using paper from a roll.

Small Printer for Low-cost, Low-volume Applications

Dot matrix impact printers are widely used with microcomputers. Their low cost makes them ideal for this purpose. Design details vary, but a typical printer will have a print head with seven or nine very small print hammers (or needles). These will be used five or more times to build up each character. These printers are relatively cheap and very flexible, being able to print a very wide range of characters. If the printer has a **graphics mode**, instructions can be sent by the computer to fire any one of the print hammers. It then becomes possible to print copies of the display screen. The computer scans the screen line by line, and wherever there is a spot of light on the screen, a dot is printed on the paper. The picture copied in this way is called a **screen dump** (see Figure 18.3, p. 223 for an example).

These printers are rather noisy and relatively slow with typical speeds from 30 to 200 characters per second. Figure 8.3 shows an outline of a dot matrix impact printer, the stages used in printing the number 8, and a dot matrix printer.

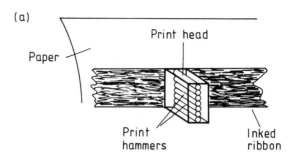

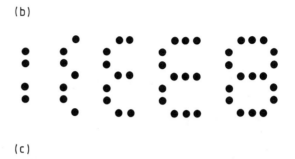

Figure 8.3 (a) A dot matrix impact printer, (b) the stages in printing the number 8 on a dot matrix printer, (c) a dot matrix printer

At present the main alternative to the dot matrix impact printer is the **daisy wheel printer**. This is a form of shaped character impact printer. The arms that carry the embossed characters are arranged in a circle round a central hub like petals round a flowerhead. Over 100 separate characters may be spaced around the wheel. In use, the daisy wheel is moved across the paper and rotated until the correct character is in position. A small hammer then strikes the character against an inked ribbon and the paper. Daisy wheel printers tend to be more expensive than dot matrix printers and are usually slower with speeds typically from 10 to 80 characters per second. They do, however, produce high-quality (letter-quality) printing, which may be essential in some situations. They are not so flexible as dot matrix printers and cannot copy a display screen but different fonts can be quite easily produced by using different daisy wheels. Like dot matrix printers they tend to be noisy in use. (See Figure 8.4.)

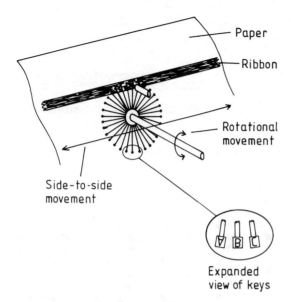

Paper

Ribbon

Rotational movement

Side-to-side movement

Expanded view of keys

Figure 8.4 An outline of a daisy wheel printer

There are many other low-cost low-volume printers, but only two will be mentioned here.

Thermal printers are non-impact dot matrix printers. In operation the printing head is either heated or produces a spark. This prints the characters on to special heat-sensitive paper. These printers are quieter than impact printers and can be produced relatively cheaply. The major disadvantage is the need for special paper which may be expensive.

Ink jet printers are non-impact printers that print characters by spraying a very fine jet of ink droplets on to the paper. A single jet may be used to spray a complete shaped character or several jets may be used to form dot matrix characters. Ink jet printers are quiet and produce good-quality printing, sometimes even in several colours. At the time of writing they are relatively new and their impact on this section of the printer market may well increase.

Exercise 30

A teacher is responsible for buying two printers for use in her school. One will be used in the school office where the secretaries use a microcomputer for various administrative tasks. Another will be used in the computer room for printing students' programs and computer output produced as part of a computer studies course. The teacher also wishes to purchase a printer for use with her own home computer. The following simplified descriptions are from the catalogue:

PRINTER A. Dot matrix impact printer. Printing and graphics modes. 120 cps. Uses fanfolded single sheet or roll paper with tractor or friction feed. Parallel and serial interfaces. £399

PRINTER B. Low-cost daisy wheel printer. 18 cps. Prints original plus two copies. Tractor feed. Other print wheels available at extra cost. £599

PRINTER C. Daisy wheel printer. 60 cps. Tractor and friction feeds. Scientific, italic and bold print wheels supplied plus Courier 10 standard daisy wheel. £1635

PRINTER D. Low-cost dot matrix thermal printer. Text and graphics modes. 30 cps at 32 char per line on $4\frac{1}{8}''$ thermal paper. Friction feed. £79.95. Paper, $4\frac{1}{8}''$ thermal, £2.45 per 60 foot roll.

1 Explain the meaning of each of the following phrases or sentences:

   a *fanfolded single sheet or roll paper*
   b *tractor or friction feed*
   c *18 cps*
   d *prints original plus two copies*
   e *Scientific, italic and bold print wheels*
   f *dot matrix thermal printer*
   g *30 cps at 32 char per line on $4\frac{1}{8}''$ thermal paper*
   h *text and graphics modes*

2 The teacher selected the dot matrix impact printer for the computer room. She was quite happy with it when it arrived but found that a problem arose if one pupil was using the printer while she was teaching another pupil. What do you think this problem was?

3 In making her decision, the teacher estimated that the average student program contained 2000 characters. Estimate the time to print a 2000 character program on:

   a the dot matrix impact printer
   b the low-cost daisy wheel printer.

4 Fanfolded paper for the dot matrix impact printer is available in boxes of 2000 sheets for £12. The teacher estimated that one roll of thermal paper was the equivalent of about 100 sheets of this paper in terms of program listing capacity. How much would the equivalent of 2000 sheets of fanfolded paper cost when bought as rolls of thermal paper? How do you think this answer influenced the teacher's decision?

5 Before making a decision about the printer to buy for the school office the teacher felt she needed more information about the tasks undertaken with the microcomputer. Explain why the teacher would need information about both the quality and the quantity of printing needed. Explain why even if the results of an investigation of the office work indicated that the £1635 printer was needed, the £599 printer might still be purchased.

6 For use with her own computer the teacher requires a printer for program listing and some printing for her own use such as recipes and class lists. Which printer would you advise her to buy and why?

Printers for Medium-to-High Volume Applications

In the commercial world, printers are required that can print at much faster speeds than the simple printers considered in the last section. These printers usually work on a whole **line** of print at a time and are called **line printers**. Print speeds of up to 2000 lines per minute are achieved.

Barrel printers (also called **drum printers**)are shaped character impact printers. Complete lines of the same character are embossed on a metal drum which rotates at high speed. As each line of characters comes level with the printing position, hammers strike the paper at all the positions in the line where that character is required. Figure 8.5 shows an outline of a barrel printer and the stages in building up the line THE RED RED ROBIN.

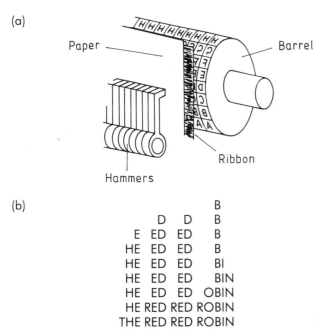

(a)

(b)

```
                              B
                  D   D       B
              E  ED  ED       B
             HE  ED  ED       B
             HE  ED  ED       BI
             HE  ED  ED       BIN
             HE  ED  ED  OBIN
             HE RED RED ROBIN
            THE RED RED ROBIN
```

Figure 8.5 A barrel printer (a) and how it builds up a line of printing (b)

Chain printers are also shaped character impact printers. In this case a continuous chain of embossed characters rotates round two pulleys (see Figure 8.6). As each character comes level with a required printing position, a hammer strikes the paper to print the character. Changing a chain is easier than changing a barrel so chain printers are more flexible. Single damaged characters can be replaced, whereas a damaged character on a barrel will mean replacing the whole barrel. Variations are **train printers** in which the characters are not connected, and push each other round in a groove, and **band printers** which have all the characters embossed on a single band of metal.

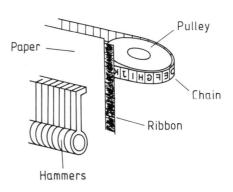

Figure 8.6 An outline of a chain printer

Dot matrix line printers exist which can print a dot at any column position along a whole line. Characters are printed from top to bottom along the whole line by firing the print hammers in the correct sequence. Figure 8.7 shows the stages in building up the word ACE using such a printer.

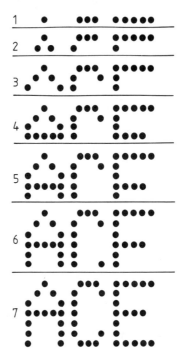

Figure 8.7 A word being built up on a dot matrix line printer

High-speed **ink jet printers** are available working at speeds of up to 15 000 lines per minute. As well as being very fast these printers are also much quieter than impact printers and very flexible because instructions can be stored to create a very wide range of characters. It may also be possible to print in several colours. Figure 8.8 shows a typical line printer in a commercial setting.

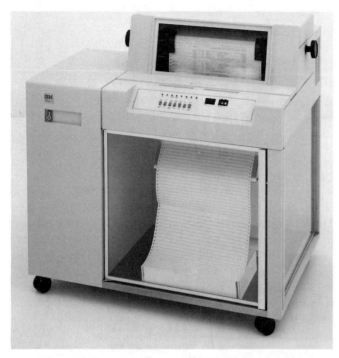

Figure 8.8 An IBM line printer in a commercial setting

To make the output of commercial printers even faster, **pre-printed stationery** is often used. This will have company names, headings, standard information, boxes and lines already printed. Only the individual details of each document will be added by the line printer. Accurate positioning of the forms is of course necessary to ensure printing occurs in the correct places on the form. (See Figure 8.9.)

Exercise 31

1 Draw a diagram to show the stages in printing the phrase PLEASE HELP ME on a barrel printer.

2 A company wishes to use a line printer for both normal printing and printing special bar code labels to be used in its stock room. Explain why a chain printer will be more suitable than a barrel printer.

3 Using squared paper, design your own 5 by 7 dot matrix character set.

4 A mail order company prints 15 000 customer statements each night with an average of 20 lines on each statement. How long will the printing take:

a on a daisy wheel printer working at one line every three seconds?
b on a dot matrix impact printer working at one line per second?
c on a band printer working at 2000 lines per minute?
d on an ink jet printer working at 10 000 lines per minute?
e writing them by hand at an average speed of 4 lines per minute?

5 When using pre-printed stationery, which of the following is the most suitable paper and feed method? Justify your answer.

a friction feed rolls of paper
b tractor feed fanfolded paper
c friction feed single sheet paper.

6 Try to obtain some samples of computer-printed documents and on each identify the pre-printed and the computer-printed information.

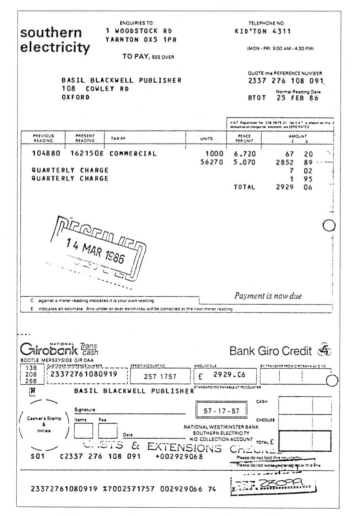

Figure 8.9 Preprinting on a domestic bill

Printing Systems for Very High-volume Applications

Page printers working at speeds of up to 40 000 characters per second are the latest development in printer technology. They are very flexible, allowing printing in different fonts, graphics and lines all on the same page. Pre-printed stationery is thus unnecessary. Because they are non-impact printers they are also quiet. They are very expensive and a very high volume of printing is needed to justify the cost. Very brief details of two of these systems follow. To understand either you will first need to understand the property of electrostatic attraction. The best way to demonstrate this is to rub an inflated balloon against a wool sweater. You will find that the balloon becomes 'charged' with static electricity. It can be stuck to a wall or used to make your hair stand on end.

In **electrographic** (or **electrostatic**) printers special paper is passed over an electronic print head (see Figure 8.10). This can form dot matrix characters as tiny spots of electrostatic charge on the paper. A rotating cylinder can also create charge on the paper for form outlines and headings. The paper is then passed over a cylinder carrying charged ink. The ink is attracted to the charged areas of the paper and the printing is formed.

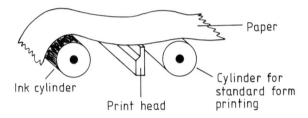

Figure 8.10 An outline of an electronic printer

In **laser** printers a cylinder is used that can be given an electrical charge over its whole surface (Figure 8.11). A laser beam 'writes' on this surface by using its concentrated light to remove the charge from parts of the cylinder. Light sources are also used to create images of any standard form outlines. The cylinder is then used to pick up charged ink and to transfer it to ordinary paper. This of course is an advantage over electrostatic printers that require special paper.

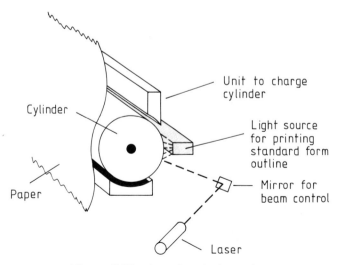

Figure 8.11 An outline of a laser printer

A page printer may be used as an off-line device controlled by its own minicomputer. The output from the mainframe computer is stored on magnetic tapes or discs and then transferred to the page printing system. This system may also include a machine to sort and collate the printed pages automatically. Such a system can be very fast but may cost hundreds of thousands of pounds. An organisation probably needs to produce half a million pages of output a month to justify the cost.

Current Developments

When ink jet and laser printers were first introduced they were thought of as high-cost, high-volume printers. Smaller and cheaper versions have been developed. Small laser printers are already being offered to business users as a direct alternative to the daisy wheel printer. At the moment these small laser printers are still quite expensive but they are twenty times faster and much more flexible than a daisy wheel printer. Their use is therefore almost certain to increase.

Exercise 32

1 Estimate (very roughly) the number of lines in this book. How long would it take to produce a copy of this book:

  a by hand, writing at an average speed of two lines per minute?
  b with a dot matrix impact printer working at 60 lines per minute?
  c with a line printer working at 1500 lines per minute?
  d with a page printer working at 20 000 lines per minute?

2 Select a suitable printer for each of the following applications and explain the reasons for your choice:

  a to produce computer listings and other output in a school computer studies room
  b for use with a computer in a school office to produce 15 copies of a letter to go from the headmistress to each school governor
  c to produce electricity bills for the customers of an electricity board
  d for an advertising campaign. In this campaign, 15 000 individually addressed letters will be produced and sent to those 'lucky' people who have won a 'valuable' prize. The letters must be produced with a very neat appearance.

Video Output (Soft Copy)

A great deal of computer output is produced on a screen like that used in a television. This is called **soft copy** because it is lost when the screen is cleared or the display switched off. Full details of this form of output are given in the chapter on interactive computing.

Output of Pictures and Diagrams as Hard Copy

When a picture or diagram is required as computer output, a device called a **graph plotter** is used.

Flat bed plotters consist of a drawing table over which is suspended an arm carrying a pen (Figure 8.12). Three movements are possible: (i) the arm can move backwards and forwards along the table, (ii) the pen can move backwards and forwards along the arm, and (iii) the pen can be moved up and down. The computer controls these movements to produce the diagram, complete with all annotations and headings.

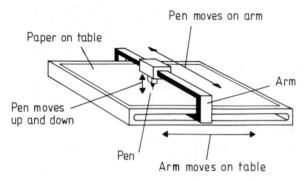

Figure 8.12 An outline of a flat bed plotter

In an alternative design called a **drum plotter**, the arm is fixed and cannot move backwards or forwards (Figure 8.13). The paper is held on a drum or rollers and is moved backwards and forwards under the arm. The computer controls this movement and the movement of the pen along the arm to produce the diagram. Drum plotters allow large drawings to be produced without the need for very large drawing tables.

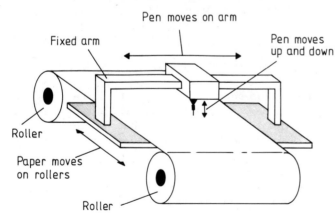

Figure 8.13 An outline of a drum plotter

Graph plotters are very widely used in science, engineering and industrial design. They are very slow devices by computer standards and may take several minutes to complete a single drawing.

Exercise 33

1 The instructions for a graph plotter are coded into a group of 8 bits, with the 8 bits being split up as follows:

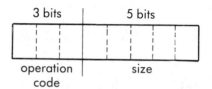

Table A

where size indicates how much movement the operation causes.

Table B gives the details of the operation code:

Mnemonic	Code	Operation
NL	000	Do nothing*
PD	001	Pen down*
PU	010	Pen up*
LT	011	Move left
RT	100	Move right
UP	101	Move up
DN	110	Move down
ST	111	Go to starting point*

*size part of code ignored for these operations.

e.g.   0 1 1   0 0 1 1 0
             LT   6

meaning move left 6 squares

Table B

a Here is a "program" for the graph plotter in the code. Write out the mnemonic version then "dry run" it, drawing the results of the program on squared paper.

```
Code
0 1 0 0 0 0 0 0
1 0 0 0 0 0 1 0
1 0 1 0 0 1 0 0
0 0 1 0 0 0 0 0
1 0 0 0 0 0 1 1
1 1 0 0 0 0 1 0
0 1 1 0 0 0 1 1
1 0 1 0 0 0 1 1
1 0 0 0 0 0 1 0
1 1 0 0 0 0 1 1
0 1 0 0 0 0 0 0
1 1 1 0 0 0 0 0
```

b Here is a shape I wish to make the plotter draw. Write a mnemonic "program" to draw it.

(EAEB 83)

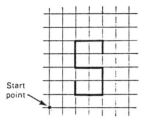

Computer Output to Microfilm (COM)

As an alternative to printing a page of output, the page of data can be reproduced on **microfilm**. The page is displayed on a video screen, photographed and then reduced to a very small size. Typically 200 pages can be reproduced on a single postcard size piece of film called a **microfiche**. The writing on each page is of course far too small to read and a special form of slide projector called a **microfiche reader** must be used. This displays a selected page on a small screen (Figure 8.14). Pages are selected by moving a tray under the screen holding the microfiche. These readers can be commonly seen in libraries and bookshops being used to read book catalogues stored on microfilm.

Figure 8.14 A microfiche reader

There are several disadvantages to the use of COM. These are:

1 A special reader is needed and must be provided in all locations where the microfilm is to be read. This can be expensive.
2 Unless a sophisticated reader/copier is used, hard copies of any given page cannot be reproduced.
3 Printed output can be manually changed and updated by a user, microfilm cannot be changed in this way.

There are also several advantages to the use of COM. These are:

1 The weight of data stored in microfiche form will be 250 times less than the weight of the same data printed on paper.
2 Storage space for microfilm will be up to 1000 times less than for paper.
3 The cost of outputting data on microfilm is up to 30 times less than printing the same data on paper.
4 Microfilm has an output speed up to 10 times faster than a line printer.
5 Since anything that can be displayed on a screen can be photographed and recorded, this is a very flexible form of output.

Exercise 34

1 The Zapper Motor Company must provide all its dealers with a full catalogue showing all the spare parts for all its models. Each time a new model is introduced or a design changed, the catalogue must be updated. These catalogues typically show a line drawing of a part, or subassembly of several parts, followed by details of part numbers, specifications and prices. At present, a master copy for each page is produced by the company's design staff and passed to an outside printer for printing. When a complete catalogue has been made up it is posted to each dealer. The details of the parts are already held on the company's main computer for use in the design department. The company is considering a plan to use COM recording equipment to produce microfiche catalogues to replace the printed ones.

   a Explain the advantages and disadvantages of the plan from Zapper's point of view.
   b Explain the advantages and disadvantages of the plan from a dealer's point of view.

2 Study the advertisement shown below and then in your own words describe:

  a what a Micrographics system is and how it is used
  b the advantages that are claimed for this filing system over an old-fashioned filing cabinet
  c what you think the disadvantages of a filing system like this may be.

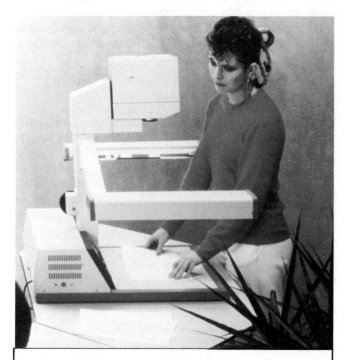

A Canon Micrographics System to cope with all the filing.

Old fashioned filing cabinets take up too much valuable space. Indexing is not always what it should be. And it takes too long to find what you want. A Canon micrographics system puts an end to all of that. A camera and a processor store the information on microfilm and a reader-printer retrieves it. Link the equipment to a computer and you can retrieve it automatically. Canon's expertise in optics and electronics has made us a world leader in micrographics. No wonder we have a wider product range than most of our rivals.

Speech Synthesis and Sound Output

If a small loudspeaker is used as an output device, it becomes possible to produce an output of sounds and spoken words.

Simple systems are used to produce the 'zaps' and 'pows' for games programs. In this case, the computer's output signals are used directly to control the pitch, amplitude and duration of the sound produced by the loudspeaker.

To produce spoken words, a **speech synthesis system** is used between the computer and the loudspeaker. The speech synthesis system converts the computer's output signals into the electrical patterns needed to produce spoken words from the loudspeaker. One type of system stores the patterns needed to produce a limited vocabulary of complete words. Another type of system stores the patterns needed to produce a range of basic sounds called **phonemes**. These devices can produce any spoken word by using a combination of these basic sounds.

Voice output is of limited use in the commercial world, but it may be of considerable use with handicapped people and to produce very 'friendly' computer programs for inexperienced users. Some computers fitted in cars can produce spoken warning messages. This is more than a gimmick because a spoken message is more likely to gain the driver's immediate attention.

Voice output has also been used very successfully in several microprocessor-based educational games. One example is the 'Speak and Spell' teaching device produced by Texas Instruments.

Output of Control Signals

When computers are used to control other machines they must output a series of control signals. If the control only involves simple switching on or off, digital output signals can be used with a suitable decoding circuit. If the control involves regulating continuously varying quantities like speed, pressure and temperature, analogue output signals may be needed. These are produced with a **digital-to-analogue converter**. This device is the reverse of the analogue-to-digital converter described in Chapter 7. In a typical application, the computer will output an 8-bit binary signal between 00000000 and 11111111. The digital-to-analogue converter will change this to an analogue voltage between 0 V and 1.5 V. Figure 8.15 shows how a digital-to-analogue is used to control a valve in a fuel line.

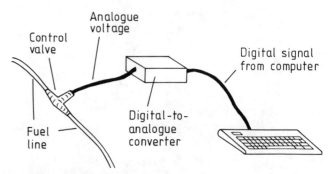

Figure 8.15 How a digital-to-analogue converter works

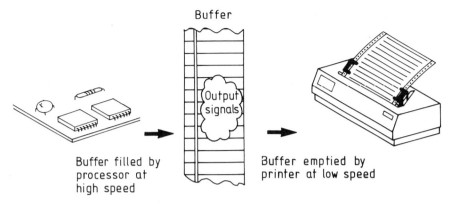

Figure 8.16 The action of a buffer

Peripherals and Buffers

Any input or output device attached to a computer is called a **peripheral device** (or **peripheral**). A keyboard and a printer are two examples. The central processing unit of a computer works very quickly, but a peripheral such as a printer is much slower. In other words, the processor can produce output signals much more quickly than they can be dealt with by the peripheral. To compensate for this difference in speed, a **buffer** is often used between the processor and the peripheral. This is a reserved area of the immediate access store where transmitted data can be temporarily stored. The processor fills this area at high speed, and the peripheral then empties it at a much slower speed. When the buffer is empty the processor refills it and the peripheral empties it again. This continues until all the data has been output. Single-user microcomputers may simply wait while a peripheral buffer is emptied. Large computers can carry on with other processing while the buffer is emptied. Figure 8.16 above shows the operation of a buffer between a computer and a printer.

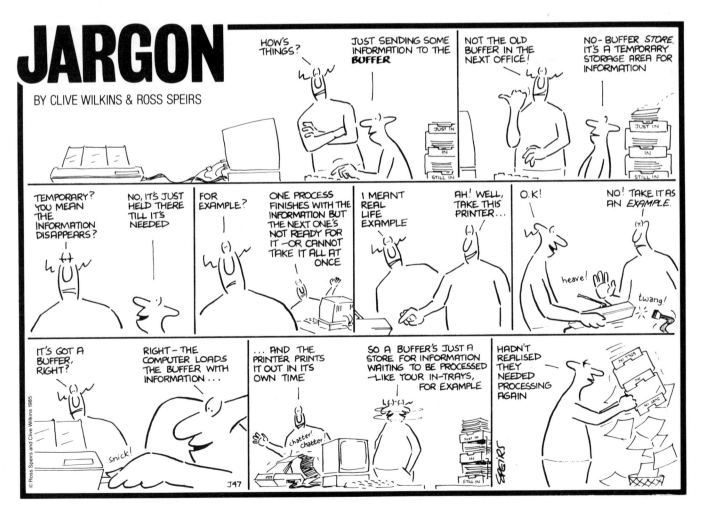

Spooling Output

Large computer systems run many different programs at the same time. This creates two conflicting problems.

1 Several programs may require the use of a printer, graph plotter or other peripheral at the same time.
2 For economic reasons, the number of printers, plotters and other peripherals should be kept to the minimum and each used for as much work as possible.

For example, it is obviously much too expensive to provide a separate printer or plotter for every program that needs one. At the same time, it will waste computer time, and therefore money, if processing is held up until a printer or plotter becomes available. The solution to these problems is to **spool** data on to magnetic tapes or discs. Data can be transferred to these much more quickly than it can be transferred to other peripherals. Each program thus sends its output to secondary storage first, where it takes its place in a queue waiting to be printed, plotted or output in other ways. When the required peripheral device becomes available, the data is transferred directly from secondary storage. In this way the number of printers, plotters or other peripherals needed is reduced and their work load is evenly spread.

Exercise 35

1 Copy and complete the following passages.

a An on-line _____ punch or _____ punch is used by the computer to punch output cards and tape. Such use is limited now but on-line punches may still be used for producing _____ and for controlling _____.

b _____ printers print one character at a time. _____ printers work on a complete _____ at a time and _____ printers print a whole _____ at a time. _____ printers work by hitting an inked ribbon against the paper. _____ printers use other techniques to produce printed characters. _____ printers print characters formed from a pattern of dots. Print quality will depend on the number of _____. _____ printers produce characters like the ones in this book.

c Friction feed printers advance the paper by _____. Tractor feed printers use paper that has _____ punched down each side. _____ wheels engage these holes and pull or push the paper through the printer. Both types of printer use _____ stationery. This is a _____ of paper, either folded into a _____ or held on a roll.

d A _____ printer has a print head with seven small _____. These are used _____ times to build up each _____. These printers are _____ and _____ but tend to be rather _____. If the printer has a _____, copies of a display screen can be produced.

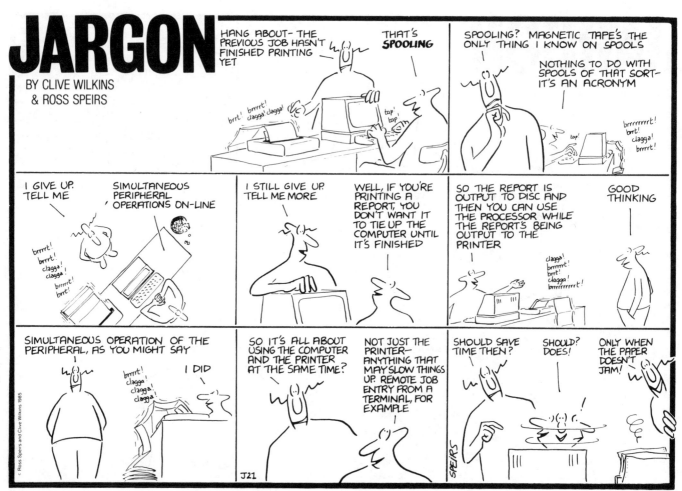

98

e _____ printers use embossed characters arranged like the spokes of a wheel. These printers tend to be more _____ and _____ than dot matrix impact printers but they do produce _____ printing. They are not so flexible as dot matrix impact printers and cannot produce _____.

f _____, _____, _____ and _____ are all types of line printer. Line printers are fast because they print _____ at a time. To increase their speed even further _____ stationery is often used. This has all _____ already printed, only the _____ are added by the line printer.

g The fastest printers are _____. These print a complete _____ at a time. They are very expensive and can only be justified if _____.

h A _____ is needed between the computer and a peripheral because they work at different speeds. This _____ is a reserved area of the _____ where data can be _____ stored. The computer fills this at _____ and the peripheral empties it at _____.

i A _____ is used to produce _____ and diagrams. A _____ moves along an arm, while this arm moves over the _____. An alternative design called a _____ moves a _____ along an arm while the paper is moved under the arm.

j COM stands for _____. Using this technique, _____ pages of data can be stored on a single post-card sized piece of film called a _____. To read the data, a _____ is needed. This is a special form of _____. The main advantages in using COM are _____. The main disadvantages in using COM are _____.

2 Explain with the aid of diagrams the difference between shaped characters and dot matrix characters.

3 For **two** named output-devices (other than magnetic stor-age-devices), explain the significant differences between them.

(O 82)

4 Barrel, chain and laser are all types of _____.

(NWREB 82)

5 Explain briefly how a line printer prints a line. Include a diagram if you wish.

(SEREB 82)

6 a (i) Contrast the output produced from a line-printer with the output from a daisy wheel printer.
  (ii) For each of these two devices, give an example of an application for which it is particularly suitable, and explain why this is so.

  b Explain what is meant by computer-output to microfilm (COM), and compare its advantages with those of printed output.

(O 82 p)

7 Describe what is meant by **pre-printed line printer stationery**, illustrating your answer by sketching an example of pre-printed stationery **underlining** what might be pre-printed.

(WJEC 81)

8 Name the hardware device shown below.

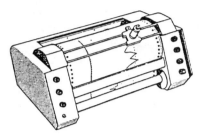

(WJEC 81 *)

9 In an application where a computer is controlling a mechanical process, such as a robot, electrical output is required to make the robot work. What is the name of the device for changing the computer output into the required electrical signals?

(EMREB 82)

10 A great many printers are now available, ranging from small, slow devices to large, versatile, fast printers. Describe various types of printer which are now in use, giving an indication of their operating speeds and paying particular attention to:

  (i) the different facilities which they provide,
  (ii) typical applications for which they are appropriate.

(C 82)

11 Make a copy of the diagram of a printer buffer. Include in your diagram the phrase HAPPY DAYS, showing the phrase stored in the buffer and printed on the printer. Use 7-bit ASCII code with an attached parity bit to represent characters in the buffer.

12 Explain why large computers often spool output on to magnetic tapes or discs.

13 The following printer descriptions are all taken from the Tandy Computer catalogue.

"Letter Quality" Dot Matrix Printer £1299⁰⁰

DMP-2100. Delivers high-speed for data processing, high-resolution for dot-addressable graphics, and a word processing mode with print quality that rivals a Daisy Wheel! Prints 32,400 dots per square inch. Change pitch and font within your text without changing print wheels. Prints 160 cps in DP mode, 770 words per minutes in WP mode. Measures just 5⅞ x 21¹¹⁄₁₆ x 5". **26-1256** £1299.00

Versatile 9½" Dot-Matrix Printer

£399⁰⁰

DMP-120. High speed data processing and graphics modes! Prints 10 and 16.7 cpi, or elongated 5 and 8.3 cpi; 120 cps at 10 cpi. Uses fanfold, single sheet or roll paper. Parallel and Colour Computer Compatible serial interfaces.
26-1255 ....£399.00

Tandy® Makes Printing Fast and Easy

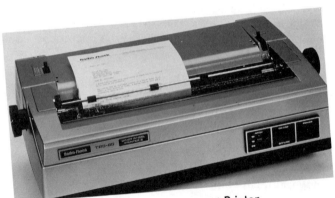

"Letter Quality" Impact Printer

£1399⁰⁰

● **Prints Over 500 Words Per Minute**

Daisy Wheel II. Our best formed-character printer. Prints over 500 words per minute with that crisp, clean, "electric type-writer" look. Interchangeable print wheels and selectable print densities, With Courier 10 print wheel, ribbon. 8 x 24½ x 1515012". **26-1158** £1399.00

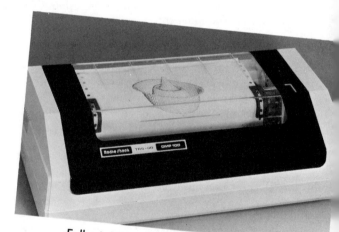

Fully-Addressable Dot-Matrix Printer

● **Bit-Image Mode Allows Printing Of High-Density Graphics**

£299⁰

DMP-100. This low-cost printer gives you black and white graphics printout of Colour Computer screen displays. Prints 7 x 5 dot-matrix upper and lower case characters on an 8" line, with underline capability. Print 50 characters per second at 10 characters per inch (80 columns at 27 lines per minute), or select expanded at 5 cpi (40 columns). Adjustable tractor, 415012 to 9½". Uses up to 9½" fanfold paper. With 480-byte full-line dot buffer. Selectable parallel and Colour Computer-compatible serial interfaces (600/1200 baud). Includes ribbon cartridge. 26-1253 ....
....£299.99

Seven-Colour Ink Jet Printer

£499·00

CGP-220. This incredibly quiet printer features a "state-of-the-art" drop on demand ink-jet printing system and lets you print text and graphics. Prints 40 characters (7 x 5) per second in text mode and 2600 dots per second in colour scan mode. Graphics resolution is 560 monochrome dot colums per line in standard bit image mode and 640 dots per line in the multi-colour mode. Parallel or Colour Computer compatible (660/2400 baud) serial interface. 26-1268

Black Inc Pack. 26-1281 .... £499.00

Tri-Colour Ink Pack. 26-1282 .... £6.95

Roll Paper. 26-1333 .... Pkg. of 3/£9.95

a Explain each of the following extracts:
   (i) 'Letter quality' dot matrix printer
   (ii) formed-character printer
   (iii) prints 40 characters (7 × 5) per second in text mode and 2600 dots per second in colour scan mode.
   (iv) Prints 10 and 16.7 cpi, or elongated 5 and 8.3 cpi; 120 cps at 10 cpi.
   (v) Uses fanfold, single sheet or roll paper.
   (vi) Prints 7 × 5 dot matrix upper and lower case characters.
   (vii) interchangeable print wheels.
   (viii) 'state of the art'
   (ix) Graphics resolution is 560 monochrome dot columns per line.
   (x) Adjustable tractor, $4\frac{1}{2}$ to $9\frac{1}{2}''$.

b Do you think drop on demand ink jet systems produce shaped or dot matrix characters?

c Given that a speed in words per minute can be roughly converted into characters per second by dividing by 10, list these five printers in descending order of speed, putting the 'letter quality' dot matrix printer into the list twice, one for each of its printing modes.

d If you were asked to decide between buying the 'letter-quality' dot matrix printer and the daisy wheel printer, what would you want to see before you made a decision?

e What advantage is claimed for the 'letter-quality' dot matrix printer over the daisy wheel printer?

f What advantages and disadvantages do you think the ink jet printer has compared with the $9\frac{1}{2}''$ dot matrix printer?

14 A friend reads the catalogue description below and asks you to describe the device and its operation and uses. Write a short account of what you might say.

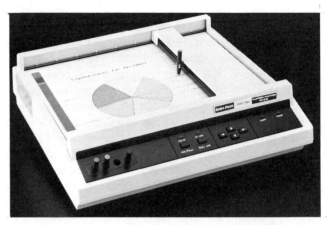

Affordable Flatbed Colour Plotter

• **Get High-Speed Plotting and High Quality Four-Colour Graphics**

£699·00

FP-215. Draws using BASIC ASCII command codes and parameters. Prints text horizontally or vertically using BASIC LPRINT command. Single pen plotting – pens can be easily changed to make multi-colour plots. Red, blue, green and black pens included. Uses 10⅛ x 14 5/16" or 8 x 11½" paper. Plot size: 7 5/16 x 10⅝" or 8½ x 11¾". Plot speed: 100 mm per second (3 15/16 ips) Step size: 1 mm. Includes parallel and Colour Computer serial interfaces. 26-1193 .... £699.00

9 Interactive Computing and Terminals

Interactive (or **conservational**) **computing** means that the input, processing and output are not separated into distinct stages but are intermixed into one continuous activity. Each user has **direct access** to the system and can directly input data and requests for output, receiving the results almost immediately. Users of microcomputers enjoy this facility automatically because microcomputers are normally only used by one person at a time. Large computer systems are much too expensive to be devoted to a single user, but techniques exist that allow many different users to *appear* to have sole use of the system. These techniques will be explained in a later chapter and for the moment we will concentrate on the main input/output devices used in such systems.

These devices are all described as **terminals** and can be classified into three main types: **teletypewriters**, **visual display units** and **graphics display units**.

Teletypewriters

Teletypewriters (or teletypes) combine a keyboard for input with a printer for output. In appearance they are like large electric typewriters (Figure 9.1). In use, instructions or data are typed at the keyboard and are automatically copied on the printer for visual checking. When the user is satisfied that the entry is correct the RETURN button is pressed and the information is transmitted to the computer. The computer then takes over control of the printer and uses it to print out its reply.

Teletypes are relatively slow in operation, typically printing at speeds between 10 and 50 characters per second.

Visual Display Units

Visual Display Units (**VDUs**) combine a keyboard for input with a screen like that in a television for output (Figure 9.2). VDUs work in a similar way to teletypes except that a copy of the user's entry and the computer's response appear on the screen rather than the printer. VDUs typically have a screen with 25 lines of up to 80 characters. Printing on the screen will be at a speed of about 1000 characters per second.

The comparative advantages and disadvantages of teletypes and VDUs are:

Advantages of VDUs

1 VDUs are silent. Teletypes can be quite noisy in operation.
2 VDUs do not require paper and ink ribbons. With teletypes these must be bought and either stored or disposed of after use.
3 VDUs are much faster at printing output.
4 VDUs contain fewer moving parts and will be more reliable and require less maintenance.
5 VDUs are very flexible and can mix simple graphical output with printed text, sometimes in several colours.

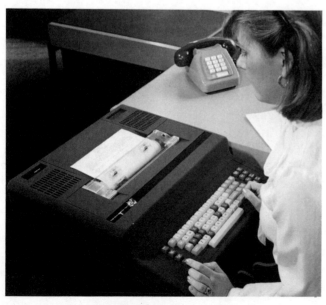

Figure 9.1 A teletype in use

Figure 9.2 A VDU in use

1 VDUs can only display a limited amount of information at one time. This can make it difficult to consult a long data list or computer program.
2 VDUs do not provide a printed record (hard copy), and this may be essential in some applications.
3 In recent years increasing fears have been expressed about the health hazard, particularly to the eyes, of prolonged VDU use.

Graphics Display Units

A graphics display unit is very similar in appearance to a normal VDU but it offers a powerful range of facilities for the display of pictures and diagrams. These pictures and diagrams can be produced in one of two ways: **raster scan graphics displays** and **vector graphics displays**.

In a raster scan graphics display, the screen is divided up into a grid of picture elements or **pixels**. Each pixel can be individually switched on or off by the computer. A picture or diagram can thus be built up on the screen by switching on the correct pixels. In more sophisticated systems, the intensity and colour of each pixel can also be controlled. **Low-resolution displays** may divide the screen into about 100 rows and 100 columns of pixels. **High-resolution displays** may divide the screen into over 1000 rows and 1000 columns of pixels. High-resolution displays can obviously produce much better pictures but also require much more computer memory. A single byte of memory may be required for each pixel, in which case a 100 by 100 pixel screen will require 10 000 bytes of memory and a 1000 by 1000 pixel screen will require 1 000 000 bytes of memory! Figure 9.3 shows a picture of a triangle produced on a low-resolution display and a high-resolution display.

Vector graphics displays should not be confused with even the highest-resolution graphics available on a pixel display screen. If you look closely at even a high-resolution pixel display, you will see that the picture is formed from a large number of small dots, as in dot matrix printing. With a vector graphics display, the picture is formed by direct control of the electron beam inside the screen. The computer controls the deflection of this beam to 'spray' the image on to the back of the screen. The final result is a display with solid lines, not closely printed dots. Vector graphics displays can produce very high-quality diagrams using far less memory than pixel displays. They are not suitable, however, for pictures requiring large coloured-in areas or for animated graphics. The use of vector display systems is normally restricted to professional design equipment used in industry. Figure 9.4 shows how a vector display system would produce the triangle shown in Figure 9.3.

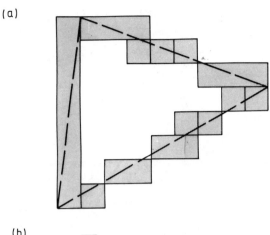

(a)

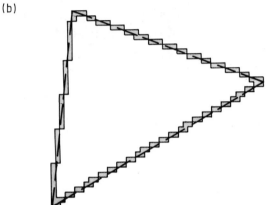

(b)

Figure 9.3   (a) A low-resolution graphics display, (b) a high-resolution graphics display

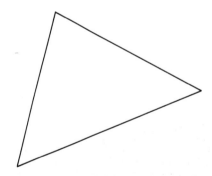

Figure 9.4   A triangle produced by vector graphics

A fully equipped graphics display unit will normally be provided with a **light pen**, **joystick**, **mouse** or **graphics tablet** for input and a **graph plotter** for output. When the light pen is pointed at the screen, the computer can sense the exact point which has been picked out. The computer can either follow the path of the light pen creating a line as it goes or the light pen can be used to identify any part of the display. (See Figure 9.5.)

Fully equipped graphics display units are highly specialized devices intended for use in **computer-aided design** (**CAD**), assisting engineers and draftsmen to produce plans and complex diagrams. The computer

Figure 9.5 A graphics display unit

controlling the unit will have a set of powerful programs to modify the completed diagram, rotating, stretching and enlarging the image, often in three dimensions. It is usually possible for the computer to calculate areas, volumes and many other factors directly from the displayed drawings. It may be possible to produce an output that can directly control the machine tools used to manufacture the final product.

Because they are such specialized devices it is not sensible to compare such systems with either a VDU or a teletypewriter. In comparison with a manual system a CAD system offers considerable advantages:

1 Designs that previously took weeks or even months to produce can now be completed in hours or days. This allows a company either to employ fewer design staff or to explore many more design possibilities.
2 The final design will be very efficient, since the computer can be used to search and test for the best solution to a design problem.
3 If the design system is linked directly to the production machines very high-quality manufacturing is possible.

Against these advantages must be balanced the high initial cost of the CAD system and the necessary training of the design staff to use it.

Point-of-sale Terminals (POS Terminals)

Many of the devices referred to as **point-of-sale terminals** do not allow interactive computing and are only used for data input. Some in fact are not even on-line to the computer; they only capture and store data on cassettes or discs that are later manually transferred to the

computer. However, the latest point-of-sale terminals are complete input/output devices on-line to the computer. They allow sales data to be input and error messages, prices and other details to be output. From the simplest (and least expensive) to the most complicated (and most expensive) systems, we have:

1 *Devices that record details of each sale directly on to magnetic media.* These tapes or discs are later manually transferred to the computer for input and processing.
2 *Devices similar to those described above but with the additional facility that they can be connected on-line to the computer at the end of each day.* The computer usually makes the connection automatically along telephone lines. Sales data can then be directly transferred to the computer without the need to move a disc or cassette manually. This technique is called **polling** the POS terminals.
3 *True terminals that are permanently on-line to the computer.* Sales data entered at these POS terminals is directly input to the computer. The data can be subjected to powerful validation checks, extra data can be accessed from records held by the computer, and the results sent back to the POS terminal. In this way full details of a customer's bill can be produced even if bar codes alone have been input. These bar codes contain only a code number and not full product names or prices.

In order to allow rapid data input at the POS terminal, many are connected to devices to allow automatic data capture. Among these devices are, bar-code readers, OCR readers, Kimball tag readers and magnetic stripe readers. All POS terminals must of course contain a normal cash drawer and a small printer for customer receipts.

A typical on-line POS terminal is shown in Figure 9.6.

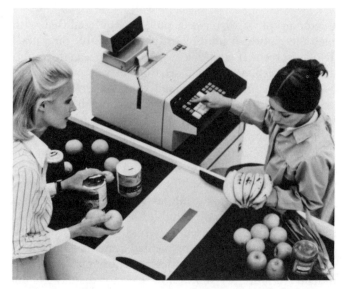

Figure 9.6 An on-line POS terminal

Connecting Terminals to a Computer

Terminals and peripheral devices can be anything from a few metres to several thousand kilometres from the main computer. When the distance is fairly short (up to a hundred metres or so), a connection will usually be by a permanent wire link. When the distance is greater (perhaps between a department store in Leeds and the company headquarters in London), the connection will be made along telephone lines. However, the square-wave pulse trains inside the computer cannot be sent directly over telephone lines. They must first be **modulated**. At the other end of the line the telephone signals must be **demodulated** before they can be input into the computer. Both these processes are carried out by a device called a **modem** (Figure 9.7). When several terminals are in use a **communications controller** will be used to handle the various incoming and outgoing signals. An outline of a typical small system is shown in Figure 9.8.

Figure 9.7 A modem

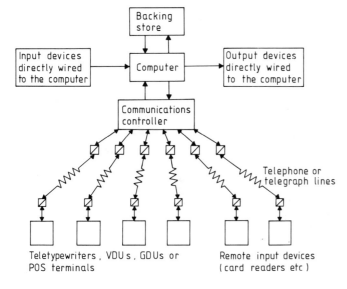

☑ Modems

Figure 9.8 A communications system using modems

Exercise 36

1   Copy and complete the following passages.

   a A _____ is an input/output device used to communicate with a large computer. One type, called a _____, combines a keyboard for entry with a printer for output. Another type, called a _____ combines a _____ for input with a display screen for output.

   b A _____ is used to display pictures and diagrams. It is usually used in a CAD system and often has facilities to _____ the picture displayed. The advantages that a _____ system offers over a manual system are _____.

   c A _____ terminal is used in shops to replace a conventional till. A fully on-line _____ terminal can input data directly to the computer. This data can then be subjected to _____, extra data can be accessed from _____, and results sent back to the _____ terminal. In this way, an itemised bill can be produced even if only bar codes are input that do not contain _____ or _____.

2   What kind of terminal would you select for each of the following applications? Justify your answers.

   a designing components for a large printing press
   b inputting the data from an experiment and then, after processing, producing complex results with many different numerical answers
   c for use by a travel agent to display seat availability and to accept booking for flights
   d reading product bar codes and then printing a bill from this information and other data
   e for an information service in a library
   f to help an architect produce a plan for a house.

3   Write a short passage outlining the comparative advantages and disadvantages of teletypewriters and visual display units.

4   In many large time sharing systems, a number of terminals are connected to a central computer using the British Telecom telephone network. Which additional piece of equipment would be required for this type of system?

   a A modem or acoustic coupler.
   b A high speed printer.
   c A verifier.
   d A switchboard.
   e A Prestel T.V. set.

   (EMREB 82)

5 a Write down in increasing order of speed of data transfer (slowest first) the following input devices: magnetic-tape reader; punched-card reader; paper-tape reader; teletypewriter.
   b For paper tape and punched cards:
     (i) name the device used to produce the codes;
     (ii) state how the information can be decoded without using a computer.
   c Compare the advantages of punched cards and visual display units as means of input of data to computers.

   (O 82)

105

JARGON

BY CLIVE WILKINS & ROSS SPEIRS

COMPUTER SHALL SPEAK UNTO COMPUTER, HUH?

VIA **MODEMS**, YES

COMPUTERS NO GOOD AT TELEPHONE CONVERSATIONS?

NO, THE TELEPHONE'S DESIGNED FOR SPEECH —IT CAN'T COPE WITH COMPUTER OUTPUT DIRECTLY

SO THAT'S WHERE THE MODEM COMES IN?

THE MODEM CONVERTS COMPUTER DATA TO SOUND SIGNALS THAT THE TELEPHONE SYSTEM CAN ACCEPT

WHO'S LISTENING AT THE OTHER END?

ANOTHER MODEM— THAT ONE CONVERTS THE SOUND TONES BACK TO COMPUTER INPUT

SO MODEMS CAN SEND AND RECEIVE

RIGHT—THE ONE AT THE SENDING END MODULATES THE TONE AND THE ONE AT THE RECEIVING END DEMODULATES IT

AHAA! MODULATE/ DEMODULATE = MODEM!

I WAS JUST COMING TO THAT

DON'T THINGS GET JUMBLED IF BOTH ENDS SEND AT THE SAME TIME?

NO—EACH END USES A DIFFERENT TONE

J07

IS THAT ALL A MODEM DOES?

THEY CAN DO AUTOMATIC DIALLING & ANSWERING, ERROR DETECTION & CORRECTION...

© Ross Speirs and Clive Wilkins 1984

COULD YOU GET IT TO DIAL MY BOSS AND CORRECT HIS ERRORS?

SPEIRS

106

6 In a supermarket chain, all goods are marked with a *bar code*, and at the *point of sale* this is read with a *light pen* attached to a *data-capture terminal*

  a Explain each of the four terms in italics in the sentence above.
  b Explain what information is probably being read.
  c Suggest **three** possible ways in which the information could be used, and for each way explain how the information would be processed.

                                 (O 82)

7 It has been suggested that in a few years' time many large shops will have facilities enabling a customer's bank account to be debited as soon as a purchase is made. Describe how such a system might be implemented, paying particular attention to

    (i) the hardware which would be needed in the shops;
    (ii) the links which would be necessary between the shops and the banks;
    (iii) the information which would have to be provided by the customers and safeguards which should be made to protect against fraud.

                                 (C 82)

8 Name three different types of interactive terminals, and in each case name one application best suited to that terminal.

                              (WJEC 81)

9 Give three reasons why a VDU would be used in preference to a tele-printer for a classroom demonstration in a Biology class of, say, river pollution.

                              (L Spec)

10 Some computer applications require facilities for processing pictures, line drawings, photographs and other images.

  a Explain how a design engineer might make use of a graphical display unit and light pen.
  b The satellite photographs of the earth used in television weather forecasts are stored in a small computer in the satellite, transmitted to earth by radio and stored in another computer before being converted back to a picture. Explain one way in which an image can be represented in a digital computer.
  c Describe two further applications where the processing of pictures, line drawings, photographs or other images is an important feature.
  d Explain the function of a digitizer by describing how it might be used.

                              (SREB 82)

11 A VDU (Visual Display Unit) is often used as a remote computer terminal.

  a What is meant by a remote computer terminal?
  b How does a VDU differ from a teletype terminal?

                              (NREB 82)

12 This article appeared in the *Sunday Times*:

But it is in CAD-CAM, computer-aided design and manufacturing, that Austin Rover has been making rapid progress in recent years. The results are to be seen in the Maestro, introduced by Austin Rover last year, and even more so in the LM11 or Montego, its big brother, which is due to go into production soon.

Computer engineering brings big improvements in the accuracy of measurements, reduces the scope for error and ensures uniformity of parts. Both are important considerations in, say, a new vehicle body shell incorporating some 300 separate panels. But the biggest gain, Barr says, is in time. And time is money.

Engineers using screen and light pen can obtain a 30% productivity improvement over counterparts working with pencil and paper, Barr says. Graphics can be produced in a third of the time. Variation — such as in engine clearances or in door opening angles — can be introduced and analysed at the touch of a button. In three dimensions and, by altering the point of vision, from different angles. "Then you're looking at an improvement of several hundred per cent," Barr says.

Design criteria, such as weight, safety, aerodynamism and the extent to which new models lend themselves to high-volume, automated production techniques, can be tested on screen using powerful computer techniques such as "finite element analysis" without resort to costly prototypes.

Once the best body shape has been identified, a life-size model in clay can be created. Measurements can be taken and fed into a computer which, using methods developed in the aerospace industry, translates the data into a mathematical surface definition.

Computer models can then be used to confirm styling, strength and safety by testing loads and stresses. Details of any size, scale or viewpoint can be summoned from this centrally-stored master data base by Austin Rover's engineers or even by outside suppliers.

Tooling and jig engineering can be developed, in a fraction of the time, from tapes carrying the same computer data. Subsequently, the information can be used to monitor manufacturing processes and quality.

a Explain the meaning of each of the following:
- (i) *CAD-CAM*
- (ii) *a new vehicle body shell*
- (iii) *And time is money*
- (iv) *Engineers using screen and light pen . . . pencil and paper.*
- (v) *Variation . . . from different angles*
- (vi) *Design criteria . . . costly prototypes.*
- (vii) *Tooling and jig . . . processes and quality*

b Make a brief summary of all the advantages of this system that are mentioned in the article. Can you think of any disadvantages of the system?

10 Backing Storage and the Structure of Files

The immediate access memory of a computer is limited in size, is relatively expensive, and in most cases ceases to store data when the power supply is disconnected. For these reasons **backing storage** is provided to store data and programs not in current use. Small microcomputers usually use cassette tapes and floppy discs for backing storage, but in this chapter we will concentrate on large (mainframe) computers.

Magnetic Tapes and Batch Processing

The magnetic tape used with computers is similar to normal audio tape but of a higher quality. The tape is typically about 1.2 cm wide and wound on a reel of about 700 m of tape. The tape has a plastic base and is coated, on one side only, with a ferric oxide that can be magnetized. Data is stored on the tape in frames like those on paper tape, except that the holes in paper tape are replaced with tiny magnetized spots (Figure 10.1). There are usually either seven or nine tracks along the tape, with one track used as a parity track.

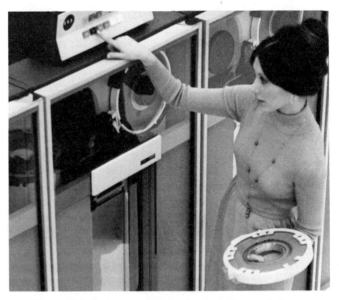

Figure 10.2 A tape unit being loaded with a reel of tape

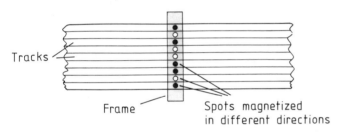

Figure 10.1 An outline of a magnetic tape

Each frame stores one character of data and typically 600 characters are stored on every cm of the tape. This means that a 700 m reel of tape stores about 40 million characters. The tape is loaded into a **magnetic tape unit** that can either read data from the tape or write fresh data on to it, overwriting any data that was there before (Figure 10.2). The speed of the tape over the **read/write heads** is very precisely controlled (Figure 10.3). It is important to avoid breaks in the tape from the sudden jerks of high-speed stopping and starting, so loops of tape are hung in vacuum columns. Tape units can read data at speeds of up to 300 000 characters per second.

A reel of magnetic tape can store far more data than can be held in the immediate access store of the computer. For this reason the data is stored in **blocks** of a convenient size for reading and processing. In use, the computer will instruct the tape unit to read a block of data and then stop the tape until it is ready to read the next block. It is essential that data is only read from the tape at the correct speed. An **inter-block gap** must be left to

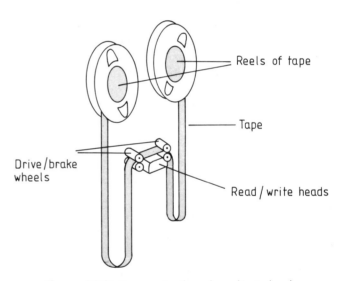

Figure 10.3 Tape passing through read/write heads

allow the tape unit to stop after reading a block and to start again and reach full speed before reading the next one. Longer blocks will increase both the speed at which a complete tape can be read and also the amount of data that can be stored on it. Shorter blocks will require less immediate access memory to store and process them and less re-reading if a parity error is detected. (See Figure 10.4.)

Figure 10.4 Inter-block gaps in a tape

Data on tapes is organised into **files**. A file of data is a collection of similar **records**. A record is a collection of related items or **fields** of data. For example, a **file** of data about your computer studies group might contain one **record** for each person in the group. Within that record there might be **fields** for the person's name, date of birth, address and telephone number. Such a file might be spread over several blocks of tape with several separate records in each block.

At the start of the tape the first block will be used as a **tape header block**. This contains details of any tape or file serial numbers plus the date of file creation and the time that must elapse before the data is overwritten. This enables the computer to check that the correct tape has been loaded. The last block will be used as a **tape trailer block**, containing details of the number of blocks that should have been read and details of any further records on another tape. Fields and hence records may be either of **fixed** or **variable** length. For example, a fixed length field of six characters can store any date of birth. Addresses will certainly not be of a fixed length, and unless blank spaces are used to pad out shorter addresses, a variable number of characters will be needed. Special characters called field separators are used to indicate the start and end of variable length fields. The first field of a variable length record is often used to record the length of the record. In practice, a programmer usually does not have to worry too much about the more awkward details of how his or her data file will be stored. **Utility routines** are provided by the computer manufacturer to handle most of the problems automatically. (See Figure 10.5.)

file. To find a second record the whole tape will need to be rewound and searched again. Magnetic tape files are thus not suitable for **interactive** computing where input, instructions, processing and output are intermixed. Tape files are, however, suitable for **batch processing** where many records are to be read one after the other and processed automatically. Examples of typical batch processing systems are given in a later chapter.

It is often useful to arrange the records in a file into a specific order or **sequence**. One data item in the record is selected as the identifying field or **key** and the records are placed into order of their keys. For example, surnames could be used as a key to organise a file. In practice it is preferable to allocate a reference number to each record to use as a key field. This will avoid any confusion between people with the same surname and can also be used to subdivide the data. For example, all the records in a school file with reference numbers between 85000 and 85240 may refer to first-year pupils.

In practice no attempt is made to change any details in a magnetic tape file directly. Instead the records are read one after the other into the computer, any required changes are made and the updated records written on to a new tape. The old tape is called the **brought forward master tape** and the new tape is called the **carried forward master tape**. The alterations needed may be stored in various ways, for example, on punched cards, paper tape, Kimball tags, OMR documents or OCR documents. To speed the updating process these details are often built up into a third tape file called the **transaction file**. To avoid constant tape rewinding it is important that this file is sorted into the same **key order** as the master tape. Figure 10.6 shows the updating process.

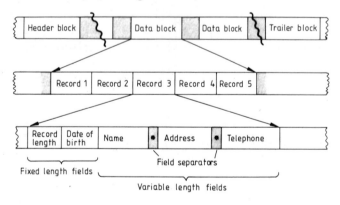

Figure 10.5 Records and fields of data

Files of data held on magnetic tape can only be processed as **serial files**. The records in a serial file can only be processed in the order in which they are stored. If we wished to find any particular record, each record must be read in order until the required record is found. It may take several minutes to locate the correct record in a long

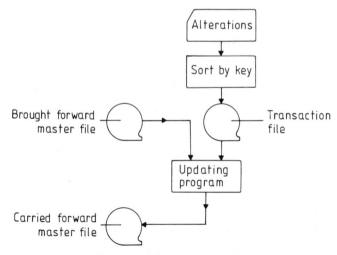

Figure 10.6 Updating a tape

Exercise 37

1 A section of magnetic tape is 70 cm long and stores 600 characters per cm.

  a How many characters can the section store if all the tape is used for storage with no inter-block gaps?
  b If the data is stored in blocks 5 cm long with a 2 cm gap between each:
   (i) How many blocks will fit into the section of tape?
   (ii) How many characters will each block store?
   (iii) How many characters will the section of tape store?

  c If the data is stored in blocks 8 cm long with a 2 cm gap between each:
   (i) How many blocks will fit into the section of tape?
   (ii) How many characters will each block store?
   (iii) How many characters will the section of tape store?

2 A file of data contains 600 000 characters. How long will it take to read the whole file if:

  a the data is read continuously at 300 000 characters per second?
  b the data is split into 200 blocks and the time to read a block, stop and then start again to read the next block is 0.015 seconds?
  c the data is split into 2000 blocks and the time taken to read a block, stop and then start again to read the next block is 0.006 seconds?

3 Explain fully this sentence from the text: *Longer data blocks will increase both the speed at which a complete tape can be read and the amount of data that can be stored on it.*

4 Make a rough estimate of the number of characters of data that can be stored in a full school exercise book of the size commonly used in your school.

  a What length of magnetic tape storing 600 characters per cm would be required to store this number of characters?
  b What length of paper tape storing 4 characters per cm would be required to store this number of characters?
  c How many punched cards storing 80 characters per card would be required to store this number of characters?

5 A library has a book loans file stored on magnetic tape. Each record contains the following fields:
Record length . . . a fixed length field
Overdue date . . . a fixed length field
Borrower's name . . . a variable length field
Borrower's address . . . a variable length field
Title of book . . . a variable length field

Draw a diagram to show the storage of a single record on tape.

6 You already have a record in several files (not necessarily computer files). For example, your teachers' markbooks, your central school records, your doctor's records and possibly at a savings bank or youth club. Try to list all the files in which you have a record and in each case answer if you can the following questions.

  a What is the name or description of the file?
  b How is the information stored?
  c Who is responsible for creating and updating the records?
  d What fields are used within each record?
  e Do you have access to your record in the file?
  f List all the people who you think could gain access to your record.
  g What steps are taken to prevent unauthorised access to your record?
  h If the file is sequential, which field in each record is used as the key field to order the records?

Magnetic Discs (Disks)

Magnetic discs, like magnetic tape, store data as a pattern of tiny magnetic spots. In this case, however, the recording surface is a flat circular metal plate coated on both sides with ferric oxide. The data is stored in a series of rings or **tracks**. These tracks are subdivided into **sectors** or **blocks** by **inter-block gaps** (see Figure 10.7). This subdivision is entirely magnetic, and no marks appear on the actual surface of the disc. The disc is typically about 35 cm in diameter and may contain between 200 and 800 data tracks. Unlike on tape, where 7 or 9 tracks are used in parallel, data is recorded along single tracks as a serial bit pattern. The recording density is varied so that each track stores the same number of characters even though the inner tracks are shorter.

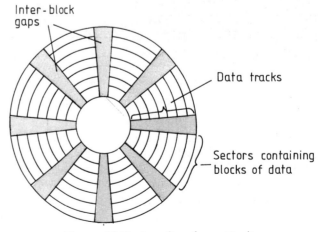

Figure 10.7 An outline of magnetic disc

Several discs are usually mounted together on a single spindle to form a **disc pack** (Figure 10.8). Usually all the surfaces are used except the very top and very bottom surface. The capacity of a single disc pack varies from 2 million to over 300 million characters. The disc pack may be an exchangeable unit that can be removed and stored or it may be fixed in position.

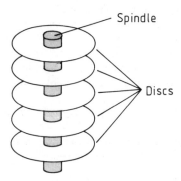

Figure 10.8 A disc pack

A **disc drive** is used to read data from and write data to the disc pack. Figure 10.9 shows an exchangeable disc pack being loaded into a drive.

Figure 10.9 The loading of a disc pack

The disc drive continually spins the discs at a constant speed of about 3600 revolutions per minute. Data is read from and written to the discs by read/write heads. These heads 'float' only 0.02 mm away from the disc surface. Since a single particle of dust can be 0.2 mm thick, great care must be taken to keep the disc surface clean. In **field head drives**, one head is positioned over each track on every usable surface (Figure 10.10). In **moving head drives** (Figure 10.11), only one head is used for each surface, mounted on an arm that can move in and out to

position the head over any given track. To access any given data block three steps are necessary:

1 The correct surface and track must be selected.
2 The disc must rotate until the correct block passes under the head.
3 The data block must be read as it passes under the head.

Step 1 is entirely electronic with fixed head drives but involves mechanical movement in moving head drives. For this reason, fixed head drives will usually offer quicker access to data. Steps 2 and 3 will depend on the speed of revolution of the discs. Transfer rates are typically between 400 000 and 2 500 000 characters per second.

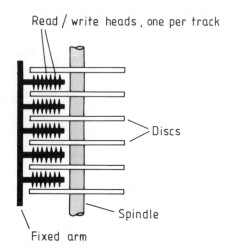

Figure 10.10 A fixed head drive

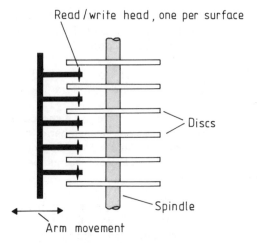

Figure 10.11 A moving head drive

One important property of disc files is that they can if necessary be processed sequentially. That is to say, the records are read and processed in key order one after the other. In order to keep head movement to a minimum, and hence gain maximum speed, when this is done the file is stored in a **cylinder** of tracks in the disc pack

(Figure 10.12). When the file is created, all the tracks in the cylinder will be used before the heads are moved one track inwards to write more data.

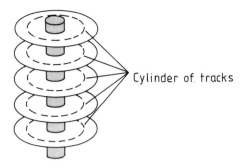

Figure 10.12 A cylinder of tracks in a disc pack

Files held on magnetic discs are divided into separate records and fields in the same way as files held on magnetic tape. Magnetic tape files can only be read and processed in **serial** – that is, by reading one record after the other. Disc files, however, offer **direct access** to individual records. A disc drive can be instructed to read or write a record using any given surfce, track and sector in the disc pack. The combined surface, track and sector numbers are called the **disc address** of the record. Thus

if the computer knows the disc address of a record it can read only the required sector of the disc. There may be several records within that block of data, but finding the required record from a single block is much quicker than searching the whole file.

The problem, of course, is how to find the disc address of any required record. To illustrate the problem we will consider a simplified version of a disc file held by a computer in an estate agent's office. The file consists of 1000 house records. Each record has the following fields:

REF NUMBER	PROPERTY DETAILS	AREA	PRICE	PRESENT OWNER DETAILS

The property details, the area, the price and the reference number are typed on a card and put in the estate agent's window. When a customer wishes to make an appointment to view a house the reference number is typed on the keyboard of a VDU and the present owner details are displayed on the screen. These details may include times at which the property cannot be visited, work telephone numbers for contact and so on.

An **indexed sequential file** is used to store the records in order of a key field. As the records are stored in blocks

Figure 10.13 Finding a record in a file

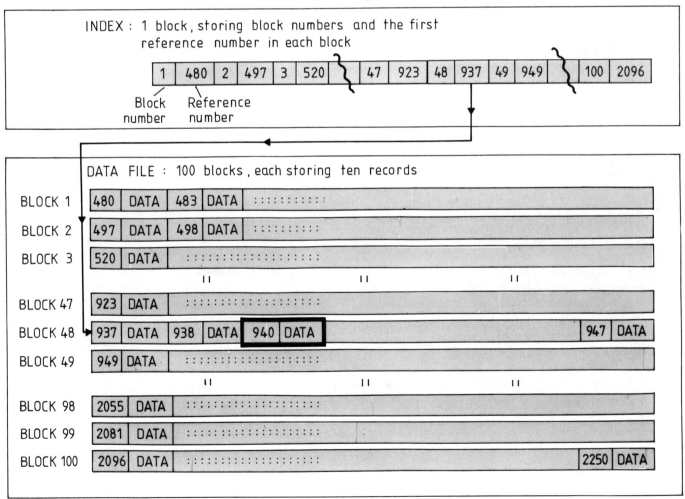

on the disc, an **index** is created and also stored on the disc. Suppose our 1000 house records are stored in 100 data blocks, each containing 10 complete records. A further **index block** will store in order the first reference number in each of the 100 blocks. This is how any given record is found.

* The index block is read into the computer's memory and searched sequentially for an index number greater than the record's reference number.
* The data block starting with the index number just before this must contain the required record.
* This block is read into the computer's memory and the record found within it.

Figure 10.13 shows how an index can be used to find record 940 in a file with records from 480 to 2250. The record numbers do not form a complete sequence because some records have been deleted from the file.

In many cases our estate agent may not wish to use reference numbers to access the data in the house file. For example, a client may request a list of all the properties for sale in a given area or all the properties selling for between £20 000 and £30 000. Separate files could be kept sorted into area order or price order. A far more powerful solution is to use a single file and to create structures that enable it to be used as a **data base**. A data base is a structured collection of data that can be searched and processed in several different ways. The full details of data base creation are well beyond the scope of this book but two of the techniques used can be illustrated.

1 **Pointers** can be added to the records in the main file linking together all the records of a similar type. For example, an extra field could be added to each record giving the reference number of the next house for sale in the same area (Figure 10.14)
   The records of all the houses for sale in a given area are thus linked. Having found the first record, we can quickly compile a full list.
2 If we wish to search for all the houses in a given price range, adding pointers to records will become too complicated. For example, a house costing £25 000 could be linked to all the houses in the £25 000–£30 000 range, the £20 000–£25 000 range, the £20 000–£30 000 range and many other possible ranges. One solution to this problem is to use an

inverted file. The structure of an inverted file to deal with a price range search is shown below.

House price (nearest £500)	Reference numbers of all records with this price
25500	480, 493, 527, . . .
26000	482, 500, 547, . . .
26500	481, 503, 526, . . .
27000	484, 490, 491, . . .

This file will be stored on the disc with the indexed sequential file of house records. By referring first to this file, the computer can find the reference numbers of all the houses within any given price range. Full details of these houses can then be accessed from the indexed sequential file.

A fully structured data base would certainly divide the property details into many fields. It might then be possible to make a search request such as this: "Find all the detached 4-bedroomed houses with a garage, in either Area A or Area B, selling for between £35 000 and £50 000 but not with oil central heating".

Because they offer both sequential processing and direct access to individual records, indexed sequential files are often used to store data on discs. They are not, however, suitable for all situations. A particular problem arises if there is no suitable sorting order to arrange the records in a sequence. In this case, a **random file** may be used. The position of any record in a random file can be calculated directly from its key field. A mathematical formula must be found that can transform any key into a disc address. As the file is created, this formula will be used to decide where each record is to be stored. When the file is accessed, the formula can be used again to retrieve the record.

A Summary of the Main Types of Data File

Four main types of data file are held in secondary storage:

* **Serial files**: files in which the records can only be accessed by reading each one in turn.
* **Sequential files**: serial files in which the records are arranged in order of a key field.
* **Indexed sequential files**: files which allow direct access to records, after an index has been used.
* **Random files**: files in which records can be directly accessed, using a calculation to turn a key into a disc address.

REF NUMBER	PROPERTY DETAILS	AREA	PRICE	PRESENT OWNER DETAILS	NEXT REF NUMBER

Pointer to the next record in the same area

Figure 10.14 How a pointer works

A Comparison Between Tapes and Discs

The cost of storing data on magnetic tapes is less than the cost of storing the same data on discs. Exact cost ratios change but disc storage may be 10 times more expensive than tape storage. So why use disc storage?

Advantages of Discs

The comparison between tapes and discs is really a comparison between the different file structures that each can support and the ways in which they can be searched and updated. Tapes can only store serial or sequential files. Discs can also store indexed sequential files and random files. It can take several minutes to locate any given record in a tape file and the file can only be updated by completely recopying it. Disc files can offer direct access to any record in milliseconds and can be updated directly. Disc files are therefore preferred whenever:

1 Quick file searching is required.
2 Interactive computing requires continuous file searching and updating.
3 No suitable sorting order exists and a random file must be used.
4 Only a few of the records in a sequential file are updated from each transaction file.

Advantages of Tapes

Apart from their lower cost, tapes have two other advantages over discs:

1 International standards for data files on tape may make it easier to use a tape file with a different computer. Tapes are also physically easier to transport than removable disc packs.
2 Tape files are more secure because they are never directly updated.

Random Access and Direct Access

The term **random access** is often used to describe any direct access disc file. This causes considerable confusion. Some of these files are indexed sequential files which provide direct access by using an index. Others are random files which provide direct access by using a mathematical formula to change a key into an address. For clarity it is preferable to refer to all disc files as **direct access files**. We can then say that these direct access files are of two types: **indexed sequential files** and **random files**.

Practical Problems

There are many problems associated with file creation and processing that have not been considered in this section. In particular, we have not considered the problem of **dynamic files** in which the data is continually updated. Dynamic files can only be created on discs. Insertions, deletions and alterations can all be made directly by overwriting the data stored on the disc. This in itself causes data security problems because overwritten data is lost and it may be difficult to recover from mistakes.

Exercise 38

1 A fixed head disc pack contains 5 discs, but the very top and very bottom surfaces are not used. Each surface contains 800 tracks divided into 30 sectors. Each sector contains a block of 512 characters of data. The pack is rotated by the disc drive at a speed of 60 revolutions per second.

   a How many surfaces are used to store data?
   b How many characters are stored in one track?
   c How many characters are stored on one surface?
   d How many characters can be stored in the whole disc pack?
   e What is the maximum possible number of characters than can be read from the disc in one second?

2 A mail order firm has 64 000 customers. A customer file contains one record for each customer with an average record length of 300 characters.

   a How many complete tracks of the disc pack outlined in question 1 would be needed to store this file?
   b How many 80 column punched cards would be needed to store the file if four cards were used for each record?
   c What length of magnetic tape storing 600 characters per cm would be needed to store the file?
   d What length of paper tape storing 4 characters per cm would be needed to store the file?
   e If each record were recorded on a separate sheet of paper and a pile of 100 sheets was 1 cm high, how high would a stack of all the sheets of paper be?

3 Draw a diagram to show the use of the index to retrieve Record 2067 from the estate agent's house file.

4 The estate agent's file contains records with house prices from £8000 to £120 000. Pointers could be added to each record linking houses of the same price. Explain why this would not be a suitable structure if a search for all the houses for sale in a given price range is required.

5 A disc file held for use by the computer in an employment agency has records with the following fields:

REF NUMBER	JOB NAME	JOB DESCRIPTION	HOURS PER WEEK	WAGE	EMPLOYER DETAILS

The file is an indexed sequential file held in reference number order.

a Explain why a search for all the records with the same job name might be required. Explain how an extra field could be added to each record to facilitate this search.

b Explain why a search for all the jobs with wages within a given range might be required. Explain how an inverted file could facilitate this search.

c Similar jobs may well be given different names by different employers, e.g. 'fork lift truck driver', 'fork lift operator', 'driver, fork lift/light van'. On the other hand, 'fork lift driver in cold storage warehouse' may not be suitable for any fork lift driver. Explain why a system might be developed that could reduce each job name to a simple number code. Describe an outline of such a coding system that could cope with up to three elements in any job name, e.g. 'driver, fork lift/light van, cold storage warehouse'.

6 A moving head disc uses 10 magnetic surfaces with 400 tracks of data on each. Each track stores 20 blocks of 1000 characters. The time taken to read a block if the heads are already in position is 1.25 milliseconds. The average time taken to move the heads to find and read a block at random is 60 milliseconds. A file of 200 records, each 1000 characters long, is stored on the disc with each record occupying one data block. Find the time taken to read the whole file in sequence if:

a the data is stored as an indexed sequential file in a single cylinder of tracks

b the data is stored as a random file.

7 a Draw a clearly labelled diagram of a magnetic disc pack containing six discs.

b (i) Using the terms *surface*, *block*, *track*, explain how information is organised on a magnetic disc pack.

(ii) After reading the outside track of the first surface, what would normally be read next if the disc was being used for *serial access*? Explain your answer.

c Give *three* advantages and *one* disadvantage of disc storage compared with magnetic tape storage.

(SWEB 82)

8 Complete the following paragraph by inserting the appropriate words from the list in the spaces provided.
memory, direct access, disc, serial, deleted, added.
_____ files are updated by making a copy of the file from one reel of tape to another. While the copy is being made every record from the old version must be copied into _____. If no alteration is required the record is copied unchanged onto the new reel. Records are _____ by not copying them onto the new file. Amending a record on a _____ file is carried out by reading it from _____ into memory, making the necessary changes and copying it back again.

(NI CSE 82)

9 The diagram shows part of a school's pupil file held on magnetic tape. Copy the diagram and write in the empty circles the correct letters to show each of the following:

a a Block
b a Record
c a Field

The circle labelled D shows a _____.

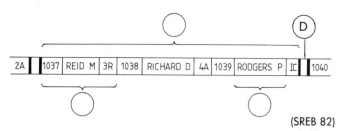

(SREB 82)

10 This is a computer print-out of a section of an employees' file in a large factory.

NAME	SEX	AGE	DEPARTMENT
WATKINS J	F	25	TYPING
WATKINS J	F	32	TYPING
WATKINS J A	M	43	MACHINE SHOP
WATKINS J L	M	27	MACHINE SHOP

a Describe this file in terms of fields and records.

b In the interrogation of this file, how could confusion between the four surnames be avoided?

(AEB 81)

Data Security

Many large organisations now hold most of their essential information on computer files. The loss of some or all of this data may well be catastrophic for the organisation. If the information is secret or contains personal employee details, even unauthorised access to the data may be damaging to the organisation or individual. There are several threats to data security.

1. Equipment failure and user mistakes. It might appear that once a brought forward master tape file has been copied it can be wiped clean and reused. If, however, the carried forward tape were to prove unreadable, get lost or stolen or be torn by the tape unit, all the data will be lost if the previous version of the file has not been retained. In practice, several **generations** of the master file and transaction files will be stored. These tapes are often referred to as **grandfather**, **father** and **son** tapes. A three-tape cycle is used to store the generations. At each update the son tape becomes the father tape, the father tape becomes the grandfather tape and the grandfather tape, after being wiped clean, becomes a new son tape (Figure 10.15).

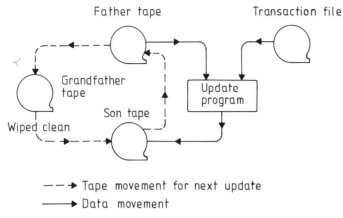

Father tape   Transaction file

Grandfather tape

Son tape

Update program

Wiped clean

--→ Tape movement for next update

——→ Data movement

Figure 10.15 Grandfather, father and son tapes

With dynamic disc files which are continually updated, file security is a major problem. Users of the system may make entry errors and destroy important records. Very occasionally the read/write heads may come into contact with the disc surface resulting in a 'head crash' and total loss of all the data on the disc. If some delay in re-creating the file can be tolerated, a solution is to **dump** the disc file contents at regular intervals on to magnetic tape. If a **log** is also kept of all alterations to the disc file between dumps it can always be re-created from the last dump and the alterations log. Dumps may be made every night or, if many alterations are made, possibly every hour.

With large interactive systems, even a few hours delay re-creating disc files may not be acceptable and a more expensive solution must be adopted. Consider, for example, a computer system dealing with all the seat bookings at a major airline. The disc files are continually updated from terminals in travel agents' offices all over the country, and it is essential that the system is operative at all times. In such cases it may be necessary to have a back-up computer duplicating all the work and files of the main computer. If the first computer fails, the other one can continue to operate the system while it is repaired.

2. Fire. A fire destroying the computer can be regarded as the ultimate in equipment failure! To avoid total loss of all the data, one generation of tapes is often kept in a fireproof safe designed to preseve them intact in the event of a fire. These tapes can be used to attempt to restart the system on a new computer.

3. Data errors. No validation routines can detect all errors in data entries and prevent them reaching the files. It is, however, essential for the programmer to incorporate the most extensive possible checks to ensure the least possible number of errors enter the file. A full set of checks on input data is often called a **data vet**.

4. Operator mistakes. The most common operator mistake is to load the wrong magnetic tape. The tape header block can be checked by the program to ensure the correct input file has been loaded. If a three-tape cycle is in use, this header block may contain a generation number so that this can also be checked. To try to ensure that files are not overwritten by mistake a **write premit ring** must be fitted into a groove in the reel before any tape can be written on (Figure 10.16).

Figure 10.16 A write permit ring being fitted in a reel

5. Criminal activity and malicious damage. A discontented or dishonest employee can do enormous damage in the computer room by destroying or altering files. Consider a bank employee creating a record of an account in his or her name with a £1 000 000 balance! Consider an employee of a large company destroying a file containing details of all the accounts owing money to the company! In practice, many checks and precautions are taken. For example, nobody should ever be allowed to gain simultaneous access to all the generations of an important file. There is, however, no complete solution to the problem and computer crime causes growing concern.

6. Unauthorised access to data. With the growth of large systems with many terminals in remote sites this is an increasing problem. Even with a home microcomputer and a simple modem it may be possible to make a telephone link to a large computer system and gain access to or even alter data files. One way of trying to stop unauthorised access is to issue a password to each authorised user. This must be entered before access to the system is allowed. A more secure system is to issue magnetic badges that must be inserted in a slot in the terminal before the system can be used. Different users may be allowed different levels of access to the system. Some may be allowed to access and update all the files. Others may be allowed to read some of the data stored on the files but not to update any files.

Exercise 39

1 Explain why it is essential to store transaction records as well as several generations of the master file.

2 A large firm stores records for 10 000 employees in a computer file used by a payroll program. Each record has the following fields:

CODE NUMBER	NAME	PAY TO DATE	TAX PAID TO DATE	TAX CODE	HOURLY WAGE RATE

Each week a transaction file is created with a record for each employee. Each record has the following fields:

CODE NUMBER	NAME	HOURS WORKED THIS WEEK

This file is used with the master file to calculate and print out the wage slips. At the same time the master file is updated and a new generation written.

a Explain why a magnetic tape file is a suitable choice for the master file.

b Explain why both the master file and the transaction file should be sorted into order of the code numbers.

c Explain why code numbers are preferred to surnames as a key to order the file.

d Describe the steps that might be taken to prevent loss of the data in the master file.

e Describe the steps that might be taken to prevent errors in the transaction file entering the master file. State the types of validation check needed, and give an example of an error that each one would detect.

f Which fields in each record of the master file will not be updated each week?

g Explain why it may be necessary both to add and to delete records in the master file. How will these alterations be made?

3 At a large comprehensive school a computer file is created each year with a record for each new first-year pupil. The first 5 fields in each record are:

ROLL NUMBER . . .   A 6-digit number, the last digit is a check digit, being the remainder when the first 5 digits are divided by 11.

PUPIL'S NAME . . .   Surname first.

PUPIL'S SEX . . .   Either M for male or F for female.

PUPIL'S FORM . . .   Either 1A, 1B, 1C, 1D, 1E, 1F, 1G or 1H.

PUPIL'S DATE OF
BIRTH . . .   A 6-digit number. All pupils should be eleven years of age by 1 September

Below are five entries that were rejected because of mistakes in these first five fields.

850235	SMITH JOHN	F	1A	130275
850279	BROWWN WENDY	F	1A	25174
850483	KAHN MOHAMMED	M	B1	320374
851534	5ONY GLOSTER	M	1J	190347
852006	JANE SMITH	N	2C	101074

a Make a list of all the errors in these records that you think a good data vet should detect. For each error:
(i) explain the kind of check used to detect it
(ii) explain the most probable cause of the error.

b There are some errors in these records that even a good data vet would probably not be able to detect. Make a list of these errors and explain why it is very difficult to detect them with a computer.

4 In each of the following examples a file is described. Explain the potential damage that could result if an unauthorised person gained access to the file.

a a file held in a newsagents giving details of when customers have cancelled their newspaper deliveries because they will be away on holiday

b a file held by a large company storing all the design details of a new product that is in a late stage of development

c a file held by the police storing records of the criminal convictions of a large group of ex-prisoners now mostly re-established as honest members of the community

d a file held by a large company storing details of the company finances and investments.

5 In each of the following cases a file is described. Explain the potential damage that could result if an unauthorised person gained access to the file *and* the ability to change some of the records.

a a file held by an examinations board storing details of all the examination passes obtained by students over the past ten years

b a file held by a bank storing details of the bank accounts of all its customers

c a markbook held by one of your teachers storing examination coursework marks

d a file held by the police storing records of the criminal convictions of a large group of ex-prisoners now mostly re-established as honest members of the community.

6 Twelve programmers were made redundant by a large company. In what seems a very inhuman manner, the programmers were called into the manager's office, told they were being made redundant, escorted by security staff to collect personal belongings from their desks and then escorted from the buildings and never allowed to return. Can you offer any excuses for the manager's behaviour?

7 Usually, when a user types his or her password at a terminal, what is written does not appear on the VDU screen or teletypewriter but is sent directly to the computer. Can you explain why this happens?

8 Some VDU terminals which are used to access sensitive data automatically clear the screen if, after a few minutes, no further keyboard entry has been made. Can you explain why this happens?

9 It is common knowledge that many people, when asked to choose a password, often choose the name of a close friend or relative. Why do you think it is a good idea to avoid such a choice?

10 Why do you think some organisations regularly change the passwords of all the authorised users?

11 In a large company the training department manager can only access the fields in the personnel records that give details of an employee's name, job in the company, previous training and age. The personnel manager is able to access many more fields, giving details, for example, of wage rates, tax codes and any past criminal record. Explain why the different managers are allowed different levels of access to the system, and how in practice the system can control the level of access.

12 If you have access to a microcomputer, find out how files of data can be created in its backing store. Write a program to create a data file of your friends' names, heights, shoe sizes, hair colours and sexes. Invent a code number for each friend that can be used to check if the sex field is correct and which also contains a check digit. Try to build as many validation checks as you possibly can into the file creation program.

Other Backing Storage Devices

Magnetic drums can be used as an alternative to discs. Data is recorded in tracks round the outside surface of a continually rotating drum (Figure 10.17). Drums offer very fast access times, but usually have less capacity and a higher cost than the latest disc packs. Drums are declining in popularity and are far less common than discs.

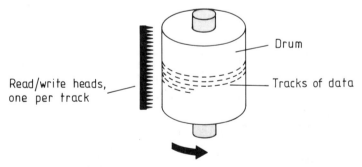

Read/write heads, one per track

Drum

Tracks of data

Figure 10.17 An outline of a magnetic drum

Cassette tapes and floppy discs. These are the microcomputer equivalents of the reel-to-reel tapes and hard discs used with large computers. All the comparisons between their larger brothers and sisters can be applied to these devices. A typical cassette is almost identical to a normal audio cassette. In fact these are often used, cut down to 10 or 15 minutes of recording time. Typical storage capacity will depend on the length of the tape and the recording density used by the microcomputer.

Storage of at least 100 000 characters should be possible on even a fairly short tape. It can take several minutes to locate a program or data file on a cassette and data transfer rates are also slow, typically about 150 characters per second. The data is recorded in a single track along the tape not, as in reel-to-reel tapes, in 7 or 9 tracks across the tape.

Floppy discs were originally developed as an alternative input medium to punched cards and paper tapes. They have now become a popular form of backing store for microcomputers. A typical floppy disc is about 13 cm in diameter and consists of a flexible plastic disc coated with ferric oxide. This is kept permanently in a rectangular cardboard envelope with a cut-out slot to enable data to be read from and written to the disc surface. Typical capacities vary from 100 000 to 600 000 characters per disc. The data layout on the disc is the same as that used for hard discs. Data transfer rates are much higher than for cassette tapes and are usually between 20 000 and 60 000 characters per second. If the much higher cost of the floppy disc drive is taken into account, the cost of floppy disc storage is about 10 times the cost of cassette tape storage.

Figure 10.18 A cassette and a floppy disc

Bubble memory. Tapes and discs need complicated mechanical devices to read and write data. They will always be far slower and less reliable therefore than the solid-state components of the computer system. On the other hand, the integrated circuits of the immediate access memory are expensive and limited in data capacity. They are also usually **volatile** — that is to say, the data is lost when the power is disconnected. Bubble memories fall between disc and integrated circuit memory in terms of both cost and speed. A bubble memory is a form of high-speed solid-state backing store. The device consists of a small (typically 1 cm^2) flat wafer covered with a thin film of magnetic material (Figure 10.19). Small cylindrical magnetic fields or **bubbles** can be created and moved about in the film by applying a magnetic field. A chain of bubbles or gaps without bubbles can thus be used to represent and store binary data. To read the data the chain is moved under a bubble detector built into the device. Bubble memories can be used for backing store because they are **non-volatile** (the data is *not* lost when the power is disconnected). The price of bubble memories is falling. They are smaller, faster and (being solid-state) more reliable than discs. It has been predicted that they will eventually replace discs as the most important form of backing store — only time will tell. Portable data-collecting devices using bubble memories are already in use and the first microcomputer with a 500 000 character bubble memory backing store is now on sale.

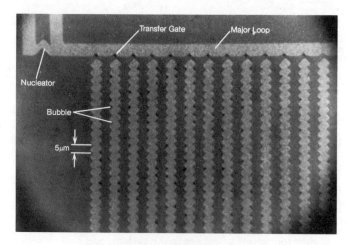

Figure 10.19   A bubble memory device

Mass storage systems. Very large organisations may have extensive libraries of data held on reels of magnetic tape. The time taken for someone to find and load the required file of data from rooms full of these tapes may become unacceptable. If so, a mass storage system could be installed. In this system the data is usually stored in

tape cartridges that can be fetched and loaded automatically by mechanical devices. Access time is still slower than with magnetic discs, but such a system can store many billions of characters of data. The cost of this volume of disc storage could be prohibitive. A typical mass storage system is shown in Figure 10.20.

Figure 10.20 A mass storage system (IBM 3802)

Optical storage systems. Optical storage systems use a rotating disc to store data. Minute indentations in the disc surface store the data as a binary code. The data is read with a laser beam reflected from the disc's surface (Figure 10.21). Because no physical read/write head is needed, the data can be very tightly packed. This means that very high storage capacities can be achieved. Present technology allows the storage of over 1000 megabytes on a single disc! Unfortunately, present systems do not allow the stored data to be changed. They can only be used to read data. Under development are read/write optical discs that use reversible chemical and structural changes in the disc surface. If this research is successful, optical discs could replace magnetic discs as the main form of computer backing store.

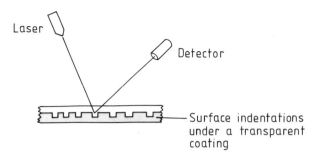

Figure 10.21 How an optical disc is read

Exercise 40

1 Copy and complete the following passages.

a _____ is always provided by computer systems to store programs and data not in current use. It is needed because the immediate access store is _____. _____ and _____.

b Magnetic tape is _____ wide and wound on a reel of about _____ of tape. The data is stored as a pattern of tiny _____. Each character of data is stored in one _____ across the tape. There are _____ or _____ recording tracks along the tape. Typically, _____ characters are stored in one centimetre of tape. The data is stored in _____ of a convenient size for reading and processing. An _____ is left between these _____ to allow the computer to stop the tape and then start it again before reading the next _____.

c A file of data is a collection of similar _____. Each _____ is a collection of related data items or _____. The first block in a tape file is the _____. This contains details of _____. The last block is the _____. This contains details of _____. Tape files can only be processed in _____. It is often useful to arrange the records in a _____. One field is selected as the _____ and records are placed in order of their _____. Tape files are never updated directly. Instead a carried forward master tape is read into the computer together with a _____ tape. Any necessary changes are made and the updated file is written on to a _____ master tape.

d The data on magnetic discs is stored in a series of _____. These _____ are subdivided into _____ by _____. A typical disc is _____ in diameter and contains between _____ and _____ tracks. Several discs are usually mounted on a spindle to form a _____. Disc files offer _____ access to records. If the computer knows the _____ of any record it can read it directly. In _____ files, this _____ is found from an index. In random files, this _____ is calculated from the key field of the record.

e Data _____ is a problem for any organisation holding most of its information on computer files. The security of data in tape files is achieved by using the _____ system. The security of data in disc files is achieved either by _____ the data regularly on to magnetic tape or by having a _____ computer duplicating all the work of the main computer. In case of fire, one _____ of tapes is usually kept in a _____. To prevent incorrect data corrupting the files, a full _____ is carried out on data entries. To prevent operator mistakes, a _____ must be fitted before a tape can be written to and the computer also checks the _____ to ensure the correct tape is loaded. To prevent unauthorised access to data, each user is often given a _____.

2 Explain what is meant by a 'cylinder of data' in a disc pack. Illustrate your answer with a diagram.

3 A salesman visits the manager of a large computer installation and tries to sell him a sprinkler system to extinguish fires. The salesman explains that the system can detect fires almost as soon as they start and can then release gallons of water through sprinklers in the ceiling. The manager decides not to buy and install the system. Why do you think he made this decision?

4 Some microcomputers are provided with connections for two separate cassette recorders. Explain why this provision is made.

5 How many tape units will be needed for an update run if both the master tape and the transaction tape hold much more data than the immediate access memory can store?

6 Explain why computer cassettes are often cut down to 10 or 15 minutes of recording time.

7 A salesman in a computer shop says to a customer, "You can store programs and data on the cassette but you will soon be frustrated with that and will want to buy the floppy disc drive." The salesman of course is more interested in selling a £150 disc drive than a £25 cassette recorder.

   a What does the salesman mean when he says the customer will be 'frustrated' with the cassette record?
   b Why should the customer consider the uses to which he or she intends to put the computer before making a decision?
   c Would you consider the extra cost of the drive justified for:
   (i) a customer who intends to use the computer at home for playing computer games?
   (ii) a customer who intends to use the computer to help with administration in a small business?

8 The diagrams below show two ways in which a transaction file and a master file can be used to produce payslips in a payroll program.

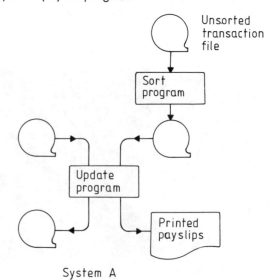

System A

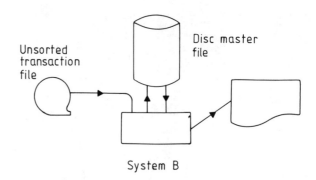

System B

   a Copy each diagram and complete the labelling on each.
   b Which of the systems uses a direct access file?
   c Why is a sort program essential in System A but not essential in System B?
   d Explain why a sort program might still be an advantage in System B.
   e Which system will use grandfather, father and son files?
   f Which system offers the better security against lost data?
   g How could the security of System B be improved?
   h If the company has 1000 employees, what kind of printer will be used to print the payslips and what kind of paper will it use?

9 If only a few of the records in a master file are changed at each update, this is referred to as a low 'hit rate'. Explain why it is more efficient to hold master files with a low hit rate on discs rather than tapes.

10 A second-hand car dealer uses a file of data on the cars he has for sale with the following fields in each record:

REF NUMBER	MAKE	MODEL	YEAR	COLOUR	PRICE

Explain in detail the file structures that could be used to create a computer data base for the dealer. Include in your answer details of at least one inverted file you would create and at least one pointer that you would add to each record. Explain the type of searches that your file structure will make possible.

11 The following extracts are from an article in *Computing*. The article is about a mass storage system called the M860 made by a company called Masstor.

Two major concerns tied to Masstor"s fastest moving products — the M860 MSS — prompt analysts to rate the stock as a high-risk long-term investment.

The M860 is a large capacity online cartridge mass storage system which directly competes against the much older (1974) and more expensive IBM 3850.

'Is IBM going to come out with a new generation product and leapfrog the M860?' wonders Gibson, 'and is Masstor going to be able to create a demand now for its product or are people going to perceive it as an old technology and wait for optical stores?'

Fortunately for Masstor, its users appear to be satisfied customers. James Mackintosh, director of information management at Hartford, says that his company will save $300,000 in 1984 by using the M860 because it reduces the need for more expensive disk drive storage ($70 a megabyte versus $8 on the M860) by putting less frequently accessed data on the M860.

At the same time Hartford can realise savings by transferring information now kept on off-line tape to the M860 and eliminate the labour intensive and time consuming process of manually searching for and loading reels of data from tape libraries.

Some observers speculate that the challenge to Masstor will come in optical storage. Storage Technology, in Louisville, Colorado, has introduced an optical disk storage system which provides faster data access time. The speed, however, comes at three to four times the cost of a megabyte of the M860 and data can be entered only once on the opitcal disks and not re-written.

a Give two reasons why analysts rate the shares of Masstore a *high-risk long-term investment*.
b Give three reasons why one customer is satisfied with the M860.
c Do you know of any current uses of *optical storage*?
d Why does the writer of the article feel the new mass storage device using optical techniques is not a threat to the M860?

12 Copy and complete the following sentences by inserting an appropriate word into each of the indicated positions.

a Magnetic tape may be used only for serial access to data; magnetic discs may be used for either _____ access or _____ access.
b The splitting into units of data stored on magnetic tape is known as _____.

(C 82)

13 Explain briefly why gaps are left between blocks of information on a magnetic tape.

14 **a** Explain the terms *serial (sequential)* access and *ramdom (direct)* access.
b Describe how information is organised on a magnetic-disc pack.
c State two factors which govern the number of characters that can be stored on a magnetic disc.
d What factors affect the access time of magnetic discs?
e How many surfaces would be used of a magnetic-disc pack that has six discs? Give reasons in your answer.

(O 82)

15 For which of the applications below is it **essential** to use random access files?
Payroll preparation; Theatre seat booking; Police files of car registration numbers; Batch processing of a series of students' programs.

(SWEB82)

16 All the estate agents in a large town use a central computer to store and retrieve data on houses they have for sale. A separate file, consisting of one record for each house, is held on disc for each agent. When a customer goes into the estate agent's shop, details of the type of house he requires are input. Immediately the computer produces a list of suitable houses for the customer.

a What is a record?
b Name a suitable input device and give an explanation for your choice.
c Write a paragraph describing the processing involved in finding a suitable house for a customer. You should consider:
  (i) **four** data items that are input.
  (ii) how the input data and file of data about houses are used.
  (iii) **four** details output for the customer.
d One estate agent decides to buy his own microcomputer system and use that instead of the central computer.
  State **one** benefit and **one** possible problem the agent is likely to find by using his own computer and give a reason for **each**.

(SEREB 81)

17 A regional gas board uses a computer to store a file of data relating to its customers' accounts. Customers can pay their bills at any showroom; each showroom is connected on-line to the gas board's computer to enable details of any transaction to be recorded and used to update the accounts file.

    (i) Outline the various measures which should be taken to prevent unauthorised access to the accounts file.

    (ii) It is possible for the accounts file to be held either as a serial file or as a direct access file. Describe in detail how the updating of the file is affected by the type of access which can take place.

    (iii) For a variety of reasons, it is possible that the data in the accounts file might become lost or corrupted. Describe safeguards which should be taken to ensure that the file can be re-created if the data is held

      a in a serial file on magnetic tape,

      b in a direct access file on disc.

(C 82)

18 a Compare magnetic **tape** storage with magnetic disc storage.

In your answer discuss methods of data access, speed of data retrieval, the amount of data stored and a typical application implemented on each storage medium with reference to the suitability of the chosen storage medium for each application.

b Name the different types of magnetic tape and magnetic disc storage media commonly used as backing store. Indicate which are used as backing storage for mainframe and which are used for microcomputers.

19 A magnetic tape unit has the following characteristics:

    (i) Packing density of 600 characters/cm.

    (ii) Tape speed of 500 cm/sec.

    (iii) An inter block gap of 2 cm.

A file of 3 000 000 characters is to be stored on this tape in blocks each holding 1500 characters.

a (i) Calculate the total number of blocks required.

    (ii) What length is each block in cm?

b How many inter block gaps will the file contain?

c What is the total length of tape (including inter block gaps) required to store this file?

d Calculate the total time required to write this file assuming that the tape has start and stop times of 0.002 secs and does not stop between blocks.

e What is meant by a frame on a magnetic tape?

(NI 82)

20 An examinations board holds records of 30 000 candidates in a computer data file as follows:

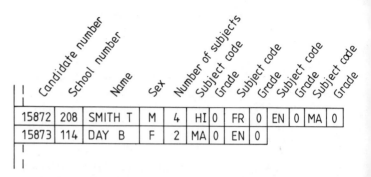

Candidate number	School number	Name	Sex	Number of subjects	Subject code	Grade	Subject code	Grade	Subject code	Grade	Subject code	Grade
15872	208	SMITH T	M	4	HI	0	FR	0	EN	0	MA	0
15873	114	DAY B	F	2	MA	0	EN	0				

The number of subjects entered by a candidate is given after the sex code. The subjects entered are shown by their codes (e.g. HI stands for history, FR for French etc.) and each code is followed by the final grade awarded to the candidate. Initially these are set to zero.

a If Henry Hutton is entered for six subjects, how many fields will be held in his record?

b Each candidate is given a candidate number of five digits. Reference to candidates is always by this number. Explain why it is easier to use the number in preference to the name

c A person sitting at a visual display unit needs information about candidate number 29347 and, by mistake, types 23947 on the keyboard. As a result, the wrong information appears on the screen. Explain how the use of check digits could overcome this problem.

d The data file is held in candiate number order. Give two reasons why this is to be preferred to alphabetical order of surname.

e Explain how it is possible for the computer to use this file to produce a list of candidates for a particular school with the girls listed first, followed by the boys and each list in alphabetical order.

(SREB 82)

11 Files and Data Processing Systems

Systems Flowcharts

We have already used systems flowcharts. In the last chapter one was used to show the updating of a tape master file. Systems flowcharts are used to describe complete data processing systems including the hardware devices and media used. Individual computer programs are simply shown as process boxes and no details of their operation are given. These are distinct from program flowcharts, which describe the exact sequence of oprations in a particular program.

There are two main conventions for the symbols used in systems flowcharts (see Figure 11.1).

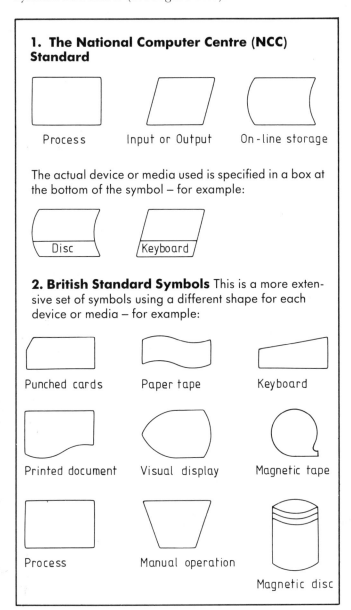

Figure 11.1 Conventions for symbols in flowcharts

Figure 11.2 below shows the updating of a tape master file from a disc transaction file drawn using the two systems. In each case pay slips are printed as the update takes place.

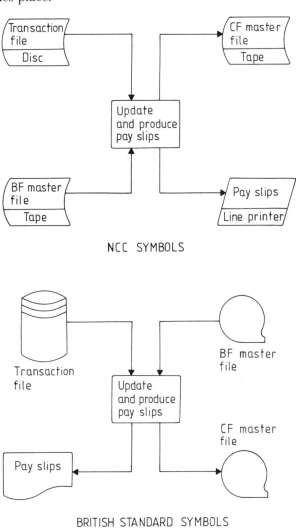

Figure 11.2 Updating a tape master file as shown in the two symbol conventions

Flowcharts using NCC symbols are usually written from left to right and flowcharts using British Standard symbols are usually drawn from top to bottom. The flowcharts in this book are drawn using the British Standard symbols. The NCC symbol example is included because it is the standard used by some examination boards. If the examination you are preparing for uses NCC symbols, you are strongly advised to convert some of the flowcharts in this book into these symbols to give you practice in their use.

The General Techniques Used to Process Files

Before we condier detailed applications, some basic file processing techniques must be explained. These techniques will be illustrated with references to tape files. All the techniques can also be applied to disc files.

Merging Files

Two or more files containing similar records will often need to be merged into a single master file. For example, files of immunisation records from several health clinics may be merged into one master immunisation file for a whole region. If we wish to merge two files they must first be sorted into order of the same key field. The system flowchart and the program flowchart for the merge routine are shown in Figures 11.3 and 11.4.

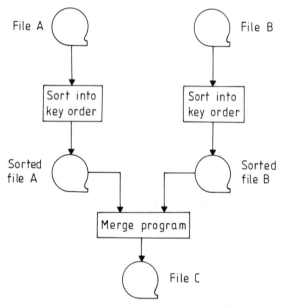

Figure 11.3 A system flowchart to show the merging of two tapes

Key (A) is the key of the record from tape A
Key (B) is the key of the record from tape B

Figure 11.4 A program flowchart to merge sorted tapes A and B into sorted tape C. The end of the tape will be detected if, when the next record is read, it is a special End of File marker rather than a normal record

Exercise 41

1 The diagram below shows the structure of the two files held on tapes A and B. Work through the merge program flowchart using these files as test data. Draw a diagram to show the structure of tape C which will be produced from tapes A and B.

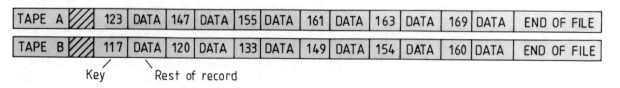

Key Rest of record

Sorting Files

To sort a file means to arrange the records in an ordered sequence using one of the fields as a key. Sorting files is a very common data processing activity and many different algorithms exist for the sorting program. If the file is small enough to be held in the CPU memory, an **internal sort** can be used. In this case the whole file will be read into the immediate access memory, sorted and written onto a new tape. With large files which cannot be held in the CPU memory an **external sort** must be used. To illustrate one type of external sort, the **classical four-tape sort**, we will consider the stages in sorting a tape

with the record keys shown in Figure 11.5. (For convenience only the key and not the whole record is shown on the tape.)

In practice of course the first tape might hold several thousand records and many more repetitions of Stage 2 will be needed. A full program flowchart for a four-tape sort is rather complicated. The program flowchart in Figure 11.6 shows just the first stage of the sort, dividing tape A between tapes C and D.

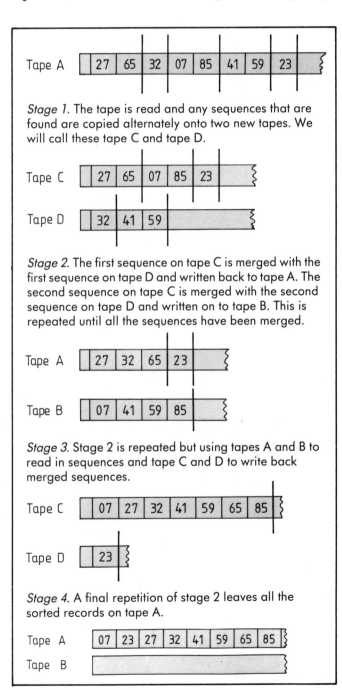

Stage 1. The tape is read and any sequences that are found are copied alternately onto two new tapes. We will call these tape C and tape D.

Stage 2. The first sequence on tape C is merged with the first sequence on tape D and written back to tape A. The second sequence on tape C is merged with the second sequence on tape D and written on to tape B. This is repeated until all the sequences have been merged.

Stage 3. Stage 2 is repeated but using tapes A and B to read in sequences and tape C and D to write back merged sequences.

Stage 4. A final repetition of stage 2 leaves all the sorted records on tape A.

Figure 11.5 Stages in sorting a file on tape

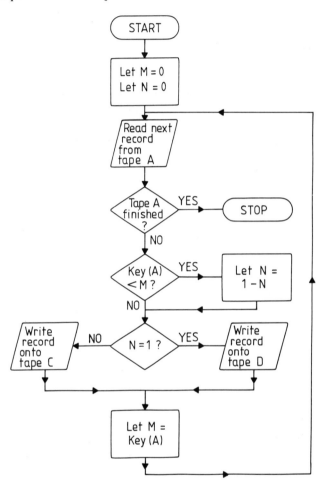

Key (A) is the key of the record read from tape A

M is set equal to the key of the last record read from tape A

N is a variable used to switch output between tapes C and D

Figure 11.6 Program flowchart for the first stage of a four-tape sort. The instruction Let N = 1 − N is designed to switch the value of N from 1 to 0 and then back to 1 again. This in turn switches the output tapes

We can illustrate one type of internal sort by using a **bubble sort** to sort a list of records with keys. We will use the following keys:

27   65   32   07   85   41   59   23

127

In a bubble sort, several passes are made through the list, comparing each key with the next in the list. If the first is larger, the records are interchanged. This is continued until a pass is made with no interchanges.

The position of each key at the end of each pass is shown below:

	Start	Pass 1	Pass 2	Pass 3	Pass 4	Pass 5	Pass 6	Pass 7
	27	27	27	07	07	07	07	07
	65	32	07	27	27	27	23	23
	32	07	32	32	32	23	27	27
	07	65	41	41	23	32	32	32
	85	41	59	23	41	41	41	41
	41	59	23	59	59	59	59	59
	59	23	65	65	65	65	65	65
	23	85	85	85	85	85	85	85
Number of swaps		5	4	2	1	1	1	0

The program flowchart in Figure 11.7 shows the operation of a bubble sort. Although the flowchart concentrates on the interchanging of keys, remember that in practice the **whole** records must be interchanged.

Exercise 42

1 Draw diagrams to show the stages in a four-tape sort of a file of records with the following keys:

015   031   012   029   095   004   010   045

2 Draw a diagram to show the position of each key at the end of each pass in a bubble sort of a file of records with the following keys:

015   031   012   029   095   004   010   045

Updating Files

Updating a file involves three basic operations:

1 Amending an existing record.
2 Deleting an existing record.
3 Adding a new record

We will illustrate these operations by looking at the updating of a **brought forward master** file from a **transaction** file. We will assume that the master file and the transaction file are sorted into the same key order sequence. The system flowchart for the updating routine is shown in Figure 11.8.

1 Amending an existing record is achieved by reading in the record from the brought forward master file and the details of any necessary changes from the transaction file. After the changes have been made, the

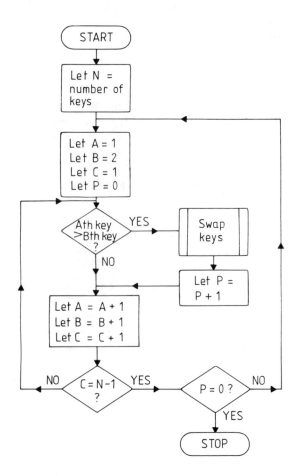

A is the first of the keys being compared
B is the second of the keys being compared
C is a counter to check the position in the list
P is a counter to check the number of swaps made in each pass

Figure 11.7   Program flowchart for a bubble sort. The subroutine Swap Keys will require the following steps:
Let X = Ath Key
Let Ath Key = Bth Key
Let Bth Key = X
where X is used as a dummy variable to store the value of the Ath Key while it is overwritten by the value of the Bth Key. The program can be made more efficient by observing that at the end of each pass the largest numbers accumulate at the end of the list. Thus the value of N can be reduced by one before each new pass

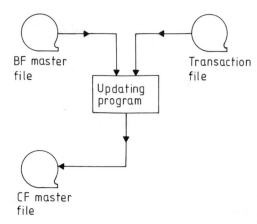

Figure 11.8   A system flowchart for an updating routine

128

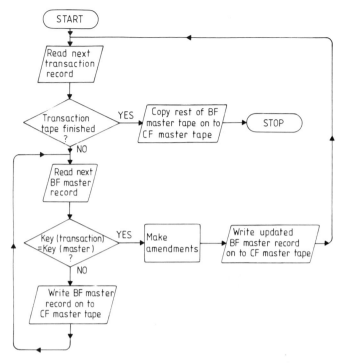

Figure 11.9 A flowchart for amending a record

updated record is written out on to the carried forward master tape. The program flowchart in Figure 11.9 shows the stages in amending a record.

2 Deleting an existing record is achieved by simply not copying it on to the carried forward master tape. The program flowchart in Figure 11.10 shows the stages in deleting a record.

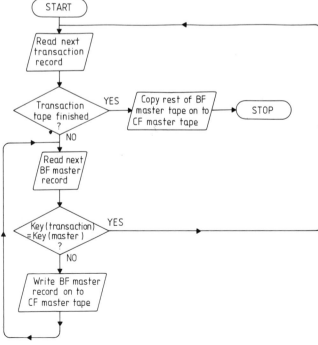

Figure 11.10 A flowchart for deleting a record

3 Adding new records is achieved by merging the new records from the transaction tape with the records in the brought forward master tape. The merged sequence of records is written on to the carried forward master tape. A flowchart to merge two sorted tapes was shown earlier (Figure 11.3, p. 126).

All three basic updating operations can be carried out at the same time if an operation code is added to each record in the transaction file. This will tell the computer if a particular transaction record is an amendment, an insertion or a deletion. Figure 11.11 shows a program flowchart that uses a code and carries out all the basic updating operations.

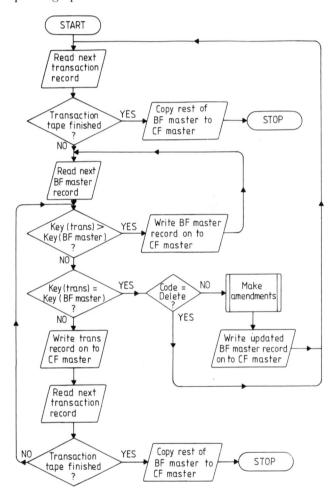

Figure 11.11 A flowchart for updating a master tape from a transaction tape

Exercise 43

The tables below show some of the records in a payroll master file and a transaction tape which is used to update it. Draw a diagram to show the contents of the master file after the updating has taken place.

Master File

Payroll Number	Name	Tax Code	Rate of Pay	Pay to Date	Tax to Date
3454	S SMITH	220	3.00	5652	1256
1234	T JONES	250	3.85	5435	1131
3355	M PATEL	290	3.85	5298	1009
2189	G SINGH	260	3.64	5372	1092
2167	G BROWN	270	3.50	5249	1035
1573	J BLOGGS	210	3.50	5700	1300
9438	D QUAN	300	3.50	5375	1013
0649	I NEWTON	280	3.85	5097	969

Transaction File

Payroll Number	Transaction Code	Name	Tax Code	Rate of Pay	Pay to Date	Tax to Date
1234	AMEND			3.95		
2189	DELETE					
2178	ADD	C WILLIAMS	250	3.50	0000	0000
2167	AMEND	D BROWN	280		5269	

Detailed Applications

In the previous sections we have looked at the basic techniques needed to process data stored in computer files. We shall now turn our attention to some detailed applications of these techniques.

A Payroll Application

We shall start by looking at the problem of calculating the wages of an hourly paid worker. We will call our worker Joseph Bloggs and imagine he works in a car factory. Hourly paid workers like Joe are paid for each hour that they work. Usually they earn a fixed rate for the first 40 hours they work each week and then a higher 'overtime' rate for any hours worked after that. This means that to calculate wages the car company needs a detailed record of the hours that each employee works. To create this record, each worker 'clocks on' each morning as he arrives for work and 'clocks off' each evening when he goes home. Clocking on or off involves placing a small cardboard 'clock card' in to a time clock which combines a clock with a small printer or cardpunch. As each worker places his clock card in the machine, it prints or punches the time on the card. These cards capture the data needed to pay the workers and are the source documents of the payroll system. (See Figure 11.12.)

Figure 11.12 Data capture for the payroll system

By Friday, Joe's card looks like this:

Name J. Bloggs				
Number 1573		Week 34		Basic £3·50
Day \ Time	In	Out		
MON.	0801	1605		
TUES.	0758	1601		
WED.	0802	1801		
THURS.	0755	1703		
FRI.	0800	1804		

Joe works an 8-hour day from 8 o'clock until 4 o'clock. He has two 30 minute breaks, but does not lose any time for these. If he works more than 8 hours, he starts to earn his 'overtime' rate, which is one and a half times his basic rate. The calculation below shows how Joe's wages are decided from the information on his clock card.

	Hours basic	Hours overtime
Mon.	8	0
Tues	8	0
Wed.	8	2
Thurs.	8	1
Fri.	8	2
Total	40	5

Total hours = $40 + (5 \times 1\frac{1}{2}) = 47\frac{1}{2}$

Total pay = $47\frac{1}{2} \times £3.50 = £166.25$

Joe has already earned £5700 this year, so his total earnings are now £5866.25.

The next stage is to decide how much tax Joe must pay this week. Income tax is collected by the Government from all workers. The Government department responsible for collecting income tax is called the **Inland Revenue**. Most people pay tax using a system called Pay As You Earn (PAYE). In this system, tax is deducted by their employers from their pay each week. The amount deducted will vary from person to person because it depends on the amount earned and the tax allowances that can be claimed.

A tax allowance is the amount of tax free money that a person is allowed to earn each year. The Inland Revenue gives everybody a **tax code** calculated from the tax allowances they are allowed to claim. This code is simply the total allowance with the last digit cut off. Thus a person who can claim tax allowances of £2107 a year will have a tax code of 210. The Inland Revenue also provide all employers with a set of **tax tables** to help them calculate how much tax they should deduct from wages each week. An extract from a typical table is shown below:

Tax Code	Earnings so far (£)		
	5800	5900	6000
200	1340	1370	1400
210	1320	1350	1380
220	1300	1330	1360

Joe has earned £5866.25 this year, or £5900 to the nearest £100. His tax code is 210. The tax tables for this week show that Joe should have paid £1350 in tax so far this year. The company records show that up to last week Joe had already paid £1300 in tax. His tax this week is thus £1350 − £1300 = £50. We have now completed the calculation of Joe's wages. His final take home pay will be £166.25 − £50 = £116.25. The company where Joe works employs 800 hourly paid workers. Fifteen years ago they decided to start using a computer for all the payroll calculations. To help you understand why they made this decision, attempt the following exercise which requires you to become a wages clerk manually calculating weekly wages.

Exercise 44

As one of the company wage clerks, you are given the source documents shown below.

Name	S Smith		
Number	3454	Week 34	Basic £3.00

Time \ Day	In	Out	
MON.	0758	1602	8
TUES.	0803	1805	10
WED.	0755	1801	10
THURS.	0759	1800	10
FRI.	0800	1801	09

47

Name	J JONES		
Number	1234	Week 34	Basic £3.85

Time \ Day	In	Out	
MON.	0755	1804	10
TUES.	0801	1801	9
WED.	0756	1800	10
THURS.	0759	1601	8
FRI.	0800	1600	8

45

Name	G. Singh		
Number	2189	Week 34	Basic £3.64

Time \ Day	In	Out	
MON.	0801	1603	8
TUES.	0749	1803	10
WED.	0800	1800	9
THURS.	0801	1701	9
FRI.	0802	1601	8

44

In your records that you have brought forward from last week you have the following details.

Payroll Number	Name	Tax Code	Rate of Pay	Pay to Date	Tax to Date
3454	S SMITH	220	3.00	5652	1256
1234	T JONES	250	3.85	5435	1131
2189	G SINGH	260	3.64	5372	1092

An extract from your tax tables for this week is shown below.

Tax Code	Earnings so far (£)				
	5500	5600	5700	5800	5900
220	1210	1240	1270	1300	1330
230	1190	1220	1250	1280	1310
240	1170	1200	1230	1260	1290
250	1150	1180	1210	1240	1270
260	1130	1160	1190	1220	1250

1 Calculate the take home pay for each of the three workers.
2 Write out in full the new records that you will carry forward to next week.

As you attempted the previous exercise, you will have realised that wage calculations are repetitive, time-consuming, prone to errors and rather boring. They are thus ideal tasks to hand over to a computer! In fact, the introduction of a payroll system is in many companies their first experience with computers.

When in the early seventies Joe's company first computerised their payroll they purchased what was then considered a medium-sized mainframe computer. The configuration of this system is shown below:

CPU	48 K bytes of immediate access store.
Input	1 card reader (800 characters per second)
	1 operator's console.

<table>
<tbody>
<tr><td>*Output*</td><td>1 line printer (600 lines per minute)</td></tr>
<tr><td>*Storage*</td><td>4 magnetic tape units
2 exchangeable disc drives.</td></tr>
<tr><td>*Data preparation*</td><td>12 keypunches for punched cards.
12 card verifiers.</td></tr>
</tbody>
</table>

Over the years, computing equipment has become cheaper and much more powerful. Its use has spread throughout Joe's company. The payroll is now considered to be a small, routine application. The configuration of the present system is:

<table>
<tbody>
<tr><td>*CPU*</td><td>4096 K bytes of immediate access store.</td></tr>
<tr><td>*Input/output*</td><td>48 VDU terminals.</td></tr>
<tr><td>*Output*</td><td>2 line printers (600 lines per minute)</td></tr>
<tr><td>*Storage*</td><td>4 magnetic tape units
8 exchangeable disc drives.
16 fixed disc drives.</td></tr>
<tr><td>*Data preparation*</td><td>8 microcomputer controlled key-to-floppy-disc stations with facilities to pool output on to magnetic tapes or discs.</td></tr>
</tbody>
</table>

The stages in using the computer system to process the payroll are as follows:

1 The data is captured on the clock cards.
2 The data is entered using the key-to-floppy-disc system. As it is entered, the microcomputers controlling the stations carry out a program of validation checks. Any errors are reported immediately to the operators.
3 A second typing is used to verify that the data has been correctly copied. Any errors are overwritten on the floppy discs.
4 The data for all the employees is pooled on to one magnetic tape.
5 This tape is sorted in to payroll reference number order. This sorted tape is the **transaction tape** for the payroll program. Each record on this tape contains the following fields:

PAYROLL NUMBER	NAME	TIME 1	TIME 2	TIME 3	TIME 4	//	TIME 9	TIME 10

The ten times are the clocking on and clocking off times for each day.

6 The transaction tape is read in by the payroll program together with a brought forward master tape. Each record on the master tape contains the following fields:

PAYROLL NUMBER	NAME	TAX CODE	RATE OF PAY	PAY TO DATE	TAX TO DATE

7 The payroll program uses the data on the tapes to calculate and print a wage slip for each worker. To do this it needs access to tax tables. These are held on a disc pack as a random file.

8 The records in the master tape are updated as they are processed and written out on to a carried forward master tape. This tape will become the brought forward master tape for next week.
9 The computer prints out an error list of all the records it is unable to process. There should be very few of these because the input data has been validated and verified.
10 The computer prints out an analysis of the coins and notes that will be needed from the bank to make up the wage packets.
11 The program prints out various statistics for the company management. For example, the total cost of the wages and the total number of hours of overtime worked.

A system flowchart for the payroll application is shown in Figure 11.13.

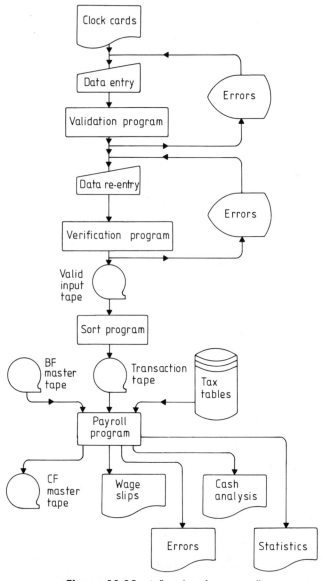

Figure 11.13 A flowchart for a payroll

Exercise 45

1 The sketch below shows part of the old manual payroll system.

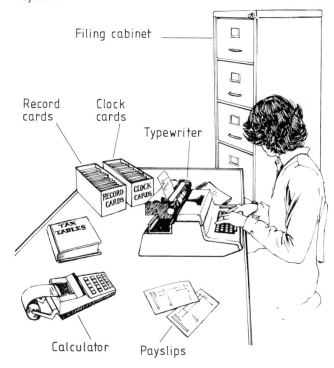

Filing cabinet

Record cards

Clock cards

Typewriter

RECORD CARDS

CLOCK CARDS

TAX TABLES

Calculator

Payslips

a Imagine that you are one of the wages clerks in the old system. Write one or two paragraphs explaining the job that you do and your feelings about your job.

b What advantages do you think the company gained by introducing a computer payroll system?

c How do you think a wages clerk felt about the new computer system;
   (i) if he or she were offered a job working with the computer?
   (ii) if he or she were made redundant?

d Which parts of the computer system correspond to the following parts of the manual system:
   (i) the typewriter
   (ii) the calculator
   (iii) the record cards
   (iv) the filing cabinet
   (v) the book of tax tables
   (vi) the clerk.

2 The company's computer system has grown considerably over the last 15–20 years. At first the payroll program was the major application. Now it is considered a small routine computer task. Compare the company's first computer system with the one it uses at the present time. Make a list of the main changes in equipment and capacities that have taken place.

3 a Why is a tape file a suitable choice for the master files used in the payroll system?

b Why is a disc file a suitable choice for the tax tables?

c The payroll program is run overnight by the computer operators, while most of the factory is closed. Why do you think this is done?

4 Design a pre-printed form which could be used to print the wage-slips. Indicate clearly on your design which parts will be pre-printed and which parts will be printed by the line printer.

5 Each week new clockcards are prepared by the factory foremen and placed in the card racks. Billy West left the factory two weeks ago but, by mistake, his foreman placed a new card for him in the rack. For a joke, his friends punched his card each day.
Explain
a why Billy West's card will pass the validation and verification checks
b why a wage slip will not be printed for Billy West
c what will be produced as a result of this invalid entry
d how the computer payroll program could be extended to reduce the foremen's work and to prevent this kind of error in future.

6 Write computer programs in any high-level language to simulate the payroll system. These could easily form the basis for a piece of computer studies coursework. If you have access to a computer with disc-based backing store, you can break the simulation down into several stages.

a Write a program to create a master file of employee records. To help you, an example of these records is given below. Include as many validation checks as possible in your program.

b Write a program to amend, delete and add entries in your master file. Include as many validation checks as possible in your program.

c Write a program to enter, validate, verify and sort clockcard data into a transaction file.

d Write the payroll program itself. This will read in the transaction file and master file and produce all the required output and a new master tape. This program will need access to a tax table. This could be created as a separate file on the disc or held as data within the program. An extract that will allow you to process the data supplied is given below.

Payroll Number	Name	Tax Code	Rate of Pay	Pay to Date	Tax to Date
3454	S SMITH	220	3.00	5652	1256
1234	T JONES	250	3.85	5435	1131
3355	M PATEL	290	3.85	5298	1009
2189	G SINGH	260	3.64	5372	1092
2167	G BROWN	270	3.50	5249	1035
1573	J BLOGGS	210	3.50	5700	1300
9438	D QUAN	300	3.50	5375	1013
0649	I NEWTON	280	3.85	5097	969

Tax Code	Earnings so far (£)									
	5000	5100	5200	5300	5400	5500	5600	5700	5800	5900
200	1100	1130	1160	1190	1220	1250	1280	1310	1340	1370
210	1080	1110	1140	1170	1200	1230	1260	1290	1320	1350
220	1060	1090	1120	1150	1180	1210	1240	1270	1300	1330
230	1040	1070	1100	1130	1160	1190	1220	1250	1280	1310
240	1020	1050	1080	1110	1140	1170	1200	1230	1260	1290
250	1000	1030	1060	1090	1120	1150	1180	1210	1240	1270
260	980	1010	1040	1070	1100	1130	1160	1190	1220	1250
270	960	990	1020	1050	1080	1110	1140	1170	1200	1230
280	940	970	1000	1030	1060	1090	1120	1150	1180	1210
290	920	950	980	1010	1040	1070	1100	1130	1160	1190
300	900	930	960	990	1020	1050	1080	1110	1140	1170

Airline Ticket Booking Systems

Airline ticket booking systems were first computerised during the late 1960s. We will look first at how the present computer systems operate and then consider their advantages over the manual systems they replaced.

When anybody wishes to travel by plane, they normally go to their local travel agent and buy their tickets in advance. Today, the travel agent will probably have a remote VDU terminal linked by modem and telephone line to the main airline computers. Small agents without terminals can telephone sales staff at the airline booking office who process the inquiry using their own terminals. Because it is essential that the booking system is always in operation, an expensive security precaution is taken. All the main units of the computer are duplicated and, in effect, two computers work in parallel. If one computer breaks down or needs regular maintenance, the other computer can take over. To coordinate the two main computers, a **front-end processor** is used. This is a third computer whose task is to supervise and control all the systems communications. Figure 11.14 shows an outline of the computer hardware used in the system.

The main computers used in the system will be large powerful mainframes. The communications controller and front-end processor must be capable of very fast communications with several hundred terminals. The backing store will need a large number of very fast direct access discs.

To understand how the booking system works, we will follow the progress of our friend Joseph Bloggs as he buys a ticket for a flight to Paris. Joe goes to his local travel agents who have a terminal link to the main airline computers. He explains that he wishes to fly to Orly Airport in Paris from Gatwick Airport near London on 16 July. The travel agent uses the VDU terminal to make a flight enquiry to discover which flights are available. She enters the details of Joe's request and the computer searches its database of flights and replies. Figure 11.15 below shows the VDU display. The information typed by the travel agent has been underlined. All the other information was added by the computer.

The travel agent explains the flight times to Joe, who decides to book a seat on the 1030 flight. The travel agent uses the VDU to check that some seats are available on this flight. The VDU display is shown in Figure 11.16. As before, the information entered by the travel agent has been underlined.

Having confirmed that a seat is available, the agent uses the VDU to make the booking. The VDU display is shown in Fig. 11.17. As before, the information entered by the travel agent has been underlined.

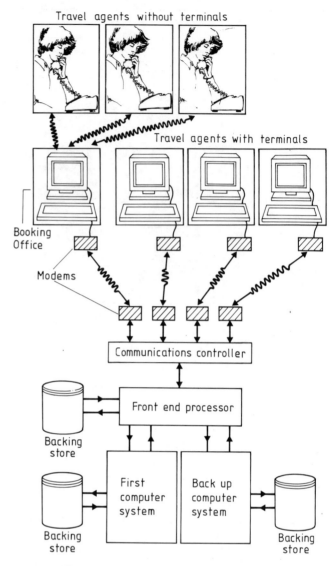

Figure 11.14 An airline ticket booking system

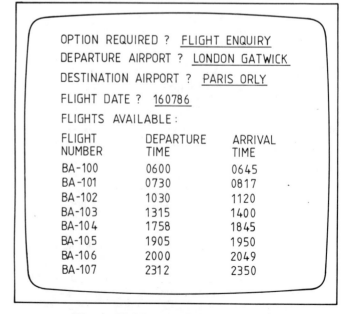

OPTION REQUIRED ?	FLIGHT ENQUIRY	
DEPARTURE AIRPORT ?	LONDON GATWICK	
DESTINATION AIRPORT ?	PARIS ORLY	
FLIGHT DATE ?	160786	

FLIGHTS AVAILABLE :

FLIGHT NUMBER	DEPARTURE TIME	ARRIVAL TIME
BA-100	0600	0645
BA-101	0730	0817
BA-102	1030	1120
BA-103	1315	1400
BA-104	1758	1845
BA-105	1905	1950
BA-106	2000	2049
BA-107	2312	2350

Figure 11.15 What flights are available?

```
OPTION REQUIRED ?  SEAT ENQUIRY
FLIGHT NUMBER ?  BA-102
FLIGHT DATE ?  160786
NUMBER OF SEATS REQUIRED ?  1
TRAVEL CLASS ?  ECONOMY
24 SEATS ARE AVAILABLE ON THIS FLIGHT
```

Figure 11.16 Are any seats available?

```
OPTION REQUIRED ?  SEAT BOOKING
FLIGHT NUMBER ?  BA-102
FLIGHT DATE ?  160786
NUMBER OF SEATS REQUIRED ?  1
TRAVEL CLASS ?  ECONOMY
PASSENGER NAME ?  JOSEPH BLOGGS
BOOKING CONFIRMED
ISSUE TICKET  BA65217-86
COST OF TICKET IS £48
```

Figure 11.17 Making a booking

```
FLIGHT NUMBER
DEPARTURE AIRPORT
DESTINATION AIRPORT
DEPARTURE DATE
DEPARTURE TIME
ARRIVAL TIME
ECONOMY SEATS AVAILABLE
FIRST CLASS SEATS AVAILABLE
  SEAT NUMBER
  CLASS
  PASSENGER NAME
  SEAT NUMBER
  CLASS
  PASSENGER NAME
  . . . . . . . . . . . . . .
  . . . . . . . . . . . . . .
  . . . . . . . . . . . . . .
  SEAT NUMBER
  CLASS
  PASSENGER NAME
```

Three fields for every booked seat

Figure 11.18 The structure of a flight record

The travel agent now writes in all Joe's flight details on a blank ticket. Joe pays for the ticket, and the transaction is complete.

If the first flight Joe asked for had been fully booked, the travel agent would have used the VDU to find an alternative flight. It is also possible to cancel seat bookings if passengers are unable to travel or change their minds.

Now that we understand how the booking system works, we will look at the files used in its operation. The records are held in a large and complex database. Each flight record has the basic structure shown in Figure 11.18.

The computer programs used to interrogate and update the database have four main modules:

1 The flight enquiry program. This is used to search all the records and produce a list of all the flights on any given day between any two given airports.

2 The seat enquiry program. This is used to retrieve the record for one particular flight and to check on the number of seats available.

3 The seat booking program. This is used to retrieve and update the record for one particular flight. It reduces the number of seats available and adds three extra fields for each seat booked.

4 The seat cancellation program. This is used to retrieve and update the record for one particular flight. It increases the number of seats available and deletes three fields for each seat booking cancelled.

The database is kept continually up to date. Every booking or cancellation results in an immediate update of the records. It is therefore impossible for any seat to be booked by two different travel agents. In the same way, seats are immediately made available for re-booking when they are cancelled. All the data must therefore be held on discs. This is the only storage medium that can provide the direct access and dynamic updating necessary in this application.

Only a simple outline of a ticket booking system has been given, and we must be careful not to make this application seem too simple. A typical airline computer will need to store details of over half a million routes, flights and fare structures. It may handle millions of enquiries each year from hundreds of terminals located all over the world. Many thousands of ticket bookings and cancellations may be made every day. As well as the operations we have looked at, many other facilities will be provided. These include: printing passenger lists both before and after check-in, checking baggage weights, allocating crew, providing data for flight planning, and controlling resources from aviation fuel to in-flight food.

Before computer systems were introduced a typical manual system made bookings at one central office and a few other offices spread around the country. In the central office a large wall board displayed the flight details for each of the company's planes. A green marker was hung at the top of the flight details if seats were still availalbe. This was replaced with a red marker when the flight was full. When an enquiry was received, the sales staff dealing with it looked at the board to see if seats were available. If they were, a booking was made. Written details of the booking were handed to a supervisor who added the details to passenger lists kept for all the flights. When a flight was nearly full, the supervisor changed the green marker to a red one to stop further bookings. The supervisor had to use personal judgment and experience to know exactly when to close a flight because bookings were coming in all the time, some by telegraph from other offices. If flight cancellations were received, all the details in the records had to be changed manually.

This manual system worked quite well in the early days of international airlines when there were relatively few flights. As air traffic grew, it became increasingly inaccurate and inefficient. Flights were often closed too early and potential bookings were lost. Sometimes passengers arrived at the airport to find that the flight had been overbooked and they did not have a seat. Before making a booking, travel agents had to consult thick volumes of flight, route and price details. Often the travel agent was responsible for calculating the cost of the fare. All these problems led to the world's airlines being the first companies to install large commercial databases. These computer systems are cheaper, because fewer staff are employed, and far faster and more efficient. They have contributed to the steady growth of air traffic. It would be impossible for airlines to change back to manual booking systems and still maintain their present level of operations.

Exercise 46

1 For each of the detailed applications looked at in this chapter, answer the following questions. A clear diagram will often improve your answers.

  a What are the tasks performed by the computer system?
  b What input data is collected?
  c How is this input data captured?
  d What data is held in secondary storage and how is it structured?
  e What data processing takes place?
  f What output data is produced?
  g What computer hardware is used?
  h What advantages does the system offer when compared with a manual system?

2 Explain in detail each of the following phrases. A clear diagram will often improve your answers.

  a remote VDU terminal
  b linked by modem and telephone line
  c front-end processor
  d interrogate and update the database
  e direct access and dynamic updating

3 The system flowchart shown below can be applied to either the flight enquiry program or the seat enquiry program.

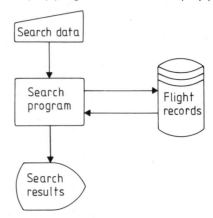

For *each* of these programs explain:

  a Which fields in the flight records are specified in the search data.
  b Which fields in the flight records are used to produce the results of the search.

4 Shown below is the record for Joe's flight before he makes his booking. Copy this diagram.

| BA-102 |
| LONDON GATWICK |
| PARIS ORLY |
| 160786 |
| 1030 |
| 1120 |
| 24 |
| 15 |
| 001 |
| JANE SMITH |
| ECONOMY |
| 002 |
| JOHN SMITH |
| ECONOMY |
| 027 |
| ROHIMA KHAN |
| FIRST CLASS |
| .... |
| .... |
| ...... |
| 098 |
| BILLY WEST |
| ECONOMY |

a Draw a second diagram to show the flight record after Joe has made his booking. Assume he is given seat 085.

b Draw a third diagram to show the flight record after John Smith and Jane Smith cancel their bookings.

5 Design a blank ticket form to be used by travel agents to write in the flight details.

6 Explain why disc files are essential in the airline ticket booking application. Do you know of any current research project which may change the secondary storage used in this application?

7 Southern Car Ferries operate a car and passenger ferry service between two ports in England and three ports in France. With five sailings per day on each route in each direction, there is a total of 60 sailings per day. The company uses a batch processing computer to record all the bookings. Each morning a listing is produced of all the bookings taken to date. As new bookings are taken during the day at the Head Office, they are written onto the listing so that no over-booking takes place. Bookings are also entered on special coding sheets and, overnight, they are recorded on the computer file by an updating program.

a In what ways in the present system wasteful of time and paper?

b Where are errors likely to occur in the present system? A new system is to be introduced which will enable ten regional offices to use visual display units connected directly to a multi-access computer in the Head Office. Bookings can be made from any office via these VDUs.

c In what ways might the customers get better service?

d How can the errors you described in (**b**) above be overcome?

e Explain why the new system must operate in real time.

(SREB 82)

Exercise 47

1 Copy and complete the following passages.

a When we wish to combine the records in two files, the files are _____. Before the files are _____ they must be _____.

b Files which are two big to hold in the _____ are sorted using an external sort. One example of an external sort is the _____. Small _____ are sorted using an internal sort. One example of an internal sort is a _____.

c There are three basic operations carried out when a file is updated. These are: _____, _____ and _____.

2 The three items of information needed by the computer to find data on a magnetic disc pack are:

a _____
b _____
c _____

(SREB 82)

3 Explain the connections between the terms record, field and file, using for an example information about the subjects taken by children in a particular class.

(SUJB 82)

4 The five terms (i) *file*, (ii) *record*, (iii) *field*, (iv) *item* and (v) *key-field* are all used in data processing.

Name one commercial application of a computer and explain each of the five terms above by giving an example of its use in that application.

(O 81)

5 With the aid of diagrams explain how the following numbers would be sorted into ascending order using a systematic method such as a Bubble Sort.

87   73   5   12

6 Magnetic discs and magnetic tapes are two common methods of storing a lot of data.

a Explain, with the aid of diagrams if necessary, how data is actually stored on discs and on tapes, referring to tracks, blocks and sectors where appropriate.

b Describe the type of access possible with both magnetic disc and magnetic tape.

c State a typical application for each of the following bearing in mind the type of access possible as answered in (b).
(i) magnetic disc
(ii) magnetic tape

(EMREB 82)

7 A particular bank has a file of customers which includes the customer's name, the customer's number, the current account balance and the deposit account balance. Draw a flowchart which includes the following:

a Data is inputted in the form
Customer name, customer number, amount.

b The file is searched for the name and a message printed if the name is not found.

c If the name is found the number inputted is checked with the number on file and if they are different a message is printed
If the amount is positive it is to be added to the current account.
If the amount is negative it is to be subtracted from the current account.

d If an amount is paid in and the current account balance then exceeds £100, the amount in excess of £100 is transferred to the deposit account.

e If an amount is to be paid out and the current account balance is insufficient a message is printed.

(SUJB 82)

8

a Using as an example the sequence of numbers given below, describe an algorithm for sorting a sequence of numbers into ascending order.

    22
    17
    38
    44
    35
    11

b Most computers have utility programs for sorting. Many of these programs allow a variety of sort algorithms to be selected. Explain why this is so.

c Describe, by means of flowchart(s) or otherwise, an algorithm for merging all the records from two sorted files, A and B, into a single file, C, having its records in ascending order of record key. You may assume that
  (i) every record has a numeric key,
  (ii) the keys of the records in file A and file B are all different,
  (iii) file A and file B are each terminated by a dummy record having the key 999.

d Describe briefly a situation in which it might be necessary to merge the records from two files.

                                  (C 82)

9 The flowchart on the opposite column is not finished. It is meant to show an algorithm for merging two files, FILE 1 and FILE 2. The merged output is to be written to FILE 3. The input files contain only numbers and they have been sorted into ascending order. At the end of each file there is a special number called END OF FILE MARKER.

Re-draw the flowchart in your answer book and complete it by using some of the following sentences to put in the boxes. Be sure to write YES and NO on the exits from the decision boxes.

WRITE END OF FILE MARKER TO FILE 1.

WRITE END OF FILE MARKER TO FILE 2.

WRITE END OF FILE MARKER TO FILE 3.

INPUT A FROM FILE 1.

INPUT B FROM FILE 2.

INPUT B FROM FILE 2.

STOP.

WRITE A TO FILE 3.

WRITE B TO FILE 3.

WRITE B TO FILE 3.

END OF FILE 1.

END OF FILE 1.

END OF FILE 2.

END OF FILE 2.

A = B.

A = B.

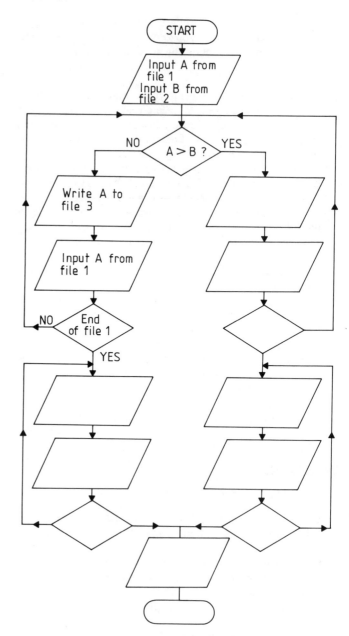

10 This is a segment from a file of athletics officials created by a file management package.

Name	Area	Duty	Grade	Experience
Tanner J L	South	Track	Senior	
Tawton H G	Wales	Time-keeper	One	
Taylor W J	Mids	Track	One	
Thomas F	South	Track	Senior	Photo finish
Thomas G D	South	Field	One	Datum
Thomas J E	North	Track	One	
Thomas V R	Wales	Field	Senior	Datum
Thornhill J J	North	Time-keeper	Chief	Photo finish
Tomkins A A	Mids	Time-keeper	Chief	Photo finish
Tomlin R	East	Field	One	Datum

a How many records are shown in this file segment?
b How many fields in each record?
c Briefly describe **three** file updating facilities you would expect this package to have.
d Explain, using the file segment shown, how a list of Chief or Senior officials from the North with photo finish experience could be produced.

(AEB 85)

11 The following segment of a system (data) flowchart shows the flow of data through a section of a payroll system.

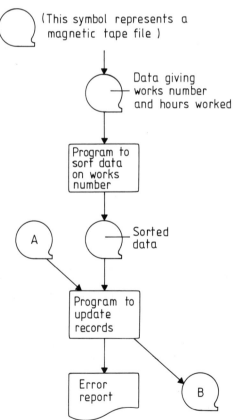

(This symbol represents a magnetic tape file)

Data giving works number and hours worked

Program to sort data on works number

Sorted data

A

Program to update records

Error report

B

Explain the function of tapes A and B in such a system.

12 The head teacher of a large school wishes to set up a computer system. It is intended the system will be used for the following tasks.

(i) To print labels for sending letters to the parent or guardian of each pupil in the school; each label will contain the name and address of the parent or guardian.

(ii) To print the name of every pupil who is due to have a medical inspection. For this purpose the head teacher might wish to identify all pupils aged between 15 years and 3 months and 15 years 9 months.

(iii) To print a list of all the girls (boys) in a given class. Classes are identified by a number followed by a letter, e.g. 5A or 2T.

a The system will require a file of data to be created. Describe the fields which must be included in this file to enable the above tasks to be performed and give examples of **two** typical records from the file.
b The data required for the file will be obtained using specially prepared forms which will be completed by the pupils. The data will be input to the computer by means of punched cards. Describe in detail a method of ensuring that the copying of the data from the forms to the cards is accurately done.
c Even if the copying of the data from the forms to the punched cards is accurately done, it is possible that the data will, nevertheless, be inaccurate. Give a reason why the data could be in error.
d (i) For the various fields in the file, describe validation checks which could be carried out on the data.
(ii) Give an example of an error which may remain even after the validation checks have been carried out.

(NWREB 82)

13 Describe a computerised system for reserving airline seats. Include in your answer a description of inputs, outputs, processing and files.

Suggest **six** benefits the system brings, **three** to the airline and **three** to the user.

12 Computer Software

Machine Code and Assembly Languages

When computers are designed, they are provided with a set of control instructions called a **machine code**. A machine code is a set of binary numbers, each of which represents one instruction that the computer can obey. For example, a very simple machine code is shown in Table 12.1.

Table 12.1 A Simple Machine Code

Code	Meaning
0000	Stop
0001	Load the accumulator from a memory location
0010	Store the contents of the accumulator in a memory location
0011	Add the contents of a memory location to the accumulator
0100	Subtract the contents of a memory location from the accumulator
0101	Jump to the instruction in a memory location
0110	Jump to the instruction in a memory location if the contents of the accumulator are negative
0111	Jump to the instruction in a memory location if the contents of the accumulator are zero
1000	Input a number and store it in a memory location
1001	Output a number from a memory location

In this particular system, each 4-bit instruction is followed by the 4-bit address of a memory location. Figure 12.1 shows how a complete instruction is interpreted.

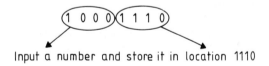

Input a number and store it in location 1110

Figure 12.1 A complete instruction in machine code

Very early computers could only be programmed by using these machine codes directly. This created problems because it is difficult to accurately write down, compare or remember binary numbers. Even a short binary code program, such as the one shown in Table 12.2, is almost meaningless to the human eye.

Table 12.2 A short binary code program

Location	Instruction
0000	10001110
0001	10001111
0010	00011110
0011	01001111
0100	01101000
0101	10011110
0110	10011111
0111	01011010
1000	10011111
1001	10011110
1010	00000000

Decimal (base 10), octal (base 8) or hexadecimal (base 16) numbers are easier to work with than binary numbers. Computers can be provided with keypads which allow a user to enter machine code programs in decimal, octal or hexadecimal numbers. Hexadecimal or octal are usually preferred because they are easier to convert to and from binary. A hexadecimal keypad would allow us to enter our binary program in the way shown in Table 12.3.

Table 12.3 A hexadecimal code program

Location	Instruction
0	8E
1	8F
2	1E
3	4F
4	68
5	9E
6	9F
7	5A
8	9F
9	9E
A	00

A trained programmer can write programs and spot and correct mistakes much more easily in hexadecimal than in binary. However, to anybody who has not learnt the hex code, the program is still almost meaningless. A further improvement is to replace the binary or hexadecimal numbers with short abbreviated words. These **mnemonics** (pronounced *neh-mon-iks*) will be used to represent binary instructions. Whenever possible they will be chosen to remind us of the full instruction they represent. A possible set of mnemonics to replace our binary instructions is shown in Table 12.4.

Table 12.4 A mnemonic code

Binary	Hex	Mnemonic	Meaning
0000	0	HLT	Stop (**Ha**L**T**)
0001	1	LDA	**L**oa**D** the **A**ccumulator from a memory location
0010	2	STA	**ST**ore the contents of the **A**ccumulator in a memory location
0011	3	ADD	**ADD** the contents of a memory location to the accumulator
0100	4	SUB	**SUB**tract the contents of a memory location from the accumulator
0101	5	JPU	**J**um**P** **U**nconditionally to the instruction in a memory location
0110	6	JPN	**J**um**P** to the instruction in a memory location if the contents of the accumulator are **N**egative
0111	7	JPZ	**J**um**P** to the instruction in a memory location if the contents of the accumulator are **Z**ero
1000	8	INP	**INP**ut a number and store it in a memory location
1001	9	OUP	**OU**t**P**ut a number from a memory location

A set of mnemonic instructions like this is written in what we call an **assembly language**. In the assembly language our program becomes:

```
          .BEGIN 0
          NUM1 :
          NUM2 :

          INP        NUM1
          INP        NUM2
          LDA        NUM1
          SUB        NUM2
          JPN        A
          OUP        NUM1
          OUP        NUM2
          JPU        B
     A :  OUP        NUM2
          OUP        NUM1
     B :  HLT
          .END
```

The program starts with **.BEGIN** and finishes with **.END**. Commands like this are called **directives**. Directives have no machine code equivalents. They are instructions to help the computer translate the assembly language program. In our assembly language, directives always start with a full stop.

At the start of the program all the locations we intend to use are given symbolic names. In this program we have declared that we intend to use two locations, called NUM1 and NUM2. In our assembly language, a colon follows all declarations of symbolic locations.

Jump instructions do not contain the actual address of the location they are to jump to. Instead they are fol-

lowed by a **label**. This label is also placed beside the instruction we wish to jump to. Labels A and B have been used in our program.

This program is much more easily understood than either its binary or hex equivalent. There is, however, a problem: the program will be meaningless to the CPU of a computer. The CPU can only deal with binary machine code instructions. If we wish to write our programs in an assembly language, we must provide the computer with an **assembler**. An assembler is a machine code program itself, designed to **translate** assembly language programs into machine code programs. The input data for an assembler is an assembly language program; its output is a machine code program. The input assembly language program is called the **source program**. The output machine code program is called the **object program**.

Sometimes the assembler is not held permanently in the computer's memory. In this case the assembly process involves:

1 Loading the assembler program
2 Entering the assembly language source program
3 Using the assembler to translate the assembly language program into the machine code object program
4 Correcting any errors found in the assembly language source program, then repeating Step 3
5 Saving the machine code object program
6 Clearing the computer's memory
7 Loading and running the machine code object program.

This form of assembly can be shown in a system flowchart (Figure 12.2).

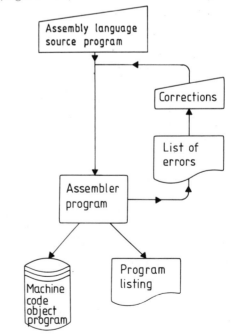

Figure 12.2 A system flowchart for an assembly process

The advantage of this method is that the minimum amount of immediate access memory is used because only the machine code version is needed when the program is run.

Alternatively, the assembler may be held permanently in the computer's memory. In this case, both the assembly language source program and the machine code object program may be present at the same time in the immediate access store. This uses more memory space but allows a more flexible programming technique. For example, the BBC microcomputer has a permanent assembler which allows the programmer to freely mix assembly language with BASIC.

Most assemblers produce the object program by scanning the source program twice. They are called **two-pass** assemblers. In the first pass, the assembler allocated actual memory addresses to all symbolic memory locations and jump labels. It stores these in a **symbol table**. A symbol table built up in a pass through our example assembly program is shown in Table 12.5.

Table 12.5 Symbol table

Symbolic name	Actual address
NUM1	1110
NUM2	1111
A	1000
B	1010

The assembler also has a fixed table which contains each instruction mnemonic and its corresponding binary code. A mnemonic table for our assembly language is shown in Table 12.6.

Table 12.6 Mnemonic table

Mnemonic instruction	Actual binary code
HLT	0000
LDA	0001
STA	0010
ADD	0011
SUB	0100
JPU	0101
JPN	0110
JPZ	0111
INP	1000
OUP	1001

In the second pass the assembler uses the two tables to translate the complete assembly language program. The directive ·.BEGIN usually contains the first storage address that the assembler is to use when storing the machine code program. In our example program .BEGIN 0 instructs the assembler to store the machine code program from location 0000 onwards. Directives have no machine code equivalents and are not translated by the assembler.

Any errors found in the assembly language source program will be reported by the assembler. Error messages will appear either as a printed list or on the display screen. Some typical errors that will be detected by an assembler are listed below.

* **Invalid symbolic name**. In most assembly languages there will be constraints on the choice of symbolic names. For example, the maximum length may be limited to four characters and the first character may have to be a letter. In this case, both NUMBER1 and 1NUM will be reported as invalid names.
* **Invalid mnemonic instruction**. The assembler will report any mnemonics that it cannot recognise. For example OUT used instead of OUP will be reported as an invalid instruction.
* **Duplicated or missing jump labels**. There must be one and only one possible destination for any jump. The assembler will report any jump labels used beside more than one instruction. For example, if label A were used beside two instructions in our example program, the assembler would report a duplicated jump label. The assembler will also report any jumps for which there is no destination because a label has been missed out.

Assembly languages are very close to the actual internal workings of the computer. For this reason they are called **low-level languages**. Almost nobody programmes directly in binary machine code, and when a new computer is designed and built, an assembler is one of the first pieces of software written for it.

Exercise 48

1 A program flowchart is shown below.

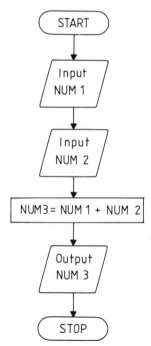

Using the codes and conventions given in this chapter:

a Write an assembly language program from this flow-chart.

b Using the symbol table given below, translate your program into machine code.

Symbolic name	Actual address
NUM1	1010
NUM2	1011
NUM3	1100

c Write your machine code program in hexadecimal code.

2 Using the codes and conventions given in this chapter:

a Write an assembly language program that inputs three numbers. The first should be added to the third and the second then subtracted from this total. Finally the result should be output.

b Construct a symbol table that can be used to translate your program into machine code. Remember you cannot use the same location for both an instruction and to store data. You will need to count the locations needed by your program instructions carefully so you know which locations are free to store data.

c Using your symbol table, translate your program into machine code.

d Write your machine code program in hexadecimal code.

3 When symbolic variable names are declared at the start of a program, we can also establish their values. For example, NUM1: 5 will automatically store the number 5 in the location allocated to NUM1. This facility is used in the program shown below. (The program lines have been numbered only to help you complete this question.)

```
            .BEGIN 0
            NUM1 : 5
            NUM2 : 1

LINE 1          LDA  NUM1
LINE 2      A:  OUP  NUM1
LINE 3          SUB  NUM2
LINE 4          STA  NUM1
LINE 5          JPZ  B
LINE 6          JPU  A
LINE 7      B:  HLT
            .END
```

a Copy and complete the following trace table for this program:

Line	NUM1	NUM2	Accumulator	Output
	5	1		
1	5	1	5	
2	5	1	5	5
3	5	1	4	
4	4	1	4	

b Translate this program into machine code using the symbol table shown below:

Symbolic name	Actual address
NUM1	0111
NUM2	1000
A	0001
B	0110

4 This is part of an assembly language program.

Instruction Number	Function Code	Memory Address	Comment
10	INP		Read a value into accumulator
11	STO	32	Transfer number in accumulator to store 32
12	INP		Read a value into accumulator
13	STO	33	Transfer number in accumulator to store 33
14	LDA	32	Transfer number in store 32 to accumulator
15	ADD	33	Add number in store 33 to number in accumulator
16	STO	34	Transfer number in accumulator to store 34
17	OUT		Print out number in accumulator

a Dry Run this part of a program, using 42 and 56 as input data.

b What needs to happen in the computer before the above program could be executed?

c In the assembly language used above there are also the following instructions:

JUP 16 Transfers control to the instruction at location 16.

JIZ 16 Transfers control to the instruction at location 16 if the accumulator is zero, otherwise continue to the next instruction.

Using this assembly language, write a program segment starting at location 10 to input positive numbers and add them together, keeping the running total in location 32. The list of numbers is terminated with a zero, and when this is found the total is output.

(AEB 84)

High-level Languages

Assembly languages offer considerable advantages over programming directly in machine code. They do, however, have four serious drawbacks.

* An assembly language programmer needs a considerable knowledge of the internal workings of the computer he or she is using.
* Each make of computer has a different assembly language. An assembly language program written for one computer cannot therefore be easily adapted to work on a different machine.
* Assembly language programs contain one instruction for each machine code instruction. These instructions are very basic and even simple programs can be quite lengthy.
* Assembly language programs are **machine-oriented**. This means that their structure reflects the design of a particular computer. Their structure is not designed to solve any particular type of problem. Writing practical data processing programs in an assembly language is therefore very difficult.

High-level languages are designed to overcome the drawbacks of assembly-level programming. They offer the following advantages over low-level languages:

* A high-level programmer needs no detailed knowledge of the internal workings of the computer he or she is using.
* High-level languages are designed to be **portable**. This means that a program written for one computer can be easily adapted to work on a different machine.
* Each instruction in a high-level language is translated into several machine code instructions. High-level programs are therefore much shorter than equivalent assembly language programs.
* High-level languages are **problem-oriented**. This means that their structure is designed to solve a particular type of problem. Writing practical data processing programs in a high-level language is therefore relatively easy.

To illustrate these points, look at the program below. It shows our example assembly language program written in the high-level language called BASIC.

```
10   INPUT NUM1,NUM2
20   IF NUM1<NUM2 THEN PRINT
     NUM2,NUM1
30   IF NUM1≥NUM2 THEN PRINT
     NUM1,NUM2
```

To write this program, no knowledge of the internal workings of the computer is needed. It will work on almost any computer which can be programmed in BASIC. It is quite short and was relatively easy to write because BASIC was designed as a simple teaching language.

There is of course one problem: any high-level program will be meaningless to the CPU of a computer. The CPU can only deal with binary machine code instructions. If we wish to program in a high-level language, we must provide the computer with a **compiler** or an **interpreter**. Compilers and interpreters are machine code programs themselves, designed to **translate** high-level programs into machine code.

We will look first at the action of a compiler. The input data for a compiler is a complete high-level program, its output is a complete machine code program. The input high-level program is called the **source program**, the output machine code program is called the **object program**. High-level programs are much more difficult to translate than assembly programs. An assembler changes each mnemonic instruction into one machine code instruction. A compiler may translate a single high-level instruction into many machine code instructions. First, the compiler must determine which binary instructions are needed and in what order. Then, it must automatically organise the storage of the program and its data and create all the necessary logical links between parts of the program. Usually comprehensive error reporting facilities are also provided. Compilers are therefore large and complex programs.

For each language we will need a separate compiler for every type of computer used. For example, FORTRAN and BASIC are both high-level languages. If we wish to use both FORTRAN and BASIC on an IBM computer, we will need two compilers. One will translate FORTRAN into IBM machine code; the other will translate BASIC into IBM machine code. If we wish to use FORTRAN and BASIC on an ICL computer, we will need two different compilers. These will translate the high-level languages into ICL machine code. (See Figure 12.3.)

Like assemblers, compilers may be either held permanently in the computer's memory or loaded from secondary storage when needed. If the compiler is not permanently in the computer's memory, the compilation process involves:

1. Loading the compiler program
2. Entering the high-level program
3. Using the compiler to translate the high-level source program into the machine code object program

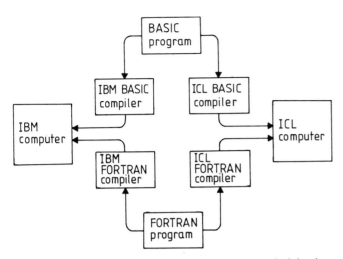

Figure 12.3 The four compilers needed to run two high-level language programs on two different makes of computer

4 Correcting any errors found in the high-level source program, then repeating step 3
5 Storing the object program
6 Clearing the computer's memory
7 Loading and running the object program

This form of compilation is shown in a system flowchart (Figure 12.4).

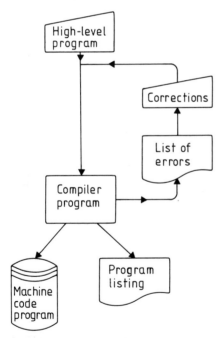

Figure 12.4 A system flowchart for a compilation process

By computer standards compilers are slow, often taking several minutes to compile even relatively short programs. However, once the machine code object program is produced it can be loaded and run as often as required.

All errors found during compilation are reported to the programmer. Corrections and modifications are made to the high-level source program and it is re-compiled.

An **interpreter** does not produce a complete machine code translation of a high-level program. Instead, the interpreter translates each line of the program as it is run. The input data for an interpreter is a single high-level instruction, its output is the execution of the equivalent machine code instructions. Any errors found in the high-level instruction will be reported and the execution of the program will stop. The program flowchart in Figure 12.5 shows the action of an interpreter.

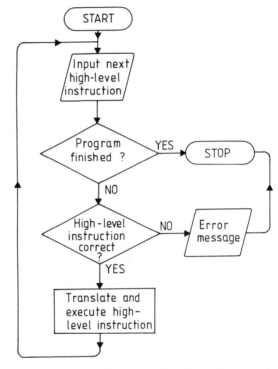

Figure 12.5 A program flowchart to show the action of an interpreter

Interpreters are less efficient than compilers because they must translate each instruction of a program every time the program is run. If the instruction is part of a loop, the interpreter will translate it each time the loop is completed. Consequently interpreted programs run far more slowly than compiled programs. However, because the high-level program is always present in the computer's memory when an interpreter is used, it is easier to modify and develop programs using an interpreter. A summary of the advantages and disadvantages of compilers and interpreters is given below:

Advantages of compilers

* Because a complete machine code program is produced, compiled programs run much faster than interpreted programs.
* A compiler need only be used once, an interpreter must be used every time the program is run.

145

Advantages of interpreters

* Because the high-level program remains in the computer's memory when an interpreter is used it is much easier to correct mistakes and make program modifications.
* An interpreter is a shorter and simpler program than a compiler.

Interpreters are a sensible choice when interactive program development is required. Compilers are preferred when large programs are repeatedly run without modification and when it is important that programs run quickly. Interpreters are used almost exclusively with the BASIC high-level language when it is implemented on microcomputers.

Both compilers and interpreters will report any **syntax errors** found in the high-level program. All high-level languages have a set of rules for the correct construction of program instructions. These are called the **syntax rules** of the language. A syntax error occurs when the rules are used incorrectly. Syntax errors may result from a programmer's misunderstanding of the syntax rules or from a simple transcription error. For example, in BASIC:

10 LET B + C = A

is a syntax error because the instruction is incorrectly constructed. The correct syntax is:

10 LET A = B + C

Alternatively, in BASIC

10 PRANT A

is a syntax error because there is a transcription mistake. The correct instruction is

10 PRINT A

Some syntax errors may occur when the rules of program structure are broken across several separate program statements. For example, in the BASIC computer language a counter-controlled loop is created with two statements, a FOR statement and a NEXT statement. If either of these statements is missed out, a syntax error will result. For example:

20 PRINT "APPLE"
30 NEXT J

will result in a 'NEXT without FOR' syntax error. The correct syntax in this case was:

```
10 FOR J = 1 TO 10
20 PRINT "APPLE"
30 NEXT J
```

Different Kinds of High-level Language

High-level languages were first developed in the 1950s. There are now a vast number of high-level languages and a summary of some of the most important ones follows.

FORTRAN
Meaning of name　FORmula TRANslation
Developed by　IBM
First use in　1956
Application area　Scientific computing
Purpose　Designed to produce programming solutions to scientific and mathematic problems. FORTRAN was the first high-level language.

COBOL
Meaning of name　COmmon Business Orientated Language
Developed by　United States Department of Defense
First use in　1958
Application area　Commercial programming
Purpose　Designed to produce programming solution to commercial data processing problems. It makes extensive use of words to make programs as much like sentences in English as possible. It contains powerful file-handling facilities.

ALGOL
Meaning of name　ALGOrithmic programming Language
Developed by　An international committee
First use in　1958
Application area　Scientific computing
Purpose　Designed to produce easily understood and well-structured programs. It contains many powerful mathematical functions.

RPG
Meaning of name　Report Program Generator
Developed by　IBM
First use in　1961
Application area　Commercial computing
Purpose　RPG is a special-purpose language designed to generate business reports from computer files. It is widely used in the commercial world.

PL/1
Meaning of name　Programming Language 1.
Developed by　IBM
First use in　1963
Application area　Commercial and scientific computing
Purpose　Designed to combine the facilities available in COBOL with those available in FORTRAN and ALGOL. PL/1 was intended as a universal programming language suitable for all applications. The widespread acceptance that was aimed for has not been achieved.

BASIC
Meaning of name　Beginners All-purpose Symbolic Instruction Code
Developed by　Kemeny and Kurtz at Dartmouth College, USA
First use in　1965
Application area　Educational computing originally, now also used for some commercial and scientific programming
Purpose　Designed as an easy-to-learn teaching language. Now greatly extended and useful for many applications, it is often preferred to FORTRAN or ALGOL. It has two major drawbacks: (i) Early versions lacked a clear program structure and encouraged a very poor programming style. (ii) Because it has been extended beyond recognition by different computer manufacturers, it is one of the least portable high-level languages.

PASCAL
Meaning of name　Named after Blaise Pascal the French mathematician and philosopher
Developed by　N. Wirth
First use in　1968
Application area　Educational computing originally, now also used quite extensively in commercial and scientific computing
Purpose　Designed as a teaching language that encourages sound program design and clear structure. It is used as a teaching language mainly in universities. It may be preferred to BASIC because of its greater emphasis on structured programming.

There are a vast range of other high-level languages. Some are designed to cover a wide area of applications. These are called **general-purpose languages**. Others are designed to cover a very narrow area of applications.

These are called **special-purpose languages**. RPG is one example of a special-purpose language. Other examples are CORAL-66 and ADA, both designed to produce programs for the direct control of physical processes. Because of the advantages they offer, high-level languages are normally preferred to low-level languages. Low-level languages do, however, have some advantages and would be used in each of the following situations.

When very efficient machine code programs are required. Compilers translate high-level programs using fixed rules and usually do not produce the most efficient machine code program possible. An assembly language programmer can usually produce a machine code program which is shorter and faster than the equivalent compiled machine code program. Therefore, if very fast and compact machine code is required, the extra time and effort to write a program in an assembly language may be justified.

When use of the full range of machine code instructions is required. Only a very simplified machine code has been explained in this chapter. A typical real machine code may have between 100 and 200 instructions. Some of these instructions will be very complex — for example, manipulating the individual bits in a storage register. Most high-level languages will not include equivalent instructions for the full range of possible machine code instructions. A programmer who wishes to use machine code instructions that are not available in a high-level language will have to use an assembly language.

When an interpreted program runs too slowly and a compiler is not available. This situation occurs most frequently with microcomputer games programming. The slow speed of the interpreter makes it impossible to write high-speed graphics programs in BASIC. Almost all microcomputer games programs are written in an assembly language.

When no high-level language exists for a particular application area. Examples may be programs to perform complex disc file updating routines or programs to control external devices. As more high-level languages are developed for special applications this is becoming a less-common situation. For example, in the past if a microcomputer was used to control another device the control program was written in an assembly language. This is no longer necessary with some microcomputers because they have an extension to BASIC called **CONTROL BASIC**. This allows high-level control programs to be written.

148

Exercise 49

1 How many different compilers would be needed to implement four different high-level languages on eight different makes of computer?

2 Ian Cook wishes to cook a recipe from a cookery book written in French. Ian does not speak French but his wife Sally does. Ian has two choices. He can ask Sally to write out a full translation of the recipe. Alternatively, he can ask Sally to come into the kitchen and translate the recipe line by line as he cooks the dish. Explain in detail why one of Ian's choices is like compiling a computer program while the other choice is like interpreting a computer program.

3 Imagine you have a friend who has just bought a micro-computer. The introduction to the machine included a brief explanation of low-level and high-level programming. She tells you she has decided to start from the beginning and learn low-level programming first, then move on to high-level programming.

  a What would you say to your friend to explain that it may be best to start by learning a high-level language?

  b What would you say to your friend to explain why she may eventually wish to learn to program in a low-level language?

4 Name **three** high level programming languages. For each give a brief description of an application for which the language is appropriate.

(C 82)

5 Explain the meaning of the terms below and the connections between the terms in each group:

  a High level, low level and assembly languages.

  b Source program, object program and translation program.

  c Interpreter, compiler, assembler and machine code.

(SUJB 82)

6 a Explain the difference between a high-level language and a low-level language.

  b Give TWO advantages of a high-level language over a low-level language.

  c Name the software used to change source programs to object programs in each case.

(ALSEB 82)

Types of Computer Software

Software is the term used to describe any kind of computer program. Software can be divided into two main types: **applications programs** and **systems programs**.

An application program is a program which enables the computer to tackle a specific task — for example, calculating and printing wage slips.

A systems program is a program which helps to control the computer's operations — for example, by selecting and controlling the input and output devices. Systems programs are designed to enable the computer to run applications programs more efficiently.

The following sections examine applications programs and systems programs in greater detail.

Applications Programs

Many computer applications are very complex, and the necessary software is usually divided into several applications programs. For example, payroll applications software may be divided into several programs. One of these programs may be used to input and validate the transaction data. Another program may be used to update the master file and print the payslips. A complete set of programs for a given application, together with all the necessary documentation is called an **applications package**.

When an organisation requires new applications programs, these may be written by programmers employed by the organisation. Alternatively, the organisation may buy a complete applications package from a supplier of computer software.

Buying a software package is a sensible alternative if an organisation does not have the time, expertise or programming staff to write tailor-made software. On the other hand, bought software will never match the organisation's system as perfectly as specially written software.

Applications packages should satisfy all the following design criteria.

* **User orientation**. The programs must be as easy to use as possible. Interactive programs should have special routines to help and guide the user. Any necessary data collection or preparation should be as simple as possible. Any output produced should be easy to understand and use.
* **Robustness**. The programs should be very hard to 'crash', no matter what mistakes the user makes.
* **Versatility**. The programs should offer the user a wide range of processing options.
* **Flexibility**. The programs should be designed to cope with differences in the detailed requirements of different users.
* **Reliability**. The programs should run whenever required. Program 'crashes' should not occur when unusual data is entered or unexpected combinations of user requests are made.
* **Portability**. The whole package should be designed to run on different computers with the minimum of modification.
* **Ease of maintenance**. The programs should be easy to modify and develop if the user's requirements change.

One of the most important parts of any applications package is the documentation provided with the computer programs. This documentation consists of explanatory notes and diagrams which help the design, implementation, day-to-day running and maintenance of the software. Many large organisations have a fixed standard for program documentation which all their programmers must use. This allows several programmers to work together on the same project and ensures that development can continue even with a complete change of programmers. Program documentation can be divided into two types: **user documentation** and **programmer documentation**. User documentation is provided to explain how to load, run and use the software. Good user documentation will contain:

* **A non-technical explanation of what the program is designed to do.** This will include the general tasks the program performs, the options offered and any limitation on the use of the program.
* **Full instructions for loading and running the program.** This will include details of any special hardware or software requirements; for example, an attached printer or a BASIC compiler.
* **Full instructions for collecting and preparing the input data.** This will include samples of any data collection forms that are used.
* **Full instructions for operating the program.** This will include details of any interactive data input and validation. A warning may also be given of any unusual features; for example, a lengthy delay while data is sorted.
* **Full instructions for using and understanding the output data.**
* **A full explanation of the error messages that may be produced by user mistakes or invalid data.** This will include details of how to correct these errors.

Programmer documentation is built up as the software package is developed. In the development stage, good documentation helps the coordination of work and provides a check on progress. At a later stage, good documentation allows programmers who wish to modify and develop the software to understand the programs quickly.

Good programmer documentation will contain:

* **Details of when, where and by whom the software was written.** These details are often included in an index number using a suitable code. This section is very important because a programmer trying to modify or correct a program may wish to consult the programmers who wrote the original software.

* **A general description of the way the program works.** This section should give a quick outline understanding of the programmer's approach, without going into details of the actual program listing. The choice of input method, output method and backing storage will be explained. This section will often be illustrated with a system flowchart.
* **A detailed description of the way the program works.** This section will include a full listing of the program. Notes will be added to the listing to explain the function of each section of the program. A list of all the variables used in the program will be given, with an explanation of their purpose. The structure of any data files used in the program will be explained in detail. This section will often be illustrated with program flowcharts.
* **Details of the way in which that the software has been tested.** This section will include sets of test data with expected and actual output that proves the program functions correctly.

A vast range of applications programs and packages exists, and new packages are always being developed. Some of these packages are designed to enable the computer to tackle a specific task. For example, software packages exist for almost all computers for stock control and payroll applications. Other packages are designed to enable the computer to tackle more general tasks. The most common software packages of this general type are: **word-processing packages, graphics packages, financial calculation packages (spreadsheets) and database creation packages.**

A third type of software package, called a **program generator**, is designed to assist users to write their own programs. A good program generator will allow a user to specify the task a computer is required to tackle in simple English statements. These statements will then be expanded by the program generator into a full computer program. Some program generators are so sophisticated that they are considered to be complete computer languages. Because they are a new stage of development after machine code, assembly languages and high-level languages, program generators are sometimes called **fourth-generation languages**.

Systems Programs

In order to run applications programs, a computer needs systems programs to control and improve its performance. The complete set of systems programs used to control a computer is called its **operating system**. An operating system will be designed to perform some or all of the following tasks:

* To control the operation of input devices, output devices and backing storage
* To supervise the loading, running and storage of applications programs
* To deal with errors that occur in applications programs
* To communicate with the user or operator, accepting requests and instructions and displaying messages
* To maintain security by protecting hardware, software and data from improper use or unauthorised access
* To maintain a record of everything that the computer does.

We can summarise the tasks of the operating system by saying that it controls and coordinates all the communications between the various parts of the computer system. This is shown in Figure 12.6.

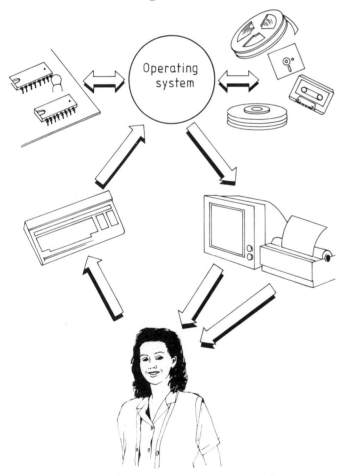

Figure 12.6 How an operating system works

The following three sections look at the most common types of operating systems.

Single Program Operating Systems

The simplest operating systems are those found on microcomputers. They are designed to allow a single user to run one program at a time. The main tasks performed by these operating systems are:

* To allow the user to enter, edit and run high-level language programs.
* To accept and execute commands entered by the user. Typical commands are:
  LOAD "INVADERS"   to transfer a program called "INVADERS" from backing store into the computer's memory
  LIST   to produce a program listing
  RUN   to start the execution of a program.
* To produce messages to help the user. Typical messages are:
  SEARCHING   to inform the user that the backing store is being searched for a program
  LOADING INVADERS   to tell the user that the program called "INVADERS" is being transferred from backing store into the computer's memory.
* To supervise data transfer between the computer and the input, output and backing storage peripherals. On a typical microcomputer, this will involve accepting input from a keyboard, sending output to a screen or printer, and copying programs and data to and from cassette tape.
* To organise the storage of programs and data on disc backing store. Discs are more complicated than other peripherals and a separate section of the operating system is usually provided to deal with them. The part of the operating system that deals with disc backing storage is usually called the **disc operating system** or **DOS**.
* To deal with errors that occur when the user's program is running. Usually, when an error occurs, the operating system halts the user's program and displays an error message.
* To carry out input/output instructions in the user's program. An example of this is the BASIC command PRINT. This actually passes data to the operating system, which then transfers the data to a screen or printer. Other BASIC commands which use the operating system are INPUT, GET, INKEY and CLS.

The operating system must be present in the immediate access memory whenever the computer is used. In microcomputers, the operating system is usually held in a special part of the memory called the **read only memory** or **ROM**. The contents of this memory cannot be changed by the user and are not lost when the computer is switched off.

Multiprogramming

Modern mainframe computers are far too powerful and expensive to be used by a single person running one program. **Multiprogramming operating systems** have therefore been developed that allow several programs to run at the same time. To understand how this is possible, we will look at a simple situation where two programs are run at the same time.

Program A is a scientific program. It reads in a small amount of data and, after lengthy calculations, produces results on a line printer. The operation of this program is shown in Figure 12.7.

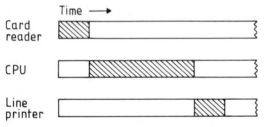

Figure 12.7 The operation of Program A

Program B is a payroll application. The program reads in the data from punched clock cards, calculates the wages and prints wage slips. The operation of this program is shown in Figure 12.8.

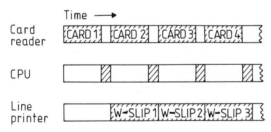

Figure 12.8 The operation of Program B

It is possible to overlap the reading of cards and printing of wage slips because buffers are used between the CPU and the card reader and printer. (The action of a buffer was described on p. 97.)

Because the CPU operates at far higher speeds than the card reader or the line printer, it is idle for most of the time that Program B is running. Figure 12.9 shows how it is possible to use this idle CPU time to run Program A at the same time as Program B.

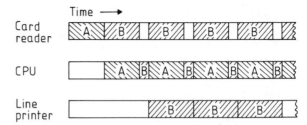

Figure 12.9 How to run Programs A and B together

In a multiprogramming system, each program is given a **priority** by the computer operator (or possibly by the operating system itself). The operating system always allows the program with the highest priority to use the CPU first. In our example, Program B has a higher priority than Program A. Program B will therefore be allowed to interrupt the processing of Program A whenever it needs to use the CPU. Program B will send an **interrupt signal** to the operating system each time it finishes reading a card. The operating system will respond to this signal by stopping the processing of Program A and switching to Program B. Having calculated the wages, the CPU is then switched back to Program A while the wage slip is printed and the next card is read.

When two programs are run together in this way, they must both be present in the immediate access memory. Usually, this memory is **partitioned** into separate sections for each program. Figure 12.10 shows the immediate access memory divided into two partitions.

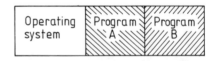

Figure 12.10 The partitioning of an immediate access memory

Our simple example only demonstrates two programs running together. In a practical multiprogramming system, as many programs as possible are run at the same time. The only limit to the number of programs that can be run is the size of the immediate access memory which must hold all the programs. To increase efficiency even further, programs and data are stored in a **job queue** on the backing store. As soon as the computer completes work on one of the programs in the immediate access store, another program is loaded from the job queue to take its place.

Output from the programs is usually stored on backing storage before it is printed. This ensures that the output from different programs is never mixed up.

To work well, a multiprogramming operating system requires two conditions:

* Most of the programs should be of the kind that do not make full use of the CPU. That is, they should involve a lot of input and output rather than a lot of calculations.
* The characteristics of each program must be known in detail so that processing priorities can be allocated.

This makes multiprogramming unsuitable for interactive computing, where the users' requirements are not known in advance. Multiprogramming is usually used for **batch processing**. Batch processing systems are of two main types:

* **Batch processing of data**. This is a system used for large commercial programs. All the input data is entered, verified and **batched** together before the program is run. An example is a payroll system, where all the clock card data is prepared using a key-to-disc system before the program is run.
* **Batch processing of programs**. This is a system used to run a series of short programs. The programs, each complete with all its input data, are collected into **batches**. Because no interactive

processing takes place, each program must also include instructions for the operating system. For example, the operating system will need to be instructed to load the correct compiler. These instructions are written in a **job control language** and placed at the start of the program. Traditionally, punched cards have been used for batched programs and the structure of a typical card deck is show in Figure 12.11.

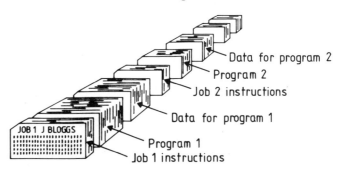

Figure 12.11 The structure of a typical batch of programs

Batch processing of programs was often used in schools and colleges during the 1960s and 1970s. The student's programs and data were written on

coding sheets and posted to a central computer department for processing. The results were later posted back to the schools or colleges. Because of the introduction of microcomputers and multi-access computer systems, batch processing of student programs is now very seldom used.

Some early computers had single-program batch processing operating systems but this is now very rare. When batch processing is used it is now almost always in conjunction with a multiprogramming operating system.

Multi-access Operating Systems

Multi-access operating systems are used to provide interactive computing at a large number of terminals. Each user works at his or her terminal and appears to have sole use of the computer. The terminals may be VDUs, GDUs, teletypewriters or point-of-sale terminals (see p. 102). **Local terminals** are connected directly to the computer. **Remote terminals** are connected to the computer with modems and telephone lines. Figure 12.12 shows a typical multi-access system.

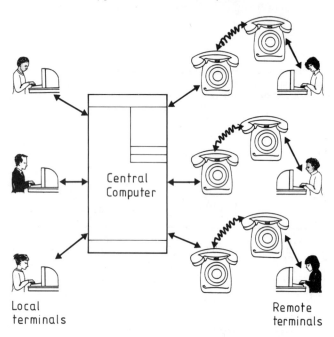

Local terminals   Remote terminals

Figure 12.12   A multi-access system

It is impossible to know in advance what work will be done at each terminal. Consequently priorities cannot be allocated to each program, and multiprogramming is therefore not suitable for this interactive system. An alternative method must be found to share the central computer between all the terminal users. One method which is often used is called **time sharing**. In a time-sharing system, each terminal in turn is allowed to use the computer for a short period of time. These short periods of time, perhaps one tenth of a second, are called **time slices**. The multi-access operating system works its

way round all the terminals, allowing each terminal sole use of the computer during its time slice. At the start of its time slice, the program being used at a terminal, with all its data, is transferred from the backing store into the immediate access memory. At the end of its time slice, the program, with all its data, is returned to the backing store. The program is stored with enough information to enable processing to continue when the terminal's next time slice comes round.

Each terminal only accesses the computer for a fraction of a second at a time, but the terminal user will hardly suspect that he or she does not have uninterrupted use of the computer. This is because of the enormous difference in speed between the computer and the human user. A typical terminal user can type at a maximum of 15 characters a second. A typical modern computer, on the other hand, can perform millions of operations each second. Very short bursts of computer time are therefore quite sufficient to meet the needs of each terminal user.

The time slices are timed by the computer's internal electronic clock. At the end of each time slice, this clock sends a **clock interrupt** signal to the operating system. The operating system interrupts the current program, dumps it on to the backing store and loads the next program. Multi-access systems need very fast backing stores because programs are continually swapped in and out of the immediate access memory. Magnetic discs or occasionally magnetic drums are used.

Multi-access systems are of two main types:

* **Program development systems**. These systems allow many terminal users to enter, edit and run computer programs. To the programmer, each terminal appears to offer all the facilities of a single-user interactive operating system. A typical example is a university computer, with a large number of terminals spread throughout the university buildings. Each terminal can be used to enter and run programs, often in a choice of several different high-level languages. Each terminal user is allocated a section of the computer's backing store to save his or her programs and data files. A password is normally used to protect this area from access by other terminal users. Most systems also have a **program library** containing complete applications programs and useful program subroutines. Any terminal user can access and use the software in this library.
* **Commercial database systems**. These systems allow many terminal users to interrogate and update a database. The computer user is not a programmer, and only requests for information or details of transactions can be entered at each terminal. A typical application is an airline ticket

booking system. Each terminal is used to request information on seat availability and to enter details of ticket purchase transactions.

In a simple multi-access system, it is usually satisfactory to allow each program to use the CPU during its time slice and then to swap the program out on to the backing store. In large multi-access systems, this approach could lead to the computer spending nearly all its time swapping programs in to and out of the main store. A method must be used which will reduce the amount of data transferred between the computer and the backing store. One solution would be to have a main store large enough to hold all the programs being run at the terminals, but this would require a very large and expensive computer memory. A compromise is to use a method called **paging**. Paging uses the fact that most programs only use a small part of the full program coding at any one time. For example, one program may provide a lengthy introduction and user explanation that is only run through once at the start of the program. Each program in a paging system is divided into a number of segments or **pages**. The computer holds in its main store one page of each program that is being developed or run. The other pages that make up the programs are held on the backing store. This allows the computer to switch from one program to another until a program requires a different page. Only at this stage is it necessary to swap a new page of the program in from the backing store to replace the one currently in the main memory. One consequence of a paging system is that a computer can run programs that need more storage space than is available in the CPU. Computers with operating systems that provide this facility are called **virtual memory** computers because they appear to have larger memories than that actually provided in the CPU.

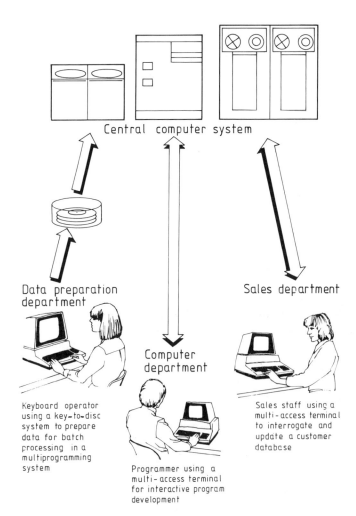

Figure 12.13 A mainframe operating system being used by different departments of a company

A Practical Mainframe Operating System

Large modern mainframe computers often have operating systems that offer both multiprogram and multi-access computing. This is possible because an interactive multi-access system will leave the CPU unused for short periods of time. These thousands of tiny time intervals can be used to run batch programs.

Tasks which include a large amount of input and output are usually run using multiprogram batch processing. An example is a payroll application, in which all the clock card data is prepared and batched before the program is run.

Tasks which are better suited to interactive computing are run using multi-access terminals. Examples are interactive program development, and database interrogation and updating. Figure 12.13 shows the outline of a system offering three kinds of computer use.

The operating systems used in these large mainframe computers are extremely complex pieces of software. As well as coordinating both multiprogramming and multi-access computing, they must control the operation of hundreds of different items of hardware.

Because they are such large complex programs, the operating systems of mainframe computers may be held on backing store rather than in a ROM memory. When the computer is switched on, a small program called a **bootstrap loader** is used to transfer the operating system into the immediate access memory. The bootstrap loader program is either entered directly by a computer operator or held permanently in a ROM memory. The phrase 'bootstrap loader' comes from the expression 'pull yourself up by your own bootstraps'. The bootstrap loader 'pulls' the operating system into the computer and the computer is then ready to start working on applications programs.

Utility Programs

A **utility program** is a systems program designed to perform a specific computer-related task. Examples of the types of task performed by utility programs are:

* The transfer of data files from magnetic tape on to magnetic disc
* The sorting, searching and merging of data files
* Copying a graphics display from a screen on to a printer.

Utility programs are either stored in ROM memory or on fast access backing store. Simple commands to the computer's operating system will allow access to these utility programs. The commands may be either entered directly by the user or included in applications programs. For example, the Sinclair Spectrum microcomputer has a utility program in its ROM memory which copies the screen contents on to a printer. The command 'COPY' instructs the Spectrum's operating system to execute this utility. The COPY command can be either entered directly at the Spectrum's keyboard or included in a BASIC program.

Computer manufacturers provide utility programs for most common tasks. This saves considerable programming time because complex routines are replaced by a simple command to execute a utility program. For example, writing a routine to sort a data file into order is a complex and lengthy programming task. If a sorting utility program is available, a simple command like SORT may be all that is required.

Execution Errors and Logical Errors

Even when an applications program is free of syntax errors, it may still contain instructions that the computer cannot carry out. These impossible instructions will cause **execution errors** (sometimes called **run-time errors**) when the program is run. The examples below show two BASIC programs that will cause execution errors when they are run.

Example 1
```
10 LET N = 0
20 LET T = 7
30 PRINT T / N
```

Note. This program will produce an execution error at line 30. This is because it is 'impossible' to divide a number by zero.

Example 2
```
10 LET X = 1
20 LET X = X * 2
30 PRINT X
40 GOTO 20
```

Note. This program is designed to print out a list of powers of two. When run, it prints 2, 4, 8, 16, 32. . . . Eventually X will become too large to be stored in the computer's memory and line 20 will cause an execution error. This type of execution error is also called an **overflow error**.

All operating systems are designed to cope with execution errors that occur when applications programs are run. When an execution error occurs, the operating system halts the execution of the program and produces an **error message** to explain the cause of the problem. Interactive operating systems will allow the user to correct the error and rerun the program. Batch operating systems will simply stop processing the program and load in a new program from the job queue. The batch user will receive back an error report instead of the expected program output. He or she must then correct the program and resubmit it to the computer department.

Even programs which are free of syntax errors and impossible instructions may produce incorrect results when they are run. This is because they contain **logical errors**. A logical error is a mistake in the design of a program. For example, the BASIC program below was designed to print out the first five powers of two. When run, it was supposed to print 2, 4, 8, 16 and 32.

```
10 LET X =1
20 LET X = X * 2
30 PRINT X
40 If X = 32 THEN GOTO 60
50 GOTO 10
60 STOP
```

When run, the program in fact printed 2, 2, 2, 2, 2, ... This is because it contains a logical error. Line 50 loops the program back to line 10, but the correct program logic is to loop back to line 20.

Logical errors cannot be detected by the computer itself because it simply carries out the user's instructions. It has no way of knowing what output the user required or what problem he or she intended to solve.

Programmers detect logical errors by using test data to complete a trace table. Some operating systems provide access to utility programs that help the programmer to detect logical errors. Examples are utility programs to produce an automatic trace table as the program runs or to print the contents of sections of the computer's memory.

Problems with Definitions

The terms **monitor**, **executive**, **supervisor** and **scheduler** are sometimes used by manufacturers to describe parts of an operating system. The definitions of these terms are, however, far from clear, and they are used by different manufacturers in different ways. It is better to avoid the use of these terms or (if you must use them) to state clearly what you intend them to mean.

Exercise 50

1 Copy and complete the following passages.

a The set of binary instructions that the CPU of a computer can understand is called the _____ of the computer. Because the binary instructions are very difficult to write down, compare or remember, _____ programs are often entered using a _____ keypad.

b Assembly languages use _____ to represent machine code instructions. An assembly language program cannot be run directly and must first be translated with a _____. The _____ takes an assembly language _____ program and translates it into a machine code _____ program.

c Assembly language programs are _____ oriented. High-level language programs are _____ oriented. An _____ programmer needs a detailed knowledge of the internal workings of the computer, a _____ programmer does not need this knowledge. A _____ language program can be easily adapted to run on another make of computer, an _____ language program cannot be so easily adapted. An _____ language program contains one instruction for every _____ instruction. A _____ language program instruction may be translated into several _____ instructions.

d A high-level program cannot be run directly and must first be translated with a _____ or an _____. A _____ translates a complete high-level program into machine code. An _____ translates a high-level program into machine code line by line each time the program is run. A _____ need only be used once to translate a high-level program, an _____ must be used each time the program is run. An _____ is a simpler and shorter program than a _____ and it is easier to correct and modify programs when an _____ is used because the _____ remains in the computer's memory.

e An _____ program is a program which enables the computer to tackle a specific task. A _____ program is a program which helps to control the computer's operations. A complete set of programs and their documentation for a given application is called an _____. The complete set of programs used to control the operations of a computer is called its _____.

f Program documentation can be divided into two types: documentation for the _____ and documentation for the _____. _____ documentation is provided to explain how to load, run and use the software. _____ documentation is provided to help software development and maintenance.

g The operating system of most microcomputers is designed to allow one _____ to run one _____. Modern mainframe computers are too powerful and expensive to be used by one _____ running one _____. _____ operating systems are used to allow several programs to run at the same time. _____ operating systems are used to allow many terminal users to use the computer at the same time. _____ operating systems are usually used for batch processing. _____ operating systems are usually used for interactive computing.

h A modern mainframe computer may have an operating system that allows both _____ and _____. If this operating system is held on backing store, a _____ is needed to load the operating system into the immediate access memory when the computer is switched on.

i A _____ program is a systems program designed to perform a specific task. One example is _____.

j Multi-access operating systems provide interactive computing at a large number of terminals. _____ terminals are connected by modems and telephone lines to the computer. One common way to share the computer between all the terminal users is to allow each terminal to use the computer for a short period of time called a _____.

k An _____ error is caused by an impossible instruction in a program. For example, if the computer is instructed to divide a number by _____ or if the computer is instructed to store a number which is too _____. When an _____ error occurs, the operating system halts the applications program and displays an _____.

l A _____ error is a mistake in the design of a program. _____ errors are detected by the programmer using _____ to complete a _____.

2 **a** Give one advantage of the use of a low level language.

b A section of a low level language program is shown below.

LABEL	OPERATION CODE	ADDRESS
	LØD	X
AGAIN	MIN	2
	JPOS	AGAIN
	PERI	

"LØD" means "copy the contents of the store named into the accumulator"

"MIN" means "subtract the number from the accumulator"

"JPOS" means "transfer control if the contents of the accumulator are positive or zero"

"PERI" means "output the contents of the accumulator"

(i) How many times will the loop be executed if the contents of store X is 9?

(ii) What will be the output of this program?

(SWEB 82)

3 Each of the "programs" below adds two numbers together. The programs are written in different languages: one is in a high level language, another is in machine code, another is in hexadecimal code and one is in an assembly (mnemonic) language.

Program P	Program Q	Program R	Program S
00111010	3 A		
01100000	6 0		
00000000	0 0	LD A. (60H)	
?	4 7	LD B, A	
00111010	3 A	LD A, (61H)	
01100001	6 1		
00000000	0 0		
10000000	?	ADD A, B	
00110010	3 2	LD (62H), A	
01100010	6 2		LET C = A + B
00000000	0 0		

a State which program P, Q, R, S is in which language.
b Find the **eight** missing bits in P if programs P and Q are equivalent.
c Supply the missing number in Q by comparing it with its equivalent in P.
d What advantage do programs R and S share compared with P and Q?
e Which program is the most portable from computer to computer?
f Which is the fastest program to execute and why?
g What kind of software converts program R into program P?
h What kind of software converts program S into program P?

(NWREB 82)

4 An assembly language has the following instructions:

Mnemonic Code	Function
RD	Read a number into the accumulator.
PR	Print the contents of the accumulator.
LC N	Load the accumulator with the constant N.
LD n	Load the accumulator with the contents of location n.
AD n	Add the contents of location n to the contents of the accumulator.
SU n	Subtract the contents of location n from the contents of the accumulator.
ST n	Store the contents of the accumulator in location n.
JP n	Jump to location n.
JZ n	Jump to location n if the contents of the accumulator is zero.
SP	Stop

a Write a program using this assembly language to read 6 numbers and output the total of the 6 numbers.
b Test your program, showing clearly the effect of executing each instruction with the following data.
3, 6, 5, 8, 11, 7.

(NI GCE 82)

5 Read the following brief description of a computer, filling in the gaps from the wordlist given below.

"A computer is an _____ machine that uses a _____ code system to represent information. The code is manipulated by a _____ to produce the _____. The computer program may have been written in a high level language (such as _____ or _____) or in a _____ language, or even in _____ code.

A computer usually completes its work much _____ than a human being could and often does jobs that would be _____ for a human to do in the time available."

computer program, machine, electronic, low-level, COBOL, output, quicker, binary, BASIC, impossible.

(EAEB 82)

6 a (i) Briefly describe the tasks carried out by a compiler.
  (ii) Give examples of two program errors which a compiler could be expected to identify, and two program errors which a compiler could *not* be expected to identify.
b (i) Describe the ways in which an interpreter differs from a compiler.
  (ii) Give one advantage and one disadvantage of using an interpreter rather than a compiler.
  (iii) Describe circumstances in which it would be preferable to run a program using an interpreter rather than a compiler.

(C 83)

7 In programming a computer, high-level languages and low-level languages both have important parts to play.

a Explain the difference between high-level and low-level languages as far as the programmer is concerned.
b When might it be desirable to write a computer program in a high-level language?
c When might it be desirable to write a computer program in a low-level language?
d Why must a high-level language computer program be translated before execution?

(EAEB 85)

8 There are many high-level languages available nowadays which are designed for particular tasks or areas of computing work.

a Name three high-level languages and explain with reasons the type of tasks for which they are particularly suitable.
b High-level languages can be either interpreted or compiled. Explain the difference between interpreters and compilers, giving their relative advantages and disadvantages.

(AEB 85)

9 "An important task of a programmer is to provide adequate documentation."

a Give **three** reasons why programs should be documented.

b State the essential sections of full documentation of a program and say what each section contains.

(AEB 83)

10 a In the table below, *tick* the **THREE** items which should be included in the user documentation of a computer program.

Item of Documentation
Operating Instructions
List of Variables
Output Format
Program Listing
Description of Procedures Subroutines
Input Format

b State **THREE** features which should be included in the Operating Instructions for a program and the reasons for their inclusion.

c Name **ONE** other item of documentation required by the user of a program

(MEG 16 + Spec. 87)

11 a Explain why computers have *operating systems*.

b State two different types of *operating systems*.

(NI 82)

12 a Describe what is meant by *batch processing*.

b Name one application where *batch processing* is appropriate.

(NI 82)

13 a What is an operating system?

b For each of the following computer systems, explain what facilities the operating system provides and what a user has to do to communicate with the system:

(i) a microcomputer system with facilities for only one user at a time;

(ii) a large computer running only a batch system, with passwords allocated to users and with several languages available — programs being 'spooled' into different queues;

(iii) a large computer timesharing 40 terminals, with passwords allocated to users and only one language available.

(O 82)

14 a Give a detailed description of multiprogramming, using as an example a situation in which three programs are being processed. Refer to the programs as PROG A, PROG B and PROG C and assume that they are held in the main store at the same time.

b Explain how your description in part (*a*) above would be altered if there were also a number of multi-access programs requiring processing. How would the operating system ensure that all the multi-access programs receive their share of processing?

(C 82)

15 a Copy this table and tick **THREE** applications in the list which would be carried out using batch processing.

APPLICATION
Airline seat reservation
Printing electricity bills
Producing payslips
A warning system for 'seat belts not fastened' in a car
Running an interactive program from a terminal
Printing examination certificates
Traffic control
Monitoring a hospital patient's heart

b Select **ONE** of the applications you have ticked and describe briefly the processing involved.

16 Give **ONE** example of a utility program and **TWO** examples of applications packages.

17 A certain computer is to be used to monitor temperature levels at intervals of 1 second. It is also to be used to process data previously recorded. Interrupts are to be used to allow both tasks to be performed efficiently.

Explain what is meant by interrupts, with reference to the above example.

(MEG Spec.)

13 Types of Computer System

The Basic Components of Computers

The first computers were built in the 1940s and early 1950s. **Valves** were used as the principle components to construct the central processing units of these early computers. Figure 13.1 shows a typical valve.

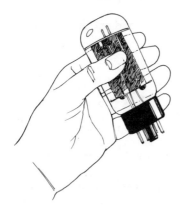

Figure 13.1   A valve

A valve is just an electronic switch with three connections. When the valve is 'open', electrical signals can flow freely between two of these connectors. An electrical signal sent to the third connector can 'close' the valve and halt this flow. Valves can thus be used to construct the switching circuits (or **gates**) used in the central processing unit. (See Chapter 5.)

Valves suffer from several disadvantages.

* They are large complicated devices and are very expensive to manufacture
* They are very fragile
* They are unreliable, often failing in use
* To work, valves require a considerable amount of electricity
* When working, valves produce a lot of heat.

As a result of these disadvantages, valve-based computers were very large, very expensive, unreliable, used a lot of electricity and needed special cooling equipment to control the heat produced. These valve-based machines are called **first-generation computers** (see Figure 13.2).

During the 1950s, transistors were developed to replace valves. A transistor is an automatic electronic switch just like a valve. Transistors are much smaller than valves (Figure 13.3). They are also cheaper, much less fragile, more reliable, use less electricity and produce less heat.

Figure 13.2   A valve-based computer

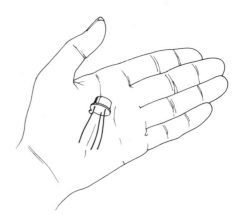

Figure 13.3   A transistor

As transistors replaced valves in computer manufacture, so computers became smaller, cheaper and much more reliable. These transistor-based machines are called **second-generation computers**.

Figure 13.4   A transistor-based computer

Transistors are made from materials called **semiconductors**. The most commonly used semiconductor is **silicon**. As research continued during the 1950s and 1960s it became possible to create more than one transistor on a single piece of silicon. Eventually, scientists learnt how to create complete transistor circuits on a small slice or **chip** of silicon. These tiny **integrated circuits**, complete with all the necessary components and internal connections, are only a few millimetres square. To provide external connections, very fine wires join the integrated circuit to a double row of pins. The whole circuit is usually embedded in a plastic case, with only the connecting pins protruding (see Figure 13.5).

At first, only a few dozen transistors were included on each chip but manufacturing techniques developed very rapidly. In 1972 the Intel 4004 appeared. This was the first **microprocessor chip**. It contained all the elements of a central processing unit in a single integrated circuit. Progress continues and some chips now contain the equivalent of over one million separate components. These chips are called **very large-scale integration** chips or **VLSI** chips. Integrated circuits have several advantages over circuits constructed by wiring together separate transistors.

* They are much cheaper to produce than wired separate transistor circuits

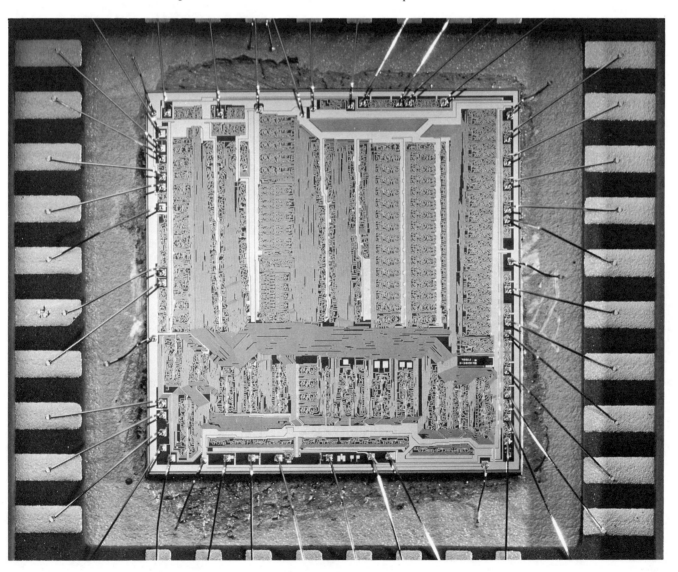

Figure 13.5 A typical integrated circuit with its case cut away to show the actual circuit and connectors, with its external connections *above* and an actual integrated circuit *below*

* They are much smaller than wired separate transistor circuits. A single integrated circuit, a few millimetres square, may contain the equivalent of hundreds of thousands of separate transistors
* They use very little electricity
* They are very reliable and robust because there are very few wired connections to corrode, work loose or break. Being made from solid silicon inside a plastic case, integrated circuits are almost unbreakable in normal use.

Integrated circuits are now the standard components from which all computers are made. The first integrated-circuit-based computers were called **third-generation computers**. The term **fourth-generation computers** is also used to describe integrated-circuit-based computers. Unfortunately, this term is used by different people in different ways. To some people, a fourth-generation computer is a **microcomputer**, a small computer based on a single microprocessor chip. To other people, a fourth-generation computer is any present-day computer based on VLSI chips.

Some people refuse to use the term fourth-generation computer and insist that any integrated circuit-based machine is still called a third-generation computer.

Types of Integrated Circuit

Random access memory chip (RAM). These chips provide immediate access memory which can be both read from and written to. RAM chips are usually used to store applications programs while they are being run by the computer. RAM chips are usually **volatile**. This means that they lose the software they are storing when the computer is switched off.

Read only memory chips (ROM). These chips provide immediate access memory which can be read from but not written to. ROM chips are normally used to store the systems programs needed to control the computer's operations. The software in a ROM chip is fixed during manufacture and is not lost when the computer is switched off.

Programmable read only memory (PROM). These chips are a special kind of ROM chip. The software is not fixed when the chip is manufactured, but is written into the chip at a later stage using a special device. After it has been programmed in this way, the PROM functions like a normal ROM, holding fixed software which is not lost when the computer is switched off. A variety of PROM called an **EPROM** (Erasable PROM) can have its contents erased with a special device and can then be

162

reprogrammed. PROMs and EPROMs are useful for developing new systems software and when only a few copies of a particular systems program are required.

Microprocessor chips. Microprocessor chips contain a single integrated circuit that can perform all the functions of a central processing unit. All microprocessor chips contain a control unit, an arithmetic and logic unit and an immediate access memory. The microprocessor's memory is usually very limited in size and RAM and ROM chips are used to provide extra immediate access memory.

Interface chips. These chips contain the electrical circuits needed to connect computers to external devices. They are connected to the central processing unit and also to the special sockets or **ports** where external devices are plugged into the computer. The computer and the external peripheral device may have many different operating characteristics — for example, speed and internal codes. The circuits in the interface chip must be designed to deal with all the problems of communication between the two devices. A **parallel input/output chip** (**PIO**) provides a means of sending and receiving parallel binary signals. A **serial input/output chip** (**SIO**) provides a means of sending and receiving serial binary signals. A computer will need PIO chips to communicate with parallel peripherals and SIO chips to communicate with serial peripherals.

Special purpose chips. Integrated circuits for any task can now be manufactured cheaply and quickly. Customers can even design their own circuit layout and then have this design etched into silicon by a chip manufacturer. This has led to a rapid growth in the use of special-purpose chips to replace conventional electrical circuits in a wide range of different devices. In computers they are used to provide analogue-to-digital converters, digital-to-analogue converters, address decoders, keyboard encoders, power regulators and speech synthesisers.

The availability of cheap special-purpose chips has led to an increase in the use of logic circuits to replace systems software. For example, some computers only have logic circuits for addition and subtraction of binary numbers. A systems program on a ROM chip allows these circuits to be used also for multiplication and division. An alternative and much faster method is to provide the computer with special-purpose chips containing logic circuits for multiplication and division. The use of these 'hardware' chips to replace systems software is likely to increase. For example, research has started on 'compiler chips' which will contain logic circuits to translate high-level languages into binary code automatically. If the research is successful, these chips may replace the machine code programs currently used to compile high-level languages.

Building Computers from Chips

Computers are built by mounting chips and other components on **printed circuit boards**. A printed circuit board is a thin sheet of insulating material on which copper tracks are formed to connect the various computer components. Most modern computers communicate binary data in a parallel form, and therefore the components must be linked with sets of parallel copper tracks. A set of parallel tracks used for communications between the components is called a **bus**. In most computers three separate buses are used, an **address bus**, a **data bus** and a **control bus**. Figure 13.6 shows a printed circuit board with chips and other components soldered on to it.

Figure 13.6 Chips mounted on a printed circuit board

Types of Computer

Dedicated microprocessors. The simplest computer systems are dedicated microprocessors used to control devices such as washing machines and calculators. A typical system consists of a microprocessor chip, a ROM chip to store the control program and an interface chip to connect the microprocessor to the device it controls. If the application is a simple one, all these functions may be combined on a single purpose-made chip. Figure 13.7 shows the essential components of a microprocessor control system.

Notice that a single data bus is used to connect all the components in the microprocessor system. The address bus is used to select which part of which particular chip has access to the data bus at any given moment. The control bus is used to decide if data will be read from or written to the bus by that chip.

Microcomputers. A microcomputer is a computer which uses a microprocessor chip for its central processing unit. Microcomputers are relatively cheap computers, usually provided with a single-user interactive

JARGON

BY CLIVE WILKINS & ROSS SPEIRS

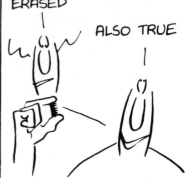

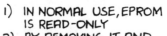
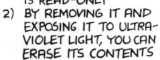

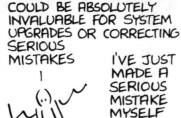

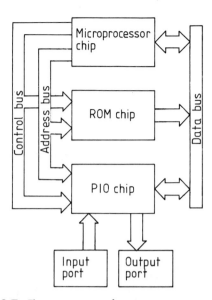

Figure 13.7 The components of a microprocessor control system

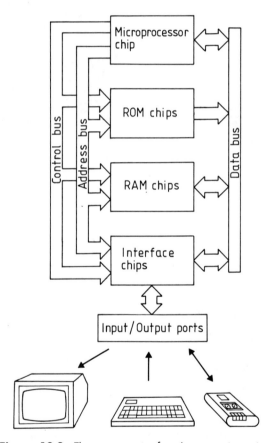

Figure 13.8 The components of a microcomputer system

usually provided on cassette tapes or floppy discs. The memory in the microprocessor chip is usually very limited, and RAM chips are used to provide additional immediate access memory. A variety of interface chips are used to link the microcomputer to keyboards, TV screens, cassette recorders, disc drives, printers and other devices. Figure 13.8 shows the essential components of a microcomputer system.

Mainframe Computers

A mainframe computer is the computer at the centre of a large computer system. Even when VLSI chips are used, the complex central processing unit of a mainframe computer will be spread over many chips. Mainframe computers are relatively expensive computers, usually provided with both multiprogramming and multi-access operating systems. Several programming languages are often provided. These are usually translated in to machine code with compilers. The operating system and other systems programs are usually held partly on ROM chips and partly on a fast-access backing store. A wide variety of input and output devices is usually provided. These peripheral devices will be expensive, high-speed, high-capacity, professional-quality equipment. Secondary storage is usually provided on reel-to-reel tapes and hard discs. Mainframe computers are usually provided with several megabytes of RAM memory. The interfaces used between mainframe computers and peripheral devices are far more complex than the simple circuits used in microcomputers. Often, **peripheral device controllers** are used that can function independently of the main central processing unit. These device controllers can supervise the transfer of data between the peripheral

operating system. The most common programming language for microcomputers is BASIC, usually translated into machine code with an interpreter. Both the operating system and the BASIC interpreter are normally stored on ROM chips. Usually a keyboard is provided for input and a TV screen for output. If desired, it is usually possible also to connect a joystick for input and a printer for output. Secondary storage is

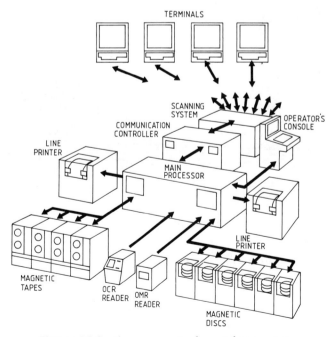

Figure 13.9 The components of a mainframe system

165

devices and the computer's memory while the computer continues with other processing. A diagram of the internal connections of a mainframe computer is too complex to be included here, but Figure 13.9 does show the main components of a typical mainframe computer system.

Minicomputers. Minicomputers were developed during the 1960s as smaller, cheaper, less well-equipped alternatives to mainframe computers. Minicomputers are often used to support mainframe computer systems, either directly by acting as front-end processors or indirectly by controlling key-to-disc data preparation. The exact dividing line between minicomputers and small mainframe computers has never been completely clear and the term has become even more vague with the introduction of microcomputers. Many of the latest microcomputers have speeds and capacities that rival those of minicomputers. (See Figure 13.10.)

Figure 13.10 This ICL System 25 mini computer can cope with 20 tasks simultaneously at 50 terminals. The processor cabinet contains up to 1.28 Mbytes mainstore with up to 600 Mbytes of disc storage.

Supercomputers. Supercomputers are the most complex computers that have yet been manufactured. By using many advanced design techniques they achieve very high computing speeds. These very high speeds allow supercomputers to tackle 'number-crunching' problems which were previously beyond the capacity of any mainframe computer. For example, the supercomputer used in the British Meteorological Office completes over 100 000 000 000 calculations in order to produce a weather forecast for the next 24 hours. The supercomputer completes this enormous number of calculations in just four minutes! (See Figure 13.11.)

Figure 13.11 A Cray supercomputer

Computer Networks

A **network** is a linked group of computers, often sharing computing power, storage facilities and other resources. The network may be spread over a wide geographical area or concentrated into a single room or building. Widespread networks are called **wide-area networks** and concentrated networks are called **local-area networks**. Wide-area networks may be linked by modems and telephone lines, microwave radio or even communications satellites. Local-area networks are usually linked with direct wire connectors.

Wide-area networks are often used to link mainframe computers in several different cities and countries. For example, one large Canadian company has factories in two English cities. The mainframe computer at the company's Canadian headquarters is linked with mainframe computers in both the English factories. The network links in England are provided with modems and telephone lines. The link to Canada is provided by telecommunications signals sent via a communications satellite. An outline diagram of this wide-area network is shown in Figure 13.12.

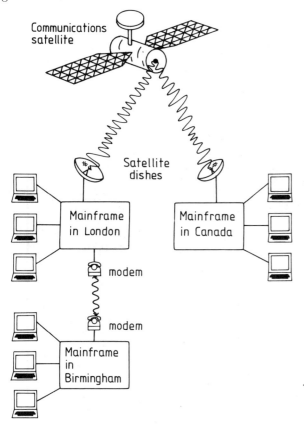

Figure 13.12 A wide-area network

The advantages of a wide-area network linking together several mainframe computers are:

* If one computer in the network develops a fault, some or all of its work can be transferred to other computers in the network
* The workload for the whole network can be spread over all the computers in the network
* The linked computers can provide a very powerful database and communications system. When data is updated on one computer, it is immediately updated on all the other computers in the network.

Local-area networks are normally used to link several microcomputers in the same room or building. One example is a network linking a group of microcomputers in a school's computer room. Another example is a network linking together microcomputers in each room of an office building. Because the distances between the computers are relatively short, local-area networks are connected by permanent wire links. Local-area networks

can be connected in many different ways. Two common ways to connect up the computers are **bus networks** and **ring networks**. In a bus network, all the computers are connected to a single cable or **bus**. In a ring network, all the computers are connected to a loop or **ring** of cable. In any local-area network, at least one computer is designated as a **file server** and at least one computer is designated as a **print server**. (Note that in some networks, one computer may be used for both tasks.) The file server will be connected to a large capacity floppy or hard disc drive. The print server will be connected to a printer. The file server micro and the print server micro will allow any other micro in the network to use the disc drive or the printer. Figure 13.13 shows the outlines of a typical bus network and a typical ring network.

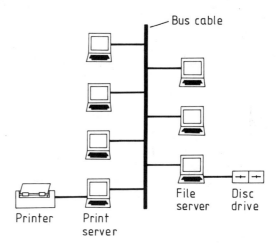

A bus network

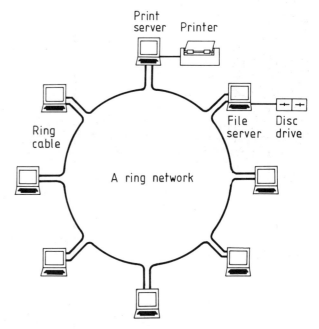

Figure 13.13 Bus and ring networks

JARGON

BY CLIVE WILKINS
& ROSS SPEIRS

The advantages of a local-area network linking together several microcomputers are:

* Expensive peripherals such as disc drives and printers can be shared between several microcomputers.
* The network can form an internal communications system. This is not important when the computers are in the same room but can be very useful when the computers are distributed round a large office building. An office manager, for example, can use a network to send a message to all the computers in the building.

Different Ways of Using Computers

In the previous chapter we looked at different operating systems and the ways in which they organised the computer's resources. We looked in detail at the operating systems that provide single-user interactive computing, multiprogrammed batch processing and multi-access interactive computing. We will now return to the topic of different computer systems, but this time looking through the eyes of the computer user. At this point, we must define exactly what is meant by a computer user. A **computer user** is the person or machine for whom the computer undertakes a data processing task. This person may or may not be a programmer and may in fact have no direct contact with the computer.

The computer user is only concerned with the way in which a computer system functions. He or she is not concerned with the details of the operating system that allows the computer to function in this way.

From the point of view of the user, there are three main ways in which a computer system can function.

Off-line computer systems are ones in which the user is not in direct contact with the computer. They are used for batch processing. In a batch processing system, the computer user supplies data which is then prepared and batched by data preparation staff. Computer operators will then supervise the actual computer processing, and the final output will be returned to the user. The user may send the data to a computer department in the same company or to an independent **computer bureau**. A computer bureau is a company which owns a large computer system and rents out its use to other organisations. For example, a small firm which does not own a computer can use the facilities offered by a computer bureau to process their payroll. Usually, the customers of the computer bureau send in the data, it is processed by the bureau's own staff, and the output is then returned to the customer.

The fall in the cost of computer equipment has led to a decline in the use of off-line systems. Today, they are usually only used for applications which require a regular updating and processing of all the records in a large computer file.

Remote job entry (**RJE**) is a form of batch processing in which the user may have a limited amount of direct contact with the computer system. A remote job entry system uses card readers, paper tape readers or document readers to input batch data from a remote site. These devices are linked to the main computer with modems and telephone lines. The input data is batch-processed by the computer, and the output is either posted back to the user or printed on a line printer at the remote site. RJE users often input their data themselves, but the batch processing features of RJE make it far more like off-line computing than on-line computing.

On-line computer systems are ones in which the user is in direct contact with the computer. They are used for interactive computing. On-line computing is usually provided in one of two ways: either by a microcomputer or by a multi-access terminal linked to a mainframe computer or minicomputer. On-line computer systems can be divided into **real-time systems** and **non-real-time systems**.

Real-time computer systems. In a real-time computer system the input–process–output sequence is carried out quickly enough to influence or control the source of the input data. There are four features which distinguish real-time computer systems.

* A real-time system is designed to control or influence a single activity
* While the system is active, it is used only to run the applications programs. No program writing or modification is allowed to take place
* The system is designed always to produce a response to any input data within a fixed time limit
* Any data files used by the system are always kept completely up to date.

There are two main types of real-time system in common use:

* **Commercial database systems**. These can be called real-time systems if each transaction immediately updates the computer's files before any further transactions can take place. Any transaction is thus influenced by all previous transactions. An example is an airline ticket booking system. If a user contacts this system at 1030, all the ticket bookings made before 1030 will have been registered in the computer's files. It will be

impossible for the user to book a ticket that has already been booked in a previous transaction. The system is therefore always up to date in the user's **real-time**. Systems like this use multi-access terminals, but usually guarantee that the user will receive a response within a fixed time limit. For example, one airline system is designed to respond to 90% of user requests within three seconds.

* **Computer control systems**. These are called real-time systems because they must produce an almost immediate response to any input data. An example is a computer control system for a space rocket. Sensors will send the computer details of the rocket engine's current performance and the rocket's position on its flight path. The computer must process this data within milliseconds and then output control signals to maintain the correct engine performance and flight path. The computer must react quickly enough to control the rocket's flight successfully. It must operate in the rocket's **real-time**.

Non-real-time interactive systems. It is often quite difficult to distinguish between on-line interactive systems that work in real time and ones that do not. The point to remember is that real-time systems are designed to control or influence an activity as it actually takes place. Thus, a real-time ticket booking system influences ticket bookings by providing a completely up-to-date enquiry service. A real-time computer control system controls machinery while it is working.

There are five features which distinguish a non-real-time interactive system:

* It is often used for many different applications
* While the system is active, users may be allowed to enter, edit and run their own programs
* The system is designed to produce an interactive response as quickly as possible, but there is no fixed time limit within which a response must be produced
* Any data files used by the system will be updated from time to time, but are not updated immediately after each transaction. At any given time, some of the data in the computer's files may be out of date
* If an on-line database service is provided, it will be for enquiries only and will not allow any immediate transactions or file updating.

Figure 13.14 shows the main types of computer system from the point of view of a computer user.

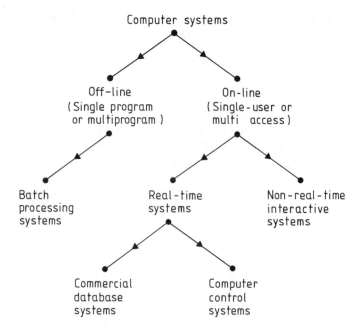

Figure 13.14 A summary of the types of computer system

Problems with Definitions

The definition of a **real-time** computer system is not clearly agreed by all computer experts. Most agree that a real-time system is one in which the input–process–output sequence is carried out quickly enough to infuence or control the source of the input data, but exact interpretations of this definition vary considerably.

Some experts focus entirely on the *speed* with which a response is produced. If a very low time limit is set for this response, most commercial database applications are excluded and the definition is effectively restricted to computer control systems. This seems (to me) a poor definition of real-time computing because it ignores two facts:

* Most commercial databases do operate in the user's real time because each transaction affects all subsequent transactions
* It is common practice in the computer industry to call commercial database applications 'real-time computing'.

Students who are used to the clear and universally accepted definitions offered in other subjects may be worried by this note. You must however realise that computing is a new and developing science. Problems with definitions are bound to occur, especially when some definitions are produced for marketing and advertising purposes rather than for purely scientific reasons. The best solution to your problem is to contact your examination board and to ask them to clarify their position on any difficult definitions.

Exercise 51

1 Copy and complete the following passages.

a The first computers were built in the 19_____s and early 19_____s. _____ were used as the principle components to construct the central processing unit of these early computers. A valve is an electronic _____ which can be used to construct logic gates. Valves suffer from several disadvantages. These are:

  *_____
  *_____
  *_____
  *_____
  *_____

b _____ were developed during the 19_____s as a replacement for valves. _____ are much smaller than valves, cheaper, less _____, more _____, use less _____ and produce less _____. Eventually scientists learnt how to create complete _____ on a small chip of _____. These tiny _____ circuits are only a few millimetres square but may contain over a million components.

c _____ chips are used to provide memory that can be both read from and written to. _____ chips are used to provide memory that can only be read from. _____ chips are a form of ROM chip which can be programmed after they have been manufactured. _____ chips are a form of ROM chip which can be programmed, erased and reprogrammed. A _____ chip contains a single integrated circuit which can perform all the functions of a central processing unit. _____ chips contain the electrical circuits necessary to connect the computer to external devices. Computers are constructed by mounting chips and other devices on to _____ boards.

d Dedicated _____ are used to control devices such as washing machines and calculators. A _____ is a computer which uses a microprocessor chip for its CPU. A _____ computer is the computer at the centre of a large computer system. A _____ is a smaller, cheaper, less well equipped alternative to a mainframe computer. A _____ is a computer which uses advanced design techniques to achieve very high calculating speeds.

e A _____ is a linked group of computers. A _____ spread over a wide geographical area is called a _____. A _____ concentrated into a single room or building is called a _____. The computers in a _____ are usually connected by modems and telephone lines, microwave radio or telecommunications satellites. The computers in a _____ are usually connected with direct wire links.

2 Read the following passage and then answer the questions which follow.
'The standard model of the B.B.C. microcomputer uses a 6502 microprocessor, has 16K RAM, 32K ROM, high resolution graphics and uses a keyboard, a domestic T.V. receiver and a cassette record. The 32K ROM includes a 16K BASIC and a 16K operating system.'

a What input devices are used?
b What is meant by 'high resolution graphics'?
c What is meant by 'RAM'?
d Explain the meaning of the final sentence to someone who has never met the terms 'ROM', 'BASIC' and 'operating system', and this particular use of the letter K.

(SUJB 82)

Early Computers

ENIAC

ENIAC was built between 1943 and 1946. It was a valve based electronic calculator.

Colossus

Colossus was built in 1943. It was a special purpose machine designed for code breaking during World War II.

Manchester Mark I

Operational in 1949, the Manchester Mark I has a wordlength of 50 bits and a 128 word internal memory.

EDSAC

First used in 1949, EDSAC had an internal memory of 1024, 17-bit words. Paper tape was used for input and output.

EDVAC

In full use by 1952, EDVAC had an internal memory of 1024, 44-bit words.

UNIVAC

In total, 46 UNIVAC computers were built between 1951 and 1958. These were general purpose computers designed for commercial data processing. The internal memory contained 1000 84-bit words. Punched cards were used for input, a printer for output and magnetic tape for secondary storage.

---

3 The diagram below shows the printed circuit board from a Sinclair Spectrum microcomputer.

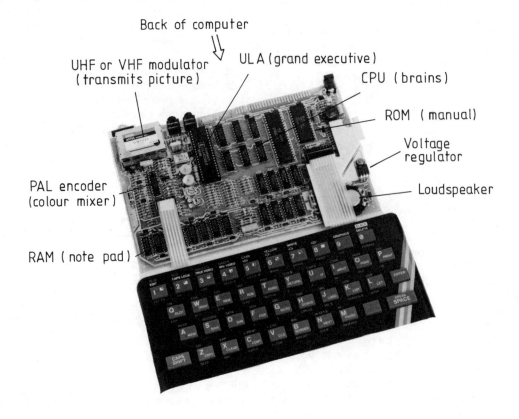

Back of computer

UHF or VHF modulator (transmits picture)

ULA (grand executive)

CPU (brains)

ROM (manual)

Voltage regulator

PAL encoder (colour mixer)

Loudspeaker

RAM (note pad)

a Why are the RAM chips labelled *Note pad*?

b Why is the ROM chip labelled *Manual*?

c Why is the CPU chip labelled *Brains*?

d The computer handbook says that the ROM chip contains a 16K BASIC. What is meant by this term?

e The ULA (uncommitted logic array) chip is manufactured as a large array of logic gates. The logic circuits needed for a particular application are created at a later stage by 'burning out' unwanted connections on the chip. The ULA in the Spectrum replaces many ROM chips found in other computers and acts as a 'communications centre' for the computer. Explain some of the functions that you think this 'communications centre' will provide.

4 The article below describes a wide-area network that allows several mainframe computers to access a large mass storage system.

NatWest goes for Masstor in £2m contract

by Eamon Quinn

National Westminster Bank is set to instal Masstor storage systems, worth £2 million, to back up customer account information from its high street branches.

The latest order will up National Westminster's total investment in Masstor M860 storage devices to £5 million; split over two computing sites in London and the Midlnds.

The M860 cassette devices supply a total of 770 gigabytes of storage as backup to online and archival customer account information collected by seven IBM 3081 and two IBM 3084 mainframes.

Masstor's high speed networking products, Massnet, will shortly be installed to link the two sites.

The National Westminster is the biggest European customer for Masstor storage and retrieval devices.

Other UK-based Masstor customers are the Royal Bank of Scotland, the Science and Engineering Research Council, the universities of Manchester and London, and British Petroleum (BP) Oil.

The M860s are typically used to back up IBM-based mainframes in preference to IBM 3380 double capacity hard disk storage devices. BP Oil, which is sticking to three mainframe suppliers, uses the M860 to back up its Sperry Mainframe.

(*Computing*, 10 October 1984)

Explain in your own words the meaning of each of the following extracts from the article:

a *to back up customer account information*
b *The M860 cassette device supply a total of 770 giga-bytes of storage. (The prefix 'giga' means one thousand million.)*
c *seven IBM 3801 and two IBM 3084 mainframes*
d *IBM 3380 double capacity hard disc storage devices*
e *Masstor's high speed networking products, Massnet, will shortly be installed to link the two sites.*

5 The article below describes how a supercomputer was used to discover a new prime number.

Numbers game

One for the mathematics fiends: scientists testing a Cray X MP super computer have claimed the largest prime number ever. A prime is a number divisible only by itself and 1, and cryptographers are keen on them. This one is the number 2 raised to the 216,091st power minus one. It contains 65,050 digits and would fill two pages of a newspaper, if any newspaper were fool enough to print it. It took the Cray three hours to test the number at 400 million calculations per second. The discoverers were Chevron Geosciences in Houston. Mind you, they were supposed to be looking for oil when their number came up, so to speak.

(*Guardian*, 26 September 1985)

a Write down the new prime number using the usual convention for writing powers of a number.
b How many calculations did the supercomputer perform to test the new prime number?

6 The extract from an article below describes part of a computer controlled cross-channel electricity link. This link has recently been completed and allows England and France to sell each other surplus electricity.

The second system Honeywell is supplying is the bi-lingual message system which will be used by both sides to order electricity and make contracts. The aim of the system is to avoid the dangers of misunderstanding through language difficulties.

The system consists of an x.25 ring network of eight DRTI-6 ruggedised microcomputers to cope with the noisy conditions inside the converter stations. The DRTIs will be located at each of the local control points, the main control points in England and France and at the national control centres in London and Paris.

The system allows pre-defined messages to be sent in English and received in French, and vice versa. Each DRTI-6 will store up to 140 messages in 27128 Eproms in the language of the country where it is located. The operator can select the appropriate pre-defined message and complete it by adding numbers in the variable parts of the message using the touch-sensitive plasma screens. A typical message would be 'We wish to exchange --- MW commencing at --- on ---,' leaving the operator to fill in the appropriate numbers.

The message number and the variable data are transmitted around the ring to the appropriate nodes. They are posted both ways round the ring for security reasons and the second message to arrive is discarded.

All contracts between the CEGB and EDF concerning trading over the Channel link will be made via the message system.

In situations where the pre-defined messages are not enough, operators can send their own message using a Qwerty keyboard, although these messages would not be translated.

If in the future either side wishes to change the range of pre-defined messages the changes would have to be decided and agreed by both sides, before creating new Eproms and inserting them into each node.

(*Computing*, 3 October 1985)

Explain in your own words the meaning of each of the following extracts from the article:

a *bilingual message system*
b *misunderstanding through language difficulties*
c *ruggedised microcomputers*
d *touch sensitive plasma screens*
e *The message number and the variable data are transmitted round the ring to the appropriate nodes.*
f *They are posted both ways round the ring for security reasons and the second message to arrive is discarded*
g *In situations where the predefined messages are not enough, operators can send their own message using a Qwerty keyboard*
h *creating new eproms and inserting them into each node*

7 Study each of the following short descriptions of computer systems. In each case state whether the system is an example of batch processing, real-time on-line computing or non-real-time on-line computing. Explain why you have decided to classify each system in the way you have.

a *A student computing facility at a university*. The system uses 50 multi-access terminals linked to a mainframe computer. Each student uses a terminal to enter, edit and run computer programs. These programs are solutions to problems that are set as part of a computer science course. The system is designed to provide quite a fast response but, when all the terminals are in use, delays become noticeable and a user may have to wait several seconds for each response from the computer.

b *A shop stock control system which used Kimball tags to capture data.* The tags are collected as garments are sold and at the end of each day sent to a central computer installation for processing.

c *A dedicated microprocessor system used to control a washing machine.* The microprocessor system receives input data on water level and temperature from sensors in the machine. It outputs control signals to the motor, water heater, water valves and pump.

8 a Give **one** example of a real time application explaining why it must be real time

b Give **one** example of an interactive non real time application explaining why real time is not necessary.

c Give **one** way in which real time applications differ from non real time applications.

(AEB 85)

9 Read the following advertisement.

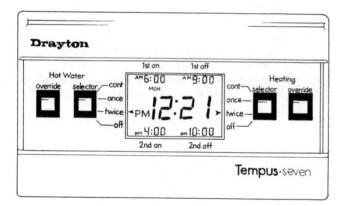

The new TEMPUS SEVEN central heating programmer knows when you're not getting up early for work!

Until now, central heating/hot water programmers have usually worked on the same time-settings every day, day in

— day out. It meant Saturday lie-ins or irregular working hours were wasting expensive fuel, because the boiler automatically came on and turned off at the same time regardless, unless you remembered to flick a switch.

Now, Drayton Controls has come up with the easiest-to-fit, simplest-to-set replacement that uses microcomputer technology to keep your heating system exactly in tune with your needs.

The Drayton Tempus seven allows each day's timings to be set differently.

By matching the day's heating programme more accurately you can cut out wasted hours of unnecessary boiler operation. The Tempus seven microcomputer programmer keeps note of each separate day's requirements in its electronic memory, protected against even momentary mains power failure by a backup battery. So if you're the sort of person who has a varied pattern of waking and sleeping throughout the week (and who doesn't?), this is the perfect replacement unit for you.

That possibly noisy, probably worn-out old electro-mechanical programmer won't last forever and it's almost certainly costing you wasted fuel. So now's the time to bring in high-tech intelligence by replacing it with the electronically accurate, virtually silent and visually attractive Tempus seven.

a Find out how an electro-mechanical central heating programmer works and write a description of an electro-mechanical programmer, illustrating your description with sketches.

b Write a description of a microprocessor-based central heating programmer, illustrating your description with sketches.

c List the advantages that microprocessor-based central heating programmers have over electro-mechanical programmers.

14 Computers in Commerce

The range of computer applications is vast and is added to almost daily. It would be impossible to list every computer application in a whole book, but the final chapters in this book attempt an overall picture.

Commercial Data Processing

Commercial data processing accounts for over 70% of all present day computer use. In previous chapters we have already looked at a payroll application and a ticket booking application. This chapter looks at some other common business applications.

Stock Control

Most businesses need to hold stocks of goods. For example, manufacturers need to hold stocks of the raw materials that they use and the finished goods that they make. In the same way, shops need to hold stocks of the wide range of goods that they sell to their customers. The task of recording and maintaining stock levels is called **stock control**. A stock control system must keep an up-to-date record of all the stock held and place orders for fresh deliveries if stock runs low. There are many different kinds of stock control system. Figure 14.1 shows the outline of a simple manual system used in a small shop once each week.

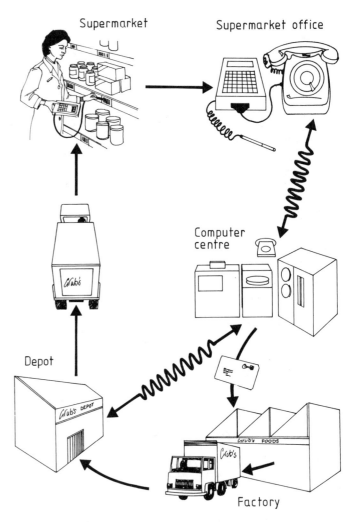

Figure 14.2 Every day, in each supermarket, a shopworker uses a hand-held data recorder to check the stock. This has a number keypad and a bar code reader. The bar code reader is used to read bar codes on the shelves. These bar codes automatically enter the coded name of the item. The shopworker then enters the estimated quantity needed using the numbered keypad. The data recorder can send the collected data directly to the computer centre using a modem and telephone link. The computer processes the order and sends direct instructions to stock depots to deliver fresh stocks to the shops. These orders are printed out on a remote line printer in each depot. The computer also has a separate stock control system to keep the depots stocked with goods. The orders for these goods are posted to the factories where they are made.

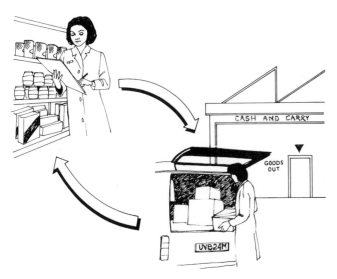

Figure 14.1 A simple stock control system. The shopkeeper checks the shelves and makes a note of the new stock needed. He then drives to a cash-and-carry warehouse and buys the new stock.

Large shops, supermarkets and factories often use computerised stock control systems. Figure 14.2 shows the outline of a stock control system used in a chain of supermarkets.

An alternative to counting stock directly is to keep a record of all stock that is sold or delivered. These stocks can then be subtracted from or added to the total stocks for the shop or factory. A system like this cannot, however, keep a check on goods that leave the shelves without being sold. A direct count of the stock will still be necessary from time to time to check that goods have not been stolen, broken, damaged or moved to the wrong shelf.

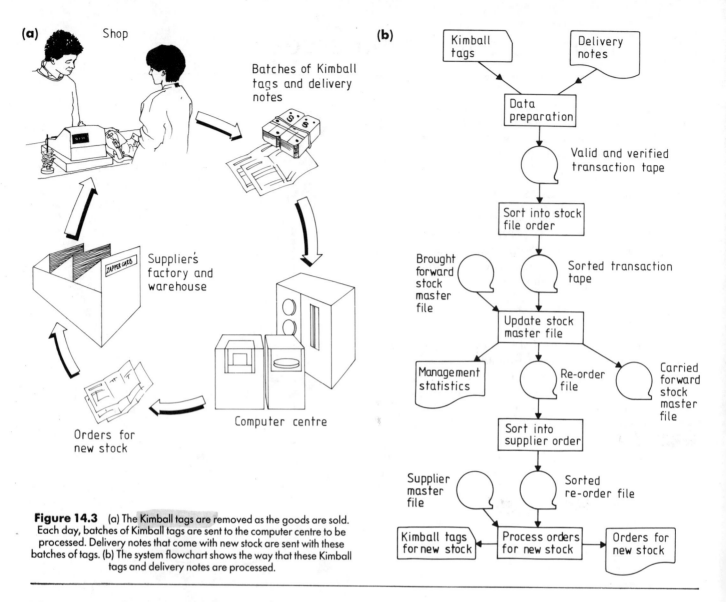

(a) Shop

Batches of Kimball tags and delivery notes

Suppliers factory and warehouse

Computer centre

Orders for new stock

(b)

Kimball tags

Delivery notes

Data preparation

Valid and verified transaction tape

Sort into stock file order

Brought forward stock master file

Sorted transaction tape

Update stock master file

Management statistics

Re-order file

Carried forward stock master file

Sort into supplier order

Supplier master file

Sorted re-order file

Kimball tags for new stock

Process orders for new stock

Orders for new stock

Figure 14.3 (a) The Kimball tags are removed as the goods are sold. Each day, batches of Kimball tags are sent to the computer centre to be processed. Delivery notes that come with new stock are sent with these batches of tags. (b) The system flowchart shows the way that these Kimball tags and delivery notes are processed.

Most systems that use this indirect method of stock control have some form of automatic data capture at the point of sale. Kimball tags, bar codes, magnetic stripe labels, OCR tags and OMR tags may all be used. Figure 14.3 shows the outline of an indirect stock control system that uses Kimball tags for automatic data capture.

A record from the transaction tape is shown in Figure 14.4. This file is sorted into reference number order. A record from the stock master file is shown in Figure 14.5.

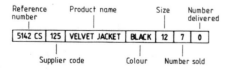

Reference number		Product name	Size		Number delivered
5142 CS	125	VELVET JACKET	BLACK	12	7	0

Supplier code   Colour   Number sold

Figure 14.4 A record from the transaction tape. 'Reference number', 'supplier code', etc. are the names of the 'fields'.

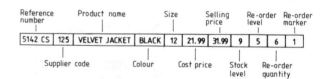

Reference number   Product name   Size   Selling price   Re-order level   Re-order marker

5142 CS | 125 | VELVET JACKET | BLACK | 12 | 21.99 | 31.99 | 9 | 5 | 6 | 1

Supplier code   Colour   Cost price   Stock level   Re-order quantity

Figure 14.5 A record from the stock file with its fields as indicated.

This file is also held in reference number order. The re-order marker is set to one when new stock is ordered and re-set to zero when the new stock is delivered. This prevents a second order being placed before a first order can be delivered. After this file has been updated, if the stock level is less than the re-order level *and* the re-order marker is zero, an order is made for the re-order quantity. This order is recorded on the re-order tape. Figure 14.6 shows a record from the re-order file.

176

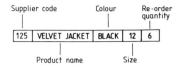

Figure 14.6 A record from the re-order file with its fields as indicated.

This file is sorted into supplier code order.

Figure 14.7 A record from the supplier master file.

Figure 14.7 shows a record from the supplier master file. This file is held in supplier code order. The re-order file and the supplier master file are used together to produce orders to be sent to the various suppliers and to punch new Kimball tags for the goods.

If an on-line terminal is installed at the point of sale, it is possible to create a real-time stock control system. Figure 14.8 shows the outline of a real-time stock control system which uses bar codes for automatic data capture.

All stock control systems attempt to satisfy two conflicting aims.

* Adequate stocks must be maintained to supply a customer with goods at any time with minimum delay. If customers find goods are regularly out of stock, they will find other suppliers and business will be lost.
* To keep business expenses to a minimum, goods must not be overstocked. By keeping stocks to a minimum, a business can limit the amount of money invested in stock and also reduce the risk of stock deteriorating before it can be sold. Minimum stock levels will also cut storage costs such as warehousing, heating, lighting and security.

Computer stock control systems allow managers to monitor stock levels very closely. With the computer's help, stock levels can be maintained at the minimum level that will meet the customer's demands. This allows a business both to increase customer satisfaction and to reduce its own costs.

In addition to these advantages, on-line stock control systems offer the following advantages:

* Customer service is much quicker. This means that either each POS terminal can serve more customers or that queues can be reduced.

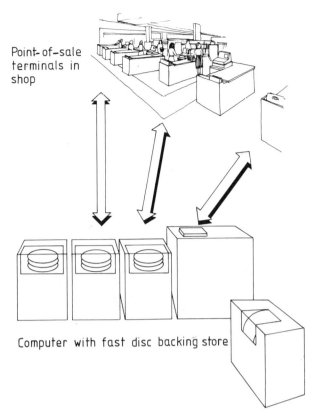

Point-of-sale terminals in shop

Computer with fast disc backing store

Figure 14.8 A real-time stock control system. The POS terminal operator only needs to pass the bar code on each item past a laser scanner. The scanner reads the code number stored in the bar code and sends it directly to a computer. The computer checks the code and, if it is valid, looks up the product's name and price in data files held on disc backing store. The name and price are sent back to the POS terminal. In this way the POS terminal can print a fully itemised bill, even though the bar code only contains a product code number. Each terminal has a keyboard that can be used if a bar code cannot be read. As each item is sold, the stock files are updated and orders are printed when they become necessary. The system uses stock master files and supplier master files with a similar record structure to those in the last example. Because these files are held on disc, they can be updated directly and separate transaction files are not necessary.

* There are very few mistakes in charging customers because the systems use on-line automatic data capture.
* Prices can be updated very easily because the price is usually marked only on the shelf and not on each separate item.
* Very accurate sales statistics can be produced.
* Because each item does not need a price label, considerable savings can be made in time and labour costs.
* A fully itemised bill can be provided for the customer.

Against these advantages, we must consider these disadvantages:

* When laser bar code readers are used, prices are usually only marked on the shelves, not on each item. This can be confusing for customers.
* The cost of the equipment is very high.

Exercise 52

1 Explain why a manual stock control system is suitable for a small shop but not for a chain of supermarkets.

2 Explain the advantages gained by using shelf bar codes and a data recorder to check stock levels.

3 Explain why a Kimball tag system is suitable for a dress shop but not for a supermarket.

4 The tables below show part of the contents of a stock transaction file and a stock master file.

Reference number	Supplier	Product name	Colour	Size	Number sold	Number delivered
0276 E	52	Check shirt	Blue	10	5	0
0277 E	52	Check shirt	Blue	12	3	6
0278 E	52	Check shirt	Blue	14	5	6
0279 E	52	Check shirt	Blue	16	3	0
0283 G	47	Jumper	Black	10	8	0
0284 G	47	Jumper	Off-white	10	6	10
0285 G	47	Jumper	Black	12	0	10
0286 G	47	Jumper	Off-white	12	5	10
0287 G	47	Jumper	Black	14	4	0
0288 G	47	Jumper	Off-white	14	3	0

Reference number	Supplier	Product name	Colour	Size	Cost price	Selling price	Stock level	Re-order level	Re-order quantity	Re-order marker
0276 E	52	Check shirt	Blue	10	7.00	17.00	12	8	6	0
0277 E	52	Check shirt	Blue	12	9.00	17.00	6	8	6	1
0278 E	52	Check shirt	Blue	14	9.50	18.00	5	8	6	1
0279 E	52	Check shirt	Blue	16	9.50	18.50	10	8	6	0
0283 G	47	Jumper	Black	10	8.50	13.50	14	8	10	0
0284 G	47	Jumper	Off-white	10	8.50	13.50	6	8	10	1
0285 G	47	Jumper	Black	12	8.50	13.50	2	8	10	1
0286 G	47	Jumper	Off-white	12	8.50	13.50	5	8	10	1
0287 G	47	Jumper	Black	14	9.00	14.50	13	8	10	0
0288 G	47	Jumper	Off-white	14	9.00	14.50	9	8	10	0

a Draw a diagram to show the new contents of the stock master file after it has been updated. Remember that if stock has been delivered, the re-order marker must be re-set to zero. If it is necessary to order new stock, the re-order marker must be set to one. In some cases, this may mean re-setting the market to zero and then immediately setting it to 1 again.

b Draw a diagram to show the contents of the re-order file that will be created as the stock master tape is updated.

c Explain why it is necessary to sort the re-order file.

d Invent a company name and then design some pre-printed stationery that could be used by your company to make the orders recorded in the re-order file. If supplier number 47 is Zap Shirts of Bee Street, Buzzwell, Honeyshire, write out the order that will be placed with Zap Shirts on your pre-printed stationery.

5 Below is a Bar Code as found on products sold in super-markets.

a Explain how the data from the Bar Code is input to the computer.

b Say how this method of data input is beneficial:
  (i) to the customer
  (ii) to the supermarket

(AEB 82)

3 020640 111611

6 A manufacturing company produces and sells a number of types of breakfast food. The raw materials for these products (cereals, sugar, cardboard for boxes etc.) are purchased from outside suppliers and stored in a warehouse until they are needed. After manufacture, the breakfast foods are packed and stored in the warehouse until they are sold.

Describe a system for keeping control of the levels of stock (both raw materials and manufactured goods) in the warehouse, indicating ways in which a computer might be used to assist in this control. Use systems flowcharts to show the flow of data both within and outside the company. Describe suitable methods for collecting the data required by the system and describe the forms of the reports which will be produced.

(C 82)

7 A firm which owns a chain of food stores and a warehouse from which they are supplied, is planning to use a central computer to control the ordering of goods and the delivery of stock between the warehouse and the shops.

  a Describe an off-line method of collecting data about current stock levels and say how this data would be sent to the computer.
  b Describe an on-line method of collecting data about current stock levels which is suitable for a real time system and say what kind of backing store would be necessary in this case.
  c A separate stock file is to be kept for each shop. List **three** items of data, apart from cost and details of the actual product, which would be kept on this file for each product.
  d There is also to be a separate stock file for the warehouse. Name **one** additional item of information which would be kept on this file.
  e What information would be output from the system
    (i) to help to keep supplies in the shops at the right level;
    (ii) to help to keep supplies in the warehouse at the right level.
  f What information could be output from the computer to reduce the amount of fuel used by the delivery lorries?
  g State **one** advantage to the customer of using stock control.
  h State **one** advantage to the firm of using stock control.
  (WMEB 82)

8 Read the article below and then write a summary of the advantages and disadvantages of electronic point-of-sale terminals.

The supermarket and hypermarket scene in the UK is dominated by a handful of very large companies. There are 444 superstores and hypermarkets operated by 55 companies but Tesco, Asda, Fine Fare and Kwik Save, operate between them over half of all such stores.

Of these, Tesco, with a turnover of £2.4 billion, has committed itself to epos. In 1981 the company stated it would spend £100 million over the next decade on new technology. However, at present it only has complete systems (including scanning) in its 30 Victor Value stores.

Asda, whose pre-tax profits for 1982–83 were £24 million higher than Tesco's, has committed all its stores to an epos programme, based on IBM equipment. With a turnover of £1.7 billion, Asda has around 9% of the grocery market.

Fine Fare has also made a commitment to epos. However, like Tesco, it has a total system with scanning only in its Shoppers Paradise outlets. Currently it has one store being implemented with scanning every week.

Robert Gavaghan, general merchandising and productivity director with Fine Fare, points out that it is easier to evaluate scanning in the Shoppers Paradise environment than in a large Fine Fare.

Kwik Save has 380 stores from Newcastle-upon-Tyne to Portsmouth but has no intention in the near future of converting to epos. Since it is a discount store, it stocks a much smaller number of lines than, say Tesco, and feels that the costs are not jusitified.

Food retailers work on very small profit margins and overheads must be nailed down as hard as possible. Since the average price of a check-out lane with epos is £5,000–£7,000 compared to some £700 for non-epos, the cost benefits have to be proven.

Sainsbury, Tesco's rival for market supremacy, is currently experimenting with ICL's Supermarket 20 in-store computer system with scanner at its Wimbledon store. It is also installing some 200 System 25 minicomputers at its large outlets. These will handle a number of sophisticated branch applications which can be linked, via an SNA network, to the mainframe computers at Sainbury's London head office.

The order was a multi-million pound one for ICL. In its last financial year, Sainsbury's turnover was £2.68 billion, with pre-tax profits of £138.1 million.

Laws Stores, one of the small multiple chains with 44 outlets is implementing scanning in two stores at present. After evaluation of these trials, with NCR and ADS equipment, it will make a decision as to whether installation will be extended.

Although some stores are still to be convinced, the benefits of epos can be counted in both financial terms and in the wealth of management information that is generated. The reason scanning is such a talked about subject in supermarkets is because now that over 90% of groceries are barcoded, scanning can provide management with a whole wealth of extra information about sales and stock levels at epos.

Epos systems can increase the retailer's turnover and gross margin while reducing running costs and losses. For instance, the reduction of the number of occasions a retailer is out of stock will have a direct effect in increasing turnover. Faster transaction times will increase turnover in the short term as a result of customers not leaving the shop because of long, slow queues.

In 1982 it was reported that the introduction of epos in Tesco stores in the US led to savings equivalent to 1% of turnover. This is near to most companies' expectations of savings of 1.2%.

Nevertheless, epos equipment is still relatively expensive, despite the fact terminals are now approximately one third of what they cost when they first appeared on the market some 13 years ago.

(*Computing Magazine* 27 Sept 1984)

Invoicing

Sometimes goods are paid for in cash immediately they are obtained. For example, when we buy an ice cream or a bus ticket we are expected to pay at once. On other occasions, goods are ordered but are not paid for until after they have been delivered. In this case an **invoice** is sent with the goods. An invoice is a list of the goods supplied, together with their prices and the total charge (see Figure 14.9).

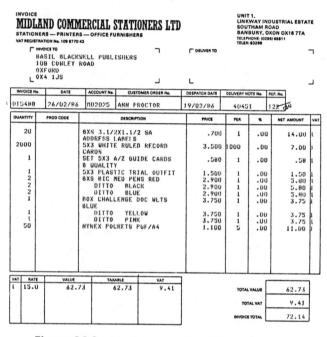

Figure 14.9 An invoice sent with a delivery of stationery

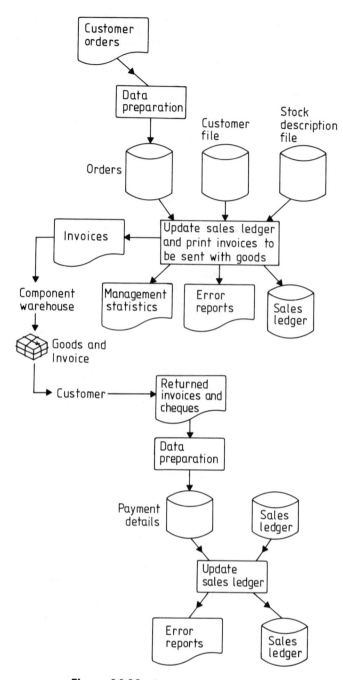

Figure 14.10 A computer invoicing system

Invoices are normally printed on multi-part stationery to produce at least three copies. One copy is retained for the firm's records and two copies are sent with the goods. One of these copies is retained by the customer for his or her records and the other copy is returned with a cheque for payment. The system flowchart (Figure 14.10) shows a computer invoicing system which uses direct access disc files. The system is used by Zap Components, a supplier of electrical goods.

When customer's orders arrive at Zap Components, they are batched together and then input using a key-to-disc data preparation system. Figure 14.11 shows a typical order that arrived from Bloggs Electricals.

The order from Bloggs Electricals, after it has been verified and validated, will take its place as one record in the **order file**.

The order file contains records with fields as shown in Figure 14.12. This file does not contain sufficient information to produce the invoices and the computer must have direct access to two other files: the **customer file**

and the **stock description file**. A record from the customer file is shown in Figure 14.13.

The credit limit is the maximum value of goods that Bloggs Electricals is allowed to order. The amount owed is the value of any outstanding invoices already sent to Bloggs Electricals. The amount owed is subtracted from the credit limit before checking whether the current order can be accepted. If the order is within the credit limit and is accepted, the total cost will be reduced by the discount level. The discount for Bloggs Electricals is 5%.

The stock description file contains records with fields like the ones shown in Figure 14.14.

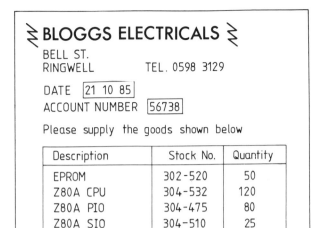

Figure 14.11 An order form

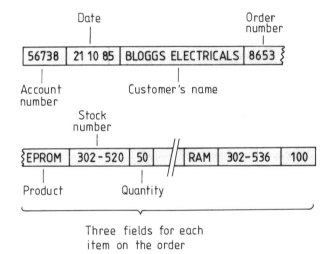

Figure 14.12 A record from the order file

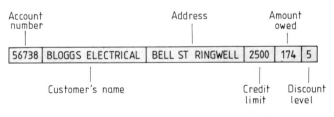

Figure 14.13 A record from the customer file

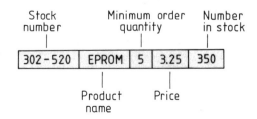

Figure 14.14 A record from the stock description file

The first stage of the invoice printing program is to check that the customer's credit is good and that all the items ordered are available. The data in the three files is then combined to print an invoice (see Figure 14.15). This invoice is sent to the customer with the goods.

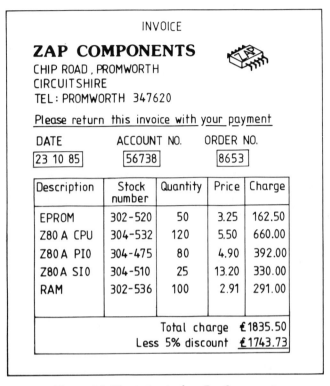

Figure 14.15 An invoice from Zap Components

As each invoice is printed, a full copy of all the details is stored in another disc file called the **sales ledger**. The sales ledger contains records with fields like the ones shown in Figure 14.16.

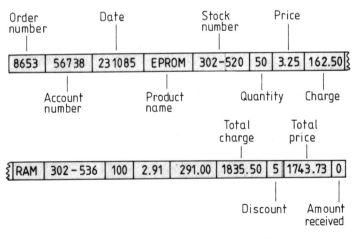

Figure 14.16 A record from the sales ledger file

When the invoices are returned, the details of the payments received are input using the key-to-disc system. Each payment, after it has been verified and validated, will take its place as one record in the **payment details file**. The payment details file contains records with fields like the ones shown in Figure 14.17.

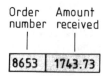

Order number Amount received

| 8653 | 1743.73 |

Figure 14.17 A record from the payment details file

The final stage of the invoicing system is to use the data in the payment details file to update the 'amount received' field in the sales ledger file. The sales ledger file is a very important file because it contains details of all the goods sold by the company and all the money received or owed. The contents of the sales ledger file form a legal document which must be made available to the firm's accountants and to the Tax Office.

Before their invoice system was computerised, Zap Components used a manual system. This system was essentially the same as the computer system, except that the files were held in books and all the work was done by clerks with pen and paper. The power and speed of the computer has produced a much more efficient system. The computer equipment cost quite a lot of money but Zap Components feel it was money well spent because of the following advantages:

* The computer system is much more accurate than the manual system. Very few mistakes occur on the computer invoices. This both saves Zap Components money and increases 'customer satisfaction'.
* The speed of the computer system has meant that it can cope with the work of many clerks. This has allowed Zap Components to cut staff and hence save on labour costs.
* The computer invoice system is combined with a computer stock control system in the component warehouse. The efficiency of the two systems allows Zap Components to dispatch most orders within twenty four hours of receiving them. With the old manual system, it could take several days to dispatch an order.
* The computer system can automatically produce many different kinds of management statistic. For example, it can produce records of total sales, sales to each customer, sales of each component and profits made from each transaction. In the old manual system this would have involved the clerks in many hours of extra work.

Exercise 53

1 **a** Explain what is meant by *multi-part stationery*.
   b What kind of printer is needed to print on multi-part stationery?

2 The order from Bloggs Electricals will be input using a key-to-disc system controlled by a minicomputer.

   a Explain how the data from the order form will be verified after it has been entered.
   b Explain how each of the following validation checks could be applied to the data from the order form.
      (i) a range check
      (ii) an invalid character check
      (iii) a control total check
      (iv) a hash total check
      (v) a check digit.

3 All the files used in Zap Components invoicing system are indexed sequential disc files.

   a Explain what is meant by an *indexed sequential disc file*.
   b For each of the five files used in the invoicing system, explain which *key field* is used to sort the file into sequence.

4 Loss of all or some of the data in the disc files would cause many problems for Zap Components.

   a Explain how data can be lost from disc files.
   b Which file would cause Zap Components the most problems if its data was lost?
   c Explain how Zap Components can increase the security of the data stored in the disc files.

5 On 18 November 1986 Zap Components receive an order from Shocking Circuits of Volts Road, Wattsville, Ampshire. The order is for 100 Z80A serial interface chips and 100 Z80A central processing units.

   a Design a pre-printed order form for Shocking Circuits and write the details of the order on your design. The account number for Shocking Circuits is 77344.
   b Draw a diagram to show how the order from Shocking Circuits will be stored in the order file.
   c Shocking Circuits have a credit limit of £3000, a discount level of 10% and owe Zap Components £345.78 from previous orders. Draw a diagram to show how these details will be stored in the customer file.
   d Draw a diagram to show the invoice that will be printed for this order.
   e Draw a diagram to show the record that will be created in the sales ledger to store the details of this order.

Gas and Electricity Bills

Gas and electricity are supplied by large companies called **boards**. Each gas or electricity board supplies a large area of the country through a network of pipes and cables. Some of the boards' customers pay for their gas or electricity by putting coins into slot meters in their houses. Other customers have meters which record the amount of gas or electricity that they use. Every 13 weeks (each quarter of a year) the boards send these customers a bill for the electricity they have used. Today, all these bills are produced and processed by computers. To illustrate the way in which these computer billing systems work, we will follow through the process of charging a customer called Judy Switch for the gas she uses in her home. In the gas board's computer system, there is a customer file with one record for each customer. Some of the fields in Judy Switch's record are shown in Figure 14.18.

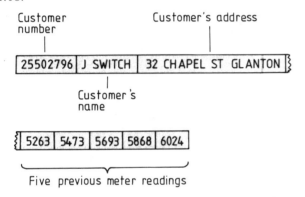

Figure 14.18   The gas board's record for Judy Switch

Judy's meter is read in January, April, July and October. The last reading, taken in October, was 6024. It is now January and Judy's meter must be read again. The first stage in this process is for the computer to print out a **meter reading sheet**.

Figure 14.19 shows the meter reading sheet which the computer prints out for Judy Switch.

This meter reading sheet is printed by the computer in an OCR font. The meter reading is recorded using the OMR section of the form. The returned meter reading sheet is then input using a **universal document reader**. This is an input device that can read both OCR and OMR data. The meter reading sheet is an example of a **turnaround document**. This document is produced by a computer and then, after extra data has been added, used as an input document. The two estimated readings on the meter reading sheet help to prevent meter reading errors. They were calculated from Judy's previous reading in the following way:

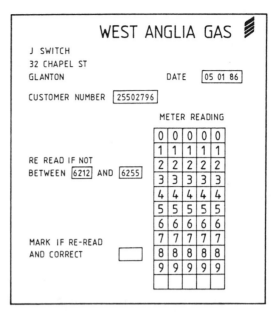

Figure 14.19   A meter reading sheet

1 The previous readings for the customer are examined. The readings for Judy Switch are

OCTOBER	5263
JANUARY	5473
APRIL	5693
JULY	5868
OCTOBER	6024

2 The amount of gas that Judy used between the previous October and January is calculated:

$$\begin{array}{r} 5473 \\ -5263 \\ \hline 210 \text{ units} \end{array}$$

3 Values 10% greater and 10% less than this amount are calculated:

$$210 + 10\% = 231$$
$$210 - 10\% = 189$$

4 These values are added to the previous reading to obtain high and low estimates of the gas Judy has used:

High estimate = 6024 + 231 = 6255 units
Low estimate = 6024 + 189 = 6212 units

If the meter reading is not between these estimates, the meter reader must re-read the meter to check that a mistake has not been made.

The gas board which serves the area where Judy lives has over a million customers. The board employs 150 meter readers who each read approximately 130 meters a day. The computer prints out a batch of meter reading sheets each day for every meter reader. Judy's sheet is in a batch given to a meter reader called Kawal Singh. Kawal calls at Judy's house and reads the meter which is inside Judy's garage. Figure 14.20 shows Kawal reading the meter.

Figure 14.20 The meter reader

Figure 14.21 shows the completed meter reading sheet.

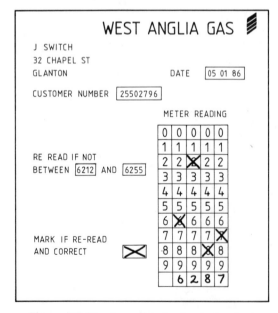

Figure 14.21 A completed meter reading sheet

Because Judy's reading was more than the high estimate, Kawal re-read the meter. When he found that the reading was correct, he entered it on the sheet and marked the box to indicate that he had re-read the meter.

Each day, Kawal and the other meter readers send their completed meter reading sheets to the board's central computer department. There the sheets are input using the universal document reader. As the sheets are input, they are subjected to a series of validation checks. Even though the OCR characters are printed by the computer, they are still checked to ensure that the OCR reading equipment is working correctly. Some of the validation checks which are used are explained below:

1 The customer reference number contains a modulus eleven check digit. If the check digit read from the sheet is incorrect, the sheet is rejected.
2 Range checks are applied to the date. If the day or month is not in the correct range, the sheet is rejected.
3 Invalid character checks are applied to the date, the customer's name and the customer's reference number. If any of these contain invalid characters, the sheet is rejected.
4 A check is made to see if the reading falls within the estimated limits. If it does not *and* the re-read box is *not* marked, the sheet is rejected.

Rejected meter reading sheets are checked by data preparation staff, corrected and entered using a visual display terminal. Sometimes it may be necessary to refer back to the meter reader before a sheet can be corrected.

The systems flowchart (Figure 14.22) shows the stages in producing the gas bills.

Judy Switch's record in the transaction file contains the fields shown in Figure 14.23.

If it has been impossible to read Judy's meter, the meter reading is replaced with the code 'E'. This instructs the computer to prepare an estimated bill based on previous readings.

The data in the customer file and the transaction file are combined to produce the bill. At the same time the record in the customer file is updated to include the new reading. Figure 14.24 shows the bill which is printed for Judy Switch.

The heating capacity of gas varies, and customers are charged for this rather than the volume of gas they use. The heating capacity of the gas is measured in **therms**. To calculate the number of therms in a given volume of gas, the gas supplied is multiplied by the calorific value and then divided by 1000.

Judy can pay her bill in any one of three ways:

* She can take her bill to any gas showroom, post office or bank and pay with either cash or a cheque

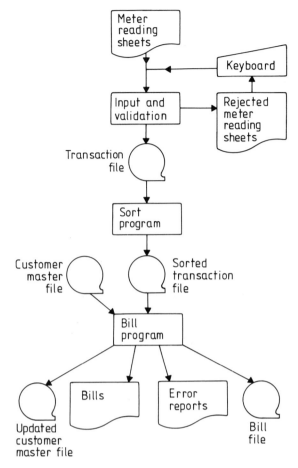

Figure 14.22 Stages in producing gas bills

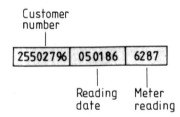

Figure 14.23 A record in the gas board's transaction file

ACCOUNT NUMBER	25502796	WEST ANGLIA GAS			
METER READINGS IN CUBIC FEET (HUNDREDS)		GAS SUPPLIED	THERMS	PENCE PER THERM	COST
PRESENT *	PREVIOUS *				
6287	6024	263	271.94	35.2	£95.72
Ms J SWITCH 32 CHAPEL ST, GLATTON				TOTAL COST	£95.72
READING DATE	CALORIFIC VALUE		* E = Estimated reading		
050186	1034 B.T.U.'s per cu ft				

Figure 14.24 A gas bill

* She can return her bill by post with a cheque or postal order
* If she has a National Girobank account, she can instruct the bank to transfer money automatically from her account to the gas board's account.

At the gas showroom, details of payments are entered at a point-of-sale terminal. These details are stored on a cassette tape. Each evening the gas board's computer automatically contacts the terminals by telephone line and modem and inputs all the data stored on the tape. Details of payments made at banks and post offices reach the gas board by various means. Figure 14.25 shows how all this data is combined to update the bill files.

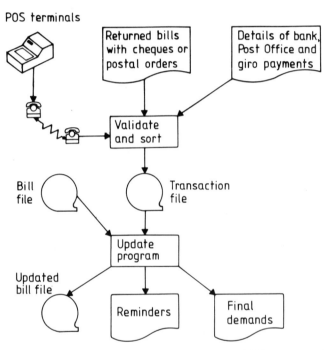

Figure 14.25 The process for updating bill files

Reminders are printed and sent to customers for any bills which are still unpaid after three weeks. If the bill is still unpaid after four weeks, a final demand is sent. This warns the customer that unless the bill is paid, the gas may be cut off. If a further week passes and no payment is received, gas board officials must decide whether to cut off the gas supply. This step is not taken lightly and Social Services are often contacted before the final decision is made.

In addition to processing customers' bills, a gas board uses its computer system for several other tasks. For example, it uses a payroll application program to pay the staff, a stock control application program for its stocks of gas appliances and spare parts and an on-line database system to provide an enquiry service in its showrooms.

Exercise 54

1 The diagrams below show the dials on two types of gas meter. Which meter uses an analogue display and which meter uses a digital display?

| 6 | 2 | 8 | 7 |

2 What advantages does the gas board gain by using OCR and OMR input devices?

3 Henry Sloane's record in the customer file is shown below.

| 16832970 | HENRY SLOANE | 2 GOON ST | BEXHILL-ON-SEA | 5369 | 5569 | 5772 | 5892 | 5997 |

On the day his meter is read, it is showing a reading of 6247.

a Draw a diagram of the meter reading sheet that will be completed for Henry Sloane.

b Draw a diagram of the bill that will be printed for Henry Sloane.

4 The Electricity and Gas Boards both make use of computers in similar ways.

a List **four** tasks that you might expect the computer to do in either of the Boards.

b Write 10 to 15 lines on **one** of these tasks. In your answer you should describe input/output and the processes carried out by the computer.

c There are both advantages and disadvantages when such large organisations make use of computers. State **one** advantage and **one** disadvantage for
  (i) the customer
  (ii) the organisation

(EAEB 82)

5 Study carefully the following description of how electricity bills are produced.

Northern Electricity Service provides electricity to private households and commercial organisations in High Town. The charge rate varies between commercial and private customers.

At the end of each quarter a Northern Electricity Service employee (the meter man) visits each customer to read the meter. He has a notebook with a page for each customer in which the quarterly readings are recorded; the appropriate customer account number is pre-recorded at the top of each page; continuation pages can be inserted in the notebook if any page becomes full. However, not all meters can be read since some customers are not at home or some commercial organisations are closed. In these cases an estimated reading is recorded based on the corresponding quarter for the previous year. When all available data is collected and all necessary estimates made the meter man hands his notebook into the Northern Electricity Service Accounts Department for processing.

The clerk in the Accounts Office uses the last two entries on each page to calculate the number of units of electricity used by each customer. The clerk then calculates the amount due for each customer for the quarter just ended and enters it in the Customer Account Book. Bills are then prepared and sent out to each customer.

Customer details such as customer account number, customer name and charge rates are kept by the Northern Electricity Service in the Customer Account Book in the Accounts Office. At the end of each month Northern Electricity Service needs to send reminders to customers who have not paid their bills. These reminders show the amount outstanding and indicate how many reminders have now been sent.

Answer the following questions.
  (i) Draw outline flowcharts for the meter reading procedure and for the bill preparation procedure. Clearly identify conditions for repetition and termination in these procedures.
  (ii) What are the inputs to and output from each of the two procedures?

A computer system is being developed to produce the electricity bills, send receipts for amounts paid and send reminders to customers.

For the computer system:

  (iii) Design a suitable document to be used for recording meter readings.
  (iv) What validation checks should be used when processing the information on this document?
  (v) Describe the contents of the Customer file.

(NI GCE 82)

A Real-time Commercial Database System

Real-time commercial database systems are often used to combine the tasks of stock control, order delivery and invoicing. The following case study illustrates the use of a real-time commercial system to control the operations of a concrete distribution company based in Stamford.

C & G Concrete are suppliers of ready-mixed concrete. They cover a large area of the East Midlands, delivering concrete from fourteen local depots. Each depot holds stocks of cement powder, sand and gravel, the basic materials from which concrete is made. These materials are stored in large hoppers from which they can be measured into the delivery trucks. When a customer orders concrete, a truck is loaded from the hoppers. Each truck also has a water tank into which the exact quantity of water needed is measured. When the truck arrives at the building site, the water and the dry ingredients are mixed and the concrete is discharged. (See Figure 14.26.)

Figure 14.26 The site of C & G Concrete

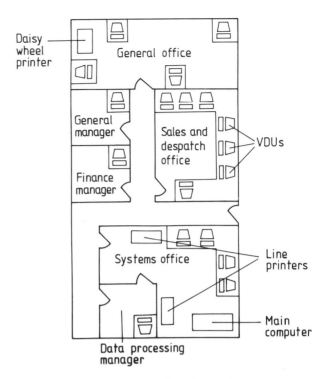

Figure 14.27 The office of C & G Concrete

All customer orders, deliveries and charges are administered from one central office. No office staff work at the fourteen local depots. The central office uses a main-frame computer system to help with this administration. The basic details of this system are as follows:

Main computer

* CPU memory   1024 Kilobytes
* fixed disc memory   800 Megabytes
* floppy disc memory   23 Megabytes

Printers
* 2 line printers (600 lines per minute)
* 1 high-quality daisy wheel printer

Workstations
* 18 VDU terminals

Programming languages
* RPGII (Report Program Generator 2)
* OCL (Operations Control Language)

A plan of the office is shown in Figure 14.27.

To understand the way in which C & G Concrete uses its computer system, we will follow the progress of a typical order for concrete. Our order is from Superhomes Ltd, a local house builder. They require five cubic metres of concrete to be delivered to their building site in Peterborough. Their first contact with C & G is the sales and despatch office. This department takes orders from customers and controls deliveries from the depots. It is also their task to ensure that all the depots are kept stocked with sand, cement powder and gravel.

Our order arrives as a telephone call from Superhomes. As the order is taken, details are written down on a special order form. The form used is shown in Figure 14.28.

The most suitable depot is selected by the salesperson, using experience and a large wall map of the area. Before

DATE	CUSTOMER	ACCOUNT NUMBER
04/07/85	SUPERHOMES	347270

DELIVERY ADDRESS	Green Meadows Development (Off) Stalford Rd Peterborough

DELIVERY DETAILS

DAY	DATE	TIME	DEPOT
WED.	10/07/85	9.30 a.m.	Peterborough

QUANTITY

5 m³

Figure 14.28 An order form used by C & G Concrete

```
CUSTOMER....... SUPERHOMES LTD
                33 BALLINGTON ST WHENINGFORD
TOTAL OWING FROM DELIVERIES .......   £245.79
CREDIT LIMIT ...........................  £8000.00
ACCOUNT........347270
```

Figure 14.29 A C & G customer on the VDU

the order is accepted, the salesperson uses a VDU to check the customer's credit rating and the work load for the day of the order. The customer's name is entered to produce the display shown in Figure 14.29.

This allows the salesperson to check that Superhomes are within their credit limit. In this case there is no problem, but if a customer was close to or over their limit, the order would be referred to the finance manager. This display also allows the salesperson to find the account number if it is not already known. If a customer does not have an account, the order is only accepted as a cash on delivery order.

A work file is selected from a screen menu, the day of the delivery is entered, and a display is produced (Figure 14.30).

```
LOADS ORDERED
DATE 10 07 85
                            DEPOTS
        1  2  3  4  5  6  7  8  9  10 11 12 13 14
 6.00   2  1  3  5  2     1  2  1     1  3  2  4
 7.00      2  1  1  3  4  1  1  1        4  1
 8.00   1        1  2  1  2  1  2  2     2  3  1
 9.00   2  1     2  3     1  1  2  1  1        2
10.00         2  3  4  6  5  1  1     1  1  2  3
11.00   2  3  2  1     2  1  2     1  1  3     1
12.00      2  1     1  2  1     1           1     1
13.00      1  1     2  3     1  1  2     3  1  1
14.00      2  1  3  4  2  5  1  1  6  1  1     1
15.00   2        1  2  1  3     1  2  3  2  2  2
16.00   1  3  3  2  1  1  2  3  4  1  1  1  3  1
17.00   1  1              1           1        1
```

Figure 14.30 A VDU display of C & G's orders for one day

This display shows the number of loads that are to be delivered from each of the fourteen depots in any one hour period. For example, there are five loads to be delivered from depot number four between 6.00 am and 7.00 am. Peterborough is depot no. 3, and because the display shows that there are no loads yet booked in for 9.00 am to 10.00 am the Superhomes order can be accepted. There is no set limit on the number of loads that can be delivered in any one hour period from any of the depots. Each salesperson must use experience and judgement of the delivery problems when accepting orders. After the order has been checked and accepted, the details are entered by the salesperson using the VDU. A copy of the order form is displayed on the screen and all the details are typed in (as shown in Figure 14.31).

The name of the customer is not entered; it is printed by the computer. The computer is able to do this by looking up the account number in the customer file. This serves

```
DATE  04 07 85
CUSTOMER ACCOUNT NUMBER   347270
DELIVERY ADDRESS   GREEN MEADOWS DEVELOPMENTS
                   PETERBOROUGH
DAY  WED        DATE 10 07 85    TIME  09.30
DEPOT  3        QUANTITY  5
CUSTOMER
                  SUPERHOMES LTD WHENINGFORD
```

Figure 14.31 A VDU display of the order from Superhomes

as a very useful check that the account number has been correctly entered. Other validation checks include:

* that the date is valid
* that the delivery time is between 6.00 am and 5.00 pm
* that the quantity is greater than 0.25 cubic metres
* that the quantity is less than 6 cubic metres.

When the order has been validated and entered, the computer adds it to a file containing all deliveries ordered for that particular day. This action ensures that when next viewed, the 'loads ordered' display will show one load for depot no. 3 between 9.00 and 10.00 on 10 July. This completes the ordering stage for our concrete. The next stage takes place on the day that the order is to be delivered. It is still dealt with in the sales and despatch office, but now by a person called the load allocator.

The computer file containing Superhomes' order has now become the delivery file for today. The load allocator has the contents of this file displayed on a VDU. Figure 14.32 shows part of this display.

```
Load Depot Time Quantity  Customer      Delivery Address
 17   SP   9.20    4       BETTERBUILD   FAIRVIEWS CLONTON
 18   PE   9.30    5       SUPERHOMES    GREENMEADOWS
                                         DEVELOPMENTS
                                         PETERBOROUGH
 19   WL   9.30    3.5     WALLYS        THE SITE
                                         DITCHFIELD
```

Figure 14.32 An extract from C & G's delivery file

On a second VDU, the load allocator has a display of all the trucks available. Figure 14.33 shows part of this display.

```
Truck      Call   Load  Delivery Address
           Sign
HPK 275V   143    17    FAIRVIEW CLONTON
FPL 875X   176
GKT 905W   121
```

Figure 14.33 Load allocation on the VDU

When he or she has selected a suitable truck for a load, the load allocator moves the cursor on the second VDU and enters the load number next to the truck details. The delivery address is added automatically by the computer, which looks it up in the delivery file.

The load allocator then makes radio contact with the truck driver. All C & G's trucks are equipped with a two-way radio for this purpose. The driver writes the details down on a delivery ticket, goes to the depot, mixes the load and delivers it. The delivery ticket (sometimes called an advice note) is signed by the building site supervisor when the concrete is delivered. (This is very important because this ticket proves that the delivery has been made and must be paid for.) As a load is allocated, the computer records the details in a delivered loads file and updates the customer file. It also deducts the quantities of sand, cement powder and gravel used from the stocks held at Peterborough.

These details are held in yet another file called the materials stock file. This system may seem very complicated but it gives C & G one great advantage. Orders which are received for delivery on the same day can be accepted and added to the delivery file for that day. As soon as a salesperson has accepted and entered the load, it appears on the load allocator's VDU and can be allocated to a truck. Thus C & G can offer its customers a very fast and efficient service. This completes the ordering and delivery stage for our concrete, but before we leave sales and despatch we will have a quick look at the work of the materials controller. This person uses a VDU displaying the contents of the materials stock file. Figure 14.34 shows the display.

	DEPOT													
	1	2	3	4	5	6	7	8	9	10	11	12	13	14
SAND	20	23	24	19	17	11	29	18	17	25	20	23	17	25
CEMENT	15	17	19	23	14	16	27	11	16	13	12	17	15	20
GRAVEL	19	23	15	27	28	13	26	14	15	25	11	27	18	23

Figure 14.34 Checking materials stock on the VDU

The display shows the number of tonnes of sand, cement powder and gravel held in the hoppers at each depot. These figures are automatically reduced each time a load is allocated. The materials controller monitors the figures and places telephone orders for more stock as it is used up. The minimum stock levels before re-ordering are stored in the computer and any stocks that fall below these levels start to flash on the screen. When the materials controller is notified that more stock has been delivered, he or she enters the details at his or her VDU and the stock figures are updated to include these extra quantities. Because of this system, C & G do not need to hold vast stocks of raw materials.

By now, you will have realised that the concrete ordering system uses a complex database. All the files used in the system, the customer file, the loads ordered files, the trucks available file and the delivered loads file are inter-linked. Enquiries and data entries often access or update several different files. All file updating takes place immediately and then influences any further transactions. This system can therefore be described as a real-time computer application.

The concrete ordering system uses seven multi-access VDU terminals in the sales and despatch office. Two of these are used by the load allocator, one is used by the materials controller, and four are used by the sales staff. Figure 14.35 shows these staff at work.

Figure 14.35 The people who deal with orders for concrete

The next stage in the processing of our concrete order takes place in the general office. At the end of each day, all the drivers' tickets are brought to this office. On the following day a secretary checks these tickets against the delivered loads file. The file contents are displayed on a

VDU and each is matched to a delivery ticket. If there are any problems (for example a missing ticket) these are dealt with by the general manager.

After the drivers' tickets have been matched to the loads delivered file and all errors corrected, customer invoices are produced. This is not as straightforward a task as it might appear, because prices are negotiated to take account of the distance of the site from the C & G depot and the quality of concrete required. For this reason, no details of concrete prices are stored in the computer system. The first stage in producing the invoices is for one of the general office staff to take a full printed listing of all the orders delivered on the previous day and to write on the list the negotiated price for each order. These price details are then entered at a VDU, giving first the load number and then the price. The price is added as an extra field in the loads delivered file. Full details of the load are then transferred from this file to the customer file. When all the prices have been entered, overnight batch processing is used to print out invoices for all the delivered loads. These invoices are then posted to the customers. The completed invoice for our Super-homes order is shown in Figure 14.36.

Figure 14.36 The invoice sent from C & G Concrete to Superhomes

The final stage in the processing of Superhomes' order takes place when their cheque for payment arrives at C & G. The finance manager uses a VDU to enter details of the payment received. The customer file is updated to reduce the total owing for deliveries, and details of the payment are stored on the computer system for account-ing purposes.

Before they introduced the computer system, C & G Concrete relied on a manual system for ordering, deli-very, stock control and invoicing. Office managers worked at each of the fourteen depots and, using pen, paper and telephone, controlled what were effectively fourteen independent operations. The system was ineffi-cient because of the lack of central control and coordina-tion. Because nobody had real-time access to the overall picture of delivery problems and stock control, customers sometimes did not receive a prompt and efficient service. By introducing a real-time computer system, C & G have been able to reduce staff, improve stock control, increase delivery efficiency and provide greater customer satisfac-tion. They have gained a well-deserved reputation in the construction industry for providing a fast, efficient sup-ply of very high-quality concrete.

Exercise 55

1 Each morning, the first task of the computer operator is to dump the contents of all the database files on to floppy discs. These discs are stored in a fireproof safe in the computer room. Explain why this action is taken.

2 There are several indications in the case study that human experience and judgement are still needed in this system.

  a Make a list of all the examples you can find of human experience and judgement playing a part in this system.
  b For each example you can find, explain why the computer is not programmed to make the necessary decisions at this point in the system.

3 At 10.30 am 5 July 1987, Superhomes need 4 m³ of con-crete at their Green Meadows site. The order is placed on 28 June 1987. Explain in detail the stages in processing this order.

4 Choose a computer data processing application which has replaced a manual system.

  a State your application.
  b How was data stored before computerisation?
  c What data capture method is used and why?
  d State **two** types of information stored in the files.
  e What backing store is used and why?
  f What is the format of the output and why is this format used?
  g Explain why computerisation was desirable.

(AEB 83)

15 Computers in Science, Mathematics and Engineering

Mathematical Subroutines and Number Crunching

Computers are often used to manipulate very large sets of numbers very quickly. This type of computer use is often called 'number crunching'. To illustrate the way in which computers are used for these 'number crunching' tasks, we will consider the problem of solving simultaneous equations. In your mathematics lessons, you have probably solved simultaneous equations such as:

$$x + y = 7$$
$$x - y = 1$$

This pair of equations only involves two unknown numbers, represented by the letters x and y. It takes only a few seconds to discover that the solution is $x = 4$ and $y = 3$.

In civil and aeronautical engineering, problems may occur which involve over one hundred equations and unknown numbers! Before the days of computers, mathematicians knew *how* to solve these problems but were unable to do so because of the labour involved. Today, by programming a computer to carry out the necessary calculations at very high speed, solutions can be found in a few minutes.

Most large scientific computer systems have libraries of standard mathematical subroutines to solve most types of problem. These subroutines can be used by any program running on the computer. This saves time for mathematicians and also allows non-specialists to use powerful subroutines that they do not have the knowledge to write themselves. Adequate documentation must of course be provided to explain how to use the library subroutines. This documentation will include details of how to include the subroutine in a program, what input data the subroutine requires and what output it produces.

Trial-and-error Calculations

Any computer can be used as a powerful calculator and 'scratch pad' to try out various ideas and problem solutions. The simplified example in Figure 15.1 shows this kind of computer use.

Suppose an engineer is designing a bridge to carry a road across a valley. Figure 15.1 shows the basic bridge design.

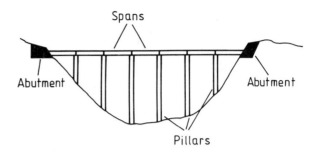

Figure 15.1 A basic bridge design

The engineer knows that the cost of the bridge can be calculated from the formula

$$\text{Cost} = (2A - P) + Pn + \frac{SL^2}{n}$$

where

- A = cost of each abutment
- P = cost of each pillar
- S = cost of a span of one metre length
- L = length of the bridge
- n = number of spans used in the bridge.

For this particular bridge, the engineer knows that

- A = £100 000
- P = £50 000
- S = £10 000
- and L = 50 metres

This reduces the cost formula to

$$\text{Cost} = 150\ 000 + 50\ 000n + \frac{25\ 000\ 000}{n}$$

The problem is: how many spans should the engineer use in a design to produce the lowest possible building cost? By writing a very simple computer program, the engineer is able to calculate the cost of the bridge in thirty different cases. The engineer's program is shown in Figure 15.2 with the output it produces. The prediction is that a bridge with 22 spans will be the cheapest solution, costing £2 386 363.

This example is greatly simplified, but it illustrates the way that the computer's speed and accuracy can be used to explore possibilities and search for ideal solutions. In many cases the engineers or scientists do not write their

```
>LIST
  10 PRINT "NU OF SPANS", "COST"
  20 FOR N = 1 TO 30
  30 PRINT TAB(5) ; N , TAB(20) ; INT(150000 + 50000 * N + 25000000 / N)
  40 NEXT N

>RUN
NU OF SPANS         COST
     1            25200000
     2            12750000
     3             8633333
     4             6600000
     5             5400000
     6             4616666
     7             4071428
     8             3675000
     9             3377777
    10             3150000
    11             2972727
    12             2833333
    13             2723076
    14             2635714
    15             2566666
    16             2512500
    17             2470588
    18             2438888
    19             2415789
    20             2400000
    21             2390476
    22             2386363
    23             2386956
    24             2391666
    25             2400000
    26             2411538
    27             2425925
    28             2442857
    29             2462068
    30             2483333
```

Figure 15.2 An engineer's program for bridge design

own programs but use special application packages designed for their type of work.

Iteration

An **iteration procedure** is a set of steps which, when applied to an approximate answer, will produce a better approximation. To use an iteration procedure to solve a problem, you first make a rough guess at the exact answer. By applying the iteration procedure to your rough guess, you can obtain a better approximation to the exact answer. If you now apply the iteration procedure to this approximation, you can obtain an even better approximation. By applying the iteration procedure again and again, you can obtain an answer to any desired degree of accuracy.

An iteration procedure is often expressed as a formula. For example, an iteration procedure to find the square root of any number N can be expressed as the formula

Next approximation =

$$\frac{1}{2} \times \left(\text{current approximation} + \frac{N}{\text{current approximation}} \right)$$

Using this formula to find the square root of 12, we might start with a rough guess of 4. Applying the iteration procedure will give:

$$\text{Next approximation} = \frac{1}{2} \text{ of} \left(4 + \frac{12}{4} \right) = 3.5$$

Applying the iteration procedure to our first approximation of 3.5 will give:

$$\text{Next approximation} = \frac{1}{2} \text{ of} \left(3.5 + \frac{12}{3.5} \right)$$
$$= 3.464 \text{ (to three places)}$$

Since the square of 3.464 is 11.999, we have obtained a good approximation for the square root of 12 after only two applications of the iteration procedure.

Iteration procedures can solve many problems in mathematics, but they were not often used before the invention of the computer because they require many tedious calculations.

The computer is of course ideally suited for the task of repetitive calculations, and as the use of computers has increased, iteration has become a very important method for solving mathematical problems.

Mathematical Models and Simulations

Many real problems can be expressed in the language of mathematics. For example, consider the problem of cooking a piece of beef. Experience has taught cooks that an ideal cooking time is achieved by allowing 20 minutes for each pound of beef plus an extra 20 minutes. This can be expressed in the language of mathematics as:

$$T = 20W + 20$$

where T = cooking time (in minutes)
   W = the weight of the beef (in pounds)

When we express a real problem in the language of mathematics, we say we have constructed a **mathematical model** of the problem. The relationship between a real problem and a mathematical model is shown in Figure 15.3.

Real problem	Mathematical model
	$T = 20W + 20$
How long should I cook a four pound piece of beef ?	Find T if W = 4

Figure 15.3 An everyday problem and its mathematical model

Mathematical models allow us to predict the results of changes in the real problem easily. For example, if the weight of the beef is changed to five pounds, the model allows us to predict easily that it should be cooked for two hours. We must, however, always remember that mathematical models are only as good as the assumptions on which they are based. Experience has shown that this cooking time model satisfies most cooks, but if you like well-done or rare meat it will not work for you.

One of the tasks of mathematicians working in Government, industry or science is to construct mathematical models of complete systems. These models are very complex and may involve hundreds of interlinked equations and formulae. They are usually written as computer programmes to take advantage of the computer's speed and accuracy of calculation. A complete mathematical representation of a physical system which allows a user to study the behaviour of the system is called a **computer simulation**. When it has been created, a computer simulation can be used to indicate how the system will behave under any given circumstances. For example, several mathematical models have been created of the British economy. These models allow a user to experiment with various ideas and see how they affect the economy. For example, a model may simulate a 2% cut in the bank interest rate and predict the effect that this will have on inflation, spending and unemployment.

These models, just like our simple cooking model, are only as good as the assumptions on which they are based. Too much faith cannot be placed in them because in many cases nobody knows the exact relationship between the elements of the system. Mathematicians can only approximate and make intelligent guesses at the way the various elements of the system affect each other. Despite this, mathematical simulations written as computer programs can be very useful when it is too expensive, too dangerous, too time-consuming or simply impossible to experiment with the real system.

Many real systems involve an element of random behaviour. For example, a supermarket manager may know that she can expect between 350 and 500 customers during a late opening evening. However, the exact number of customers and the exact times at which they arrive will be random numbers which cannot be predicted in advance. Mathematical simulations of such systems can make use of the computer's ability to select random numbers. Figure 15.4 shows how a simple random system can be simulated in the BASIC computer language.

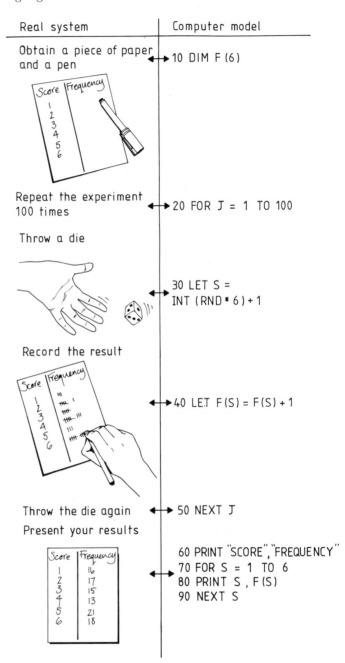

Figure 15.4 Simulating a real system with a computer model

Returning to our supermarket manager, let us look at her problem of deciding how many checkouts to use for her late opening evenings. If she uses too few checkouts, queues will build up and customers will become angry and may shop elsewhere in future. If she uses too many checkouts, there will be no queues but she will be wasting staff wages. A computer model of the supermarket system can help her to make a balanced decision on the number of checkouts to use. This model will select random numbers of customers and random times for them to arrive at the store. It will also select a random checkout time for each customer as their time in the store expires. The computer simulation can be run with different numbers of checkouts in use and will predict the lengths of the queues that will build up (see Figure 15.5). The manager can use her judgement to decide on the number of checkouts that will keep all her staff busy and all her customers happy. If the computer model is to be of practical use, it must be based on sensible assumptions. The random numbers used must be selected within sensible ranges which have been established by observing the real system. Before the program is used, the manager will need to discover sensible values for

* the number of customers that can be expected to use the store
* the pattern and rate of arrival of the customers
* the average time taken by a customer to pay at the checkout.

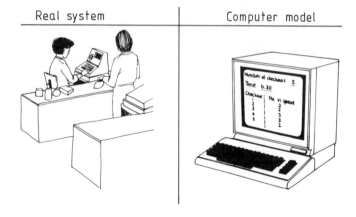

Figure 15.5 A computer model of a supermarket queue

The supermarket simulation is a very simple example of a computer model which could be easily run on a microcomputer. There are many other, far more complex, simulations which require the computing power of a mainframe or supercomputer. In almost all fields of research, computer models can be used to take experiments to an advanced stage before actually undertaking a physical test. Examples of their use include:

* **Financial simulations**. These allow managers to experiment with different business strategies and predict their likely effects and outcomes.
* **Scientific simulations**. These allow scientists to predict the results of dangerous, difficult or expensive experiments before they are actually undertaken. Examples range from a teacher simulating a dangerous experiment in a school laboratory to a nuclear scientist simulating the effects of an atomic explosion! One advantage of such simulations is that the user can slow down or stop the simulation at any stage to examine it in greater detail. It is not possible to stop a real nuclear explosion half way through!
* **Engineering simulations**. These simulations allow engineers to predict the likely strengths and weaknesses of their designs without building prototypes or physical models. This saves time and expense and allows the engineer to explore many more design possibilities.
* **Weather simulations**. These simulations allow weather forecasters to predict the weather patterns that are likely to develop from the present weather situation. This is a type of simulation which involves an enormous number of repetitive calculations and requires the calculating power of a supercomputer.
* **Geological simulations**. These simulations allow geologists to predict the way in which rock structures are formed and the results that different mining and drilling techniques will produce.
* **Flight simulators**. A flight simulator consists of an artificial aircraft cockpit mounted on a hydraulic suspension system. A computer system provides the control signals needed to allow the flight simulator to behave like a real aircraft. Lifelike scenes are projected on to the windscreen of the cockpit and the pilot's use of the controls is monitored. The computer then makes the projected scene and the cockpit move just as it would if the pilot were flying a real plane (see Figure 15.6).

Statistics

Statistics is the branch of mathematics which deals with the collection, organisation, description and analysis of data. Simple statistical techniques include calculating averages and drawing graphs. More complicated techniques are used to try to discover the relationships between variables. For example, a statistician may try to discover the relationship between the number of cigarettes smoked and the incidence of lung cancer. To do this, he or she must collect and analyse data on smoking habits and lung cancer deaths.

This analysis will involve many tedious calculations and the computer is an ideal tool to help with the work.

Figure 15.6 Flight simulation by day and night

Operational Research

Operational research is the branch of mathematics which deals with the solution of real management problems. These problems usually involve making decisions about the best course of action to take in a given situation. Operational research was developed during the Second World War as a scientific and systematic method of decision making. It has since found many uses in commerce, industry, Government and military fields. Today, most operational research exploits the power of computers to carry out many tedious calculations rapidly. Three operational research techniques that are often offered as computer programs are **linear optimisation**, **timetabling** and **critical path analysis**.

A **linear optimisation program** allows a user to search for the most effective solution to a given problem. Some examples of the use of linear optimisation include:

* finding the most efficient blend of ingredients in animal feed
* finding the best route for a delivery truck to take
* finding the best way to deploy rolling stock around a railway system
* marking out the most efficient garmet cutting pattern on a piece of cloth.

Timetables must be constructed in all schools and colleges and in many other institutions. Each year, many difficult decisions must be made as the timetable is constructed. A major difficulty for any timetabler is that he or she has no way of knowing if a solution to a particular problem exists. If a solution cannot be found, it may be because one does not exist. On the other hand, it may be because the timetabler is not clever enough to find the solution. It is not uncommon for timetablers to scrap their work and start again several times as they struggle to find a satisfactory timetable. Computers have not as yet proved a great success as timetablers. The limited educational market has reduced the effort that has gone into attempts to write timetabling software, and conventional VDUs and printers are unsuitable for displaying complete timetables. Most software that is available is designed to provide aids for a human timetabler rather than a complete timetable solution.

Critical path analysis is used to find the best schedule for tasks that can be broken down into several separate actions. The first stage in critical path analysis is to construct a chart or **network** showing all the separate activities and the way that they depend on each other. A critical path network for frying fish and chips is shown in Figure 15.7.

Today, almost all large-scale statistical analysis is done by computers. The computer does not replace the human statistician, it simply takes care of the tedious elements of the work.

One of the most famous uses of a computer to analyse statistical data was undertaken by Professor MacGregor and the Reverend Morton at Glasgow University in 1961. They analysed the frequency and pattern with which certain words were used in the writings of St. Paul. The research indicated that the writings of St. Paul were in fact probably the work of several different authors. Similar statistical work has attempted to demonstrate that Shakespeare's plays are not the work of a single author.

195

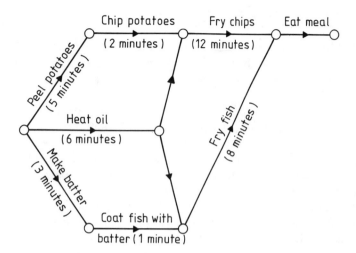

Figure 15.7 A critical path network for frying fish and chips

By studying this diagram, we can see that the shortest possible time to prepare the fish and chips is 26 minutes. Figure 15.8 shows how each of the activities is spread over the 26 minutes.

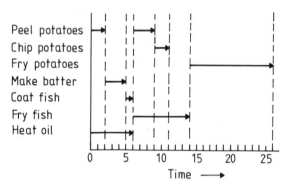

Figure 15.8 Using Figure 15.7 to work out the critical path with the shortest time

Our simple example of a critical path network can be easily solved. The type of network produced by an industrial task may, however, involve hundreds of separate activities. To analyse a network of this complexity without the help of a computer would be a very long and difficult task. Several software packages exist, however, that allow the user to enter the details of complex networks. The computer can usually produce the most efficient schedule of activities in a few minutes.

Computer-aided Design

A computer-aided design (CAD) system usually consists of a graphics display unit with a light pen or joystick for input and a graph plotter for output. In the past, the power of a minicomputer or mainframe computer has been needed to run the software for the system, but recently packages have become available for microcomputers. Figure 15.9 shows a computer-aided design package.

Figure 15.9 A computer-aided design package

The user of a CAD package usually has a keyboard to enter instructions and a light pen or joystick to identify a point on the display screen. The software package supplied with the system will understand a large number of drawing commands, such as

Line	to draw a line on the screen
Circle	to draw a circle on the screen
Arc	to draw a curve on the screen
Text	to insert headings and measurements on the finished drawing
File	to store a copy of the finished drawing on the computer's backing store
Plot	to plot a copy of the finished drawing on a graph plotter.

The user builds up a drawing by identifying points on the screen and instructing the computer to draw lines, circles and arcs between these points. Titles or measurements can be added and the final drawing either stored or plotted. To make the process even easier, a menu of commands may be provided on the side of the screen or on a special keypad. CAD systems allow very quick production of drawings and plans, but this is not their only advantage. Most systems will offer some or all of the following advantages:

* **Ease of modification**. A stored drawing can be retrieved from the backing store and detail changes easily made before it is filed away again or plotted.
* **Ease of calculation**. It may be possible automatically to calculate surface areas, volumes, cross sections and many other values directly from the drawing. This can save many hours of tedious work.
* **Ease of manipulation**. A drawing stored in the CAD system can be easily rotated, enlarged, stretched, reflected, reduced and distorted in many other ways. A designer can thus enter a basic design and then experiment to find the best possible solution.
* **Ease of production**. Some CAD systems include the facility to produce control instructions for the machines used to make the actual product. These control instructions may be produced on paper tape, magnetic tape, magnetic disc or even sent directly to an on-line machine.

Today, CAD systems are widely used by architects, mechanical engineers, electronic engineers, civil engineers, artists and designers of all kinds (see Figure 15.10).

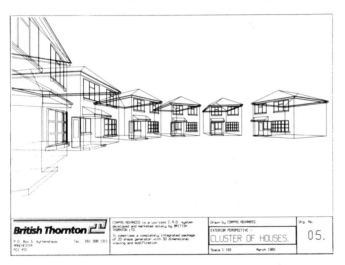

Figure 15.10 Designing houses using CAD

Exercise 56

Several questions in this exercise will require the use of a microcomputer.

1 Write a computer program to solve any pair of equations of the form

$$ax + by = c$$
$$dx + ey = f$$

where a, b, c, d, e and f can be any six numbers.

2 Using the bridge cost formula given in the text, find the minimum cost of a bridge built under the following conditions:

Cost of each abutment = £120 000
Cost of each pillar = £24 000
Cost of one metre span = £15 000
Length of bridge = 120 metres

3 Read the following article which describes how and why British Gas use computer modelling. Explain in your own words the advantages that British Gas obtains from its computer simulation.

One of the main problems facing British Gas over the next decade, whether it is privatised or not, is the rising cost of its raw material, natural gas, which it buys from the producers and distributes throughout the country.

For this reason, it is highly important that the corporation makes the right decisions when deciding to buy gas from a particular reservoir. Because of the nature of gas and oil exploration, these decisions have to be taken before the reservoir is developed, based on data from a number of different sources — such as gravitational, magnetic and seismic surveys — which has to be pieced together to build as complete a picture as possible of the reservoir before it is drilled.

British Gas has developed its own computer modelling software to enable it to adopt the position of an informed buyer when negotiating with the producers of gas, who are mainly oil companies. The software, called Progress, builds a computer simulation of the reservoir in question using all the scientific data available at the time, and the corporation uses this to predict the production capacity of the reservoir before it signs any contracts with the producers.

'We want to know they can produce the amount of gas we need before we sign any contracts,' explained Martin Leigh, group leader of the exploration and production team at British Gas London research centre, where the software was developed. 'Although we can put clauses into the contract to give us financial compensation if the gas is not produced, that does not help us get the gas to the customer on the day,' he said.

(*Computing Magazine*, 23 May 1985)

4 Read the following article and then draw up a list of all the supercomputer owners mentioned in the article and the uses to which they put their supercomputers.

Code-breaking played a big part in the very first days of computers and has played an even bigger role in the development of supercomputers.

When Seymour Cray began his career, in the early 50s, it was as an electrical engineer building code-cracking machines for Engineering Research Associates, a US Navy contractor specialising in cryptography equipment.

After a spell building computers with Control Data (CDC) Seymour made his own machine — the Cray 1 — which is reputed to have gone straight into the basement of the US spy centre, the National Security Agency (NSA). The first Cray 1 was delivered to the NSA in the spring of 1976, according to James Bamford, author of a history of the NSA (*The Puzzle Palace*, Sidgwick & Jackson).

Today, the Cray still plays a vital role in intelligence work. The UK's misleadingly named Government Communications Headquarters (GCHQ) at Cheltenham is widely believed to have one if not two of these superfast number crunchers to race through millions of possible combinations in search of the key to a code.

James Bamford said GCHQ is also networked to the Crays and dozens of other computers at NSA headquarters in Fort Meade, Maryland.

However, despite the Cray's beginnings, the most important use found for the supercomputer has turned out to be in something quite different to code-breaking. Most Crays have been put to work on modelling and simulation tasks. The latest machines are being used to mimic wind-tunnels, nuclear explosions, galaxies, oil fields and the weather. One is even being used by Hollywood to make life-like cartoons.

Before the powerful Cray came along and led people to coin the word 'supercomputer', the fastest computers used by scientists were made by Control Data. CDC dominated from the mid-60s to the mid-70s with its Cyber 6000, 70 and 170 series.

Then, in 1976, the first Cray 1 rolled out of the factory gates at Chippewa Falls, Minnesota. It could run at 150 million floating point calculations a second (megaflops) by virtue of its vector processing architecture. Such a computer stores data in registers and can race across each one at lightning speed, carrying out simple and repetitive calculations.

It is too inflexible to manage the variety of tasks that a commercial mainframe is called upon to perform. But it has turned out to be tailor-made for modelling where a few bits of data need to be added to millions of points to build up a total picture.

The Cray very quickly found its way into this niche. The first officially acknowledged Cray was delivered to the Los Alamos Scientific Laboratory in New Mexico in 1976 where it was used to simulate nuclear explosions.

In the environment-conscious 70s, there was a great pressure to cease the testing of nuclear weapons. The Cray was seized upon as the answer. Los Alamos staff could take warhead designs to a highly advanced stage simply by feeding data into their Crays.

Still Cray's most important customer, the Los Alamos Laboratory now has more than 10 of these multi-million pound machines.

Chris Windbridge, Cray's UK marketing manager, said another US nuclear research site, the Lawrence Livermore Laboratory in California, owns seven Crays and has been the first to buy Cray's two latest machines, the XMP/48 and the long awaited Cray 2.

The UK's own nuclear industry has been a keen customer of Cray. It has bought three of the 10 Crays now officially installed here. But the nuclear industry cannot claim to have had the first Cray to land on these shores. That was delivered to the European Centre for Medium Range Weather Forecasts in Reading in 1977, a joint project funded by 17 European nations.

The second Cray went to the Atomic Weapons Research Establishment (AWRE) at Aldermaston and the third to the UK Atomic Energy Authority at Harwell, soon after.

Aldermaston used its $8.6 million Cray 1 for simulating the new Chevaline multiple warheads on the Polaris missile, among other projects, and the AWRE bought its second Cray — the four times faster Cray XMP/24 — late last year.

Harwell bought a Cray in 1980 and uses it for modelling nuclear power plants, nuclear reactor accidents and other safety studies.

Cray made its first commercial sale in the UK to the Shell oil company. Shell bought a Cray 1b in April, 1981, to analyse seismic survey results and to model oil fields so the best way of extracting crude can be worked out.

Another oil industry company, Merlin Profilers of Surrey, bought a Cray 1s/1300 in August last year, for seismic work in the North Sea.

The cost of a Cray has nevertheless meant that most of the 10 machines officially in the UK have been sold to Government-funded research establishments.

As well as Aldermaston and Harwell, Crays have been bought by the Royal Armament Research and Development Establishment (Rarde) at Fort Halstead, Kent, in 1983 and the Royal Aircraft Establishment (RAE) at Farnborough, Hampshire, in 1984.

The other two Crays in the UK are accounted for by the machine at the University of London Computing Centre and one at Cray's own sales headquarters in Bracknell, west of London.

(*Computing Magazine*, 7 Feb 1985)

5 a What is meant by the term "computer simulation"?
b Give **three** reasons why computer simulations are used.
c Describe briefly a computer simulation program which you know about. State
   (i) what the program does;
   (ii) who might use it;
   (iii) why it is used;
   (iv) what input information it needs;
   (v) how its result are output.
d Explain how the effects of chance are sometimes introduced into a simulation.

(WMREB 82)

6 Each morning when he gets up, Bill Clean goes through all the following activities.

* fill sink with hot water (1 minute)
* fill bath with hot water (5 minutes)
* shave (3 minutes)
* brush teeth (2 minutes)
* take bath (15 minutes)
* towel dry (4 minutes)
* get dressed (5 minutes).

The diagram below shows a possible critical path network for these activities. Copy the network and label it with the activities. Find the least possible time for Bill to complete all these activities.

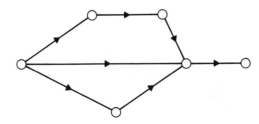

7 Read the article below and then write a summary in your own words of the ways that CAD can be used in the clothing industry.

Garment designs have to be drawn up and turned into a sample for presentation to the client, often a retail chain. Taking the client's modifications into account, the rough sample then has to be turned into an accurate pattern. Once the basic pattern has been created, it has to be expanded and contracted into a range of sizes, a process known as grading. The creation of the initial design is still mainly done by hand. But it can be entered using a digitiser into a computer system to establish a basic 'block', stored in the system's memory.

The computer system can automate the time-consuming process of grading. It also gives the clothing manufacturer much more flexibility to model designs. Maitland Menswear makes a range of medium-priced suits, and is one of Com Plan's clients. Paul Hanson, personal assistant to Maitland's managing director, explained: 'From the point of view of speed, computerisation cuts about 70% off the time taken to turn existing designs into cut patterns, and about 30% off new designs.'

Once the pattern has been transformed into a range of sizes, the next stage is to work out how the pattern pieces can best be cut out of a roll of fabric so as to minimise fabric wastage; this is known as lay planning, and is an important factor in achieving the cost savings the industry needs to maintain profits. Existing computer systems speed up the lay-planning process by displaying all the pattern pieces on a vdu.

Most of the industry's system suppliers are now working on software that will calculate the most economic lay automatically; Investronica, for example, has a system due for release 'any time', according to sales executive David Worgan.

Future developments in clothing design systems are likely to evolve in three directions. One is the emergence of small micro-based systems that small companies can afford. Com Plan is currently working with an associate company in Sweden on one such range, to run on Unix-based micros.

Secondly, companies are looking at ways of integrating the design and pattern making process with manufacturing, to produce systems that would also be capable of automatic costing.

But many in the industry, including Walsh, believe that cad is the major area where the technology will develop. Emerging now are sophisticated sketchpad systems which allow for far more detailed designs to be produced by manufacturers for the customer's inspection. On show at this year's Clothing Fair in Cologne was a system from OEM which is now beginning to be offered as a standard package by Gerber, Investronica and US firm Microdynamics.

Running on an IBM PC, with video camera and a digitising board, this produces high quality sketches that can form an alternative to samples. The digitising board allows fabric patterns to be put into the system to enhance the sketch's realism, and the system will display a wide range of colours.

A link between sketchpad systems and pattern design systems would be the first stage in developing a 3D clothing design system that would drastically cut down on the need to make sample garmets for customers.

(*Computing Magazine*, 15 August 1985)

16 Communications and Information Systems

Information Technology

Information technology is the technology associated with the storage, manipulation, organisation and communication of information. There is nothing new about the idea of applying the latest technology to information handling. When Samuel Morse invented his telegraph system in 1837, he was simply applying the latest technology of his time to information handling. Figure 16.1 shows some of the most important stages in the development of information technology.

Recently, the technologies of computing, telecommunications and microelectronics have been applied to information handling. The ways in which these technologies have changed the storage, manipulation, organisation and communication of data are examined in the following sections.

COMMUNICATIONS

Smoke signals and bonfire beacons (pre-history to 1850)

Runners, riders and pigeons (pre-history to present)

Naval signal flags (1770 to present)

Semaphore (1816 to present)

Morse code (1837 to present)

Postal service (1840 to present)

Analogue telephone system (1876 to present)

Radio (1901 to present)

Television (1929 to present)

Modem (1950 to present)

Optical fibres (1966 to present)

Digital telephone system (being introduced)

Figure 16.1 The history of information technology

DATA MANIPULATION AND ORGANISATION

Abacus (pre-history to present)

Mechanical calculators (1614 to present)

Computers (1945 to present)

DATA STORAGE

Stone and clay tablets (3500 BC)

Papyrus and hieroglyphics in Egypt (3000 BC)

Paper and writing in in China (100 BC)

First printed book in Europe (1450)

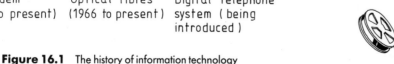
First typewriter (1800 ?)

Microfilm data storage (1871)

Magnetic storage (1900)

Optical disc storage (1980)

Information Storage and Retrieval

Before the introduction of computers, most information was stored on printed or hand-written documents. The documents were organised into books, folders and filing cabinets to provide easy access to the information. This is of course still a very common form of information storage, but computers have offered the alternatives of magnetic and electronic information storage. The advantages of magnetic and electronic storage devices are:

* they store information in a very compact form
* they are re-usable
* they can be searched automatically at very high speeds by a computer.

As we already know, magnetic tapes and discs are the main form of storage device used in modern computer systems. Magnetic tapes allow serial access to the stored data and magnetic discs allow both serial and direct access to the stored data. Serial access is of limited use in information retrieval because all the records in a file must be read one after the other until the required record is found. It may, however, be the only possibility if the records are not held in any order or if we are uncertain which records will be relevant in our search. Serial information retrieval is also used in some cases where a number of records are to be retrieved from a large file. In this case, the information requests are usually batched together and built up into an enquiry file. This file can then be batch processed with the master file and all the required information retrieved in a single search. The enquiry file must of course be sorted into the same order as the master file. One example of the use of a batch enquiry system is the enquiry service provided by the Driver and Vehicle Licensing Centre (DVLC) in Swansea. The DVLC maintains a file containing one record for every vehicle in use on British roads. Some of the fields in this file are shown in Figure 16.2.

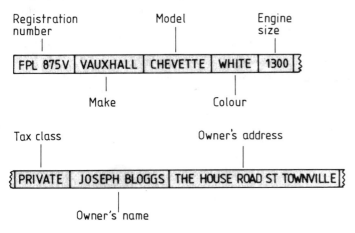

Figure 16.2 Fields in a file at the DVLC, Swansea

Other fields in each record provide a complete history of the vehicle. For example, details are stored of all previous owners, their addresses and any modifications they made to the vehicle. This enormous file is stored on over 150 reels of magnetic tape. Every day the DVLC receives many requests from vehicle owners for information about the history of their vehicles. The system flowchart in Figure 16.3 shows the way that these enquiries are processed.

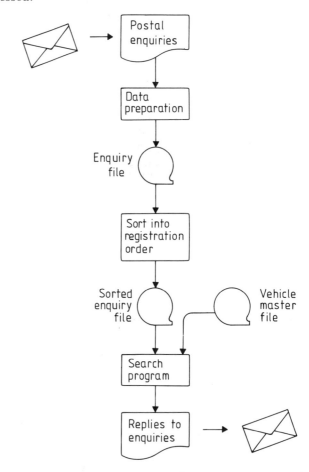

Figure 16.3 A system flowchart used for processing enquiries at the DVLC, Swansea

It takes over two weeks for an owner to receive a reply to an enquiry, so this type of information retrieval is only satisfactory for non-urgent off-line enquiries.

When data is held on direct access backing store, a rapid on-line information retrieval service can be provided. Often users of this enquiry service will wish to search the same data in several different ways. In manual information retrieval systems, this has often meant that the same data must be held sorted into several different orders. For example, a manual library enquiry system will need to hold the same data sorted into three different orders (see Figure 16.4).

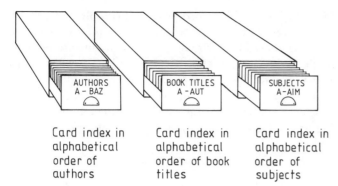

Card index in alphabetical order of authors   Card index in alphabetical order of book titles   Card index in alphabetical order of subjects

Figure 16.4 A manual library enquiry system

These three files will enable a library member to find Computer Studies for GCSE by Mark Bindley either by looking for BINDLEY in the author file or COMPUTER STUDIES FOR GCSE in the book title file or COMPUTERS in the subject file. To avoid this duplication of records, data held on direct access backing store is often structured as a **database**. Databases are often created from indexed sequential files with structures added to the files to allow them to be searched in many different ways. For example, a single-indexed sequential book file could be structured to allow searches for any author, any book title or any subject. (Database construction was explained on p. 114.)

Databases often allow searches to be made with a combination of keys. The keys are combined with words like **and**, **or**, **not**, **containing** and **between**. For example, a book enquiry database might allow a search instruction such as:

FIND :
    SUBJECT ? : COMPUTER SCIENCE
    OR COMPUTER STUDIES
    AUTHOR ? : WHALLEY **OR** WALLEY
    OR WALLY
    TITLE ? : **CONTAINING** BASIC

Suppose you are the witness to a crime and see the criminals escape by car. Perhaps the light was poor and the best description you can offer the police is "It was a Vauxhall Cavalier saloon, I think, grey or perhaps white, fairly new, certainly not more than three years old, the number plate ended with FPT." The police could turn your description into the following database information request:

    Registration number **containing** FPT
    and Make Vauxhall
    and Model Cavalier
    and body saloon
    and colour gray **or** grey **or** white
    and registered **between** 1984 **and** 1987

The result of this enquiry will be a list of the names and addresses of the owners of all such cars.

To be useful, a database must provide a large amount of **high-quality information**. High-quality information is **complete**, **accurate**, **up-to-date** and **precise**. In contrast, **low-quality information** is **incomplete**, **inaccurate or misleading**, **out-of-date and vague**.

Initially, all the information in a database must be input, usually with a keyboard. At regular intervals, records must be amended, added and deleted to keep the information up to date. It is essential to verify and validate all the entries to prevent incorrect data entering the database.

The use of computer information retrieval systems is increasing rapidly. Anyone with a microcomputer and a modem can now link themselves by telephone to a large variety of databases. There are already a number of companies who sell specialist on-line information. These companies own large computers which support complex databases. Customers pay to be allowed to contact the database with their computers and retrieve information. Some companies charge an annual subscription fee, and others make a charge for the time a customer is connected to the database. The kind of information which is sold in this way includes general news, financial information, technical and scientific information, business information and legal information.

If data is held in order on direct access backing store or in the main memory, it can be searched rapidly even if a full database is not created. The technique most commonly used to access ordered data rapidly is the **binary search**.

In a binary search, we begin by inspecting the record in the middle of the ordered list. If this is not our required record, it will at least tell us which half of the list does contain this record. For example, if we are searching for Mr Smith's record, finding Mr Jones in the middle of the list will tell us that the required record is in the second half of the list. We continue our search by inspecting the record in the middle of the remaining half of the list. If this is not our required record, it will again tell us which part of the list does contain this record. We continue this strategy, each time reducing the number of records left to search by a factor of 2, until the required record is found. Figure 16.5 shows the stages in a binary search for the name Smith in a list of eight names.

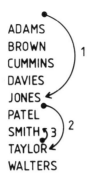

ADAMS
BROWN
CUMMINS   1
DAVIES
JONES
PATEL
SMITH 3   2
TAYLOR
WALTERS

Figure 16.5 How a binary search works

Expert Systems

An expert system is a computer program which has access to a large database of knowledge. It can draw conclusions, make decisions and offer advice based on that knowledge. In use, an expert system is supplied with some basic information about the problem it is to solve. It then examines its knowledge base and asks for other information until it can solve the problem and offer a decision. For example, an expert system designed to produce a medical diagnosis will be told a patient's age, weight, height, sex and general symptoms. The expert system will then take on the role of a human consultant and ask for further information until it can offer a firm diagnosis. If at any point the doctor using the expert system is puzzled by the computer's line of questioning, he or she can ask it to explain why it is asking those questions. Expert systems can be programmed with the knowledge and experience of many human experts. The program can also be designed to learn from mistakes and thus improve its own performance. It seems inevitable that the use of expert systems will increase as they become available in more and more fields of knowledge. Some successful present-day expert systems include:

* MYCIN   a medical diagnosis expert system.
* PROSPECTOR   a geology and mining expert system.
* DENDRAL   a chemical analysis expert system.

Teletext and Viewdata

Teletext systems provide an information service using adapted television sets. The information is broadcast from the same transmitters used for normal television programmes using part of the normal TV signal. There are two teletext services in Britain at the moment: **Ceefax** provided by the BBC, and **Oracle** provided by ITV. The information provided by a teletext service is divided into **pages**, each of which fills a TV screen. A typical page might contain the latest sports news or a recipe for the day or some travel news. One very useful service provided for deaf viewers allows teletext subtitles to be added to normal programmes. Each teletext system

provides about 200 pages of information which can be selected using a special hand-held keypad. Index pages are provided to help the user select the information he or she requires. Teletext systems like Ceefax and Oracle can provide only a limited database of information and are **not interactive**. A user can select a teletext page providing entertainment information, but cannot use the system to book a ticket for a cinema or theatre. However, both Ceefax and Oracle have the advantage that they are free; the only expense is in buying an adapted television set. At the moment a teletext set costs between £50 and £100 more than a normal set. Figure 16.6 shows an outline of a teletext system.

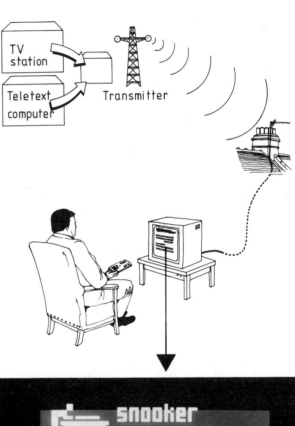

Figure 16.6 The outline of a teletext system

Viewdata is a more powerful form of teletext which allows interactive use of the system. The largest viewdata service in Britain is the **Prestel** service provided by British Telecom. Prestel information is transmitted over the telephone network, and to access Prestel a user needs an adapted television or microcomputer, a telephone and modem, and a Prestel keypad. Like Ceefax and Oracle, Prestel information is divided into pages. Unlike Ceefax and Oracle, Prestel provides hundreds of thousands of pages of information. Prestel is not a free service. Companies and organisations pay to rent Prestel pages from British Telecom and then use the pages to display information about their services and products. Information is provided on travel services, business news and services, entertainment, banking, financial news and services, exchange rates for foreign currency, share prices, weather forecasts, farming services, computer programs, importing and exporting services and many other areas of interest. The people who rent Prestel pages are called **information providers**. The other users of the Prestel system are the people who access the information. To access information, a user must first use the Prestel keypad to dial the Prestel computer and establish a telephone link. The user then uses the keypad and the extensive Prestel index to select the information required. Prestel is an **interactive** service. Using the keypad a user can send signals to the computer and enter into various transactions. For example, having consulted the entertainment pages, a user can actually book a ticket for the event he or she wishes to attend. Prestel is quite an expensive service because the user must pay an annual rental and the cost of all the telephone calls made to the Prestel computer. Some information providers also make a charge each time a user accesses one of their pages. Figure 16.7 shows an outline of the Prestel system.

If information services such as teletext and viewdata increase, they may eventually compete with (or even replace?) more traditional sources of information. Traditional paper and ink, books, newspapers, catalogues, directories and brochures could all be replaced by electronic alternatives. Initially, the cost of the electronic hardware would be very high, but in the long term there would be considerable savings and other benefits. The display screen of an information system could be used again and again, and there would be no need to cut down millions of trees each year to produce the paper for books and newspapers.

Word Processing and Electronic Mail

A word processor is a computer system which can input, store, retrieve, manipulate and print text. Word processing facilities can be provided in three ways:

* with a microprocessor-based machine used only for word processing
* with a general purpose microcomputer running a word processing application package
* with a terminal connected to a minicomputer or mainframe computer which has a word processing package in its software library.

Whichever system is used, a word processor has the following components:

* a keyboard for data entry
* a monitor screen for the immediate display of the input data
* a floppy disc or hard disc backing store
* a printer to produce the final document.

The hardware of a typical word processing system is shown in Figure 16.8.

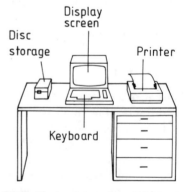

Figure 16.8 The hardware of a word processing system

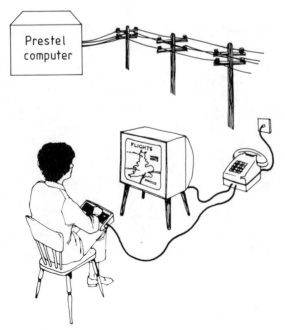

Figure 16.7 The outline of the Prestel system

Initially, the text is typed into the word processor and displayed on the screen. A small spot of light called the **cursor** marks the current typing position. Having entered the text, the user has many options available. Here are some of them:

* The cursor can be moved to any position in the text and mistakes can be deleted and corrected.
* Whole sentences or paragraphs can be moved to different places in the text.
* Previously stored material can be retrieved and inserted in the text.
* The text can be **formatted** in many different ways. For example, the user can experiment with different margin widths and line spacings.
* A spelling check can be made by asking the word processor to check each word in the text against a dictionary held in its backing store. (This is, however, quite a lengthy process and can create problems when correctly spelt names are not found in the dictionary.)
* The user can instruct the machine to replace one word with a different one wherever it appears in the text.
* The corrected text can be stored for later recall.
* A **hard copy** of the text can be obtained on the printer. This is usually a high-quality (letter-quality) printer such as a daisy wheel or ink jet printer.

Because text typed into a word processor is first displayed on a screen, it is possible to correct all mistakes and make any alterations before the text is printed. Standard letters need only be typed in full once. They can then be recalled each time they are needed, detail changes can be made, and then a copy can be printed. If the only detail change is the name of the person receiving the letter, the machine can often work automatically from a stored **mailing list**. This is a disc file with the names and addresses of all the people who are to receive the letter. The word processor can extract details from this file and print a copy of the letter addressed to each person on the mailing list. Some word processors are linked by modem and telephone into computer networks. Copies of documents can then be sent directly to other computers and word processors linked to the network. This **electronic mail** is faster, more reliable and often cheaper than sending documents by post.

Now we shall look at an example of how a word processor is used. Imagine a personnel manager called Siloben Patel who, after holding interviews, has decided to employ Fred Wheel as a lorry driver. Siloben has a word processor which she often uses herself rather than wait for her work to be done by an office typist. Her first step is to recall on the screen the standard format she uses for letters offering people a job. The display is shown in Figure 16.9.

Figure 16.9 A standard letter on a VDU

Moving the cursor around the display, Siloben adds the details of Fred's letter to produce a new display (Figure 16.10).

Figure 16.10 A letter specifically addressed to Mr Wheel

Siloben then prints a copy of the letter and signs it. To prepare the contract of employment, Siloben calls up a standard contract form. This contains many separate conditions of employment, some of which apply to Fred and some of which do not. For example, the clause

* The employee must hold a current Heavy Goods Vehicle driving licence

applies to Fred but the clause

* The employee will be provided with a company car

does not.

Siloben deletes any conditions of employment that will not apply in Fred's case and prints out a copy of the contract to enclose with her letter.

Communications

Communications by spoken word, picture image, computer signals and printed text are all sent from place to place using the methods shown in Figure 16.11.

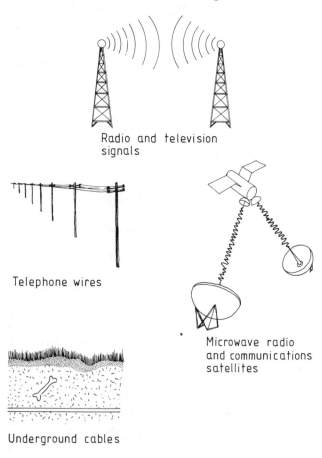

Radio and television signals

Telephone wires

Microwave radio and communications satellites

Underground cables

Figure 16.11 Systems for communications

At the moment the computer's first link into any communications system is usually by telephone and modem. Do you remember why a modem is needed? It is because the telephone system uses *analogue* equipment. This analogue equipment is, however, being slowly replaced by **digital** telephone equipment that will send all messages as digital signals. This will allow direct computer telephone links and will also provide a better-quality voice transmission service. France already has an extensive digital telephone network, and Britain has started to install its **System X** digital telephone exchanges in several cities.

Note that there is another alternative to a modem: an **acoustic coupler**. A modem converts a computer's digital signals directly into analogue signals that can pass

through the telephone system. An acoustic coupler uses a small speaker to turn the computer's signals into sounds. These sounds are then picked up by a normal telephone headset. Acoustic couplers are cheaper than modems, but transmit data at a much slower rate and with many more errors. Acoustic couplers are, however, very useful for portable computers because they need no special wiring and can be used with any telephone.

Exercise 57

1 Explain why the DVLC enquiry system is satisfactory for its task but would not be satisfactory if the police were trying to trace a car used in a serious crime.

2 Explain the different ways in which a manual library enquiry system can be searched.

3 The following account was given by a witness to a murder, "The man drove off in a dark blue (or was it black?) car. I only saw the front, it was either a Ford Escort or an Orion, I only caught the first part of the number, it was C 372 I think". Turn this account into a database information request.

4 The following article describes a new police database system. Read the article and write a summary of the advantages that the new system will have over a traditional card index.

Holmes computer memory to aid fight against crime
Almost a century after Conan Doyle invented the world's greatest detective, another Holmes is being pressed into the service of the British police. On order is a tailor-made computer system designed to take some of the slog out of investigations like the current hunt for the hooded rapist known as The Fox.

Holmes — Home Office Large Major Enquiry System — will store all the information that pours into a police incident room and give detectives rapid access to it by scanning statements at speeds of up to one million words a minute.

Many police forces have already bought their own computers — largely as a result of lessons learned during the hunt for the Yorkshire Ripper — and Holmes is intended to equip all 41 forces with a compatible software system enabling them not only to conduct their own inquiries but also to co-operate efficiently in joint investigations.

Computer firms have been called to the Home Office for the moment only as a specification; the Home Office wants it operational by next January. It has to have more extensive facilities than Miriam — Major Incident Room Index Action Management — a system set up for trials at Kent police headquarters last year and now regarded as too elementary.

Holmes will replace the traditional card-index. For example, if one witness recalls seeing a red car, an officer will receive from the computer every other reference to red cars in previous statements. It has other sophisticated facilities.

* When an officer keys in a word, the computer will find it everywhere it appears in statements; even part of a word — thus 'cort' will reveal not only every Ford Cortina but also every Ford Escort.
* The computer will be able to combine information on two different investigations if they are thought to be linked, and separate them again if there is found to be no connection. There was speculation last week that the crimes of The Fox might be linked to rape attacks in the north-west.
* Like-sounding names and words: officers hunting "Reid" will also get "Reade", "Reed" and "Reede".
* The search for names such as Elizabeth will also turn up the shortened forms Liz, Betty and Beth.
* Synonyms: an officer making inquiries about, say, a blue jumper, would be given references to jerseys, sweaters and pullovers from other statements.

A Home Office spokesman said: "The chief police officers monitoring the Miriam project have indicated that they would like more extensive facilities than the experimental system. That's why the specification for Holmes has been drawn up." He explained that "large" had been inserted into the title to make the initials read as Holmes — "After all, we couldn't call it Homes".

Several computer firms have spoken to the Home Office about supplying Holmes. The Home Office intends to approve several different makes to keep the price competitive while ensuring that the systems used by different forces are compatible. By writing new software, manufacturers hope to be able to use existing hardware.

(*Sunday Times*, 29 July 1984)

5 Read the following article and then draw up a list of the advantages and disadvantages it mentions for and against on-line databases.

On-line databases — libraries of computerised information which can be searched by people using a desk-top computer and the telephone — once promised to revolutionise the way we work: we would twiddle a few buttons and, whoosh, the world's knowledge would appear on our screens.

But like a lot of high-tech promises the reality is, unfortunately, quite different.

Financial information, such as currency movements and share prices, has transferred easily to telephone lines and monitors. The financial community has also been prepared to pay a premium to get the information quickly, sometimes literally within seconds. Scientists have also provided a profitable, if small, market for computerised information on esoteric subjects such as chemical structures and patents.

And people such as Mike Spelman, chief economist at

the BOC Group, can hum or whistle favourite tunes without incurring the wrath of librarians, while searching through libraries to gain access to the vast amount of information stored electronically around the world.

"Today I might be looking for economic statistics about Japan and tomorrow I'll need information about a company based in Brazil. I can't always specify in advance what I'll need. To go through the traditional routes of researching in a library takes too long,' he says.

Spelman's company supplies industrial and medical gasses and operates in most parts of the world. His job is to keep a constant surveillance on global commerce, look at the competition and identify trends among customers or potential customers.

'The electronic databases I use don't contain anything that was not available before, they just make the information more accessible and the process of getting at it less time-consuming,' he says.

But general-purpose information, the sort carried by newspapers, radio and magazines, has not been an electronic hit, mainly because the public has not understood the benefits and has been unwilling to pay much more for the convenience of reading news on a computer screen. Not many mothers rush for the computer to check a recipe or theatre programmes and few business people flip through the *Economist* on their PCs, although these services are available.

There are a number of reasons for reality being a lot duller than early expectations: some are technical, most are commercial.

First, organising the information into easily accessible categories on computers is relatively difficult. This means that users have to learn a number of, sometimes quite complex, procedures before they can search the database successfully. Users have to go on courses and also keep in practice, otherwise they can waste their time and money.

Business people who spend most of their time doing other jobs and only a small proportion searching for information have refused to put up with the problems. Methods of searching are, fortunately, getting easier and some databases, such as World Reporter from Datasolve, make limited demands on the user.

Second, not everyone has a computer at their disposal. Without one it is impossible to make a search. Some on-line databases insist that users use a special terminal which has to be rented. While the terminal can make it easier to use the database, the extra cost and space it takes up puts people off.

Third, telephone costs can be quite high and to use the cheaper 'packet switched' lines involves a certain amount of organisation which, combined with other problems, complicates the job of signing on.

Fourth, newspapers and magazines are concerned that their revenues will decline if they also appear in electronic form. It has taken some time to persuade the main newspapers to sell their information in this way. To overcome copyright problems, some services still offer only a precis of articles.

Fifth, databases cost about £1 a minute to use. If the telecommunications costs and that of the hardware is added the whole bill can be quite daunting.

'But we can now do work and take on projects which we couldn't have done five years ago. I can also spend far more time thinking and analysing. And that's partly to do with databases,' says Spelman.

(*Observer*, 27 October 1985)

6 Two contrasting headlines from articles about expert systems are shown below. Explain what an expert system is and how each of the headlines may be true.

Expert systems aid cancer research

Expert systems put jobs in question

7 Explain the differences between teletext services like Ceefax and Oracle and viewdata services like Prestel. Draw up a list showing the advantages and disadvantages of each service.

8 **a** Explain what is meant by Word Processing.
  b Choose three different jobs where word processing might be used.
    (i) State the job and explain how word processing might be used.
    (ii) For each job give a different benefit of using word processing.

(AEB 84)

9 **a** Describe **two** ways in which word processing machines can be used to help improve the working life of an office typist or secretary.
  b Why is it likely that an office manager would welcome the introduction of a word processing machine?
  c Why might some typists be worried by the introduction of a word processing machine?

(UCLES 82)

10 "The laborious process of moving a letter from one part of the world to another shows the limitations of traditional methods of coding and transmitting information." (The Mighty Micro — Dr. C. Evans)

  a (i) Describe the traditional methods referred to by Dr. Evans
    (ii) Give four different limitations of these methods.
  b The traditional methods may be replaced by "Electronic Mail".
    (i) Show how this might operate.
    (ii) Explain **two** advantages and **one** disadvantage it would have over the traditional methods for a large company.

(AEB 82)

11 Read the following article, which describes the use of an agricultural expert system.

  a Explain how a farmer can use this particular expert system.
  b Explain the advantages that ICI gain from this expert system.

c Explain the advantages that a farmer gains from this expert system.

d If you were a farming expert, explain why you might be worried by the introduction of a computer expert system.

e If you were a member of an ecology movement trying to stop the use of chemicals in agriculture, explain why you might be worried by the use of this particular expert system.

In the complex business of modern agriculture, expert systems may soon be playing a growing role, says Jim McCarten

Advanced technology is becoming a marketing tool in one of the UK's oldest industries — agriculture. Farmers buying ICI's agrochemicals now get access to an expert system on the use of fungicides for wheat crops.

For ICI, which claims the service is a world first, the commercial advantage is clearcut — an edge over its competitors. For farmers, use of expert systems may soon become a trend, as they face a mass of decisions on crops and slimmer profit margins.

The expert system, Wheat Counsellor, was introduced in autumn 1984, and is the first in what ICI hopes will be a series of applications for the arable farming community, covering a number of different crops. It is available to farmers on viewdata sets installed at ICI dealers who already use them to provide for advanced business management systems.

ICI clearly hopes Wheat Counsellor will act as a powerful incentive for farmers to visit its dealers — the service will *not* be made available to farmers at home.

In use, Wheat Counsellor begins by asking for the particular farmer, farm and the specific field to be analysed. Information is then retrieved from ICI's database about the field's geochemical and farming history, and the type of wheat grown in it.

The farmer can be asked for further information about seeds and fertiliser being used, and how they are being applied. The risks from various strains of disease are then evaluated, and explained to the farmer.

Treatment recommendations are made, and along with them cost/benefit analyses for the recommended course of action, or for alternative treatments. This last point is the crucial one — if the system's decision can be justified in hard cash terms, then technological niceties can be forgotten.

ICI has been involved in expert systems research for five years. It took about 12 months to develop, using the Savoir expert system shell developed by software house Isis. Recently, a videodisc facility has been linked into the system. This can elaborate on information presented on videotex, by supplying extra information and high resolution graphics for diagrams/pictures.

Expert systems have sometimes been accused of being products in search of a useful application. Because of this, ICI's developers selected a specific problem area and tried to ensure that the information built into the expert system was appropriate. They identified one particular problem in need of a solution: a lack of expert agricultural sales staff to go round at peak times.

Selecting crop protection chemicals is a complicated business. Decisions have to be taken each year at different times during the seasons and the conditions are constantly changing. The weather, soil composition, previous year's crops, and the particular geology beneath a specific field affect conditions for parasites. Suppliers like ICI are constantly researching their products to maintain position in a fiercely competitive market. Consequently the products available are constantly changing.

At key times like autumn, when planning for the new crop is under way, the number of farmers seeking advice far exceeds the number of people qualified to give it. So ICI needed to improve the productivity of its human experts. Two members of its plant protection division, Mike Jones, commercial services development manager and Derek Crates, system analyst, produced a paper describing the development of Counsellor, which was presented at Videotex International conference in Amsterdam in October. Their paper pointed out that "Computers have for some time been used as an aid in this area, but have been hampered by their lack of ability to provide reasoning to back up the advice and recommendations given, normally done by the scarce and expensive human expert".

Before starting work on Counsellor, the team looked carefully at the advantages of using an expert system. They came up with these key points:

* Ease of expressing knowledge: The data in the system is stored in a form more akin to ordinary English than in conventional systems.
* Flexibility of expression: The sources of data for the system can range from text-book definitions of fungi to farmers' folklore.
* Explanation of reasoning: Expert systems, in addition to arriving at an answer, can explain how it got there.

Creating user confidence is a major part of selling an expert system. Justifying its answers in a way the farmer can follow, and agree with, is crucial to doing this.

According to Richard Walker, ICI Plant Protection Division's trade affairs manager, an important part of the dialogue between farmer and computer was the ability to cope with an individual's likes and dislikes. Some farmers just do not like dealing with certain suppliers or products and want an alternative solution, even if it is not a 'first choice' option.

The fourth key consideration in favour of the expert system is its ability to handle uncertainty and 'reason' a best result. Treatment recommendations are made, and along with them, cost/benefit analyses for the advice or for alternative treatments — a crucial final stage.

One area ICI did not have to worry about was persuading farmers to use new technology. Mark Rogers, head of ICI's Decision Support Systems Group, said that computers are now a common sight on farms. Young farmers going to agricultural college are trained in the applications of computers in business and return to the industry armed with lots of new ideas.

A number of companies already specialise in management and finance software for the farming community and ICI has a unit devoted to this area — Agricultural Information Technology (AIT). AIT's main efforts are concentrated on Adviser, a viewdata service that farmers can access from terminals in their own home.

The system can act as an information service for weather forecasts, prices and so on. It can also download programs for accounting, stock control and tax returns.

In the long run, ICI's plan is to extend the use of expert systems by giving farmers home terminals to interrogate ICI's mainframe computer. The mainframe will have data files on individual farmers and will be able to relate those to its own main data files, offering an informed 'opinion' on the user's problems.

Rogers said the next step would be to aim for more software integration between systems running on the central mainframe.

Jim McCarten is a staff writer on Computing.

(*Computing*, 5 December 1985)

17 Computer Control

Input and Output

A computer which is provided with suitable input and output devices can be used to control a machine directly. The task of the input devices is to provide the computer with information on the performance of the machine under its control. The task of the output devices is to move the gears, valves, switches and levers which affect the performance of the machine.

The input devices can be selected from a vast range of *sensors* which measure quantities such as temperature, sound, pressure, liquid flow and magnetic fields. The sensors usually measure the quantity with an analogue voltage. For example, Figure 17.1 shows a temperature sensor being used to monitor the temperature of a liquid. As the temperature of the liquid goes from 0 °C to 100 °C, the voltage produced by the sensor will go from 0 V to 1.5 V.

Temperature from 0°C to 100°C

Voltage from 0 V to 1.5 V

Figure 17.1 A temperature sensor

Other sensors, called **proximity switches** can detect the close presence of various substances. They produce an electrical signal if the substance comes close to the sensor. Figure 17.2 shows how two proximity switches can monitor the level of sand in a hopper.

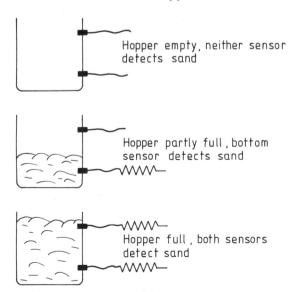

Hopper empty, neither sensor detects sand

Hopper partly full, bottom sensor detects sand

Hopper full, both sensors detect sand

Figure 17.2 Sensors to detect the level of sand in a hopper

Many types of sensor produce analogue signals, but analogue signals cannot be processed directly by digital computers. Before the analogue signals from a sensor are input they must therefore be converted to digital signals with an **analogue-to-digital converter** (or **ADC**). Figure 17.3 shows a magnetic sensor mounted near a gear wheel to monitor its speed. As the teeth of the gear wheel pass the sensor, they create a magnetic field which rises and falls. This produces a varying analogue voltage from the sensor. The ADC changes this to the digital signals needed for input to the computer.

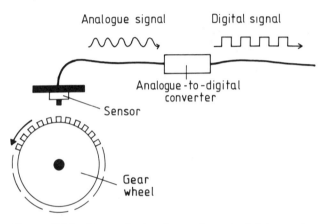

Analogue signal   Digital signal

Analogue-to-digital converter

Sensor

Gear wheel

Figure 17.3 One application of an analogue-to-digital converter

A computer sends control signals to other machines through an **output port**. A typical output port with eight parallel output lines is shown in Figure 17.4.

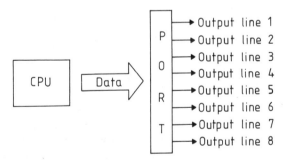

CPU   Data

P O R T

→ Output line 1
→ Output line 2
→ Output line 3
→ Output line 4
→ Output line 5
→ Output line 6
→ Output line 7
→ Output line 8

Figure 17.4 Signals passing through an output port

To the CPU, the output port is simply a memory location in which it can store any 8-bit number. Figure 17.5 shows how the computer can turn 8 switches on and off by storing binary numbers in the output port.

If more than 8 switches are to be controlled, suitable decoding logic circuits can be constructed to interpret the computer's output signals. Figure 17.6 shows a logic

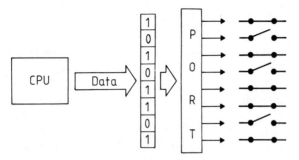

Figure 17.5 How an output port can control switches

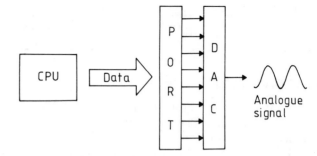

Figure 17.7 How a digital-to-analogue converter is used

circuit that will only turn a switch on if the computer outputs the control signal

$$1\ 0\ 1\ 0\ 1\ 0\ 1\ 1$$

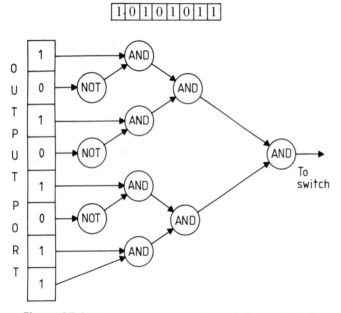

Figure 17.6 How an output port can be used with a logic circuit

The CPU can store any binary number from

$$0\ 0\ 0\ 0\ 0\ 0\ 0\ 0 \quad \text{to} \quad 1\ 1\ 1\ 1\ 1\ 1\ 1\ 1$$

in the output port, and logic circuits can be constructed to interpret any one of these binary numbers as a signal to turn a switch on or off.

If an analogue output signal is required, all the output lines can be fed into a **digital-to-analogue** converter (or **DAC**). The **DAC** will convert the range of output binary numbers into an analogue signal. For example, a DAC may convert a range of binary numbers from

$$0\ 0\ 0\ 0\ 0\ 0\ 0\ 0 \quad \text{to} \quad 1\ 1\ 1\ 1\ 1\ 1\ 1\ 1$$

to a voltage between 0 V and 1.5 V. Figure 17.7 shows a DAC connected to the output port.

The signals from the output port may be used to control another machine directly or they may be used to control **activators**. These activators in turn move the gears, valves, switches and levers which affect the performance of the other machine. The most common activator is a

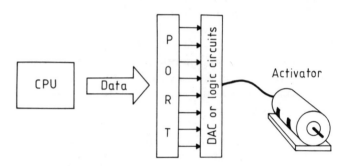

Figure 17.8 The stages by which a CPU controls an activator

small electric motor. Figure 17.8 shows a complete system for the output of control signals.

In a complete computer control system, sensors monitor a machine's performance and input this information to the computer. The computer uses a control program to analyse the information and to decide on the correct control signals to maintain or improve the machine's

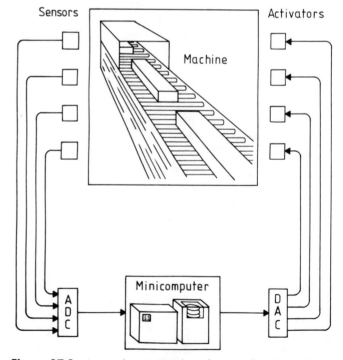

Figure 17.9 A control system in industry for controlling the production of steel bars

212

performance. These control signals are then sent to the activators, which physically control the machine. The sensors monitor the effects of the control signals, and the whole control sequence starts again. A complete record of the input information and output control signals is normally built up on backing store for analysis of the machine's performance. Figure 17.9 shows the outline of a control system used for a machine producing steel bars.

Microprocessor Control Applications

Small computer control applications are usually based on a dedicated microprocessor. These microprocessors and their necessary sensors and activators are usually built into the machine which they control. As an example we will look at the system used to control an automatic washing machine (see Figure 17.10).

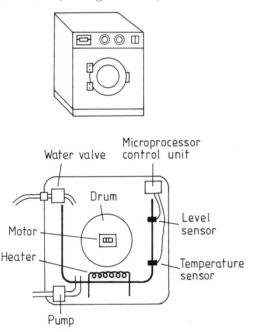

WASHING MACHINE

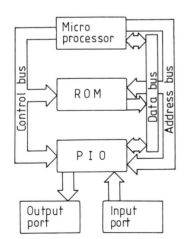

MICROPROCESSOR CONTROL UNIT

Figure 17.10 A washing machine and its basic components

The microprocessor has links from two of the lines in its input port to the level and temperature sensors. Four lines from the output port are connected to the water valve, heater, motor and pump. Figure 17.11 shows these links and the codes and control signals which are used.

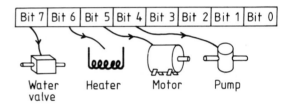

INPUT PORT

Code Signals Used

If BIT 7=0, the drum is empty.
If BIT 7=1, then drum is full.
If BIT 6=0, the water is not hot enough.
If BIT 6=1, the water is hot enough.

OUTPUT PORT

Control Signals Used

If BIT 7=0, the water valve is closed.
If BIT 7=1, the water valve is opened.
If BIT 6=0, the heater is switched off.
If BIT 6=1, the heater is switched on.
If BIT 5=0, the motor is switched off.
If BIT 5=1, the motor is switched on.
If BIT 4=0, the pump is switched off.
If BIT 4=1, the pump is switched on.

Figure 17.11 How the input and output ports control a washing machine

To control the washing machine, the microprocessor has a **control program** in its ROM memory. This control program will contain instructions for several different types of washing cycle. For simplicity, we will only consider the simplest of washing cycles. The stages in this washing cycle are:

1 Fill the machine with water
2 Heat the water
3 Wash the clothes
4 Empty the machine

The control program for this very simple washing sequence is shown in Figure 17.12.

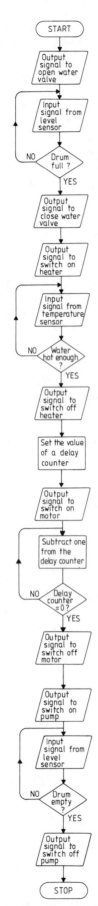

Figure 17.12 The control program for a washing sequence in a washing machine

This application has been simplified to make it easier to understand. We must remember that a real washing machine would need several other valves and pumps and a much more complex control program. Most modern microprocessor controlled machines offer a wide range of washing cycles with different temperatures, wash times, spin times and number of rinses.

Before microprocessors became easily available, the control of a washing machine was achieved by mechanical or electro-mechanical means. A complex assembly of gears, levers and electric motors switched the various components on and off. Microprocessor control systems have rapidly replaced these systems because they are cheaper, more reliable and more flexible, being able to offer a much wider range of washing cycles.

For the washing machine manufacturer, the microprocessor control unit offers these advantages:

* There are fewer parts to assemble. This leads to a reduction in jobs and savings in labour costs.
* The microprocessor control systems are cheaper than mechanical or electro-mechanical control systems. This leads to either greater profits or a cheaper and more competitive product.
* The greater reliability of microprocessor control systems leads to a better reputation for the manufacturer and to a reduction in the cost of repairs carried out under the product's guarantee.
* There is considerable advertising potential in products which contain microprocessor control systems. This may create sales to people who already own serviceable machines but who want to buy the new 'electronic' model.

For the buyer and user of the washing machine, the microprocessor control unit offers these advantages:

* Microprocessor control systems are much more versatile than mechanical or electro-mechanical control systems. This means that the machine can be provided with a far wider range of washing options. It should be noted, however, that this wide range of options does make the machine more difficult to use.
* The greater reliability of microprocessor control systems leads to a reduction in repair bills.

For the people who service and repair washing machines, microprocessor control systems create the following changes:

* Repairs are often carried out by a method of **module exchange**. This simply means that a defective unit is removed and replaced with a new one. The defective unit is thrown away or

214

returned to the factory; the service personnel do not attempt to repair it themselves. There is thus a great reduction in the skill needed by the service personnel.

* The greater reliability of microprocessor control units leads to fewer breakdowns and less actual repairing of parts. This in turn leads to a reduction in the number of service personnel needed and hence to loss of jobs.

Digital Watch. Digital watches contain a microprocessor to control their operation. Usually a very small crystal timing device is used to produce a series of very fast and accurate time pulses. The microprocessor is used to count the pulses and to convert them into seconds, hours and minutes. A digital display panel is used to show the time. When a button is pressed the same display can be used to show the date. A stopwatch and alarm function may also be included. The control program automatically adjusts the date for months with thirty days and for leap years. When the date, stopwatch or alarm display is in use, the microprocessor continues to keep the correct time. Apart from occasionally changing the battery, these watches require no regular maintenance because they contain very few moving parts.

Traditional watches contain hundreds of small mechanical parts to control their operation. The manufacture and assembly of these parts is a complex, highly skilled and expensive operation. In use, the parts start to wear and the watch needs regular maintenance and cleaning. Date, alarm and stopwatch functions are difficult and expensive to provide, since each requires a separate mechanism and display. (See Figure 17.13.)

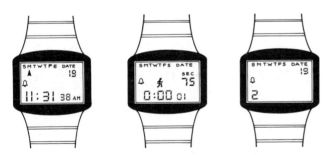

Figure 17.13 The different displays on a digital watch

Supermarket Scales. Many supermarket scales now contain microprocessors. In use, the produce is placed on a normal weighing pan. The price per kilogram or pound is then entered using push buttons. Sometimes a separate button is provided with a picture of each item. In this case, it is not necessary to enter the price, this is already stored in the memory of the microprocessor system. From the weight and the price per kilogram or pound, the microprocessor calculates the price of the produce. This is shown on a digital display panel. Usually a small printer is also connected to print out a price label.

Traditional scales work with springs, levers and gear wheels. Usually only the weight of the produce can be shown. The operator must then calculate the price and write out a price label. (See Figure 17.14.)

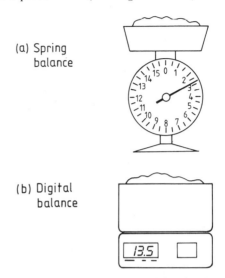

(a) Spring balance

(b) Digital balance

Figure 17.14 Analogue and digital scales

Telephones. Some telephones now contain microprocessor systems which enable them to offer many extra facilities. The traditional dial is usually replaced with a number keypad which is easier to use. If a number is engaged, the telephone can be left to keep trying the number automatically until a connection is made. The most frequently used numbers can be stored and obtained using a one-digit or two-digit code. If somebody knows they will be at a different number, the system can automatically re-route all calls for them. Traditional telephones can offer none of these facilities. (See Figure 17.15.)

Figure 17.15 Microprocessors are changing the action and appearance of the telephone

Cameras. When a photograph is taken, two important factors must be considered: the distance of the object from the camera and the light level. Cheap cameras have no adjustments and can only be used in good light. Often the picture is poorly focused and the image blurred. Good cameras allow the user to adjust the light entering the camera, the speed of the shutter and the focus of the lens. Working out the correct settings is difficult, however, and poor pictures are often taken with even the most expensive cameras. Some cameras now include microprocessor control systems. Sensors are used to measure the light level and the distance of the object from the camera. ADCs allow these values to be input to the microprocessor. The correct settings are calculated and signals are output to small activators. These set the shutter speed, lens aperture and focus automatically. If the light is poor, an electronic flash may be automatically used. A perfect picture should (at least in theory) result every time.

There are many other examples of microprocessor-controlled systems. It is a list that is added to almost daily as new applications are found. Some common applications not considered in detail here are:

* cookers
* alarm systems
* traffic control (see Figure 17.16)
* lifts
* car fuel and ignition systems
* heating and ventilation systems
* calculators
* electronic toys and games
* petrol pumps
* cash registers
* radio tuners
* time switches
* numerically controlled machine tools

Of course, many older examples of the above devices still use mechanical or electro-mechanical control systems. These are, however, being steadily replaced with micro-processor control systems. Many new applications of automatic control are also being developed where in the past traditional mechanisms were too large or expensive to install. This very rapid growth is sometimes referred to as the **microprocessor revolution**.

Summary of the Advantages of Microprocessor Control Systems

* **Speed**. They can work much more quickly than a human or a mechanical device.
* **Flexibility**. Being programmable, the same basic system can be used in many different ways.
* **Reliability**. They are very reliable because there are no moving parts.
* **Low power consumption**. They can easily be run from batteries as well as mains power.

Figure 17.16 Metropolitan Police traffic control at New Scotland Yard

* **Low cost**. They can be used even in devices sold for a few pounds.
* **Very small size**. They can be used in devices that must be very small and light.
* **Robustness**. The circuits are embedded in solid silicon and a plastic case. They are virtually indestructible in normal use.
* **Data storage**. All input data and output instructions can be stored for later analysis.
* **Decision-making ability**. A microprocessor control system can function in many different ways, depending on decisions made by the control program.

Process Control

Large-scale computer control applications are common in **process industries**. Process industries take in raw materials and convert them to a more useful form. Some examples of process industries are:

* Metal works
* Chemical plants
* Cement plants
* Food processing factories
* Oil refineries
* Paper mills
* Power stations
* Brickworks

During the conversion process, it is necessary to control pressure, temperature, rate of flow, chemical composition and many other physical factors. Very fast and accurate control is needed in processes that are potentially very dangerous. Fires and explosions have sometimes occurred when processing machines have gone out of control. This has in turn caused a great deal of suffering and loss of life. Usually the control needed is too fast and accurate for a human to provide, and mechanical and electrical controllers have traditionally been used. Because they are faster, more reliable, cheaper and, being programmable, more flexible, computer control systems are increasingly used. Large-scale control applications often require hundreds of sensors and activators, and the power of a minicomputer or mainframe computer is usually needed. The latest and most powerful microcomputers can, however, cope with some large-scale control applications.

The tasks of a computer controlling a manufacturing process are:

* To maintain the quality of the finished product
* To raise the alarm if the process goes out of control and to shut down the machinery if necessary
* To keep a complete record (log) of the performance of the production machines. Usually all sensor inputs and activator outputs are dumped on to backing store to build up this data log
* To analyse the data log and present production statistics in an easy to understand form
* To produce the maximum output possible at the minimum cost possible.

As an example of a large-scale control application, we will look at the production of float-glass. The raw materials from which float-glass is made include charcoal, soda, salt, limestone, sand and feldspar. These and other materials must first be mixed and melted in a furnace at a temperature of 1600 °C. When the raw materials have been melted, they are poured out on to the surface of a bath of molten tin. The liquid glass floats on the surface of the tin, forming a perfectly flat sheet 3 millimetres thick. As the glass flows along the tin bath, it is gradually cooled to 650 °C. From the tin bath the glass passes into a cooling oven which slowly cools the glass to 120 °C. Accurate control of the cooling process is essential,

because if the glass cools too quickly it may crack or blemish. Because the surface of the molten tin is perfectly flat, the glass needs no further finishing apart from cutting into sheets. When the production machines are in action, the glass-making process is continuous, with raw materials flowing in to one end of the production line and glass sheets emerging at the other end. Figure 17.17 shows the outline of the float-glass production line.

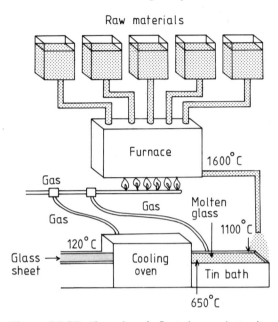

Figure 17.17 The outline of a float-glass production line

In this much simplified diagram, no attempt has been made to show the valves, switches, activators and sensors used by the computer to control this process. The computer inputs information from over 700 sensors and outputs information to over 100 activators! The computer monitors each of the 700 sensors 30 times a second and compares each signal with optimum values stored in its memory. It then decides on any necessary action and outputs control signals to the activators. The computer can maintain very accurate pressures, temperatures and rates of flow in the process system. For example, the temperature in the furnace can be maintained to within one degree of its optimum level.

Control of Transportation Systems

Process industries are not the only users of large-scale computer control systems. Many transportation systems, by road, rail and air are now under direct computer control. Let us look at the problem of moving road traffic through a large city. Traditionally, city traffic has been controlled with traffic lights. In most traffic lights, small clocks switch the lights on and off at regular intervals. The clock controllers have some flexibility and can, for example, be constructed to vary the times of red and green lights to match the direction of rush-hour traffic.

217

However, an accident or unusual traffic flow can create chaos because these systems cannot respond to what is actually happening on the roads. To solve these problems, many large cities have installed computer-controlled traffic light systems. Sensors under the roads are used to detect and measure the traffic flow. This information is sent to a central computer where it is analysed and used to build up a picture of traffic flow throughout the city. Control signals can then be sent to the traffic lights to vary their timings and to relieve any hold-ups or delays. Figure 17.18 shows the outline of a computer-controlled traffic light system.

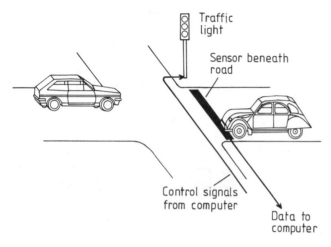

Figure 17.18   The outline of a traffic light system controlled by computer

Movement Control and Robotics

Large computers, microcomputers and microprocessors can be used to control the movements of various machines. In small applications the most common device used is the **stepper motor**. This is an electric motor that can be very precisely controlled. The motor rotates through a precise angle each time it receives a pulse from the computer. It can be run continuously at various speeds and can also be turned through exact fractions of a single turn. With several motors, very complicated movements can be controlled. Larger applications normally use hydraulic or pneumatic systems, which can produce far more power and force than stepper motors.

In simple movement control systems, the computer issues a series of control signals and assumes that these instructions are carried out. In more complex systems, sensors are used to feedback information to the computer about the effects of its instructions. The current position of the machine can be continually monitored and obstructions in its path can be detected and avoided.

The **turtle** crawler that can be attached to microcomputers is an example of simple movement control. Two stepper motors are used to control the drive wheels. By turning the wheels at different speeds, movement in any direction is possible. Sensors can be attached to the crawler to allow it to follow lines and detect and avoid objects. If a pen is attached, the path of the turtle can be traced out as it moves. (See Figure 17.19.)

Figure 17.19   This BBC 'buggy' is controlled by a micro

Industrial robots are a more complex example of movement control. In its most typical form an industrial robot resembles a human arm. Several mechanical joints, all of which can be controlled independently, allow considerable freedom of movement. A control program for a robot arm consists of a series of instructions to turn the mechanical joints through various angles. Figure 17.20 shows how a simple control program can instruct a robot arm to pick up a small box.

In small arms, a stepper motor is used at each joint but large arms normally use hydraulic systems. The 'hand' at the end of the arm may be a general purpose gripper like a crab's claw. Alternatively, special tools like spot welders or paint sprayers may be attached. The control program stores the sequence of movements necessary for the robot to complete its task. These movements can be worked out by a programmer or they can be recorded as part of a 'learning' process. In the latter case, the movements of a human operator are monitored and recorded as he or she leads the robot arm through a task. The computer can then direct the arm to repeat this exact sequence of movements at a fast pace, never growing tired and never making mistakes. A few robot arms were in use before the introduction of computer control systems. The control mechanisms were individually constructed from mechanical and electrical components. If the robot was required to undertake a new task, a new

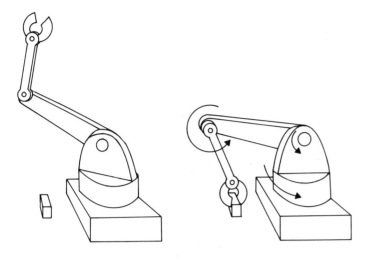

Control program

1. Rotate base through 45°
2. Rotate lower arm through 5°
3. Rotate upper arm through 190°
4. Close jaws

Figure 17.20 A control program for a robot to pick up a box

control mechanism was developed and built. This led to high costs and the use of industrial robots was restricted. A computer-controlled robot simply needs a new computer program to complete a new task. This often only means plugging in a new ROM chip. Computer control systems, having few moving parts, are also far more reliable than electro-mechanical controllers. These advantages have led to a great increase in the use of industrial robots. Factories already exist where all the major assembly tasks are carried out by robots. (See Figure 1.3, p. 2.)

Data Logging and Alarm Systems

Strictly speaking, the example which follows is not an example of computer control. It is included to illustrate a very useful application of using sensors to input information directly into a computer. The example concerns the way that computers are used to monitor patients in hospitals. Patient monitoring involves keeping a constant watch on the patient so that immediate help can be given if his or her condition deteriorates. Most hospital patients do not need this close attention, but for some it can be critical. In 1974 it was estimated that half of all the patients who died in hospital from heart attacks could have been saved by constant watching. The problem is that such watching by doctors or nurses would require a lot of staff. In most hospitals it is very difficult to free a nurse just for one or two patients. The problem has been solved by using computer-controlled patient monitoring systems. These systems use a microcomputer or minicomputer which can input data from a number of sensors attached to the patient. Sensors exist to measure

a wide range of body variables — for example, blood pressure, respiration rate, heart rate, body temperature, brain activity and urine output. The computer inputs data from each sensor several times a minute. The input values are compared with levels which a doctor has set as normal for the patient. If any of the sensor inputs are too low or too high, the computer can raise the alarm with a buzzer and a flashing light. In most applications the computer also builds up a log of all the input data on its backing store. At regular intervals the computer will analyse this data log and produce an easy to understand summary of the patient's condition. This summary may be printed out or presented in graphical form on a VDU screen. (See Figure 17.21.)

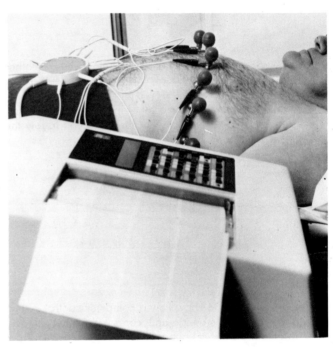

Figure 17.21 Computer monitoring can save lives

Exercise 58

1 Explain the advantages that digital watches have compared to traditional watches.

2 Explain how apples are likely to be weighed and sold:

    a from a market stall;
    b in a large supermarket.

3 Sometimes the prices of the goods are stored in supermarket scales.

    a Explain why it is essential that these prices are stored in RAM and not ROM.
    b Who do you think updates the prices stored in the supermarket scales? How often do you think this is done for scales used to weigh fruit and vegetables?
    c What advantage is gained by storing the prices in the supermarket scales?

4 A secretary in England must regularly telephone an office in France. The telephone number is 0103332609764. The number is a busy one and is often engaged. Explain how a microprocessor-controlled phone will make the secretary's task easier.

5 Sketch a design for a new household gadget that uses robot arms. Do not worry too much about technical details; just use your imagination.

6 The diagram shows a design sketch for a simple 'turtle'. It uses two stepper motor-controlled drive wheels and one small nose wheel.

If one wheel turns through half a revolution while the other does not move, the turtle turns through an angle of 90°. If both wheels complete two revolutions, the turtle moves forward 1 metre. Write out a set of instructions for turning the left and right motors so that the turtle can follow the path shown below.

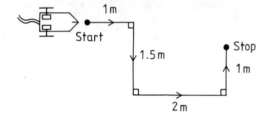

7 Draw a diagram to show how a computer control system can be used to monitor and control the flow of acid through a pipe. Label each of the components used in your system.

8 The diagram below shows a system which is to be placed under computer control. When in use, the heater tank will first be filled with chemicals from tanks A and B. These chemicals will then be heated to 100 °C. When they reach the correct temperature, they will be run off into tank C.

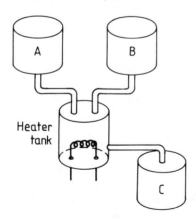

a Three types of sensor are described in the advertisements shown below. Explain what they are and how they could be used in the computer control system for the above chemical process.

Optical proximity switch
300 mm range

A high quality proximity switch operating on the principle of the emission/detection of modulated infra-red light. This mechanically and electrically rugged unit is housed in a threaded aluminium case with a glass end window and has many applications where any material is required to be detected.

Temperature
sensor
590 kH

Liquid flow sensor

A versatile, simple to use and install liquid flow sensor. Provides a pulse output, the frequency of which is proportional to the flow rate through the device.

b Explain what other devices will be needed in the computer control system.
c Draw a sketch of the complete computer control system and write a short explanation of the way it will function.

9 Explain the advantages of a computer patient-monitoring system:

a for the hospital
b for the patient.

10 Write a short summary of the following article.

The basic problems faced by London Underground's signals division are to ensure that trains go to the right destinations, by controlling signal devices along the line, and to keep as closely as possible to schedule. Both functions require railway controllers to know the identity and location of individual trains.

The tracking problem was solved at a relatively early stage, by monitoring the electrical current in different segments of the line. The first automatic route setting devices were installed in the 1950s, employing punched data on paper rolls to set points and signals along the track.

It was an obvious step to replace the type of mechanical program device employed here by a computerised version, and the first of these was installed at Watford in 1972.

However, by then a new problem had arisen. In the early 1970s staff shortages led to a surge in train cancellations, and a resulting deterioration in services. The problem was that once route information had been fed into the system it had to be changed manually, and this led to serious delays. 'The system was too inflexible', says Ray Blakey, development engineer for signalling on London Underground.

A team looked at this problem and concluded that what was needed was a centralised computer system that would control all the movements on a line. Alan Hooper, principal signalling assistant, explained the thinking behind this: 'Under the old system, if you cancel a train on one program machine, you must cancel it on every subsequent program machine it will pass. A computer system can work out each junction the train will pass, and cancel the train accordingly.'

The first stage of tackling this problem was to develop a system that would monitor all the train movements on a line. A project was initiated for the Victoria and Northern lines, and eventually went live in 1981, operating from a control room near Euston Station.

A valuable spin-off from this system is the dot-matrix signs on the Northern Line, which indicate how long passengers must wait for the next train, and are being extended to provide further information.

A second scheme, involving the north end of the Piccadilly Line, was the first to provide control functions, and was implemented in January 1982. It used a ring network specially engineered by Ferranti to control signals along the line.

London Underground's signalling division is currently working on the most ambitious scheme to date, which will be implemented on the Jubilee Line and a parallel stretch of the Metropolitan Line and will be introduced from mid-1986. 'We took the best ideas from the other two schemes and put them together for the Jubilee', said Blakey.

In recognition of the advances that have been made since the early 1980s, this system will use a proprietary packet switching network from Hewlett Packard, the DS-1000. Centralised computers at Baker Street will be linked to local computers at each junction on the line, in a joint ring and star configuration that increases the reliability of the system.

One of the advantages that London Underground has when it comes to installing networks is that cables can be easily distributed along the existing railway tunnels. Tunnels are cabled in both directions for extra security.

For monitoring purposes, a 'snap-shot' is taken every 30 seconds to provide the location of each train on the line. This information will feed through to a GEC 4090 minicomputer at Baker Street that displays fixed line diagrams, both on individual display units, and a giant 30 ft long LED screen in the control room. Two other logs are also kept: a summary of each trip that can be used to verify subsequent complaints about delays, and an exception report that records the worst cases of delayed trains.

A second 4090 provides command functions. Standard timetables are distributed to local computers at each junction, which control the signals at the same location. Under normal circumstances, signals will be automatically set for each trip from the route information contained in this timetable. Using the picture on the line diagrams, which record the progress of each train, control room staff can monitor delays and act accordingly.

For example, if a train has to be taken out of service, staff in the control room can cancel the trip by editing the timetable — and this information will be sent to all the affected stations.

If a replacement train is to be brought into service, this information is invaluable at an early stage to station managers who will have to allocate staff. With 160-odd trips per day on the Jubilee Line in each direction, it is essential to act quickly to prevent a backlog building up.

(*Computing*, 18 July 1985)

18   More Microcomputer Applications

A microcomputer is a computer which uses a micro-processor chip for its central processing unit. Most microcomputers are used in homes and small businesses as general purpose computers running a wide range of applications programs. Early microcomputers were normally 8-bit machines and used a cassette recorder for secondary storage. Their internal memories were small by present standards, 8K being a typical memory size.

The development of the microcomputer has been very rapid. A wide range of machines is now available, ranging in price from less than one hundred to several thousand pounds. At the bottom end of this scale, the micro-computer will still be an 8-bit machine, probably still with cassette backing store and an internal memory of between 16K and 64K. At the top end of the scale, the microcomputer will be a 16 or 32-bit machine with floppy or even hard disc backing store and an internal memory of between 256K and 1000K.

Early microcomputers suffered from slow and unreliable backing store, small internal memories and poor quality peripherals. Often the range of applications software was limited and of poor quality.

Recent developments have included fast reliable backing store, internal memories of up to 1000K and a wide range of good-quality peripherals. Some makes of micro-computer still suffer from a lack of good software but the popular makes usually have lots of good quality software easily available. This software is designed to be as easy to use as possible and the computer user is often led through the program with a series of graphics displays and option menus. Figure 18.1 shows a microcomputer running an application package designed to guide the user with graphics display of the options that are available.

Before the development of the microcomputer, most small organisations could not afford to buy and use a computer. There were other applications in which the size and power consumption of a mainframe computer made its use impossible. The microcomputer has sold very well in both these situations. In practice, it is very rare for a choice to be made between buying a microcom-puter or a mainframe computer. A small organisation could not afford a mainframe and would not need its vast backing store or high-speed peripherals. A large organi-sation, on the other hand, needs a mainframe computer to cope with the volume of data processing that it requires.

The following sections look at some common microcomputer appli-cations.

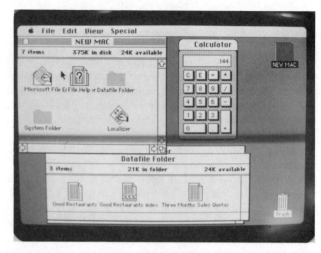

Figure 18.1 A graphical option display on an Apple Macintosh

Microcomputers in Schools

Before the introduction of microcomputers there were few computing facilities in schools. Some schools used a postal batch processing service for their student's pro-grams but this was a poor substitute for 'hands-on' experience. A few lucky institutions did have interactive terminals connected by telephone to mainframe com-puters, but with a single keyboard it was very difficult to allocate students very much computing time. During the last few years this position has radically changed. Many schools now have 20 or more microcomputers, often linked in a local-area network to share discs and printers. The use of these microcomputers can be divided into four areas.

1 Administration. Microcomputers are increasingly used in school offices and staffrooms. Some applications have proved more successful than others, and there are some problem areas. For example, all schools keep records of their students. Basic details stored include name, address, date of birth, sex, form and year group. Much more sensitive data includes information about the student's home background, medical history, aca-demic achievements, criminal record (if any), discipline record and teachers' opinions of character and persona-lity. Some schools have started to store records in micro-computer systems, but there seems to be little advantage in this. Even in a school with over 1000 pupils, it is rare for more than 20 individual records to be retrieved each day. Manual systems can easily cope with this level of demand. Also, if the microcomputer is used to store sensitive data, access to the system must be very care-fully controlled. At least one authority has plans to link all its schools with a computer administration network.

Many students, parents and indeed teachers will be very worried if sensitive pupil data is stored in computer networks.

Timetabling is another area where computers have been only partly successful. Several computer timetabling programs exist, but none offers a complete solution. Most programs are designed as aids for a human timetabler. The help provided ranges from checking for clashes in the use of teachers or rooms to printing out individual timetables for the students.

Computers have been more successful when employed to run subject option program packages. Most schools offer students a choice of subjects in the fourth and fifth years. When the students have made their selections these are entered into the microcomputer. The choices can be validated and sorted into group lists. These lists can then be manipulated to achieve suitable group sizes and to maximise the number of students getting their first choice subjects. Finally the completed group lists can be printed and distributed.

As in all offices and administrations, word processing is of great use to increase productivity. The word processor can be used in schools for all the routine office tasks and also for the creation, storage and reproduction of worksheets, tests and examinations.

2 Computer-based instruction (CBI). CBI involves individual interactive use of a microcomputer or terminal. A teaching program takes the student through a carefully controlled learning sequence. Teaching material and problems are presented on a VDU. Answers are entered with a light pen or keyboard. If a student copes easily with the tasks, the program will branch to a more difficult level. If a student makes incorrect responses, the program will branch to further explanations and simpler problems. Students can work at their own pace, receiving immediate feedback to their answers. The machine will never grow impatient or angry with slow students. Usually details of each student's progress are stored for evaluation by teachers or instructors. At the moment, the use of CBI is limited. Good programs take a long time to develop and require a large computer memory. CBI may be very useful to teach straightforward factual material, but many subjects require group discussions and the development of creative skills. It is hard to see how CBI can provide these facilities and it may well be better suited to industrial training courses rather than schools.

3 Computer-assisted learning (CAL). CAL involves using the computer as an aid to normal teaching. As schools have acquired more and more microcomputers, the number of CAL packages has grown.

Some CAL programs try to improve basic skills with "drill and practice" exercise. The advantage of using a computer for these exercises is the extra motivation it can provide. Figure 18.2 shows the screen of a CAL program designed to improve basic arithmetic. The user must enter the correct answer in the gun at the bottom of the screen before each space invader can be shot down.

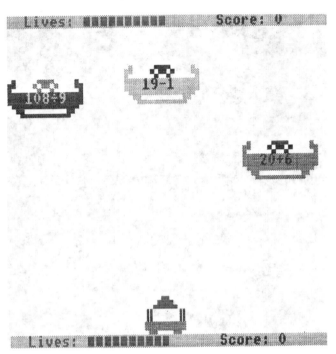

Figure 18.2 A drill-and-practice CAL program

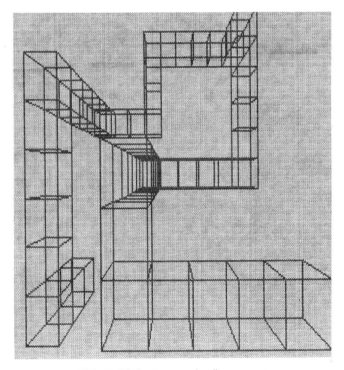

Figure 18.3 A screen doodler program

Some CAL programs are much more open ended than the "drill and practice" programs. Figure 18.3 shows the screen of a program which allows the user to construct a block diagram on the screen. Starting with a single cube, the user can move up, down, left, right, in or out. The program aims to improve a users understanding of perspective as he or she doodles on the screen.

Other CAL programs offer simulations of real situations. In geography and history the student can enter decisions to questions the computer asks as it develops a geographical or historical simulation. The computer can quickly calculate the consequences of these decisions and display an updated situation. Other simulations are used to replace difficult, dangerous or lengthy science experiments.

4 Computing courses. The availability of cheap microcomputers has made computing courses very popular. Many schools now provide short courses for all pupils as well as the traditional examination courses.

Microcomputers in Small Businesses and Organisations

Almost every mainframe computer application package now has its scaled-down microcomputer equivalent. Most organisations have found it more economical and practical to buy the software they need rather than develop their own programs. Packages are available for payrolls, invoicing and accounts, stock control, financial planning, word processing and information storage and retrieval. Communications networks have also been developed that allow microcomputers to be linked to local, regional and national databases. A brief description of some common applications follows, but it must be remembered that the range of applications is vast. Indeed it is hard to think of any small business or organisation where no use could be found for a microcomputer!

* **Solicitors**. The work in a solicitor's office often involves typing several copies of standard legal documents. Word processors are ideal for this type of application and their use is widespread.
* **Estate agents** need to store and frequently retrieve details of a large number of properties for sale. By storing these details in a database, rapid searches can be made for all the available properties of any given type. When a chain of estate agents covers a large area, the computers may be linked so that details of any property for sale by the chain can be retrieved.
* **Used car dealers** and **antique shops** often get requests for vehicles or items that they do not have in stock. There have been several recent attempts to set up national or regional computer networks for this type of dealer. Using modified microcomputers as terminals, any dealer using the system can access details of the available stock of any other dealer in the scheme. Dealers can thus earn commission from another supplier even if they do not have a particular item in stock.
* **Doctors and dentists** can use microcomputers for storing patients' records. Fast and reliable backing storage is of course essential, and file security must be carefully considered. The micro can also be used to handle National Health Service claims and payments.
* **Farms** may seem unusual places to find microcomputers but they are widely used. Modern farming requires a great deal of office work. There are national and EEC regulations to be complied with, and all kinds of forms and documents to complete. The microcomputer can help with all this general paperwork. Expensive fertilisers, weedkillers and pesticides are used in growing crops. The use of these chemicals can be planned, organised, recorded and analysed using a microcomputer. Dedicated micros can be used to monitor and control the feeding of animals and to record and analyse egg, milk and meat production. Milk sterilisation and bottling is an example of process control and most modern dairies use microprocessor controlled machinery. (See Figure 18.4.)
* **Shops** of all kinds can use microcomputers for stock control, sales analysis, accounts and VAT records.
* **Transport, distribution and shipping companies** can use microcomputers for planning routes and to optimise cargo loading and storage. A complete software package to plan the loading of container ships is available for use on microcomputers.

Microcomputers in the Home

A general-purpose microcomputer is now a common feature in British homes. Many people buy these computers intending to use them for household budgeting, tax calculations, games playing and information storage and retrieval. Often they hope that the micro can help their children's education and future employment prospects. In many cases the microcomputer is in fact used mostly for playing games! Often this is because of unrealistic expectations of the capabilities of a cheap microcomputer. It is easy to say you intend to catalogue your stamp collection with your new micro. It is not so easy to enter, store and update details of thousands of stamps, particularly using a slow and unreliable backing store. Computer companies and sales staff often exaggerate the

Figure 18.4 Computerised monitoring and control of milking machine

ease with which people can learn to program the computer. This can lead to frustration and disappointment when programming is found to be a difficult and time-consuming task. Available software, apart from many excellent games programs, is often very poor, frequently failing to live up to advertising claims. This situation may of course change as more powerful microcomputers become cheaper and better software becomes available.

This may seem a rather negative picture of computer use, but one group of people can gain very real benefits from the use of a home computer. For a handicapped person the microcomputer can become a trusted and faithful friend. Many special input devices have been developed to allow even the most severely handicapped to communicate with the computer. Once communication is established, the computer can be used to monitor and control other equipment. Heating, lighting, radios, TVs, tape recorders and many other items can easily be brought under direct control. The micro can even monitor its owner and raise the alarm if he falls and needs help. In some cases the microcomputer has enabled handicapped people to work and earn a living again. Some already run small businesses from their homes, offering word processing facilities or programming skills.

Exercise 59

1 Explain why details of each of the following items might be included in a student's school records. In each case, state with your reasons whether you are in favour or against schools storing this information.

   a Home background
   b Medical history
   c Academic achievements
   d Sporting achievements
   e Activities outside school
   f Criminal record
   g School discipline record
   h Teacher's opinions of character and personality.

2 In each of the following cases, discuss the security of the record system. Explain in detail the ways in which loss of data can occur and the knowledge and actions necessary to gain unauthorised access to the data.

   a Records recorded on paper and stored in a locked filing cabinet in a school office.
   b Records recorded on floppy discs and stored in a locked cupboard in a school office. A microcomputer in the office is used to access the records.
   c Records stored in the backing store of a large central computer. A terminal and a modem in a school office are used to access the records.

3 List some of the tasks that a word processor could be used for in your school office.

4 Explain the advantages and disadvantages of computer-based instruction.

5 Which of the following tasks is more suitable for computer-based instruction. Explain your answer.

   a Learning to add and subtract fractions
   b Learning to write poetry.

6 If you have experienced the use of a computer-assisted learning program:

   a Describe the program and how it was used.
   b In what ways do you think the program added to your understanding or enjoyment of the topic?
   c Can you suggest any ways in which the program, or the way in which it was used, could be improved?

7 If you had access to a database creation program:

   a On what subject would you choose to create a database?
   b List the details that you would store for each item in your database.
   c What kinds of searches would you want to make of your created database?

8 Why do some schools run short computer courses for all their pupils?

9 Explain why early microcomputers were not suitable for business use.

10 From magazines and newspapers, obtain some advertisements for business microcomputers. Compare the prices and capacities of these machines with the machines you use at school.

11 List some of the general tasks that business micros are used for.

12 With the permission of your teacher, ask a local shop or business about its use of microcomputers. Write a report under the headings:

a Computer hardware used.
b Computer software used.
c Staff who work with the computer.

13 Explain why computer companies sometimes exaggerate the ease with which people can learn to program a microcomputer.

14 Explain why some people who have bought home computers have regretted the purchase.

15 Write a short story about a handicapped person and his or her microcomputer.

16 There are many microcomputers available for use in the home, ranging in price from about £70 upwards. Describe **three** different uses of a home computer system.

(EAEB 82)

Exercise 60

This exercise revises all the contents of Chapters 14–18.

1 Select five of the applications looked at in Chapters 14–18 and for each application answer the following questions. A clear diagram will often improve your answers.

a What are the tasks performed by the computer system?
b What input data is collected?
c How is this input data captured?
d What data is held in secondary storage and how is it structured?
e What data processing takes place?
f What output data is produced?
g What computer hardware is used?
h What advantages does the system offer compared with a manual system?

2 Write a short summary of the use of computers in each of the following areas:

a Commercial data processing
b Scientific, mathematical and engineering applications
c Communications and information systems
d Computer control systems
e Microcomputer applications.

3 This systems flowchart shows the stages in the updating section of a stock control system in a wholesale warehouse. Customers take their purchases to point of sale terminals linked directly to a mainframe computer, which uses sequential files.

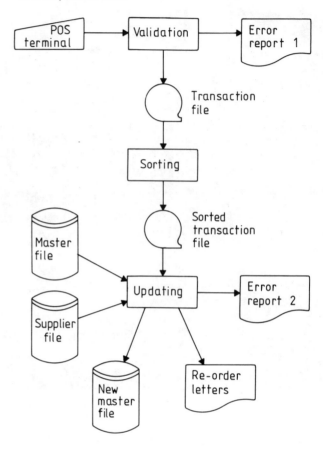

a For what purpose is the transaction file used?
b What happens to the records during sorting?
c Why is sorting necessary?
d What happens during updating?
e Explain the terms grandfather, father and son in relation to file generation and explain why they are necessary.
f Describe **three** different types of error that might be reported and state at which stage they will be reported.
g Explain the output at the "Re-order" stage.

(AEB 84)

4 Home-Warm is a company which specialises in installing central heating systems in houses. The various items which are used in the central heating systems (radiators, boilers, pipes etc.) are bought from suppliers and stored in the Home-Warm warehouse until they are needed. Home-Warm employs fitters to install the heating systems and also employs office staff to carry out clerical work.

Home-Warm is considering using a computer to assist in the management and operation of the company. Identify and describe **four** tasks for which the computer could be used.

For **two** of these tasks, describe and give examples of the data which would be input to, and output from, the computer. Also indicate suitable methods of collecting the data.

(C 82)

5 Glendale School has its own microcomputer consisting of a 32K processor, keyboard, television set and twin mini-floppy disc drives. Recently a teacher has written some programs, in BASIC, to allow a file of pupil records to be set up and processed. The record for each pupil contains data that includes date of birth and home address.

a List **two** advantages of writing the programs in a high level language rather than a low level language.

b The date of birth is held in the form: day/month/year e.g. 11th March, 1967 is held as: 11/03/67
   (i) List **four** checks that a **program** could make, to detect errors, on the date of birth of any pupil.
   (ii) Give an example of an error in the date of birth which could **not** have been found by checks built into a program.

c The school wishes to use its microcomputer to produce address labels for sending letters to parents.
   (i) What extra piece of equipment is needed?
   (ii) Suggest **one** advantage for the school of using a computer to produce address labels.

d Suggest **one** reason why some parents were worried when the school decided to computerise pupil records.

Give **one** advantage of using a microcomputer at the school rather than a large computer at a local college.

(SEREB 82)

6 The following text gives details of a case study. Read it carefully, and then answer ALL the questions that follow. You should assume:
   (i) a slip is submitted for every period on the timetable;
   (ii) that the transaction file contains **all the data** submitted by the school and that it is all correct;
   (iii) the easy availability of a utility program which will sort any named file into ascending order using any named key field.

A school of approximately 1500 pupils and seventy staff uses a computer to help keep detailed attendance records of its pupils. The school works a five day week and each day is divided into eight periods. For each period taught, the teacher must record attendance details on a printed slip.

Teachers send these slips to the school office at the end of each period. At the end of the day, the slips are sent to the computer centre where the data is keyed onto magnetic tape to form the daily transaction file. This transaction file, the pupil master file and the teacher master file are processed during the evening so that printout can be delivered to the school early next morning.

The daily printout consists of details of pupils who were absent the previous day, printed in form order for each period.

The weekly printout is produced after the last daily printout for the week and contains:
   (i) for each pupil, the attendance records for the last three weeks and an overall percentage attendance for the year so far;
   (ii) for each teacher, the number of pupils who were absent from each period taught by that teacher during the previous week;
   (iii) for each period, the number of pupils who were absent in each year group.

The master files for teachers and pupils are held in ascending key order on magnetic tape at the computer centre. The computer has approximately 16K eight-bit bytes available for data storage after the program has been loaded. Magnetic tapes are the only backing storage available while the programs are running but there are sufficient tape drives available for any reasonable application.

a Design an attendance slip which could be used as a data preparation document. Write brief notes to explain why each data item is necessary and to justify your choice of field lengths.

b (i) Specify a suitable format for the pupil master file giving field names and lengths.
   (ii) Specify a suitable format for the transaction file giving field names and lengths.
   (iii) Specify a suitable format for the teacher master file giving field names and lengths.

c (i) Describe an algorithm to update the teacher master file each day.
   (ii) Draw systems flowcharts to show how the daily and weekly reports are produced.

(L 81)

7 a Explain the basic elements of an information-retrieval system including an account of how the information is kept up to date.

b For **two** of the following examples, describe an information-retrieval system which could be used. Include details of the information held and how it is maintained, and the information that can be obtained from the system and how this is done.
   (i) airline booking-system;
   (ii) patients' medical records;
   (iii) personal records;
   (iv) lending-library records.

(O 82)

8 Real-life situations are often simulated using a computer. Choose a simulation from science, business or commerce.

Explain that simulation in detail showing;
   the purpose of it,
   how it operates,
   who uses it,
   why it is used,
   the disadvantages of it.

(AEB 83)

9 A word processor consists of a keyboard, visual display, floppy disc drive, a limited amount of main store and a printer. It is used to process and output information.

   a What form of backing store is used?
   b How is the information input?
   c Give a **specific** example of information that is stored on a word processor.

                       (SEREB 81)

10 A creamery uses a computer in the processing of over 100 000 gallons of milk a day.

   a How does the use of a computer in this situation differ from that in a bank?
   b Give **two** distinct advantages of using a computer in the creamery.

                       (AEB 83)

11 **a** Name **three** everyday articles which depend upon microprocessors and which cost under £40 each.
   b Compare and contrast the input, output and processing of the three articles.
   c What are the advantages and disadvantages of having microprocessors in the articles?

                       (NW REB 82)

12 The Hand Calculator and the Digital Watch are two examples of the use of the microprocessor for a specific application. Name TWO other specific applications of the microprocessor with a brief description of the function of each device. Include in your description the particular properties of the microprocessor which are used in each case.

                       (ASLEB 84)

13 Describe the architecture of a microprocessor-based computer system using suitable diagrams. How could such a system be adapted to deal with real-time signals in analogue form?

                       (O&C 82)

14 Describe typical hardware configurations which would be needed for the systems indicated below. For each give an indication of the tasks which the system could be expected to perform.

   a A process control system, for two liquids being mixed together in a heated container; the temperature and the rates of supply of the liquids must be kept under control.
   b A word processing system.
   c An airline booking system.

                       (C 83)

19 Professional Computer Staff

The staff who work with computers can be divided into two broad categories: those concerned with the development of new computer applications, and those concerned with running existing applications programs.

It is very difficult to describe the staffing of a typical computer department. Some departments have only three or four staff, whereas a large department may have hundreds of staff. There are wide variations in the structure of the departments, and the job titles given to the staff employed in them. However, most computer departments will employ some or all of the staff shown in the following 'chain of command' (Figure 19.1).

Running Existing Applications Programs

To illustrate the way that large-scale commercial applications are often run, we will look at the processing of a payroll program.

The data arrives from the wages department in the form of factory timesheets. **Control clerks** batch the timesheets together and pass them to the **data preparation supervisor**. The data preparation supervisor gives out the batches of timesheets to **keyboard operators** who enter and verify the data. When the data has been built up on to a tape or disc, it is loaded into the computer by a **computer operator**. This computer operator also retrieves the necessary master files from the **media librarian**. When all the files have been loaded and the correct stationery put in the printer, the operator runs the program. The output is collected by a control clerk and returned to the wages department.

This is a summary of the tasks of the staff who are concerned with running applications programs.

Keyboard operators
* To enter and verify data using keypunch or key-to-tape-or-disc equipment

Data preparation supervisor
* To allocate work to keyboard operators
* To control the quality of the keyboard operators' work
* To train new keyboard operators
* To liaise with other supervisors and managers

Data control clerks
* To accept and check input data supplied on forms and documents by the computer users
* To batch input data and pass it to the data preparation supervisor
* To return the output data to the computer user

Data controller
* To allocate work to data control clerks
* To liaise with computer users
* To keep a record of the work processed by the computer
* To liaise with other supervisors and managers

Media librarian
* To take charge of all the files used by the computer department. These may be on magnetic tape, magnetic discs, punched cards or paper tape
* To issue files when they are needed

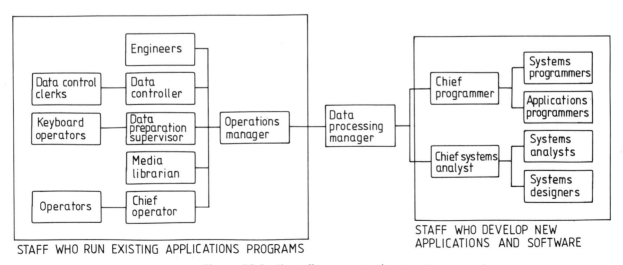

Figure 19.1 The staff in a computer department

* To ensure that files are returned after use
* To keep a record of all the files used
* To ensure that unauthorised staff are not allowed access to files
* To ensure that copies of important files are held in a fireproof safe

Computer operators
* To load the correct tapes and discs
* To run the applications programs
* To keep the printer supplied with the correct paper
* To make security dumps on to tape from important disc files
* To maintain a log of everything that happens while applications programs are being run

Chief operator
* To allocate work to computer operators
* To organise computer operators into two or three teams (or shifts) so that the computer can be kept working for 16 or even 24 hours a day
* To liaise with other supervisors and managers

Engineers
* To carry out regular maintenance
* To carry out repairs

Operations manager
* To be responsible for the efficient day-to-day running of the data processing operations
* To coordinate the work of the data control, data preparation and computer room staff
* To work out staffing timetables
* Staff training
* To liaise with the data processing manager

Many small computer departments will of course not employ all of the above staff, and a single person may carry out tasks listed under more than one of these job titles. As the price of computer equipment has fallen, there have been two trends which have reduced the need for traditional data preparation departments. First, more users have been provided with on-line terminals and allowed to enter their own data. Secondly, methods of automatic data capture such as bar codes and OCR documents have become more widely used. Data preparation staff will always be needed, however, to prepare and input large volumes of data and to correct and re-input documents rejected by OCR and OMR readers.

Figure 19.2 shows the way that data circulates in a traditional data processing department.

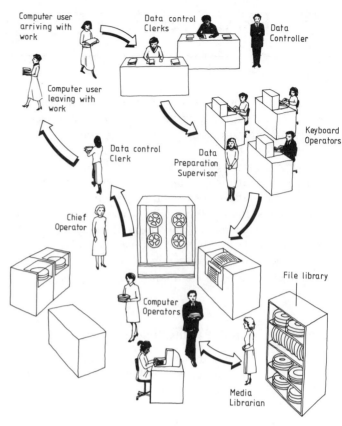

Figure 19.2 The flow of data through a computer department

Developing New Computer Applications

Every major new computer application goes through several stages of development and testing. The complete task of developing and testing a new computer application is called a **systems project**. The stages in a typical systems project are explained in the following sub-sections.

The identification of a problem. Most new computer systems are created because the systems currently in use start to cause problems. For example, the manager of an expanding company might identify the following problem.

"When we were a small company, a manual system for processing customers' orders worked quite well. Now that our business has grown, the system is becoming too slow and inefficient. Mistakes and delays are occurring which cost us money and make our customers angry".

The assignment brief. After a problem has been identified, the company managers will start to consider possible solutions. If the problem involves data processing, the managers will almost always consider the use of computers to solve the problem. If the company already has computer development staff, the data processing manager will be asked to set up a **project team** to investigate the problem. If the company does not have its own staff, a team of outside consultants will be asked to come into the company and investigate the problem. The project team will be given an **assignment brief**, specifying their exact task. The assignment brief to investigate our customers' orders problem is shown in Figure 19.3.

ZAP COMPONENTS
CHIP ROAD, PROMWORTH
CIRCUITSHIRE

ASSIGNMENT BRIEF TO INVESTIGATE THE CUSTOMER ORDER PROCESSING SYSTEM

1. The aim of the study is to establish the feasibility of using a computer controlled customer order system.

2. The objectives of the study are:
   * To reduce the time taken to process customer orders.
   * To reduce the number of mistakes made in delivering customers orders.
   * To reduce the number of mistakes made in charging for customer orders.

3. The project team has full authority to investigate all the current activity in the sales department. All company staff are expected to co-operate fully with the project team.

4. Initially, the project team will consist of two systems analysts, Mr Fog and Mrs Smog.

5. The project team will report weekly to the chief analyst, Mr Mist. The final report must be handed to the D.P. manager Mr Brume within five weeks.

Figure 19.3 An assignment brief at Zap Components

The feasibility investigation and outline systems design. Armed with their assignment brief, the systems analysts start to investigate the present system and to look for possible ways to computerise it. The analysts will start by talking to the staff who use the present system and observing them at work. The analysts will also examine all the documents and forms and any manual filing systems used. The analysts will try to measure the volume of data the system processes and also the time taken for each item of data to be processed. While they are doing this, the analysts will often discover inefficiencies in the present system. (See Figure 19.4.)

Figure 19.4 The systems analyst investigating a pre-computer system

For example, they may discover that separate invoices and delivery notes are being used which could be replaced by a single document. The analysts will avoid these inefficiencies when they start to design the computer system.

When they are satisfied that they have a complete description of the present system, the analysts can start to prepare a **project report**.

The project feasibility report. The project report will contain a complete description of the present system and the outline design of a computer system to replace it. The costs, savings and benefits of the new computer system will be estimated. In some cases several alternative new computer systems may be outlined. Figure 19.5 shows a flowchart used to describe the manual order system. Figure 19.6 shows the proposed computer order system.

The costs, savings and benefits identified for our computer order system are as follows.

Costs
   * Two new microprocessor controlled key-to-floppy disc systems
   * Staff training time
   * Redundancy payments

Savings
   * The staff involved in processing orders can be reduced from ten people to three people

Benefits
   * The computer system will process customer orders within 24 hours (on average). The present system takes 5 days (on average) to process orders.

231

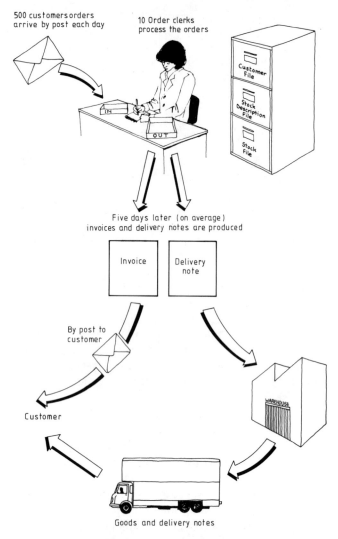

Figure 19.5   The old 'manual' order system

* The new system should significantly reduce mistakes in delivering customer orders because all stock descriptions will be verified, validated and checked with a computer file.
* The new system should significantly reduce mistakes in charging customers because all pricing will be done automatically by the computer.

Project approval. The systems analysts will give their report to the data processing manager who will in turn present it to the company managers. They will decide to go ahead with the proposal, scrap the whole idea, or ask for a further report. If the plan is approved, a detailed systems design is prepared.

Detailed systems design. When a new systems project has been approved, the data processing manager will ask the project team to prepare a detailed design for the new computer system. At this stage the membership of the team may be changed and expanded. Sometimes the same systems analysts who carried out the investigation will also produce the detailed systems design. In other

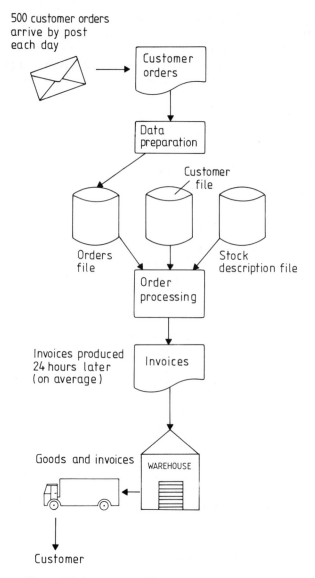

Figure 19.6   A proposal for a computer order system

cases different systems analysts or possibly specialist **systems designers** will be asked to produce the detailed systems design. In either case, the project team will take the outline design and expand it into a complete and very detailed design.

First, the project team will specify the *exact* output required from the new system. A possible output specification for our order system is shown below.

Output for customers
* Invoices printed by line printer on multi-part pre-printed stationery

Output for other departments
* Management statistics giving the sales figures for each stock item and each customer. Full line printer listings or VDU graphical displays are to be available for management statistics

* Error reports and analysis reports on the systems performance

The project team must carefully consider the format of all the output data. They must design any necessary documents and screen displays and select the most suitable media for each type of output. They are likely to consider any of the following forms of output:

* Line printer
* Microfilm
* Text on a VDU screen
* Graphics on a VDU screen

Obviously the project team must have a detailed and up-to-date knowledge of all these techniques.

Having specified the exact output required, the project team can turn their attention to the data needed to produce this output. They will need to consider carefully which of this data will be input and which can be held in backing storage. The input data needed for our ordering system is as follows.

For each order
{
Account number
Date
Customer's name
Order number
Product name
Stock number } For each item
Quantity required } ordered
}

The backing storage data for our ordering system is as follows.

Account number
Customer's name
Customer's address } For each
Credit limit { customer
Amount owed
Discount level

Stock number
Product name } For each stock
Minimum order { item
quantity

For the input data, the project team must select suitable input methods and design any necessary forms, documents and VDU screen displays. They must also devise suitable methods for verification and validation of the input data. They are likely to consider any of the following methods of input:

* Key-to-disc data preparation
* Key-to-tape data preparation
* Key-to-floppy-disc data preparation
* OCR equipment
* OMR equipment
* Merchandise tags
* Bar codes
* MICR equipment

It is very unlikely that any present-day new system will include paper tape or punch card data preparation.

For the backing storage data, the project team must select suitable storage devices and file structures. They are likely to consider any of the following methods of storage:

* Magnetic tape serial access files
* Magnetic disc serial access files
* Magnetic disc direct access files

The record structure in all the master files and transaction files must be specified exactly. If files are to be held in sequence, suitable key fields must be selected. If the codes used in the manual system are not suitable for use as key fields, it will be necessary to devise new coding systems. The project team must also consider the problem of data security and specify the precautions that will be taken and the back-up files that will be kept.

As the project team complete the detailed systems design, it is essential that they consult the staff in other departments. Input designs must produce systems that allow data preparation staff to enter data quickly and accurately. Output designs must produce data which is easy to understand and use. This can only be ensured by asking the opinions of the staff who will actually run the application.

The systems designers will document their work with systems flowcharts, written descriptions, specimen input and output documents, diagrams and various other design aids. Standard documentation is essential for two reasons:

* Many different systems designers may work on large projects. If they do not all use the same form of documentation, it is impossible to supervise and coordinate their work
* The systems designers do not write the actual computer programs needed for the new system. It is therefore essential that their work is fully documented so that others can write programs by following the design.

Software development and testing. When the systems designers have designed the complete system, their work is passed to a team of computer programmers. Working from the detailed systems flowcharts and other design information, the programmers write the necessary programs and program documentation. In large systems projects, software production will start as soon as each part of the system design is finished. Applications programmers will write the new applications programs in a high-level language. Systems programmers will write any new systems software needed in a low-level or special-purpose language. The systems analysts and designers will help the programmers to test the software fully with realistic test data.

When all the software has been written and tested, the next stage of the project is to implement the new system.

Implementation. This is the most important stage of any new system, and planning for the implementation of the project will start at an early stage. Implementation of a new system involves the project team in the following tasks.

* Ordering any new computer equipment needed
* Selecting and training the computer staff who will run the applications programs
* Preparing an installation timetable and a checklist showing each activity and individual task
* Ordering special supplies — for example, floppy discs, pre-printed stationery, data collection forms, etc.
* Training the staff in other departments to collect the input data and to use the output data
* Making physical preparations in the computer room — which may involve making space for new equipment, putting in extra power supplies, wiring extra terminals and providing storage space for paper and magnetic media
* Collecting all the data needed for the computer master files, preparing it for conversion and storing it on magnetic tapes or discs
* Drawing up plans for either a period of **parallel running** or for a **pilot run**. Parallel running means that the new computer system and the old system are *both* used for a period of time. This is expensive but provides security against a failure in the new system. Pilot running means that the work is gradually transferred to the new system over a period of time
* Monitoring the actual conversion to the new computer system
* Evaluating the new system and comparing its performance with the original design brief

This is a summary of the tasks of the staff who are concerned with developing new applications and software.

Systems analysts
* To define the exact nature of problems in present systems
* To carry out a complete analysis of the present system
* To produce a feasibility report and an outline design for a new computer system

Systems designers. (In many computer departments there are no separate systems designers and these tasks are carried out by combined systems analyst/designers.)

* To produce a detailed design of a new computer system
* To work with programmers to develop and test the software necessary for the new computer system
* To implement, monitor and evaluate the new computer system

Chief systems analyst
* To supervise the work of systems analysts
* To allocate systems analysts to project teams

Programmers
* To write the software necessary for a new computer application
* To work with the systems designer to test the software
* To produce program documentation
* To maintain the software by correcting any 'bugs' which are discovered and by updating variables such as tax rates and tax allowances

Chief programmers
* To supervise the work of programmers
* To allocate programmers to project teams
* To help train new programmers

Data processing managers (computer managers). The tasks of a data processing manager are to supervise, coordinate and control the work of the entire computer department.

It must be remembered that the development and testing of large new computer applications usually only happens in companies employing a considerable number of computer staff. Most small companies buy applications packages which are supplied ready to use on their computers. These applications packages are developed by teams of analysts, designers and programmers working for the **software houses** who market and sell computer software. The assignment brief for these project teams is to produce applications software that can be applied in a wide range of different organisations.

Even a company which does employ its own large computer department may buy some software packages 'off the shelf' from software suppliers. This is because there are several advantages in buying an applications package rather than producing your own specially written software. These are:

* The applications package is ready for immediate purchase and use. Specially written software will take weeks, months or even years to develop.
* The applications packages supplied by good software companies have been subjected to extensive testing. If they are already in wide use, this testing has been extended by all the current users of the package. If software 'bugs' have been found, they will have been corrected in later releases of the package.
* Help and advice will be available from the software suppliers and possibly from other users. Sometimes groups of users have formed organisations to help each other.
* It is much cheaper to buy an applications package then to employ staff to write special software.

Against these advantages must be considered the following disadvantages:

* Applications packages are written so that they can be applied in a wide range of different organisations. They use standardised approaches which often do not allow for the special methods used in one particular organisation. If an application and the available package are not exactly matched, it is the application which will have to be modified, not the package.
* The buyer of a software package will have to rely on the software supplier to provide staff training. This may not be as comprehensive as training provided by the organisation's own computer staff.
* The buyer of a software package will have to rely on the software supplier to provide corrections for any 'bugs' found in the software and updates which become necessary as circumstances change. This should not be a problem with large and reputable software suppliers, but may be a problem if a package is bought from a software supplier who then goes out of business.

Exercise 61

1 Copy and complete.
When data arrives in the computer department, it is received by _____, who check and batch the data and pass it to the _____ who in turn gives it out to _____. These _____ enter and verify the data. Computer _____ load the correct disc and tapes into the computer and the correct stationery into the line printer. They obtain the master files from the _____ who keeps track of all the files used by the computer.

2 Use this list of computer personnel to draw up a 'family tree' diagram showing the structure and deployment of staff in a computer department.
  Operations Manager, Systems Analyst, Data Processing Manager, Operators, Data Controller, Chief Programmer, Senior Operator, Control Clerks, Data Preparation Supervisor, Key Punch Operators.

(ASLEB 82)

3 Copy and complete the following paragraphs by inserting the appropriate words from the given list in the spaces provided.

Interviewing, design, feasibility, analysis, calculating, investigation.

The systems analyst's job has two main parts: _____ of the present system and the _____ of the new one. The initial investigation usually starts with a _____ study to determine if it will be profitable to use the computer. When this study is complete the analyst will carry out a detailed _____, collecting information about the existing system. He will do this by _____, observation and sending out questionnaires.

(NI CSE 82)

4 A company wishes to computerise its system of ordering. By referring in some detail to the crucial work of the systems analyst, and briefly to the part played by programmers, describe the sequence of events which would lead to a satisfactory implementation of the new system.

(NWREB 82)

5 Identify a simple data processing task with which you are familiar. For example, you could choose a task involved in:

* Administering school meals
* Keeping a record of pupils' marks
* Maintaining a catalogue of a stamp or record collection
* Running a small club
* Managing a local sports team
* Running a small shop
* Running a milk round
* Organising the school library.

a Prepare an assignment brief to be given to a systems analyst investigating your chosen task.
b Carry out an investigation of your chosen task and produce a project report recommending ways to computerise it.
c Prepare a detailed design of your proposed computer system.
d Write some or all of the necessary software for your system.
e Test your software.

235

20 Computer Users

A computer user is the person or machine for whom the computer carries out a task. This section first looks in detail at two important groups of computer users and then provides some extracts for you to read on other types of computer use.

The Police

The popular image of police work is often one of individual detectives solving crimes by pondering clues like Sherlock Holmes or taking part in American gun fights. The reality of police work is a long way from this glamorous image. Most major crimes are solved by large teams of officers taking hundreds of statements from the public and sifting through these statements for connections that lead to suspects. When a serious crime occurs, the police set up a **major incident enquiry**. At the centre of this enquiry is the **incident room**. Figure 20.1 shows the layout of a typical traditional incident room.

Figure 20.1 A police incident room

The police officers attached to the case start to collect statements and other information from witnesses and the general public. Telephone messages will be received giving more information and sometimes a 'tip-off'. All this information arrives on the desk of an officer in the incident room called the **information receiver**. He or she classifies the information into statements, general information and information requiring urgent action. The urgent information is passed to the **action officer** who can direct the officers working on the case to take appropriate actions. The statements are passed to another officer who reads through and checks them. All the information arriving in the incident room is filed by **indexers**. The task of these officers is to build up a card index file storing all the information relevant to the crime. By searching this file, the police officers hope to spot connections and coincidences which will lead them to suspects. Unfortunately, building up the card index is a difficult and tedious task. For example, a detective may wish to search the file to find all the references to a particular car. Key fields could include the owner's name, the colour, the make, the model, the age and the registration number. This means that to include a reference to a single car in the file the indexers must fill out six separate cards! As the investigation continues, the card index may eventually build up to several thousand cards. It then becomes a daunting and lengthy task to search the file to try to connect small pieces of evidence. This can mean that connections and coincidences are overlooked. After Peter Sutcliffe, 'the Yorkshire Ripper', was caught, it became obvious that the police files held several references to his name. If it had been possible to search the files in a quick and flexible way, he might well have been caught much earlier.

Such problems have led the police to introduce computer indexing systems for major crime enquiries. In the incident room, the card index is replaced with a large microcomputer or minicomputer running a special database applications package. The indexers use this computer to build up a computer file of all the information relevant to the crime. A computer database is far more flexible than a card index system. Because the records are structured so that they can be searched in many different ways, duplication of records is not necessary. A search that could take officers weeks using a manual card index takes the computer a few seconds.

An officer might be told by a witness "I saw a man run off, he was wearing a green sweater, he lives round here I'm sure, I think his name might be Read". The officer can ask the computer to tell him if any other statements contain references to a man in a sweater or to a Mr Read.

The computer can be programmed to pick out references to all words with the same meaning. Thus an officer searching for all references to a sweater will also receive references to jumpers and pullovers. In the same way, when searching for all references to a Mr Read, the computer can pick out references to Mr Reid, Mr Reed, Mr Reade and Mr Reide. The computer allows the police officers to carry out frequent, accurate and fast searches, and it is much less likely that connections and coincidences will be overlooked.

The first success of the computer system was its help in the capture of Malcolm Fairley, 'the Fox'. Fairley's name appeared on a list of suspects produced by the computer index system. All these suspects matched the details that the police knew about 'the Fox'. One of the crucial details was that 'the Fox' wore his watch on his right wrist.
Other police uses of computers include:

* Storing databases of criminals' names, addresses and past records
* Controlling the distribution and allocation of manpower, police cars and other resources
* Storing databases of fingerprints
* Storing databases of vehicles and owners' names. These details are obtained from the DVLC computer at Swansea
* Storing databases of missing persons.

The police use of computers is expanding, and a network of microcomputers, minicomputers and mainframe computers is being rapidly created. At the centre of the developing network is the **Police National Computer** (PNC). This is a large powerful mainframe computer set up in Hendon in 1968. It currently has two separate central processing units, and over 2000 megabytes of direct access backing store. The computer system currently stores over 40 000 000 entries. There are eight main indexes of which by far the largest is the file of vehicle owners. There are 900 multi-access terminals, shared among the 51 police forces in Britain. The computer system receives 31 000 000 requests for data each year through these terminals.

Two new major national computers are under development. The **National Fingerprint Computer** will store over 3 000 000 sets of fingerprints. Technology is being developed to allow the computer to read and compare fingerprints automatically.

The **National Major Incident Computer** will be used when any regional major incident enquiry becomes too large for local computers. It will also coordinate enquiries that cover several different police authorities. When the police network is completed, it will probably look like Figure 20.2.

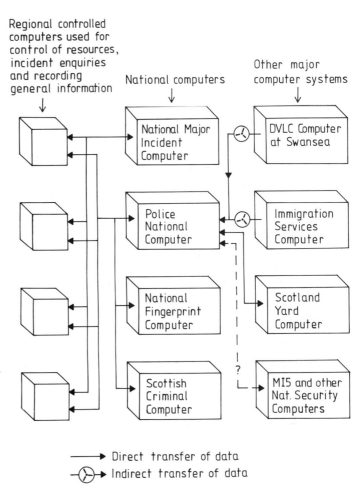

Figure 20.2 The network of police computers that will probably emerge from current developments

Exercise 62

1 Write a summary of a major incident computer application under the following headings. A clear diagram will often improve your answers.

a The main tasks of the computer system
b The input data collected
c The method of capturing the input data
d The data held in secondary storage
e The main processing tasks
f The output produced by the system
g The type of computer hardware used
h The communications used by the system
i The main advantages offered by the system over alternative systems

2 Describe the other uses the police make of computers.

Banking

Paying by cheque. There are several major banks in Britain, each with many branches in towns and cities around the country. Banks became one of the first major users of computers when, in the late 1950s, they started to computerise the handling of cheques. Before we look at the system used by the banks, we must first examine the process of paying for goods by cheque. Sue Black has an account at a branch of Barclays Bank and Jim White has an account at a branch of Lloyds bank. Let us suppose that Sue buys an electronic keyboard from Jim and pays him with a cheque for £20. Jim takes the Barclays cheque that Sue has given him and pays it into his account at Lloyds bank. At the end of the day, this cheque, together with all the other cheques that the Lloyds branch has received, will be sent to a special bank in London called the **Clearing Bank**. Over 6 000 000 cheques arrive at the clearing bank each day. Piled up, these cheques would be five times as high as Big Ben! The Clearing Bank sorts the cheques into bank and branch order, and they are returned to the correct banks. Eventually Sue's cheque will arrive at her branch and the value of the cheque will be deducted from her account.

If you think carefully about this transaction, you will realise that Barclays Bank now owes Lloyds bank the £20 which has been deducted from Sue's account and added to Jim's. Because hundreds of thousands of cheques pass between branches of Barclays Bank and Lloyds Bank every day, they do not bother to send each other individual sums of money. Instead, the Clearing Bank keeps a total of all the money transferred and passes these details each day to the Bank of England. The Bank of England is a very special banker's bank where both Barclays and Lloyds have accounts. Daily adjustments are made to these accounts based on figures received from the Clearing Bank. Figure 20.3 shows the outline of the Clearing Bank system.

In the late 1950s, banks started to introduce computers and automatic sorting machines to handle cheques. Before then, all cheques were processed entirely by hand. Many clerks worked long hours at the boring and repetitive tasks of sorting cheques and adjusting accounts. The manual system was expensive and also reaching the limit of its capacity to handle cheques. If the banks wanted to expand, it was essential that they developed a more efficient system. The system chosen by the banks is based on **magnetic ink character recognition** (**MICR**). All cheques are printed with magnetic ink code numbers for the bank, branch, account and cheque. Figure 20.4 shows these details printed on a typical cheque.

When the cheque is paid into a bank, a machine called a **magnetic ink encoder** is used to print the value of the cheque on it in magnetic ink. Figure 20.5 shows a cheque with the value added to it in magnetic ink.

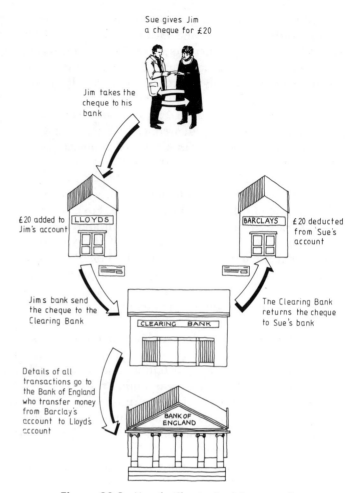

Figure 20.3 How the Clearing Bank System works

Figure 20.4 A typical blank cheque

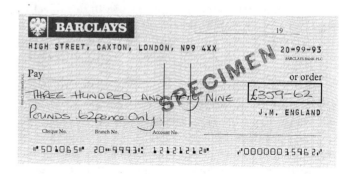

Figure 20.5 A cheque with the value added in magnetic ink

238

All the cheque details can now be read automatically by sorting machines and computers. There is no need for any further human processing apart from the physical transfer of the cheques between the banks. The actual cheque processing cycle remains unchanged. The difference is that all the processing is now done by machines. This has produced considerable savings in labour costs and also allowed the banks to expand their business far beyond the limits that a manual cheque processing system imposed.

Branch accounting. At each branch of a bank, records must be kept of all its customers' accounts. Before the introduction of computers, much of this accounting work was done by hand. Large books called **ledgers** were used to record the amount of money that each customer had in his or her account. The ledgers also recorded all the money paid into and drawn out of the account. This meant that every time a customer withdrew money, paid in money or used a cheque, the ledger needed to be updated. Every month the details in the ledger were copied by hand on to **statements** which were sent to each customer. These statements showed all the payments into and out of the account during that month.

This accounting was a time-consuming, tedious and difficult task. Because humans often make mistakes, all the figures were checked twice. Before the staff left the bank at the end of the day a complete check was made that everything was correctly recorded and that no money was missing.

Today, most of this work can be done by the bank's computer. Much of the necessary input data can be captured directly from the MICR printing on the cheques. The ledgers have become computer files. All the arithmetic is done by the computer and the monthly statements are printed on a line printer. This has allowed banks to reduce staff, provide an expanded and more efficient service, and also provide a more pleasant job for the staff they still employ.

Standing orders. If you have to pay a regular bill to somebody who has a bank account, you can arrange to pay the bill by **standing order**. This is an instruction to your bank to pay the regular bill for you. Standing orders are often used to pay insurance premiums, mortgage repayments and hire purchase debts.

In the old manual banking system, diaries were kept of all standing order payments. Each day a bank clerk checked the diary, wrote out credit slips to pay all the bills and posted them to the receivers' banks. The bank clerk then deducted the amounts paid from the accounts of the customers who had made the standing order requests.

Today, the banks operate the **Bankers Automated Clearing Service (BACS)**. This is a magnetic tape exchange system. The banks' diaries of standing order payments are now held as computer files. Each day banks dump details of all standing order payments *from* its customers accounts to other banks on to magnetic tapes. At the same time the amounts are automatically deducted from the customers' accounts. The tapes are sent to the BACS computer which sorts all the payments into bank and branch order. Each bank receives back from BACS a magnetic tape with details of all standing order payments *into* its customers' accounts from other banks. The computer automatically adds these payments to the customers' accounts.

Direct debiting is a slightly different alternative to standing order payments. If you sign a direct debit agreement with an organisation, the organisation can request the money directly from your bank each month. They do this by sending a magnetic tape to the BACS computer. Direct debiting is only used by large organisations like gas or electricity boards, and the magnetic tape will contain details of many different direct debit payments. These details will be distributed to the banks of the people who signed the direct debit agreements. Currently, over 450 million standing order and direct debit payments are handled every year by the BACS computer. This would be quite beyond the capacity of a manual system. Figure 20.6 shows the outline of the BACS system.

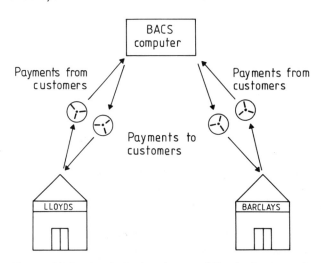

Figure 20.6 How the Bankers Automated Clearing Service works

Cash dispensers. Cash dispensers are on-line terminals outside banks which are used to provide an out-of-hours banking service. From the terminals customers can obtain cash, and also order a statement or a new cheque book. To provide security, each customer is issued with a small plastic card which has the customer's identity stored in a magnetic stripe. The customer is given a

Personal Identity Number (or **PIN**). This number is also stored in the magnetic stripe and is known only to the customer and the bank's computer. To obtain cash from the dispenser, the customer must insert the card and also type in the correct PIN number (Figure 20.7). This system prevents lost or stolen cards being used to withdraw money.

Figure 20.7 A cash dispenser in action

The use of cash dispensers provides customers with a 24 hour banking service, but has also caused some problems. A small number of customers claim that money has been withdrawn from their accounts when they have not used the cash dispenser. The banks insist that this is impossible and that the customers have forgotten they used the card or that it was used by somebody else who knows the PIN number. Some customers, however, remain adamant that they have been cheated by the bank's computer.

Electronic Funds Transfer Systems (EFTS). Recently there has been a great deal of interest in the paperless banking method called **Electronic Funds Transfer**. This method removes the need for cheques and provides an on-line banking service available in any shop with a special POS terminal. At the moment EFT systems have been limited to small experiments in a single town or group of shops, but their use seems likely to increase. At the heart of an EFT system is the bank's computer. This is connected on-line by telephone line and modem to POS terminals in shops. Each of these terminals has equipment to read the magnetic stripe on a plastic card issued to each customer. When a customer makes a purchase he or she pays with the plastic card which is inserted in a slot in the POS terminal. The POS terminal can contact the bank and check if the customer has enough money in their account. If they do, it will transfer the correct amount directly into the shop's account. The plastic card is then returned to the customer.

This system is very attractive to banks because it is completely automatic and involves no cheque handling or cash deliveries. Figure 20.8 shows the outline of an EFT system.

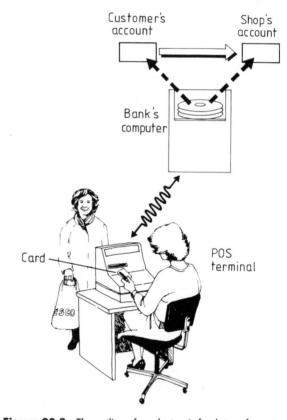

Figure 20.8 The outline of an electronic funds transfer system

Exercise 63

1 Write a summary of the banks' computerised cheque handling system under the following headings. A clear diagram will often improve your answers.

  a The main tasks of the computer system
  b The input data collected
  c The method of capturing the input data
  d The data held in secondary storage
  e The main processing tasks
  f The output produced by the system
  g The type of computer hardware used
  h The communications used by the system
  i The main advantages offered by the system over alternative systems

2 Describe the other uses the banks make of computers.

3 When a customer pays by cheque, it normally takes three days for the cheque to pass through the clearing system and for the money to be deducted from their account. When a customer pays by electronic funds transfer, the money is deducted immediately from their account. Bearing this in mind, can you think of any disadvantages that EFT has for customers?

Exercise 64

On the pages following are some extracts from articles in *Computing*, a combined magazine and newspaper for the computing profession. At this point in your course you should have acquired the knowledge needed to read and understand these articles, though you may find *some* parts of the articles difficult to understand. Unlike this book they were not written with school or college students in mind, and nothing has been simplified or omitted. Having read each article, prepare a summary of the application under the headings given in Exercise 62, Question 1 (p. 237).

EXTRACT 1: THE LONDON MARATHON The scale of the London Marathon, however, is somewhat larger than that of the Reading event — in Reading there were 4,000 runners selected from 16,000 applicants, while in London this year there will be 22,000 runners selected from around 80,000 applicants.

The DEC system has been installed at the London Marathon office in Richmond Park since last October, and is being used to process all the applications and runners' details, in addition to calculating the results on the day.

The system is based around a VAX 11/730 minicomputer at the Richmond office, which contains a database of all the original applicants to run as well as details of all those who have been selected and their race numbers.

Almost all the administration for the marathon has been done from this office, which has a full-time staff of four, including one employee seconded from the GLC especially to work on the marathon. Although the bulk of the data entry to the system was done in Reading, by school-leavers at Reading's government sponsored Information Technology Centre (Itec), the Richmond office took over the task in February after the Itec ran out of time.

Meanwhile, on the day itself, the results system will operate from a caravan on Westminster Bridge, containing two VAX 11/730s and two MicroVAX 1s networked together. The MicroVAXes will be used to collect data from timers on the route, supplied by Seiko. This data will enter the computers through RS232 connections and will enable the system to gauge the running time of each runner who completes the course. Two MicroVAXes are being used so that in the event of one breaking down the other will be able to accept the data which continues to come in from the timers whether the system is working or not.

The timing information will be checked against data on the 11/730 machines giving the sequence of runners completing the course. This data will come from bar-coded badges which each runner is given with his race number and instructed to wear during the race. When the runner goes past the finishing barrier, the bar code badge is sent down a chute where it is collected and read into the VAX machines.

Ian Sams, one of the DEC employees working on the marathon project, is confident that by checking these two sources of information against each other, the chances of human error creeping in will be greatly reduced: 'The Seiko timers are operated by operators who enter runners' numbers manually as they go past, which means there is a likelihood that numbers will be entered wrongly or not at all, so we are using the computer to validate them by checking them against the bar code information.'

As well as the results system and the office system, a Micro-VAX will be given to the race commentator on Westminster Bridge, containing a complete database of all the runners. This will enable the commentator to enter the number of a particular runner and access the runner's name, nationality and any other details.

Identical systems will be available in the press area in County Hall and at the television centre for the television commentators to use.

(*Computing*, 18 April 1985

EXTRACT 2: HEPWORTH AND SON Hepworth has so far spent over £1 million on updating its computing and already there are tangible results.

For example, after the Next ⓜ stores shut at 5.30 on Saturday evening, sales information can be on the central computer by the end of that same evening, and by Monday morning vans can be on their way to the stores bearing fresh stock tailored to the sales profile of each outlet.

Up-to-date information like this is a vital competitive tool in the clothing business, as data processing manager Ian White explained: 'If a line is selling well, we want to know as early as possible, so that we can place a repeat order. Unless you can react quickly, it's not always possible to do a follow-up on a successful fashion line.'

Hepworth & Son has used computers for years, but until the current project began to take effect, it relied exclusively on batch systems, running on an IBM 3031 and 4341. Coopers & Lybrand advised that this was risky; because the systems were so old, each modification made to fit the company's changing needs was in danger of making the systems less reliable. The consultants suggested bringing all the different retail operations within the Hepworth group together under a single group merchandising system based on a large common database, and moving to online rather than batch operations.

The system now operating in Next ⓜ is, White says, all about 'putting the right styles in the right sizes in the right branches, to achieve maximum sales'. Fifty IBM 3684 point-of-sale (pos) terminals in the Next ⓜ branches can be polled over telephone lines as often as head office wants; in practice, once a week for most of the year, but more frequently during crucial periods like the run-up to Christmas and in January, when new ranges of clothes are being launched.

The central system consists of seven modules. These are:

* Purchase order management, which copes with orders from head office to suppliers.
* Merchandise processing and distribution, which deals with the initial allocation of merchandise to branches.
* Planning, both financial and also assortment planning which ensures, for example, that the correct number of jackets to trousers is issued to branches.
* Merchandise reporting, which tells the merchandisers how well the various styles have performed in the various branches, as well as overall. On the basis of

information from this module, head office can decide whether to increase demand for a line that is selling badly by dropping the price, or to increase the supply of a popular line by placing repeat orders.

* Inventory management. This controls the physical inventory, and contains information on pricing and inter-branch transfers of stock. It can be used to speed up the auditing process.
* Sales and returns.
* Forecasting and replenishment.

HCS believes that the system now operating for Next ⓜ is ahead of the field. Firstly, its stores are among only a handful of chains in the country that use terminals which can be directly polled over phone lines. Most stores still have to do what Hepworth used to do: use a courier service physically to collect up the tapes containing sales information from each store and take them to head office.

Before the new system came into operation the last of the tapes only arrived at HCS in Leeds late on Sunday. It is also more reliable. With the old methods, staff might forget to leave the tapes for the courier, or bad weather could slow the delivery service down, meaning that the merchandiser had to send out fresh stock to branches without knowing whether the last lot had been sold. Hepworth also uses a system of stock codes, which are entered into the pos by the sales assistant when a customer pays for an item, and which display the price automatically.

A further boon is that the pos system gives greater control over overseas stores. Hepworth now has four branches in West Germany equipped with pos terminals which can be dialled from the UK via the Bundespost.

In the long term, HCS intends to develop both the pos and the central system further. It plans to start using bar codes for stock entry and add a facility for automatic capture of Access and Barclaycard transactions. A more elaborate pos system, probably involving a master terminal with several 'slaves', is planned for two Next mini department stores which are being set up in Bristol.

Later on, the idea is to use the pos terminals to send not only sales but also general branch information to head office. 'We will develop the pos system to use it for wage information and stock transfer. We could even use it for electronic mail,' said Martin Chatwin, director and general manager of HCS.

(*Computing*, 10 January 1985)

EXTRACT 3: STRATHCLYDE FIRE BRIGADE Over the last two years, fire brigades up and down the country have been installing computer-based command and control systems for the mobilisation of emergency services. These systems, in turn have provided a method of collecting statistics on fire accidents which has paved the way for more ambitious computer systems for management information.

An official for IAL Gemini, a specialist in command and control systems, highlighted the care that computer vendors must exercise in developing these systems. 'They take a great deal of time to construct and debug, because people's lives would be at risk if they failed. The last thing we want is for loss of life due to one of our systems,' he said.

An IAL Gemini installation at Strathclyde Fire Brigade went live earlier this year, and IAL Gemini claims it is one of the largest of its kind. It has taken the Strathclyde brigade four

years and a £3 million budget to get to this point, but Neil Ronnie, divisional officer and project manager for the system, firmly believes that for large regions the time and the expense is worth it.

Strathclyde Fire Brigade is an amalgam of five old brigades, brought together during local government re-organisation in 1975. The new Strathclyde brigade inherited five different control rooms from each old brigade and found that they had incompatible operating systems. 'For example, the old Lanarkshire brigade had a British Telecom, VFA System, while the Glasgow area had an RFL hardware system,' says Ronnie.

The first step was to instal a basic, common system for automatically operating the bells in each station, and a Dowty RFL Firecat system was chosen. But then Strathclyde decided that a computer-based system was needed which could co-ordinate the strategies involved in responding to emergency calls.

Strathclyde Fire Brigade took two years researching the market and conducting feasibility studies before it finally chose IAL Gemini to supply and instal the command and control system.

Strathclyde's chosen IAL Gemini system provides the fire service both with controls for its operations and with management information. The management information system is fed from the main operational activities of the brigade, which mobilise the service in response to emergency calls.

The command and control system starts its work as soon as an emergency call is received at Strathclyde's central control room in Johnston. When a call comes in, the operator types the address of the incident immediately into a vdu, which triggers the system to activate the Firecat system in the appropriate fire station. The Firecat system is operated from the IAL Gemini system via radio signals, but if the radio links fail, the system automatically switches onto telephone links.

The IAL Gemini system also provides a gazetteer of the Strathclyde area giving the fire service the exact location and condition of an address, and the best route to it from the alerted station.

The communication between a mobilised fire engine, and the central control office, supplies information for a resource availability system. In each engine there is a 'button-box' which sends radio signals to central control on the location of the engine, and on the state of its activities.

The resource availability system has a visual display at Johnston in the form of a large illuminated map of the area. A series of different coloured lights shows immediately the distribution of the service's resources to the controlling officers. This serves two purposes, according to Ronnie. First, it displays whether manpower and facilities need to be redistributed over the area in response to specific, resource consuming problems. 'For example, in the forest fire season the services in the forested north and south of the areas are under great pressure, which the stations in the urban areas can help out with,' says Ronnie. 'The illuminated display gives the supervisor an overall view.'

Secondly, the display gives a fall-back procedure. In the unlikely event of the system crashing completely, the screen can be updated manually.

An official for IAL Gemini said that the development of management information systems was where the future lay for command and control systems. Though the operational system can provide help for the immediate needs of the service, the management information system holds out the hope of improving fire prevention; it can also ensure that the equipment used is kept in peak condition.

Strathclyde's management system has 13 sub-systems live at the moment, including vehicle information, communications stock control, personnel system, and fire prevention records and statistics. Ronnie said that over the next two years, Strathclyde would be expanding this side of its system, to include subsystems for information such as operational equipment stock control.

The Central Fire Brigades Advisory Councils in England, Wales and Scotland are doubtful that these systems can be cost-effective for the smaller regions at the moment, but the prospect of the increasing experience in their development, thereby bringing about reduced prices, holds offers of bigger markets for command and control system vendors like IAL Gemini.

(*Computing*, 2 May 1985)

EXTRACT 4: A NEW NEWSPAPER

Eddie Shah will be taking on Fleet Street with a newspaper produced with the aid of £12 million worth of computer technology.

There are 10 million people who do not read newspapers in this country, he said. 'Most of them are in the 16 to 36 age group. They are used to good magazines, good colour television and a better quality life in general so they expect quality in a newspaper.'

The Daily Shah, as it has been dubbed for want of a proper name, will be halfway between a magazine and a newspaper. It will be printed on near magazine-quality paper, and readers will not get dirty fingers from it, said Shah.

He maintains people buy the Fleet Street tabloids only for lack of something better. 'They are rubbish, they are so badly printed you can barely read the type and the ink comes off in your hands.'

But it is computer technology rather than new inks that makes Shah's paper — due to be launched in March — radically different from its rivals.

Computers are at the heart of the whole operation and at work at every level. The paper should be better designed than the older tabloids because it will have good quality colour pictures and it will have later, more up-to-date news.

The look of a paper is important because the advent of better designed magazines has made design all-important. But good design is no guarantee of good editorial.

An achromatic process is being used to produce high definition colour pictures.

Chris Wood, assistant editor, said 'Men expect sport in colour as they see it on the television.'

Fashion is popular with young female readers and smudgy black and white pictures are not enough when there are good colour ones of the Paris fashion shows in the glossy magazines.

Computers will also dramatically speed up production of the paper, which will go to bed much later than other Fleet Street papers — around 1.30 am rather than 6 pm to 8 pm, and Shah's presses will keep on rolling until 6 am.

New equipment will enable staff to lay out even the most graphically complex colour page in under an hour — a process which usually takes about two to three hours.

Finished pages can then be sent instantly by Monotype Lasercomps to five regional centres with the aid of two Datrex 7601 readers, which will convert the page into digital format for transmission by microwave down a dedicated line. The page will then be etched directly on to a plate for immediate printing using Datrex 760X writers.

The five regional centres are all near motorways to enable fast distribution and to speed things up even more Shah has developed a project management system — using just a micro. With the aid of a built-in-clock, this will keep track of the variables in the production process, so if bad weather is causing a hold-up on the M6, delivery schedules can be adjusted accordingly. Shah claims computer scheduling is unheard of in Fleet Street.

Reporters equipped with portables will speed things up even further. By transmitting their stories via a modem direct to the sub-editors they will cut out the copytaking stage.

Sub-editors and layout artists, in advertising as well as editorial, will also have their tasks speeded up by working directly on to screen. Shah does not anticipate any health problems.

Indeed, he talks about provincial journalists who can spend long hours in front of the screen without any ill effects. The unions do not agree.

Shah also dismisses the claim that word processors lead to bad writing.

Computers will speed things up in advertising sales too — an area where creativity is not at such a premium.

Shah himself uses a personal computer.

'I can sit down at home and say what will happen if I do this and this. I can, in effect, play a game with the computer and at the end I will have the answers to what will happen in certain business situations.

'So I can go into meetings better prepared — without having to wait three weeks while the accountants work the figures out,' he said.

Computers have saved Shah a massive amount of money as well as time, mostly on staff — he has recruited only 465 staff compared to the 3,000 he would need for a conventional newspaper.

Investment in the paper has been only £22.5 million — a quarter of what it would have cost to set up a national newspaper using conventional technology.

However, Shah does not have absolute faith in new technology. He has invested in a small back-up manual system in case of a computer breakdown.

(*Computing: The Newspaper*, 10 October 1985)

EXTRACT 5: A DEFENCE SYSTEM

Nestled in the undulating countryside of Nebrasks, in the state capital of Omaha, is the United States Air Force Strategic Air Command Headquarters at Offutt Air Force base.

Strategic Air Command (SAC) at Offutt looks much like any other base: hangars, runways, a variety of airplanes, from fighters through to bombers and transporters. But Offutt is unlike any other in the world, for here lies the computer centre which controls two-thirds of the nuclear strike force of the US, the world's strongest nuclear power.

Reassurance is the name of the game at SAC headquarters and much of it rests with the computer system: 'At SAC, our primary mission is the deterrence of war, by providing the ready, strategic, offensive forces, capable of responding decisively to all threats that endanger the security interests of the United States. Therefore, SAC must be prepared to deploy its forces to any part of the world through all phases of the conflict. We do this with information systems.'

This statement formed part of the briefing given to visitors to the Strategic Information System, Division (SISD) at SAC headquarters. SISD commander, Brigadier General Ludwig, serves as deputy chief of staff for information systems and answers to the commander in chief at SAC, General Bernie Davies, (or CINCSAC). CINCSAC is a direct advisor to President Reagan on military matters. Thus the computer system provides information which enables the joint chiefs of staff and the US president to evaluate, command and control US response to conflagration, or the threat of war, around the world.

SISD has four major functions: intelligence; war planning; command and control; and support (such as administrative data processing and air traffic control). Each of these functions is based around a computer system. Over 2,500 personnel work with these systems at Offutt and another 6,000 people for 26 subordinate units across the US continent and throughout the world.

The intelligence function uses a variety of devices for its data collection which would be very much out of place in most data processing environments: SR-71's fly high altitude missions worldwide, U-2's photograph landscapes and targets and RC-135 aircraft gather electronic intelligence. All of these aircraft gather and store data which is subsequently processed by SISD for immediate use by the appropriate commanders. A number of separate intelligence computer systems control such tasks as production of target kits loaded into intercontinental ballistic missiles (ICBM), and the maintenance of offensive and defensive orders-of-battle.

The second SISD function, war planning, helps the joint chiefs of staff co-ordinate deployment of the Strategic Triad. The Strategic Triad comprises SAC land-based ICBM, SAC's bombers and the US Navy's sea-launched ballistic missiles (SLBM).

This means that the computer system must help produce war plans which are operable and credible while translating concepts and guidance into detailed plans.

Once the plan is complete each detail of it must be related to where that information is needed. Data must be distributed to each nuclear missile, launch control centre, submarine, bomber and aircraft in the nuclear theatre.

The introduction of cruise missiles, now stationed in a number of sites in the UK, including Greenham Common, has added a new dimension to the data processing requirements at SISD.

The innocuous-looking mass storage scrolls contain the data which describes terrain over which cruise missiles will fly. Just before a missile is launched terrain maps are loaded into its on-board computer. A model of over 18 million square nautical miles of terrain is being produced and stored in the computers at SISD in Offutt.

SISD's third function, command and control, has grown considerably in complexity since the simple telephone system of the 1950s. The response time to a 'Soviet threat' has dropped from 10 to 12 hours in the 1950s to 10 to 20 minutes in the 1980s. That timing is from warning of a threat through decision-making to deployment of nuclear weapons.

Global Command is controlled from the basement of building 500 at Offutt. Should that be destroyed an airborne command would take over control. As Major Feldbauer com-

mented during a tour of the computer centre of building 500: 'If we went missing our job would already have been done.'

A variety of networks using a mixture of modes and media provides the communications capability. This has increasingly become satellite-based. Although the most sophisticated technology is deployed for most systems the primary alerts are still handled by the telephone system designed and installed in the 1950s.

SISD's fourth function is providing support systems which include transmission, data processing and air traffic control.

The dozens of computer systems at SAC headquarters in Omaha regulate and control the major defence systems of the Western hemisphere. It has become the role of the data processor, the computer expert, to carry out the awesome task of maintaining the balance of nuclear power, of keeping the threat of annihilation credible.

Perhaps it would depend on your faith in computer systems just how reassured you will be by the technological marvels we have constructed to defend ourselves.

Mike Norton is a senior writer on Computing.

(*Computing: The Magazine*, 31 January 1985)

EXTRACT 6: A HOSPITAL COMPUTER   By the end of the century hospitals may be using computers in a variety of specialised applications ranging from expert diagnostic systems to image processing of X-rays. As the implementation of artificial intelligence techniques becomes increasingly feasible, computers are set to become just as essential a tool in hospital wards as they now are in the office. But for the time being, the everyday use of computers in hospitals is rather more mundane, albeit none the less important.

St Thomas' Hospital, situated on the south bank of the Thames facing Westminster, is typical of the general purpose hospitals throughout the country. Situated in the district of Lambeth, it provides medical attention for some of the UK's worst areas of inner city decline, armed with budgets that have been relentlessly squeezed by the Government in the last few years.

In the struggle to reconcile unequal ends and means, the overriding requirement for data processing at hospitals like St Thomas' is to streamline the administration of enormous registers of patients. Although there are only 950 beds at St Thomas' — enough in itself to cause a headache — the total number of patients registered with the hospital is over half a million, roughly equivalent to the entire population of Manchester.

The central core of the hospital's computer operations is the patient administration system, which provides a database of information on all registered in- and out-patients.

There are three main components to the patient administration system in use at St Thomas'. The first of these is registration, which provides basic personal details on each patient: name, address, age and so on. Each patient is identified on the system by a unique seven-character code.

Stokes expects the newly created Data Protection Act to have some effect on the hospital's administration although the full repercussions cannot yet be measured. 'We are already conforming with the main requirements of the Bill regarding security of information,' he said. 'The major difference it will make will be to give patients the right to look at their own personal, but not medical, details. It's not clear at present what exemptions there will be.'

A second component of the patient administration system is known as bed-state, and is concerned with recording who is in which bed at any one time. As the shortage of available beds becomes increasingly acute, it is vital to ensure that beds are allocated with maximum speed and efficiency, to avoid wasting resources.

The third part of the patient administration system deals specifically with out-patients, generating a list of people visiting each of the clinics in the district. By giving the clinic this information in advance, clinic staff can pull out the necessary files and medical records, again speeding up the overall process of treatment.

The major application outside of the patient administration system at St Thomas' is in the laboratories, where computers are used to record details and results of all work carried out. Three laboratories are involved: microbiology, haematology and chemical pathology, the last of which has recently been implemented.

In the microbiology laboratory specimens are taken for analysis, some 500–600 each day, arriving from both inside and outside the hospital. Specimens are usually delivered by porters, who place them in fridges according to the specimen type.

The analysis is performed by Medical Laboratory Scientific Officers (MLSOs), who are organised on separate benches according to the type of specimen involved. Each specimen comes with a request card from the doctor sending it, and this holds such details as the patient's name, the doctor's name, the specimen type and instructions for the analysis to be performed. The MLSO keys these details into the system in a series of codes which are translated by the main database.

A unique laboratory number is allocated by the computer and all the details are printed on a standard report form, on which the MLSO can mark results during analysis of the specimen. When tests are completed, the forms are automatically read with the help of an optical mark reader, and matched with the existing laboratory record.

The computer system uses a simple rule-based procedure to check that valid conclusions have been reached. If the result is classified as negative, a report can be sent to the commissioning doctor automatically.

According to Neil Bone, a principal systems analyst at St Thomas', this is one of the chief benefits of a computerised system in the hospital's laboratory: 'Normally the pathologist has to check the results of each analysis, but by eliminating the negative cases, they are able to pay greater attention to those which are positive,' he explained.

'As a safeguard all specimens from babies and most children are looked at by the pathologist and there is also an option to override negative results on the basis of supplied clinical details,' he added.

Another benefit of this system is the provision of a standard format for bench work, enabling technicians to pick up each other's work when necessary. Once the results of laboratory work have been filed on the computer, they can be accessed by consultants in any of the wards, providing fast information on in-patients.

(*Computing*, 17 January 1985)

EXTRACT 7: WINNING SAILORS AN ON-BOARD ADVANTAGE

US-developed CompuSail sets out to fine tune the instincts of experienced sailors by providing the data they need to win top races. Gordon Black reports on the progress of the father and son team who built the system.

CompuSail, a computerised sailing system under development in California, could be the key ingredient in next year's America's Cup. If, as seems possible, the system is adopted by one of the US entries, Australia's victory in the 1984 event is unlikely to be repeated.

Trials with prototypes of CompuSail have already illustrated the system's ability to increase the performance of boats. In fact when the system was fitted to a new and unraced boat it managed to beat other ships in its class on its first outing.

That win by *Dream Factory*, skippered by Dennis Durgan, has served to confirm that the on-board computer can outstrip the instincts of even the most experienced sailor.

But in designing the software and hardware for CompuSail, father and son team Bob and Dale Winson expected end users to be proficient and knowledgeable sailors.

'A computer cannot sail a boat,' says Bob Winson. 'This program will not make a bad sailor better, but it should give a great sailor an extra edge.

'Right now the amount of information available to a sailor is enormous,' he comments. 'To sail a boat unaided is an immensely complex process.'

A dynamics engineer by profession and a hobbyist sailor for 30 years, Bob Winson has spent more than five years developing the software for CompuSail. The program is written in C and is designed to operate on an IBM PC or compatibles.

Apart from expecting the operator to be a competent sailor, the system is designed to be user-friendly. 'We have gone to a lot of trouble to make this program as foolproof as possible,' says Bob Winson.

Certainly for someone unfamiliar with computers the system is easy to follow. A help utility guides the user through the detailed menus available on the program. A master menu contains all 10 features of the program, from race course entry and selection to timing functions and automatic polar data generation. It is a comprehensive sailing system program.

By taking four inputs from the boat's instruments the program is able to produce a series of calculations which would not be easy or possible otherwise. Information on boat speed, magnetic heading, apparent wind direction and velocity, as well as longitude and latitude position, are fed into the computer from the boat's instruments through a single cable connection. Because the software is interrupt-driven both the data collection and calculations are completed in real time.

'As a result of the processing one of the things the computer does is measure performance and store information as to what performance is,' explains Bob Winson. 'In other words, how fast the boat is moving for a particular wind velocity and for a particular mag-wind direction.'

By storing this information the computer builds up an array of data on the boat's performance. Comparing this data with future information allows a comparison or performance factor to be determined. 'Ideally if the boat was being sailed perfectly you would sail with a performance factor of 100% — but that is not the case,' claims Bob Winson.

Other capabilities of the program give the user a flexibility and wealth of information which even veteran sailors never attain in a lifetime.

By keying in the latitude and longitude of a particular race course the program will produce distances and direction. It is even capable of allowing the user to name waypoints on a course or simply identify them by a number. Where distances and headings between waypoints on a course are provided, the program will generate the appropriate latitude and longitude. Once a particular course has been fed into the machine it can be retained, modified or amalgamated with other course data. Courses can be displayed or sorted using true north or magnetic north bearings.

In order to produce courses the program has to undertake some fairly complex vector equations, hence the powerful 8087 co-processor.

While the navigational aspects of CompuSail effectively remove the time-consuming aspects of working a course, the aim of the system is to increase efficiency. At the heart of its computational ability is what is known as polar data gene-ration. When a boat sails, polar details (the relationship between boat speed and true wind angle) are collected automatically through the instruments. but they may also be manually altered. These polars are used to determine the best sailing position.

'As you're sailing it is constantly computing what the optimum mag-heading is to get to the next waymark. And it will be telling you whether you are reaching to the mark or are going to tack to the mark. If you're going to tack to the mark it will tell you how far it is to the lay line and what the heading will be,' explains the program writer. 'It's a very, very busy program' he adds. 'This thing is solving some rather complex vector equations.'

Put simply, it will tell sailors the ideal sailing course to reach a given point. On top of such information of immediate interest, the program can generate the predicated values for the next leg of a race. This is particularly valuable in major events navigated over a series of points.

(Computing the Magazine 29 August 1985)

21 The Social Effects of Computers

Changes at Work

Those who work can be divided into four broad categories:

* Manual workers
* Clerical and office workers
* Professionals
* Creative workers

The introduction of computers has affected these groups of workers in different ways.

Manual workers

Many manual jobs have been lost because of the introduction of computers. For example, each new industrial robot replaces an average of four factory workers. In the same way, the introduction of microprocessors-controlled digital watches has put nearly twenty major Swiss watch manufacturers out of business. As time progresses, it seems certain that computer-controlled machines will replace more and more manual workers. Many jobs will also be lost in industries which manufacture electrical and mechanical devices that can be replaced by microprocessor devices. Some workers will of course still be needed to make industrial robots and microprocessor devices, but on balance it appears that many more jobs will be lost than gained. However, almost all the manual jobs that are being lost are boring, repetitive, dirty and often unpleasant and dangerous. Very few people *want* to work on a dirty, noisy factory production line. Problems are caused only when it is impossible to find alternative tasks for these workers.

Many of the more interesting manual jobs are still too difficult for a computer-controlled machine. For example, no lorry driver, gardener, house builder or farm worker has yet lost his or her job to a computer. (See Figure 21.1.)

Clerical and officer workers

The nature of clerical work has been drastically altered by the introduction of computers. Before the 1960s, clerical workers maintained paper and ink records and ledgers and processed numbers by hand or with mechanical calculators. Today, most large record systems are stored on magnetic tapes and disc, and most processing is done by the computer. The main effect of this appears to have been a vast expansion of business services rather than massive unemployment of clerical and office workers. Certainly many current banking, ticket booking and information retrieval services would be quite impossible to operate with manual methods.

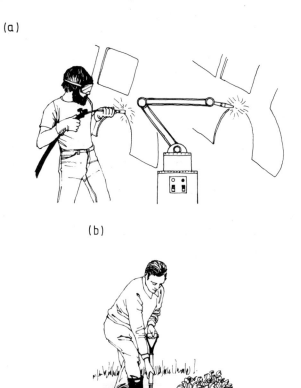

(a)

(b)

Figure 21.1 (a) Many boring, dirty manual jobs are being lost to computer-controlled machines, but (b) some interesting manual jobs cannot yet be computerised

Talking to office workers, the author has found many who have welcomed the computer. They have found that the computer can relieve them of their more tedious tasks and allow them to work in a more flexible and enjoyable way. On the other hand, some office workers say they feel the computer has robbed them of their job satisfaction. They used to feel they were doing a difficult and important task, but now they feel they are mindless servants feeding information into the office computer.

One area of office work that seems certain to see a large loss of jobs is typing. A large bank was recently able to cut its typing staff from over 150 to less than 50 by introducing word processors. If this pattern were spread over the whole country, some 500 000 typists could lose their jobs. (See Figure 21.2.) If word processors are networked, they can provide an electronic mail service. Any large increase in the use of electronic mail could see the loss of many postal workers' jobs.

Figure 21.2 Word processors may mean fewer typists

Professional workers

Professional workers are people such as scientists, teachers, engineers, doctors, lawyers, accountants and systems analysts. They earn their living by offering their clients a combination of factual knowledge and practical experience. As yet, very few professional workers have lost their jobs to computers. Where computer use has entered a profession, it has mainly been used to increase productivity rather than to replace staff. For example, most CAD systems have been used to allow designers to explore more design possibilities, not to reduce the number of designers. Certainly no teacher or doctor has yet lost their job to a computer (Figure 21.3).

Figure 21.3 The computerised teacher? Not yet!

It is possible that some professionals may be replaced by expert systems, but at the moment this seems unlikely. It seems more probable that expert systems will be used by professionals to allow them to offer a better and more extensive service.

Creative workers

Creative workers are people such as musicians, painters, actors, authors and poets. The reaction of many of these people to computers has been to ignore them. There is certainly no need for any creative worker to feel their job is threatened by computers. Real creativity is one of those mysterious human powers that is completely beyond any known computer technology. Nobody can say that creative computers will never be built, but at the moment nobody even knows how to start.

Although no creative workers are likely to lose their jobs to a computer, many of them use a computer as a powerful tool to aid their work. Artists use CAD packages to explore design possibilities, authors use word processors to write and edit their books, and animators and cartoonists use computer graphics to produce their work more quickly and with less effort. In the theatre, computers are used to control lighting and sound systems. In films and on television, computers are used to edit visual material and to create special effects. Musicians, both pop and classical, use computers to help them compose and create music. In short, computer technology can open up many new possibilities for expressing human creativity. Figure 21.4 shows an example of 'computer art'. The cover of this book shows another.

There are many different views of the patterns of working that will emerge over the next few years. Table 21.1 presents one viewpoint that is extremely pessimistic and one that is very optimistic.

Figure 21.4 *The Fisherman* by Kerry Strand, drawn by a computer-guided digital plotter

Table 21.1 Two views of the computer future

For the pessimist	For the optimist
Computers will cause massive unemployment. This will lead to social unrest and confrontation between those with jobs and the unemployed. Computers will devalue humans who will be condemned to a life of enforced idleness while computers do the real work.	The high productivity of computer systems will produce the profits to employ more people for drastically cut working hours. This will eventually lead us back to full employment, but with people doing jobs they really want to do. All the boring and unpleasant work will be done by machines, and humans will be free to do socially useful and satisfying jobs such as nursing, teaching and community care. Everybody will have the time and resources to enjoy far more leisure activities.

Exercise 65

1 Many people now use computers in their jobs. This has often meant that they must change the way they work and also has led to less people being employed. Select any three jobs and for each explain:

   a one way in which the job has been changed by the introduction of computers
   b one way in which the computer has led to less people being employed
   c one advantage and one disadvantage that you feel have been created by the use of computers in the job.

2 Read the following extract from *Player Piano* by Kurt Vonnegut Jr, published in 1952.

   a Explain in your own words what has happened to Bud and why Paul is unable to help him.
   b When you read the text, what is it that tells you this book was written when computers were at an early stage of development?
   c To what extent do you think Kurt Vonnegut's vision has come true over the last 30 years?
   d To what extent do you think Kurt Vonnegut's vision will come true in the next 20 years?

   The motor took hold with assurance and swept Paul over the hilltop and up to the gate of the Ilium Works. A watchman waved from his pillbox, a buzzer sounded, and the iron, high-spiked gate swung open. He came

now to the solid inner door, honked, and looked expectantly at a thin slit in the masonry, behind which another guard sat. The door rumbled upward, and Paul drove up to his office building.

He went up the steps two at a time — his only exercise — and unlocked two outer doors that led him into Katharine's office, and beyond that, his own.

Katharine hardly looked up when he came in. She seemed lost in melancholy, and, on the other side of the room, on the couch that was virtually his, Bud Calhoun was staring at the floor.

"Can I help?" said Paul.

Katharine sighed. "Bud wants a job."

"Bud wants a job? He's got the fourth-highest-paid job in Ilium now. I couldn't equal what he gets for running the depot. Bud, you're crazy. When I was your age, I didn't make half — "

"Ah want a job," said Bud. "Any job."

"Trying to scare the National Petroleum Council into giving you a raise? Sure Bud, I'll make you an offer better than what you're getting, but you've got to promise not to take me up on it."

"Ah haven't got a job any more," said Bud. "Canned."

Paul was amazed. "Really? What on earth for? Moral turpitude? What about the gadget you invented for — "

"Thet's it," said Bud with an eerie mixture of pride and remorse. "Works. Does a fine job." He smiled sheepishly. "Does it a whole lot better than Ah did it."

"It runs the whole operation?"

"Yup. Some gadget."

"And so you're out of a job."

"Seventy-two of us are out of jobs," said Bud. He slumped even lower in the couch. "Ouah job classification has been eliminated. Poof." He snapped his fingers.

Paul could see the personnel manager pecking out Bud's job code number on a keyboard, and seconds later having the machine deal him seventy-two cards bearing the names of those who did what Bud did for a living — what Bud's machine now did better. Now, personnel machines all over the country would be reset so as no longer to recognize the job as one suited for men. The combination of holes and nicks that Bud had been to personnel machines would no longer be acceptable. If it were to be slipped into a machine, it would come popping right back out.

"They don't need P-128's any more," said Bud bleakly, "and nothing's open above or below. Ah'd take a cut, and go back to P-129 or even P-130, but it's no dice. Everything's full up."

"Got any other numbers, Bud?" said Paul. "The only P-numbers we're authorized are — "

Katharine had the *Manual* open before her. She'd already looked the numbers up. "P-225 and P-226 — lubrication engineers," she said. "And Doctor Rosenau's got both of those."

"That's right, he does," said Paul. Bud was in a baffling mess, and Paul didn't see how he could help him. The machines knew the Ilium Works had its one allotted lubrication engineer, and they wouldn't tolerate a second. If Bud were recorded as a lubrication engineer and introduced into the machines, they'd throw him right out again.

As Kroner often said, eternal vigilance was the price of efficiency. And the machines tirelessly riffled through their decks again and again and again in search of foot draggers, free riders, and misfits.

"You know it isn't up to me, Bud," said Paul. "I haven't got any real say about who's taken on."

"He knows that," said Katharine. "But he has to start somewhere, and we thought maybe you'd know of some opening, or who to see."

"Oh, it makes me sore," said Paul. "Whatever got into them to give you a Petroleum Industries assignment, anyway? You should be in design."

"Got no aptitude for it," said Bud. "Tests proved that."

That would be on his ill-fated card, too. All his aptitude-test grades were on it — irrevocably, immutable, and the card knew best. "But you *do* design," said Paul. "And you do it with a damn sight more imagination than the prima donnas in the Lab." The Lab was the National Research and Development Laboratory, which was actually a war-born conglomeration of all the country's research and development facilities under a single headquarters. "You're not even paid to design, and still you do a better job of it than they do. That telemetering arrangement for the pipeline, your car, and now this monster that runs the depot — "

"But the test says no," said Bud.

"So the machines say no," said Katharine.

"So that's that," said Bud, "Ah guess."

"You might see Kroner," said Paul.

"Ah tried, and didn't get past his secretary. Ah told her Ah was after a job, and she called up Personnel. They ran mah card through the machines while she held the phone; and then she hung up, and looked sad, and said Kroner had meetings all month."

"Maybe your university can help," said Paul. "Maybe the grading machine needed new tubes when it went over your development aptitude test." He spoke without conviction. Bud was beyond help. As an old joke had it, the machines had all the cards.

"Ah've written, asking them to check my grades again. No matter what Ah say, Ah get the same thing back." He threw a piece of graph paper on Katharine's desk. "Theah. Ah've written three letters, and gotten three of these back."

"Uh-huh," said Paul, looking at the familiar graph with distaste. It was a so-called Achievement and Aptitude Profile, and every college graduate got one along with his sheepskin. And the sheepskin was nothing, and the graph was everything. When time for graduation came, a machine took a student's grades and other performances and integrated them into one graph — the profile. Here Bud's graph was high for theory, there low for administration, here low for creativity, and so on, up and down across the page to the last quality — *personality*. In mysterious, unnamed units of measure, each graduate was credited with having a high, medium, or low personality. Bud, Paul saw, was a strong medium, as the expression went, personality-wise. When the graduate was taken into the economy, all his peaks and valleys were translated into perforations on his personnel card.

"Well, thanks anyway," said Bud suddenly, gathering up his papers, as though embarrassed at having been so weak as to bother anyone with his troubles.

"Something will turn up," said Paul. He paused at his office door. "How are you fixed for money?"

"They're keepin' me on a few more months, until all the new equipment gets installed. And Ah've got the award from the suggestion system."

"Well, thank God you got something out of it. How much?"

"Five hundred. It's the biggest one this year."

"Congratulations. Is that on your card?"

Bud held the rectangle of cardboard up to the window and squinted at the nicks and perforations. "Think thet little devil raht there's it."

Data Protection

Today, almost everybody has some information about them stored in computer files. A typical adult has data about them stored in their employer's computer, the DVLC computer, their bank's computer, the Inland Revenue computer, the DHSS computer, the NHS computer, and many other computers. It is estimated that there is an average of 50 K of data stored on every person in Britain! Many people are very concerned about the growing amount of data which computers store about us all. The main reasons for this concern are:

* Some of the data may be inaccurate or out of date, but may still be used to make decisions about the person to whom it refers.
* It is difficult for individuals to find out exactly what data is stored about them and who is storing it.
* It may be possible for unauthorised people to gain access to stored data. It is very difficult to ensure that the data will always stay private.
* The data may be passed on without the consent of the person to whom it refers.
* Governments and others may try to use the data as a source of control over the people to whom it refers.

Of course, before the introduction of computers, much of this data was already stored in manual filing systems. People have become more concerned now the data is stored in computer filing systems for three reasons:

* Computer filing systems can store vast amounts of information in a very small space. The sheer size of manual filing systems limited the amount of data that could be stored on each individual. These restrictions do not apply to computer filing systems.
* The data stored in a computer system can be retrieved very quickly and accurately. It might take hours to find data in a large manual filing system. A computer filing system can be searched in seconds.
* Data can be easily transferred from one computer filing system to another. Computers can also be linked so that a complete 'data picture' can be built up on any individual. In the wrong hands this data could prove very damaging to the individual concerned.

Figure 21.5 shows the potential computer network that surrounds us all. To some people this is a menacing picture which demonstrates that 'Big Brother' is already closing in on the lives of ordinary people.

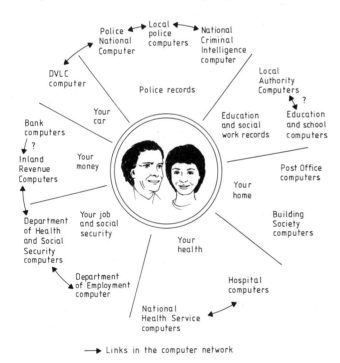

Figure 21.5 We are becoming surrounded by computers

The growing level of public concern over data stored in computer systems led the Government to pass the Data Protection Act. This act received the Royal Assent on 12 July 1984. The introduction to the Act contains the following passages:

The Data Protection Act 1984 meets two concerns:
— that arising from the threat which the mis-use of the powers of computing equipment might pose to individuals. This concern derives from the ability of computing systems to store vast amounts of data, to manipulate data at high speed and, with associated communications systems, to give access to data from locations far from the site where the data are stored;
— that arising from the possibility of damage to our international trade which might occur if the United Kingdom were not to ratify the "Council of Europe Convention for the Protection of Individuals with regard to Automatic Processing of Personal Data". Countries ratifying this Convention might place restrictions on the transfer of personal data to countries which have not ratified it.

You can see from this extract that the rights of its citizens were not the Government's only concern. The Act established the following rights for any individual:

* To seek compensation, through the courts, for damage or distress caused by the loss, destruction or unauthorised disclosure of data or by inaccurate data.
* To apply to the courts for the rectification or erasure of inaccurate data.
* To obtain access to the data of which he or she is the subject.

The Act defines a *data user* as 'an organisation or individual who controls the contents and use of a collection of personal data processed, or intending to be processed, automatically'. In other words, a data user is just about anybody who stores personal data on a computer. The Act lays down the following obligations for data users:

* All data must be collected and processed fairly and lawfully.
* All data must only be held for specified, lawful, registered purposes.
* All data must only be used for registered purposes or disclosed to registered recipients.
* All data must be adequate and relevant to the purpose to which it is held.
* All data must be accurate and, where necessary, kept up to date.
* All data must be held no longer than is necessary for a stated purpose.
* All data must be protected by appropriate security measures.

The Government has created the office of Data Protection Registrar to implement and enforce the provisions in the Act. All data users must register with the registrar, who will establish a public register of all data users. Using this register, individuals will be able to find out who holds data about them and then demand to see that data.

Some data users will be allowed exemptions from part or all of the Act. The Police for example will not be forced to reveal data if it would prevent or hinder the arrest or prosecution of criminals. Other exemptions may be made on the grounds of National Security or for the assessment and collection of taxes.

Exercise 66

1 Explain in your own words why many people are concerned about the increasing amount of computer stored data which relates to individuals' private lives.

2 Explain in your own words the way in which the Data Protection Act will give individuals some control over the data stored about them on computers.

3 One of the provisions of the Data Protection Act is that appropriate security measures must be taken to protect stored data. Explain the security measures that can be taken to prevent the loss of data and also unauthorised access to data.

4 Explain why it is necessary to provide some exemptions to the general provisions of the Data Protection Act.

Changes in Lifestyles

Nobody knows what will happen in the future, and from past experience most guesses turn out to be wildly inaccurate. For example, in the late 1940s, many experts predicted that between five and ten computers would be the maximum number that Britain would ever need. Today, computers are commonplace in shops, factories and homes.

What does seem certain is that we are living through a period of social change brought about by many new technologies, not just computer technology. The car, for example, has made considerable changes in our lifestyles, enabling people to work and shop at much greater distances from their homes. Television has changed the way we think about the world, bringing scenes of war, famine and disaster into our living rooms.

This is not the first social change brought about in this way. The **Industrial Revolution** during the 19th century was also a period of great social change brought about by new technology. Before the industrial revolution, almost all workers were employed in farming. In 1700, over 90% of the population worked on the land.

During the industrial revolution, people changed from being labourers working with their own strength to machine-users controlling the power of machines many times stronger than themselves. New inventions led to the setting up of large factories in Britain's towns and cities. Workers gradually moved from the farms to these new factories, adapting from a country lifestyle to a city lifestyle. Today, less than 3% of workers are employed in farming. The farms still produce enough food to feed us all, but machinery has replaced many of the farm workers of the 18th and 19th centuries. Many people believe that we are now going through a similar period of social change. This is sometimes called the **Post-industrial Revolution**. We are already seeing some of the effects of this revolution. Traditional clerical work is becoming obsolete, and the task of controlling machines is steadily declining. Our houses are packed with gadgets our parents never dreamed of when they were children. Microcomputers, word processors and microprocessor-controlled devices that were unheard of until the mid 1970s are now commonplace. As has already been noted, most predictions of the future turn out to be wildly inaccurate, but if we do guess, what new developments seem likely? The following sub-sections examine some of the developments which are possible.

The cashless society. If electronic funds transfer systems spread, paper money and coins could eventually become obsolete. All purchases and payments would be made with a personal card read by an on-line POS terminal. The POS terminal would contact banking computers and 'money' would be transferred from the buyer's account to the seller's account. People would be paid in a similar way by transferring 'money' from their employer's account to their account. No physical notes and coins would need to exist. 'Money' would simply be the total recorded in each person's account in the banking computers.

Although this development is technically quite feasible, it seems likely that many people will resist it. Hard cash is useful for many different reasons. How else would you give pocket money, tip the taxi driver, pay the window cleaner, make small bets with friends, make street donations to charity or make a million and one other small transactions? It is possible that all these *could* be accomplished with EFT, but it seems highly unlikely that hard cash will ever disappear *completely*. One concern which the growth of EFT systems will cause is the possible loss of individual privacy. All EFT transactions will leave a computer record, and it would become possible for Governments, tax officers and many other agencies to gain access to every minute detail of our earnings and spendings. On the other hand, in a complete EFT system, bank robberies and wage snatches would become things of the past.

Electronic shopping. An extension of Prestel and other similar viewdata systems might eventually lead to most shopping being done from home. Shops could display their goods on viewdata screen pages and customers could use interactive terminals to order them. In a few minutes, a customer could compare the price of an item from several different suppliers and arrange a delivery direct to his or her home. If the shopping system was linked to an EFT system, payment for the goods could also be handled automatically.

Electronic shopping will probably increase, but it seems unlikely that it will become any more important than catalogue shopping is today. Some people like to buy from catalogues, but many more prefer to visit the shops to try things on and generally have a good day out. There seems little reason to suppose that electronic shopping will have any more to offer than selecting goods from today's colour catalogue.

Artificial intelligence. One prospect which fascinates many people is the possibility of building a truly intelligent computer. Such machines are common in science fiction stories, but nobody has ever built a real one. In fact, people find it very hard to agree on what exactly is meant by an 'intelligent' computer. But this is not surprising because people also find it hard to agree on what exactly is meant by an 'intelligent' person. Some of the abilities which we do seem to associate with 'intelligence' are listed below:

* Ability to calculate
* Ability to remember and recall information
* Ability to communicate by natural spoken language
* Ability to communicate by natural written language
* Ability to recognise shapes and patterns
* Ability to use tools and to move and manipulate objects in a controlled way
* Ability to laugh at and make jokes — in other words, having a sense of humour
* Ability to create new ideas and insights into problems
* Ability to feel a range of needs — hunger, thirst etc.
* Ability to feel a range of emotions — happiness, sadness, etc.
* Ability to reason and make logical conclusions
* Self-awareness, knowing that you exist.

In some of these abilities, computers have already far surpassed human performance. For example, no human can hope to match the calculating speed of a computer. In most of the other abilities, the human brain is still far in advance of any computer yet built. Research projects are under way to try to equip computers with some of these abilities. For example, attempts are being made to produce computers that can communicate by natural language. However, for several of the abilities listed, nobody at present has any idea of how they could be transferred to a computer. For example, nobody has even suggested how a computer could be made aware of its own existence.

One problem with any artificial intelligence project is the lack of real understanding of the functioning of the human brain. All present-day computer programs depend on algorithms. An algorithm, remember, is a fixed set of rules used to solve a particular type of problem. Whatever mysterious things happen inside the human brain, it is very hard to believe that they depend on algorithms. Who can sensibly believe that there is a 'music-composing' algorithm or a 'picture-painting' algorithm or a 'book-writing' algorithm? Nobody can say for certain that a truly 'intelligent' computer will never be built. What we can say for certain is that if 'intelligence' is taken to include creativity, emotions and self-awareness, then nobody has even begun to design such a computer.

Even if we do not see 'intelligent' computers within our lifetimes, we are almost certain to see **fifth-generation computers**. Fifth-generation computers are the object of research projects in several countries, notably Japan. As with any research project, we cannot be completely certain what kind of computer will emerge but these fifth-generation computers should have some or all of the following facilities:

* The ability to communicate with the user in natural spoken language
* The ability to store a vast and complex database of knowledge
* The ability to search and process the database at very high speeds, retrieving information and also drawing logical conclusions and inferences from the data
* The ability to be programmed by a natural language 'conversation' with the user
* The ability to process images and 'see' things in the way that humans can.

Even though fifth-generation computers will still fail many tests for true 'intelligence', they may come very close to human abilities in several areas (as in Figure 21.6?). If all the aims of the research projects are met, by the mid-to-late 1990s we may be faced with a situation where the jobs of many office, clerical and professional workers are under threat. All fifth-generation research depends on four main developments which are necessary before the computers can be built:

* Very large memories will be needed with very fast access times.
* Very fast processors will be needed.
* More powerful programming languages must be developed.
* The major problem of voice recognition and natural language analysis must be overcome.

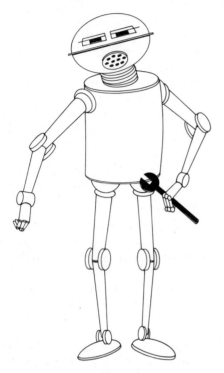

Figure 21.6 A fifth-generation computer?

Possible loss of freedom. There is no such thing as a completely free society. All societies must strike a balance between the freedom of each individual and the protection of society in general. For example, a balance must be struck between the freedom of an individual to drive his or her car as fast as he or she likes and the need to protect other road-users from reckless driving. All societies have a system of laws which establish this balance between individual freedom and the protection of other members of the society. There is no 'correct' balance, and the extent to which any given society allows too much or too little individual freedom is a question of personal preference and opinion.

Democratic countries such as the UK, France, India, Australia and the USA are considered to offer their citizens a high level of individual freedom. In these countries the legal system concentrates on the restriction of anti-social **physical** activity and usually allows the citizen freedom of speech and the right to belong to any political party.

Totalitarian countries such as Poland, Russia, East Germany, Iran and some South American dictatorships are considered to offer their citizens a low level of individual freedom. In these countries there is often strict censorship of all forms of communication and only one official state political party. Citizens who do speak out against the system are often harassed by state employees who restrict their ability to work, meet with friends and live where they choose.

On the other hand, representatives of countries such as Russia might well point out that their systems have produced 100% employment, 0% inflation and a marked absence of problems like drug abuse that plague some democratic countries.

Some people fear that computers will allow governments to impose far greater control over individual citizens. They see this as a threat to the freedom of people living in democracies and a threat of even greater control to people living in totalitarian states. There are several ways in which present and predicted computer technology could be a threat to freedom:

* The linking of computer systems into one vast national database could allow a complete 'data picture' to be created on any citizen very quickly. Financial history, medical records, past criminal convictions, membership of clubs and political parties, educational qualifications, names of friends and relations, and many other details could be recalled at the touch of a button. Any blemishes at all in this past record could be used as a source of pressure, control and even blackmail.
* Extensive use of Electronic Funds Transfer systems would enable a government to monitor the details of all the financial transactions of any individual.
* Powerful voice recognition computers could monitor all telephone conversations (if fifth-generation computer research is successful).
* State employees could harass individuals by creating false computer records — for example, by creating a false record of unpaid debts, an individual's credit rating could be ruined. This in turn could cause the collapse of their business or loss of their home.
* Adapted OCR readers could be placed on all roads to read the number plates of the vehicles that pass. If these OCR readers were linked to a central computer, it would be possible to monitor the movements of every vehicle.

It must be noted that all these developments are only possibilities. They will be implemented only if governments wish to do so and are allowed to do so by their citizens.

Gadgets. Almost every day new computer-controlled gadgets are introduced. Some of these are little more than toys. For example, who actually *needs* a pen that also contains a digital watch and a miniature radio? Others are very useful new inventions. For example, a micro-computer controlled device is being developed which may allow paralysed people to walk again by electrically stimulating the muscles in their legs. It is impossible to give an extensive coverage of the thousands of useful devices already introduced or under development. The reader is highly recommended to watch the BBC programme 'Tomorrow's World' and to obtain a school copy of *Computing Magazine* in order to stay up to date with new developments.

Exercise 67

1 Write a short essay with the title 'Life in the Year 2000', concentrating on the changes that you think computer technology will have created by this date.

2 Read the following article about the Police National Computer.

Police computer lists five million 'criminal' names by James Naughtie, Chief Political Correspondent

A new dispute over the national police computer broke out at Westminster last night when published figures revealed the extent of its records.

Written parliamentary answers from the Home Office showed that in May 4,974,479 people were listed under the criminal names index and that more than 3.5 million sets of fingerprints were on file.

Mr Gerald Kaufman, Labour's home affairs spokesman, said last night: "This is extremely disturbing. We want to know who these criminals are, whether they have been convicted and how long these records are kept."

The Home Office said that the "criminal names" index was restricted to those convicted of serious offences and that people acquitted by the courts were removed. Those awaiting trial on serious charges have their names listed.

A spokesman said that the index was weeded regularly to remove those whose offences were committed long ago. However, the first publication of the size of the computer's indexes is bound to start a bout of detailed questioning from the opposition about the guidelines used by police in deciding which names to keep on file and which to remove.

The Home Office said last night that it would be unfair to present the figures as meaning that about one person in 10 was listed in the criminal names index at any given moment, since there was a regular weeding.

However, the scope of the indexes was worrying Labour MPs, and ministers can expect a host of detailed questions about the rules under which police officers have access to them and the safeguards used to ensure that the names of the innocent are not mistakenly kept on file after acquittal.

The series of answers, to Mr Harry Cohen, Labour MP for Leighton, said that the entries in the various indexes on the computer were as follows on May 18: stolen and suspect vehicles, 349,620; chassis, engine and plant numbers, 542,713; vehicle owners, 35,610,660; criminal names, 4,974,479; fingerprints, 3,512,434; convictions, 467,377; wanted and missing persons, 109,659; and disqualified drivers, 298,436.

Malcolm Dean adds: About 600,000 people are found guilty or cautioned for an indictable (serious) offence every year. Another 500,000 are found guilty of summary (less serious) offences and more than one million convicted of summary motoring offences.

Only the indictable offences will usually be placed on the computer but within 10 years this means five million or more names have been collected. Mr Derek McClintock, the Edinburgh criminologist, estimated that one man in every three will be convicted of an indictable offence during his lifetime.

(Guardian)

a Imagine you are a senior police officer. Write a short speech you might give in support of the Police National Computer.

b Imagine you are an MP. Write a short speech you might give expressing some fears about the Police National Computer.

3 Read the following article.

PHONE GUARD Big brother is watching Lidia Munoz.

Lidia, 20, of Delray Beach, Florida, is under electronic house arrest using the latest technology available. She has been fitted with an electronic transmitter, programmed to inform the local police if she strays more than 120 feet from her home.

It is the latest example of a system that has been under trial at the Palm Beach County Sheriff's department since December last year, as a method of avoiding prison for people who have committed minor crimes. It started with five offenders, now covers 45, and will expand to 125 within two years.

In the scheme, an offender is placed in the responsibility of a sponsor — say a girlfriend, father or mother — and, in effect, kept under police surveillance.

Anklet : Property of Palm Beach Sheriff's Office.

Judge Garrison approached Gene Garcia, divisional commander of Palm Beach Sheriff's Office, who started the electronic surveillance scheme. A band containing a transmitter was fitted, with rivets, to Lidia's leg. It happily survives baths, showers and swimming.

The second part of the system is an electronic box of tricks — a dialler-receiver — attached to the offender's phone. It is programmed to interrogate the transmitter at 35 second intervals to check that it is in the right place at the right time and pass the information, via telephone, to a police computer.

The system can be programmed to allow the offender to go to work and back.

The system will continue to keep on eye on Lidia until she faces trial on 5 November or sooner.

The system saves the Sheriff's Office money. Instead of spending $30 a day to keep someone in jail, the offender pays $63 a week, to remain under electronic surveillance, which goes towards the initial outlay on the system of $53,000. When the payment is made each week, the device is checked to ensure it has not been tampered with.

The system prevents overcrowding of cells, 'and believe me, we are overcrowded,' says Garcia. Most important, it cuts down violations.

(*Observer*, 13 October 1985)

a Explain the advantages of this system from the point of view of the prison authorities.
b Explain the advantages of this system from the point of view of a minor offender.
c Explain how the system could be mis-used by a government to control its citizens.

4 a Describe how future developments in microtechnology may affect our shopping, banking and use of money.
b Describe TWO common household items where a microprocessor might be found in the latest models. What is the reason for the use of the microprocessor and what advantages does it bring?

(SUJB 82)

5 Read the following article and write a summary of the advantages of this microprocessor controlled aid for blind readers.

BLIND AID
Braille, essentially a dox matrix code embossed on paper, is expensive to produce. Only a relatively limited number of books are available in this form and, to make matters worse, the embossed surface wears quickly with repeated use.

Now there is another way to get the benefits of the tactile basis of braille, yet still use the printed page. A team at the University of Chicago's bioengineering department have

developed a hand held scanning device, which reads a printed braille text and translates it into a tactile image.

The image is perceived through the fingertips just like conventional braille via a series of electrically powered points which pop up and down. The scanning unit itself, which is smaller than the average television remote control unit, contains a solid state camera and the tactile output. The heart of the unit is a small microprocessor which is connected to the scanner via a lightweight cable. Its advantages are obvious. The inkbraille text is much cheaper to produce than the embossed text and there is no problem of wear and tear. The average blind reader can learn to use the machine in less than an hour.

(*Observer*, 6 October 1985)

6 Read the following passage taken from an article on computers:

"Doctors, hospitals, the police, Government departments and loan companies have always stored files of personal information. Today such information is being stored in computer data banks. Some people believe that this increases the threat to an individual's privacy."

a What is a data bank?
b Give **one** reason why data banks are thought to be a threat to an individual's privacy.
c How might the misuse of such information be prevented?

(EAEB 82)

7 a It is generally accepted that personal data (data about people) which is stored in a computer system should be *accurate, secure* and *private*. With the help of examples briefly explain the meanings of these three terms.
b Computer systems used by government, local authorities and commercial organisations all store personal data. Describe **three** computer systems which use personal data and indicate any dangers which would arise if the data were not accurate, secure and private.

(C 83)

8 The 'Computer Revolution' is frequently referred to as a problem which is imminent. Well-meaning and authoritative articles are to be found warning of the social problems that will occur. The reality is that the revolution has been successful. Many businesses could not now function without their computers. Microcomputer automation in engineering has been found to be essential if firms are to remain competitive. Computer based information systems are available on everybody's television.

a Name a business that is committed to the extent suggested in the above passage, and explain why it would not be able to manage without computers.
b Give an example of microcomputer automation and explain why it is more efficient than the system it replaced.
c Name a system that provides computer based information via home television. State TWO advantages for people obtaining information in this way.

(ASLEB 82)

9 The increasing use of computers to store personal data is believed by some to be a threat to people's privacy.

a Name three different applications where personal data may be held on a computer. In each case describe briefly the type of information that could be stored.

b Describe three possible safeguards which can be used to prevent unauthorised access to personal data.

c Why is it important that personal data is accurate? What steps can be taken to ensure that data is accurate and up-to-date?

d Explain briefly why people are more worried about giving private information now than they were before computers were in use.

(SREB 82)

Glossary

Accumulator. A register in the arithmetic and logic unit. It is used to hold data transferred from the memory unit for processing and also to store the results of calculations.

Acoustic Coupler. A computer communications device which sends and receives digital data as sound waves using a normal telephone.

Address. The number used to identify a storage location.

Algorithm. A set of rules which will always produce a solution to a particular type of problem or indicate that no solution exists.

Analogue-to-digital converter. A device used to convert analogue (continuously varying) signals to digital (discrete number of values) signals before input.

Applications package. A complete set of programs and their associated documentation for a particular computer application.

Arithmetic and logic unit. The part of the central processing unit where arithmetic and logic operations are carried out.

Assembler. A computer program designed to translate assembly language into machine code. Usually a complete assembly language *source program* is translated into a complete machine code *object program*.

Assembly language. A low-level programming language in which each machine code instruction is replaced with a mnemonic code and symbolic names are used for actual memory locations.

Backing store. A large non-volatile store used to hold programs and data not in current use by the computer.

Bar code. A code made from a pattern of lines, normally used to store the identity of the article on which it is printed.

Batch processing. A method of computer processing in which all the programs and data are collected together (i.e. *batched*) before processing starts.

Baud. A unit for measuring the speed with which data is transmitted. For convenience, one baud is taken to be a transmission rate of one bit of data per second.

Bistable. A component which has two stable states — for example, a small area on a magnetic tape which may or may not be magnetized.

Bit. A **BI**nary digi**T**, either one or zero.

Block. A group of data items treated as a complete unit for transfer to and from backing store.

Buffer. A temporary store for data while it is transferred between the central processing unit and a peripheral device.

Bureau. An organisation which hires computing hardware and software facilities.

Bus. A common data pathway connecting together several components of a computer system.

Byte. A set of bits used to represent a single character. Usually eight bits are used.

Ceefax. The teletext service provided by the BBC.

Central processing unit. The main part of the computer where all processing takes place. The CPU contains the immediate access memory, the control unit and the arithmetic and logic unit.

Character. One of the symbols that can be represented in a computer.

Character code. The set of binary patterns used to represent characters in the computer. One common character code is ASCII (American Standard Code for Information Interchange).

Character printer. An output device which prints one character at a time.

Character set. The full set of characters which can be represented in the computer.

Check digit. An extra digit calculated from the original digits of a number and then attached to that number. It is used as a means of later checking the validity of the number.

Compiler. A computer program designed to translate a complete high level *source program* into a machine code *object program*.

Computer. A machine, controlled by a stored program of instructions, which accepts input data, processes the data and then supplies the results of the processing.

Computer output on microfilm (COM). A method of producing computer output in very compact form, recorded photographically on microfilm.

Control switch. A set of logic gates built into a data bus and used to control the flow of data in the computer.

Control total. A total calculated by adding a specified field from several records. Control totals are used to check that data has been input correctly.

Control unit. The part of the CPU which directs and synchronises the execution of program instructions.

Cylinder of data. The set of tracks in a magnetic disc pack which can be read without movement of the read/write heads.

Daisy wheel printer. A shaped character impact printer using a rotating ring of characters arranged on the spokes of a small wheel.

Data. Information coded into a suitable form for computer input, processing and output.

Database. An organised and structured collection of data. The structure is independent of any particular application and designed to allow the data to be processed in a variety of ways.

Databus. A common data pathway linking together the units of a computer.

Data capture. Collecting data for use in a computer application.

Data channel. The physical path followed by data as it flows through the computer. Control switches allow a single data bus to provide many different data channels.

Data preparation. Preparing data for input by transcribing it on to a media that can be read directly by the computer.

Data processing. A general description for the work done with a computer. It is particularly associated with commercial computing.

Data processing manager. The person responsible for all the work of the computer department.

Data terminator. See *Rogue value.*

Deck. A set of punched cards.

Dedicated computer. A computer, usually a microprocessor, which is used for only one task.

Direct access. Storing or retrieving data items without the need to read through any other stored data items.

Direct data entry. A term which causes confusion. It can be taken to mean either data entry using a key-to-disc-or-tape system or data entry while the processing program is running. (The second definition is preferred by the author.)

Documentation. The written description of a computer program. This usually includes notes, listing, specimen test data, flowcharts, specimen output and full user instructions.

Document reader. An input device for reading either optical marks or optical characters.

Dot matrix printer. A printer which produces characters by printing a pattern of dots.

Dry run. Working through a computer program by hand, using test data and a trace table to record the results at each stage of the program.

Electronic funds transfer (EFT). A method of transferring money directly from one bank account to another using a computer communications network.

Electronic mail. A method of transferring letters and documents between computer systems using a communications network.

EPROM (Erasable Programmable Read Only Memory). A type of memory chip which in normal use is non-volatile read only memory. When required the chip can be removed and its contents erased by exposure to ultra-violet light. It can then be reprogrammed.

Error message. A message produced by the computer system when a fault is detected in the program.

Even parity. A property of any binary code which is devised so that each binary pattern contains an even number of 1s. Binary codes with even parity can be checked after they have been transmitted from one part of the computer to another.

Exchangeable disc pack. A magnetic disc pack which can be removed from the disc drive.

Execute phase. The part of the fetch/execute cycle in which the program instruction is decoded and carried out.

Execution error. An error which is detected while a program is running — for example, an overflow error or a division by zero error.

Expert system. A computer system which can access a large knowledge base and draw reasoned conclusions from that knowledge.

Feedback. Using sensors to monitor the effects of control instructions output by a computer.

Fetch/execute cycle. A two-phase cycle by which the central processing unit processes a computer program.

Fetch phase. The part of the fetch/execute cycle in which the next program instruction is transferred from the immediate access memory to the instruction register.

Fibre optics. The use of very thin glass strands to transmit signals in the form of light waves.

Field. The storage area allocated to a single item of data. A field forms one section of a record.

File. An organised collection of related records.

File librarian. The person responsible for the library of magnetic tapes and discs in the computer department.

Flip-flop. An electrical circuit that can be in one of two states. A pulse of electricity can switch the device from one state to the other.

Flowchart. A graphical representation of the flow of data through a computer system or computer program. *Systems flowcharts* show the flow of data through a complete computer system, describing the equipment and clerical steps involved but giving no details of the actual computer programs. *Program flowcharts* show the flow of data through a computer program, detailing the exact sequence of operations required to process the data.

Frame. The part of a paper tape or magnetic tape that is used to store the code for a single character of data.

Front end processor. A small computer used to coordinate and control the communications between input/output devices and large computer systems.

Full adder. A logic circuit which can add together two binary digits and a carry from a previous addition. The circuit produces a sum bit and a carry bit for the next addition.

Gate. An electronic device used to control the flow of data in a computer. Gates are the basic building blocks from which logic circuits are built to combine, modify and direct data as it flows round the computer.

Generation (of a computer). A term used to distinguish between computers based on different kinds of technology. Valves were the principle components of *first-*

generation computers. Transistors were the principle components of *second-generation* computers. Integrated circuits are the principle components of *third generation* computers.

Generation (of a file). A term used to distinguish between updated versions of a master file. Usually the latest version is called the *son* file, the version before the last update is called the *father* file and the version before that is called the *grandfather* file. For security reasons, it is usual to retain at least three generations of all important files.

Graphics tablet. An input device in which the movements of a pointer or cross-wire over a pad are converted to digital input signals giving the coordinates of a picture or diagram.

Graphics terminal. A terminal designed to display pictures and diagrams on a screen.

Graph plotter. An output device which produces diagrams and pictures by drawing onto paper with a pen.

Half adder. A logic circuit which can add together two binary digits. The circuit produces a sum bit and a carry bit.

Hard copy. Computer output printed on paper.

Hardware. The physical components that make up a computer system.

Hash total. A control total calculated in a way that would otherwise be meaningless.

Hexadecimal numbers. Base sixteen numbers.

High-level language. A problem-oriented language which is independent of the machine code of any particular computer.

Immediate access memory. The memory in the central processing unit, used to store programs and data in current use.

Information retrieval. A computer application that provides access to a large database of information.

Input device. A peripheral device used to convert input data into the coded electrical signals which can be processed by the computer.

Instruction decoder. A logic circuit used to decode machine code instructions during the execute phase of the fetch/execute cycle.

Instruction register. A register in the control unit used to store program instructions while they are executed.

Instruction set. The full set of instructions which can be executed by the computer.

Integrated circuit. A complete electrical circuit created on a single piece of semiconductor material.

Interactive computing. A type of computer use in which the input, processing and output are inter-mixed. The user is involved in a 'conversation' with the computer.

Inter-block gap. A gap left between blocks of data stored on magnetic tape or discs.

Interface. The hardware and associated software needed to link peripheral devices to a computer. The interface must compensate for differences between the computer and the peripheral – for example, operating speeds, signal levels and internal codes.

Interpreter. A computer program designed to execute a high-level program by translating one statement at a time as the high-level program runs.

Interrupt. A signal which causes a temporary break in the execution of a program while some other activity is performed by the computer.

Job control language. A special purpose computer language used in a batch processing system. The language is used to identify each job and describe its requirements to the operating system.

Joystick. An input device in which the movements of a small lever are converted to input instructions to move an object on a display screen.

K. A unit of memory size. A 1K memory can store 1024 characters of data.

Key. A selected field in a record used to identify the record and possibly to sort a file of records into order.

Key-to-disc system. A data preparation system used to input data and store it on magnetic discs.

Key-to-tape system. A data preparation system used to input data and store it on magnetic tapes.

Large scale integration. A technique for producing a large number of components on a single integrated circuit. *Very large scale integration* is an even more advanced technique.

Laser printer. A printer which uses an electrostatic drum on which characters are created using a laser light beam.

Light pen. An input device used to identify a point on a display screen.

Line printer. An output device that prints a line of characters at a time.

Local area network. A computer network linked by cable, usually in a single building or room.

Logic gate. See **Gate**.

Low-level language. A machine-oriented language in which each instruction corresponds to a single machine code instruction.

Machine code. A set of binary instructions which can be executed by the computer without the need for any translation.

Magnetic ink character recognition. An input technique which uses a special device to read characters printed in magnetic ink.

Mainframe. A large computer with a fast processor, a high-capacity backing store and a range of peripheral devices.

Master file. A file of data which is the main source of information for an application program. The data from a transaction file may be used to update and amend the master file.

Memory unit. The part of the computer where data and programs in current use are stored.

Merge. To combine two or more files of data into a single file.

Microcomputer. A computer which uses a microprocessor for its central processing unit.

Microfilm. An output medium which allows very compact data storage by using a technique of photographic reduction.

Microprocessor. A single integrated circuit containing all the elements of a central processing unit.

Minicomputer. A computer offering scaled-down facilities of a mainframe computer at a reduced cost.

Mnemonic code. An assembly language code selected to remind the user of the machine code instruction it represents — for example, LDA used to represent LoaD the Accumulator.

Modem. A computer communications device which converts digital data to and from the analogue electrical signals used for transmission along telephone lines.

Multi-access system. A computer system which allows several users to use the computer apparently at the same time. This is usually achieved by allowing each terminal in the system to use the computer in turn for short periods of time.

Multiprogramming system. A computer system which allows several programs to be run at the same time. The programs are usually allocated priorities and the program with the highest priority will use the CPU until it requires an input or output operation. While this operation takes place, a program with a lower priority can use the CPU.

Object program. A machine code program produced by an assembler or compiler from an assembly language or high-level source program.

Octal numbers. Base 8 numbers.

Odd parity. A property of a binary code in which each binary pattern contains an odd number of ones. See **Even parity**.

Off-line processing. Computer processing carried out while the user is not in direct contact with the computer.

On-line processing. Computer processing carried out while the user is in direct contact with the computer.

Operating system. The systems software which coordinates and controls the running of applications programs on the computer. The operating system allows applications software to be run easily and efficiently on the basic computer hardware.

Operator. The person responsible for operating the computer.

Operator's console. An input/output device used by the computer operator to send instructions to the computer and to receive messages from the computer. It is usually a VDU or teletype terminal.

Optical character recognition (OCR). An input technique which uses a special device to read characters printed in a special font or possibly characters drawn by hand.

Optical mark recognition. An input technique which uses a special device to detect marks made in predetermined positions on an input document.

Output device. A peripheral device used to convert the coded electrical signals that are processed by the computer into output data. The output data is usually either printed or displayed on a screen.

Overflow error. An error caused when an attempt is made to store a number too large for the available storage location.

Parallel data transmission. A method of communication in which the bits which represent a character are sent at the same time along a set of parallel wires.

Parity bit. An extra bit added to a binary code in order to create binary patterns with either even parity or odd parity.

Parity check. A check that the parity of a binary code number is correct.

Peripheral device. Any input, output or storage device connected to the central processing unit.

Pixel. A single picture element. The smallest area of the screen which can be used to build up a picture.

Point-of-sale terminal (POS terminal). Any device used to capture data directly at the point of sale. POS terminals range from relatively simple devices which record sales on discs or tapes to fully on-line terminals directly connected to a computer system.

Port. A connector used to link devices to a computer.

Prestel. The viewdata service provided by the Post Office.

Program. A set of instructions used to control the operation of a computer.

Programmable read only memory (PROM). A type of read only memory which is programmed after manufacture. A PROM memory can only be programmed once, after this the software is fixed and cannot be erased.

Program counter. A register in the control unit which stores the address of the next program instruction. It is sometimes called the *sequence control register*.

Programmer. A person who writes, documents and maintains computer programs.

Random access memory (RAM). Memory which may be both read from and written to. Its main use in a computer is to store application programs and data.

Range check. A check that a data item is within sensible limits.

Read only memory (ROM). Memory which can be

read from but not written to. The software in ROM memory is fixed when it is manufactured. Its main use is to store systems software.

Real-time system. A computer system which can receive input data and process that data quickly enough to be able to output signals to control the source of the input.

Record. A collection of related data items or fields.

Register. A memory location used for a specific purpose.

Remote access. Computer access from a remote site, usually by means of a terminal, modem and telephone line.

Remote job entry. A method of entering programs and data for batch processing from a remote site.

Rogue value. An invalid value in a set of input data items which can be detected as a signal to end data entry. Sometimes called a *data terminator*.

Rounding. Approximating a number to the nearest equivalent value with a given number of significant figures.

Rounding error. The error produced by rounding a number.

Sequence control register. See **Program counter.**

Sequential file. A file in which the records are held in order of a particular key field.

Serial access. The process of locating a record by reading through all the previous records.

Serial data transmission. A method of communication in which the bits which represent a character are sent one after the other along a single wire.

Software. Computer programs and their associated documentation.

Source documents. The documents used to capture data for input to a computer system.

Source program. A program in a high-level or assembly language which is translated into a machine code object program by a compiler or assembler.

Spooling. The temporary storage of input or output data on magnetic tape or discs before use in a program or printing.

Syntax. The set of rules which define the way in which a programming language may be used to construct program statements and complete programs.

Syntax error. An error resulting from the incorrect use of the syntax rules of a programming language.

Systems analysis. The analysis of the requirements of a task and the production of feasibility study and design of a computerised system to complete the task.

System analyst. The person who completes a systems analysis.

Systems software. The set of computer programs used to control the operation of the computer.

Teletypewriter (Teletype). A terminal which uses a keyboard for input and a character printer for output.

Terminal. An input/output device used to communicate with a large computer system.

Time sharing. A method of providing multi-access computing by allowing each terminal in turn to access the computer for a short period of time called a *time slice*.

Transaction file. A data file used to update a master file.

Truncation. Approximating a number by ignoring all the digits after a given number of significant figures.

Truncation error. The error produced by truncating a number.

Truth table. A table showing every possible combination of inputs and outputs for a logic circuit.

Turnaround document. An output document which is later used as an input document after extra data has been added to it.

Two's complement. A method of representing positive and negative binary numbers. The most significant bit of a two's complement number represents a negative quantity.

Utility program. A systems program designed to perform a specific task — for example, copy a screen display on to a printer.

Validation. Checking input data to ensure that it is accurate, complete and reasonable.

Verification. Checking that input data has been correctly transcribed onto computer media. This is usually achieved by entering the data twice and comparing the two entries.

Viewdata. An interactive communication system which uses telephone lines and modified television sets. The best known system is the Post Office's Prestel network.

Visual display unit (VDU). A terminal which uses a keyboard for input and a screen for output.

Wordlength. The number of bits in each location of a computer's memory.

Word processor. A computer system used to enter, edit, store, retrieve and print letters and documents.

Write permit ring. A ring which must be fitted into a reel of magnetic tape before data can be written on to the tape.

Index

265